Defending the Political Constitution

OXFORD CONSTITUTIONAL THEORY

Series editors:
MARTIN LOUGHLIN,
JOHN P MCCORMICK, AND
NEIL WALKER

Oxford Constitutional Theory has rapidly established itself as the primary point of reference for theoretical reflections on the growing interest in constitutions and constitutional law in domestic, regional, and global contexts. The majority of the works published in the series are monographs that advance new understandings of their subject. But the series aims to provide a forum for further innovation in the field by also including well-conceived edited collections that bring a variety of perspectives and disciplinary approaches to bear on specific themes in constitutional thought and by publishing English translations of leading monographs in constitutional theory that have originally been written in languages other than English.

ALSO AVAILABLE IN THE SERIES

Animals and the Constitution
Towards Sentience-Based Constitutionalism
John Olusegun Adenitire and Raffael Fasel

New Constitutional Horizons
Towards a Pluralist Constitutional Theory
Cormac Mac Amhlaigh

Constitutional Ratification without Reason
Jeffrey A. Lenowitz

Legitimation by Constitution
A Dialogue on Political Liberalism
Frank Michelman and
Alessandro Ferrara

Authoritarian Liberalism and the Transformation of Modern Europe
Michael Wilkinson

Constitutionalism and the Paradox Principles and Rules
Between the Hydra and Hercules
Marcelo Neves

Constituent Power in the European Union
Markus Patberg

Religion, Law, and Democracy
Selected Writings
Ernst-Wolfgang Böckenförde
Edited by Mirjam Künkler and Tine Stein

Constituent Power and the Law
Joel Colón-Ríos

Law and Revolution
Legitimacy and Constitutionalism after the Arab Spring
Nimer Sultany

After Public Law
Cormac Mac Amhlaigh, Claudio Michelon,
Neil Walker

Europe's Functional Constitution
A Theory of Constitutionalism Beyond the State
Turkuler Isiksel

Constitutionalism
Past, Present, and Future
Dieter Grimm

Unconstitutional Constitutional Amendments
The Limits of Amendment Powers
Yaniv Roznai

Euroconstitutionalism and its Discontents
Oliver Gerstenberg

Popular Sovereignty in Early Modern Constitutional Thought
Daniel Lee

Defending the Political Constitution

RICHARD BELLAMY

Professor of Political Science, University College London, UK

OXFORD
UNIVERSITY PRESS

OXFORD
UNIVERSITY PRESS

Great Clarendon Street, Oxford, OX2 6DP,
United Kingdom

Oxford University Press is a department of the University of Oxford. It furthers the University's objective of excellence in research, scholarship, and education by publishing worldwide. Oxford is a registered trade mark of Oxford University Press in the UK and in certain other countries.

Published in the United States of America by Oxford University Press
198 Madison Avenue, New York, NY 10016, United States of America

British Library Cataloguing in Publication Data
Data available

Library of Congress Control Number: 2025946027

ISBN 9780198784494

DOI: 10.1093/9780191826986.001.0001

Printed and bound by
CPI Group (UK) Ltd., Croydon, CR0 4YY

The manufacturer's authorised representative in the EU for product safety is Oxford University Press España S.A. of Parque Empresarial San Fernando de Henares, Avenida de Castilla, 2 – 28830 Madrid (www.oup.es/en or product.safety@oup.com). OUP España S.A. also acts as importer into Spain of products made by the manufacturer.

MIX
Paper | Supporting responsible forestry
FSC® C013604
FSC www.fsc.org

Preface and Acknowledgements

This book seeks to defend both the normative attractiveness of a political constitution and its empirical plausibility. If the initial criticisms of my earlier defence of *Political Constitutionalism* in 2007 centred on its coherence as a normative ideal, the more recent critiques have focused increasingly on its ability to withstand certain real-world contemporary challenges. Taken on their own, the normative criticisms have not altered much over the intervening eighteen or so years. By contrast, the real-world challenges have changed dramatically—both in kind and urgency. Back in 2007 and the immediate years that followed, these challenges mainly stemmed from what was heralded as the unfolding triumph of legal constitutionalism, both domestically and internationally. With regard to the UK, for example, this development was traced to the constitutional reforms of the first Labour administration of Tony Blair—most particularly the Human Rights Act and the creation of the Supreme Court, on the one hand, and the growing impact of the jurisprudence of the Court of Justice of the European Union, the European Court of Human Rights, and of international law more generally, on the other. However, more recently the apparent global expansion of legal constitutionalism has met with—and, on some accounts, even provoked—a populist backlash, a shift associated in the UK with the ultimately successful campaign to leave the European Union.

One response to this assault has been to seek to strengthen the available legal constitutionalist counter-measures, including the adoption of so-called militant democracy constitutional clauses that allow the banning of certain parties or kinds of party programme. Those advocating this approach often point to the ways that certain apologists of the populist attacks on legal constitutions have deployed political constitutionalist arguments to legitimize their actions. In this way, the empirical critique of political constitutionalism has lent support to criticism of it as a normative ideal. However, militant democratic measures have often proven hard to trigger and provided mechanisms and arguments that the very parties they are aimed against have used themselves. As a result, legal constitutionalism arguably finds itself in a parallel dilemma to that allegedly bedevilling political constitutionalism: namely, that of aiding and abetting those forces it seeks to contain.

This book proposes a different response to both the initial, legal, and the current, populist, real-world challenges. First, I continue to defend a democratic form of political constitutionalism as resting on similar normative foundations regarding political equality to a liberal form of legal constitutionalism, albeit more coherently and consistently so and in a way that relates to the republican notion of freedom as non-domination. However, I have tried to make clearer than in the earlier book how the political constitution gives rise to a form of legal constitution. Legal rules and norms inevitably play a part in the functioning of any political regime—including a democracy. Within a political constitution, however, this legal constitution plays a subordinate, if complementary role. Moreover, the type of legal constitution supported by a political constitution is both more flexible and more detailed than the standard liberal model of an entrenched and abstract constitution, which operates as higher rather than ordinary law. Not only does the standard liberal model hand arbitrary power to the judicial and other authorities charged with applying the legal constitution's general norms and rules to particular cases—thereby raising the stakes for capturing that power, as populists have done in recent years, but also—notwithstanding its predominance among constitutional theorists—that liberal legal model proves more the exception than the rule in practice. While I have used the UK as my main example of a political constitution, the underlying reasoning extends to the growing number of flexible and detailed constitutions which aim at ensuring that judicial as well as executive decisions are democratically responsive and controlled.

Second, this last point links to my claim that legal constitutions of both the entrenched and the flexible kind prove to be only as good as the political constitutions in which they are embedded. As a result, we need to pay attention to those features of a democratic system that support its constitutional qualities. I argue that for a political constitution to guard against arbitrary rule in practice, it must be capable of reflecting the plurality of ideas and interests in contemporary societies that makes democratic decision-making necessary—something populists deny. In doing so, democracy acquires certain core constitutional qualities by creating a series of democratic checks and balances that guard against domination by obliging citizens and their representatives to treat each other with equal concern and respect by hearing and harkening to the other side. Such democratic mechanisms also offer a potentially robust response to the rise of populist regimes. Here too we find an instance of how politics comes first.

The book charts a path towards this conclusion by engaging with the normative critique of the political constitution in Part 1; then turning to the claim of its being undermined by the spread of legal constitutionalism in Parts 2 and 3—where the thesis regarding the subordination of legal to political constitutionalism is developed, along with the complementarity of a flexible and detailed legal constitution, involving 'weak form' judicial review, with a political constitution; and, finally, by confronting the populist challenge in Part 4. Taken together, these chapters aim to provide a restatement and defence of the continuing normative appeal and practical relevance of a political constitution.

Many people over many years have played an important role in the writing of this book. In alphabetical order, with abject apologies to anyone I may have unintentionally omitted, I am grateful to Albena Azmanova, Luca Baccelli, Tom Bailey,

Nick Barber, Or Bassok, Seyla Benhabib, Enrico Biale, Adrian Blau, Chris Brooke, Bojan Bugaric, Basak Cali, Peter Cane, Dario Castiglione, Thomas Christiano, Mark Dawson, David Dyzenhaus, Cristina Fasone, Alessandro Ferrara, Andreas Føllesdal, Rainer Forst, Steffen Ganghof, Valentine Gentile, Oliver Gerstenberg, Tom Hickey, Jeff Howard, Joanna Innes, Peter Jones, Aileen Kavanagh, Jeff King, Matthew Kramer, Sandra Kröger, Harshan Kumarasingham, Cecile Laborde, Cristina Lafont, Christine Landfried, Jean Leclair, Bruno Leipold, Annabelle Lever, Jacob Levy, Dominique Leydet, Nicola Lupo, Cormac Mac Amhlaigh, Giuseppe Martinico, Emily McTernan, David Miller, Darrel Moellendorf, Margaret Moore, Glyn Morgan, Sam Moyn, Peter Niesen, Colm O'Cinneide, Markus Patberg, Carmen Pavel, Bilyana Petkova, Philip Pettit, Alan Renwick, Enzo Rossi, Philip Sales, Emilio Santoro, Eric Schliesser, Geoffrey Sigalet, Quentin Skinner, Adam Swift, Christine Sypnowich, Stephen Tierney, Jim Tully, Mark Tushnet, Laura Valentini, Jeremy Waldron, Neil Walker, Albert Weale, Jeremy Webber, Daniel Weinstock, and Antje Wiener for their written and/or verbal recommendations for, and observations on, one or more of the book's chapters. Needless to say, the many remaining flaws are all my own responsibility, no doubt due to a failure to respond adequately to their criticisms. I owe a special debt to Gregoire Webber, who kindly read almost the whole of the revised manuscript, and offered encouragement and helpful suggestions on it, and to Cosmin Vraciu, who provided invaluable research assistance in getting a first draft into the format desired by Oxford University Press and thereby spurred me to revise and complete the book.

Most of the chapters draw on, and considerably revise and extend, previously published articles and chapters. I am grateful to the publishers and editors for allowing me to use material from the following:

'Political Constitutionalism' in P. Cane and H. Kumarasingham (eds), *The Cambridge Constitutional History of the United Kingdom*, vol. 1 *Exploring the Constitution* (Cambridge: Cambridge University Press 2023) ch. 3, 59–87 in the Introduction.

'Rights as Democracy' (2012) 15(4) *Critical Review of International Social and Political Philosophy (CRISPP)* 449–71 in Chapter 1.

'Can the Rule of Law Meet the Hobbes Challenge? Democracy and the Rule of Law' in Enrico Biale, Federica Liveriero, and Roberta Sala (eds), *Public Ethics for Real People* (Cham: Palgrave Macmillan) 131–50 in Chapter 2.

'Political Constitutionalism and the Human Rights Act' (2011) 9 *International Journal of Constitutional Law (I-Con)* 86–111 in Chapter 4.

'The Democratic Legitimacy of International Human Rights Conventions: Political Constitutionalism and the ECHR' (2014) 25(4) *European Journal of International Law* 1019–42 in Chapter 5.

'Turtles All The Way Down? Is the Political Constitutionalist Appeal to Disagreement Self-Defeating? A Reply to Cormac Mac Amhlaigh' (2016) 14(1) *International Journal of Constitutional Law (I-Con)* 204–16 in Chapter 6.

'The Democratic Qualities of Courts: A Critical Analysis of Three Arguments' (2013) 49(3) *Representation* 333–46 in Chapter 7.

'Political Constitutionalism and Populism' (2023) 50 (Suppl. 1) *Journal of Law and Society* S7–S25 <https://doi.org/10.1111/jols.12401> in Chapter 8.

'Political Constitutionalism and Referendums: The Case of Brexit' (2023) 32(6) *Social & Legal Studies* 973–95 <https://doi.org/10.1177/09646639231153129> in Chapter 9.

'Losing Control: Brexit and the Demoi-cratic Disconnect' in Uta Staiger and Benjamin Martill (eds), *Brexit and Beyond: Rethinking the Futures of Europe* (London: UCL Press 2018) 222–8 in Chapter 10.

Contents

PART 3. THE JUDICIAL CHALLENGE—DEMOCRACY THROUGH COURTS?

PART 4. THE POPULIST CHALLENGE: DEMOCRACY AS THE WILL OF THE PEOPLE?

Introduction

The Political Constitution—A Genealogy

1. INTRODUCTION: ON LEGAL AND POLITICAL CONSTITUTIONALISM

This book defends the superior merits of a political constitution of a democratic kind compared to those of a legal constitution of a liberal hue. Political constitutionalism locates the constitution in the character and design of the political system and the modus operandi of its component political processes.[1] Though the approach predates democracy, the form defended here emphasizes the role of democratic mechanisms—such as the electoral system, party competition, the interaction of different parliamentary chambers, and the balance between central and local government—and of the political actors empowered and controlled by them, in securing such standard liberal constitutional goals as the upholding of individual rights, the rule of law, legal and political equality, and the constraint of arbitrary rule by the executive and administration. As such, it can be contrasted with a liberal form of legal constitutionalism, which identifies the constitution with a codified and entrenched written document with the status of 'higher law', and allots the upholding of the aforementioned constitutional goals to legal institutions and actors, such as the judges on a constitutional or supreme court, who are responsible for its interpretation and application.

Naturally, a political constitution will encompass many legal elements, just as a legal constitution includes many political elements. Courts will play a key role in the application of those written elements of a political constitution enshrined in law,[2] including insofar as they relate to the behaviour of political actors. However, these written legal embodiments of the political constitution, such as the UK Representation of the People Act, will take the form of ordinary legislation, with a due political process ultimately responsible for determining their content,

[1] Richard Bellamy, *Political Constitutionalism: A Republican Defence of the Constitutionality of Democracy* (Cambridge: Cambridge University Press 2007).

[2] The UK is sometimes deemed to have an 'unwritten' constitution—but a great deal is written down even if it is uncodified. (For a recent overview, see David Torrance, 'The United Kingdom Constitution: A Mapping Exercise' Research Briefing House of Commons Library, 18 December 2024 <https://commonslibrary.parliament.uk/research-briefings/cbp-9384/>.) Indeed, even where codified constitutions exist, many important constitutional norms rest on conventions (such as the number of judges on the US Supreme Court) or are written but uncodified (such as the employment of the plurality electoral system for elections to the US congress).

Defending the Political Constitution. Richard Bellamy, Oxford University Press. © Richard Bellamy 2026.
DOI: 10.1093/9780191826986.001.0001

applicability, and interpretation. There will also be certain unwritten yet widely accepted conventions that can be applied by courts, though their continued legal standing will ultimately be a political decision. Likewise, a legal constitution will detail many aspects of the operation of the political system, which will have the main responsibility for putting flesh on constitutional essentials through legislation and administrative acts, while many aspects of a legal constitutional regime will be either ordinary law or unwritten conventions. The key distinction between the two consists in where final authority concerning the operation of the legal and political systems ultimately lies—in the courts, with judges as interpreters of the 'higher law' of the constitution; or in the legislature, with political actors operating through a duly constituted and constitutive legislative process.[3]

Political constitutionalists contend that the constitutional qualities of the law and legal system reflect those of the political system more generally. This insistence on the primacy of politics involves both an empirical contention and a normative proposition.[4] While the empirical claim plays a role in assessing some of the real-world challenges confronting constitutionalism more generally, such as the populist challenge explored in Chapter 8, this book largely focuses on the normative claim. Political constitutionalists see law not as framing the political system, as legal constitutionalists propose, but as being inevitably framed by politics—and rightly so within a democracy. On their view, identifying and upholding the rights and obligations of those subject to the law is a political act that can only be legitimately undertaken via a democratic process by those duly authorized to do so by these self-same subjects of the law and to whom these elected representative actors must ultimately remain accountable.[5] Political constitutionalists consider the constitution of a polity to consist precisely in the way the democratic processes of authorization and accountability frame the exercise of authority and the degree to which its members regard these processes as legitimate.[6] The task of the legal system becomes to implement democratically determined laws in a consistent and impartial manner, though that role is likely to be fostered by its officials possessing

[3] Aileen Kavanagh, *The Collaborative Constitution* (Cambridge: Cambridge University Press 2024) ch. 1 portrays Ronald Dworkin and Jeremy Waldron, as theorists of legal and political constitutionalism respectively, as engaged in a Manichean debate, in which each side ignores the complementary role of the branch they object to: legislatures in the legal constitutionalist case (e.g. Dworkin) and courts in the political constitutionalist case (e.g. Waldron). However, this Manichean picture caricatures their respective positions (think of Waldron's extensive writing on the rule of law, for example, in 'The Concept and the Rule of Law' (2008) 43 *Georgia Law Review* 1–61). Both explicitly acknowledge the complementary role of courts and legislatures and regard them as collaborating, albeit in contrasting ways, much of the time. They diverge on the degree to which the legislature is a forum of principle and courts stray into policy-making, to deploy Dworkin's terminology (e.g. Ronald Dworkin, *Freedom's Law: The Moral Reading of the American Constitution*, (Cambridge, MA: Harvard University Press 1996) 30), and where—in those cases in which the two branches diverge—the final say should reside.

[4] Bellamy, *Political Constitutionalism*, 4–5.

[5] Jeremy Waldron, *Law and Disagreement* (Oxford: Clarendon Press 1999) chs 10, 11.

[6] Waldron, *Law and Disagreement*, ch. 5; Bellamy, *Political Constitutionalism*, ch. 6.

a degree of political independence, as will generally be the case for the state bureaucracy more generally. From this perspective, legal constitutionalism, and in particular 'strong form' rights-based judicial review, whereby courts can disapply and strike down legislation on the grounds that it infringes the constitution, and which is discussed in Chapters 1, 2, 4, 5, and 7 in particular, involves judges illegitimately adopting a political role without either authorization or accountability by those subject to their judgments, so that they become judge and jury over their own authority.[7] However, political constitutionalism is compatible with 'weak form' review, whereby the legality under existing law of certain administrative acts and laws can be challenged through the courts, so long as the ultimate decision on their constitutionality and continuing applicability lies with Parliament, including through the revision or withdrawal of existing law or the enactment of new law.[8]

The United States has come to provide the exemplar of a liberal form of legal constitutionalism, especially in the large literature produced by North American legal and political philosophers, such as Ronald Dworkin and John Rawls and their many followers.[9] Of course, there are other legal constitutional traditions in Europe, Latin America, Africa, and Asia, with significant differences with regard to their content and operation both between each other and with the US constitution. Nevertheless, they share a number of common features—including those elements stressed by Dworkin and Rawls regarding the primacy of certain legally enshrined constitutional principles and the superior role of courts in upholding them with regard to the procedures and outputs of the political system.[10] Similarly, a democratic political constitutionalism has been identified with the British constitution and the Commonwealth model of constitutionalism more generally,[11] though elements also exist elsewhere, such as the Nordic countries.[12] Within the British constitutional system, democratic processes provide the core constitutional mechanisms whereby citizens can hold governments and the administration accountable—most notably, directly through elections and indirectly via their elected representatives, as a result of the need for the government to govern

[7] Jeremy Waldron, 'The Core of the Case Against Judicial Review' (2006) 115 *Yale Law Journal* 1346–1406; Bellamy, *Political Constitutionalism*, ch. 1.

[8] Waldron, 'Core Case' 1354–55; Richard Bellamy, 'Political Constitutionalism and the Human Rights Act' (2011) 9 *International Journal of Constitutional Law (I-Con)* 86–111 [revised as Chapter 4 of this book].

[9] e.g. Dworkin, *Freedom's Law*, 6; John Rawls, *Political Liberalism* (New York: Columbia University Press 1993) 216.

[10] e.g. Jürgen Habermas, *Between Facts and Norms: Contributions to a Discourse Theory of Law and Democracy* (William Rehg tr., Cambridge: Polity Press 1996) clearly has the post-war (West) German constitutional settlement as a reference point, as is even more the case with regard to the Latin American constitutional tradition for Roberto Gargarella, *Latin American Constitutionalism, 1810–2010: The Engine Room of the Constitution* (Oxford: Oxford University Press 2013). Nonetheless, both can be seen as, in part at least, engaging in a dialogue shaped to some degree by debates among US scholars.

[11] Stephen Gardbaum, *The New Commonwealth Model of Constitutionalism: Theory and Practice* (Cambridge: Cambridge University Press 2013).

[12] Andreas Follesdal and Marlene Wind, 'Nordic Reluctance towards Judicial Review under Siege' (2009) 27 *Nordic Journal of Human Rights* 131–41.

and legislate with the support of a plurality of the population and a majority of MPs.[13] Obviously, even elected governments, like ordinary citizens, must abide by existing law and can be challenged through the courts should they act in an *ultra vires* manner, for example. Nevertheless, laws can be changed through a due parliamentary process—either to accommodate or overturn an adverse judicial decision. However, Parliament is constitutionally sovereign not only because it makes the law, but also—and most importantly—because the democratic cast of its operations produces those attributes we associate with constitutional government, such as the restraint on arbitrary rule or the need to accord equal concern and respect to individual citizens in both the framing and administration of law and in executive actions. The constitutional character of the British political constitution ultimately depends on the quality of its democratic processes. If these latter get eroded, then so does its constitutional credentials.

Thinking about the political constitution with reference, in part at least, to the British constitution should not be regarded as an instance of Podsnappery any more than thinking about legal constitutionalism with regard to the US constitution should be associated with its American equivalent. True, Dworkin regarded judicial review as practised by the Supreme Court as 'providing the most important contribution our [US] history has given to political theory'.[14] But writing towards the end of his life, he admitted that 'If I had to judge the American Supreme Court only on its record during the last few years, I would judge it a failure'.[15] As I shall suggest in Chapter 7 in particular, we should consider such a failure as a challenge to the normative as well as the empirical claims of the theory—especially in light of the challenges posed by democratic backsliding to legal constitutionalism as practised around the world. However, that challenge can be regarded as motivating an attempt to produce a revised and stronger theory. In like manner, if the positive aspects of an actually existing political constitution, such as that of the UK, can add to the plausibility of such a conception, its many negative aspects pose problems to be addressed. In defending the political constitution, this book aims not only to respond to academic criticisms but also to the real-world issues confronting it.

So, in offering a genealogy of the political constitution in the UK by way of introduction, the aim is to provide a context for normative theorizing and reflection rather than a complacent description of an existing arrangement that ignores unpleasant facts.[16] Mr Podsnap, it will be recalled, opined that 'We Englishman are

[13] J. A. G. Griffith, 'The Political Constitution' (1979) 42 *Modern Law Review* 1–21; Adam Tomkins, *Our Republican Constitution* (Oxford: Hart Publishing 2005) 1–6.

[14] Dworkin, *Freedom's Law*, 6.

[15] Ronald Dworkin, *Justice for Hedgehogs* (Cambridge, MA: Harvard University Press 2013) 399; and see too his *The Supreme Court Phalanx: The Court's New Right-Wing Bloc* (New York: New York Review of Books 2008).

[16] It is sometimes argued that there have been three phases or waves of political constitutionalist theorising (e.g. Marco Goldoni and Chris McCorkindale, 'Three Waves of Political Constitutionalism' (2019) 30 *King's Law Journal* 74–96): a first, descriptive, wave associated with Griffith's 'The Political

Very Proud of Our Constitution ... It Was Bestowed Upon Us By Providence. No Other Country is so Favoured as This Country'.[17] Asked how other countries, less favoured by Providence, did, he replied—regretfully—that they must simply 'do ... *as* they do'. By contrast, the account offered here notes how the idea of a political constitution has historical roots in the ancient ideal of mixed government—a conception that not only shaped constitutional developments in the UK but Western democracies more generally—including the political components of legal constitutionalist systems such as that of the United States. Meanwhile, it explores the development and adaptation of this ancient ideal to modern mass democracy, within an international context that has become in part shaped by global elements of legal constitutionalism. It is within this setting that a contemporary defence of a democratic political constitution, which takes up the rest of the book, has to start.

The sections of this chapter that follow trace the evolution of the UK's political constitution from the seventeenth century to the present, noting how it has drawn on different ideas and taken different forms over time, and highlighting the contingent nature of its current representative and parliamentary character. The next section explores how the English system of government came to be conceived as embodying the classical idea of mixed government in a novel form, that of the balanced constitution. Involving elements of what became the separation of powers, it located sovereignty in the Crown in Parliament: that is, in the combined rule of the monarch and his or her ministers, the House of Lords and the House of Commons.

Constitution', centred on describing how the British political system operates; a second, normative, wave, usually linked to my *Political Constitutionalism*, among the work of other authors; and a new, third, 'reflexive' wave, that seeks to explore a broader role for politics than that allowed by the Westminster system of representative democracy, and to examine the role of different types of political activity outside formal channels and within a wider range of different constitutional systems and settings, e.g. Marco Goldoni and Chris McCorkindale, 'Why We (Still) need a Revolution' (2013) 14 *German Law Journal* 2103–2292. However, I have always regarded the descriptive, normative, and reflexive as complementary tasks of any satisfactory constitutional theory—be it legal or political (see Richard Bellamy and Jeff King, 'Introduction: Of Constitutions and Constitutional Theory' in *The Cambridge Handbook of Constitutional Theory* (Cambridge: Cambridge University Press 2025). As I've argued elsewhere (in Richard Bellamy, 'Between Utopianism and Realism: The Limits of Partisanship as an Academic Methodology' (2021) 69(3) *Political Studies* 481–91), building on Rawls's notion of 'reflective equilibrium', one necessarily thinks within the normative horizon of the present while seeking to apply and elaborate broadly held principles to new circumstances in a way that 'extends what are ordinarily thought of as the limits of practical possibility'—a mode of argumentation Rawls termed 'Utopian realism' (John Rawls, *The Law of Peoples* (Cambridge, MA: Harvard University Press 1999) 6, 7–9). That approach informed my political constitutionalist reading of the European Union (EU) (Richard Bellamy, *A Republican Europe of States: Cosmopolitanism, Intergovernmentalism and Democracy in the EU* (Cambridge: Cambridge University Press 2019) esp. 15–20), elements of which I summarize in Chapter 10. This book can be regarded as an attempt to do something similar with regard to political constitutionalism more generally. It departs from a normative analysis of a plausible description of a working political constitution and extends and elaborates those principles and mechanisms to address the challenges confronting that settlement. (In suggesting how the three waves interact I am indebted to the analysis in Graham Gee and Grégoire Webber, *Political Constitutions* (Cambridge: Cambridge University Press 2026).

[17] Charles Dickens, *Our Mutual Friend* (Harmondsworth: Penguin 1971 [1864–65]) Book 1, ch. 11, 179.

The subsequent section traces how Montesquieu offered a canonical account of this mixture as a form of constitutional government that preserves liberty and generates the rule of law. Adopted by Blackstone, later thinkers such as Hume, Bagehot, and Dicey then adapted this account into a theory of parliamentary government to accommodate the emerging superiority of the Commons, whereby this mix became expressed through the influence of Crown and aristocracy on parties within the lower house. In the process, as the succeeding section shows, the conceptual basis was established for a democratic version of parliamentary government based on representation through electoral competition between parties. Developed over the twentieth century, this version is most commonly associated with political constitutionalism today. A final section sets the scene for the rest of the book and looks at the prospects for the political constitution in the twenty-first century.

2. FROM MIXED GOVERNMENT TO THE BALANCED CONSTITUTION: CHECKS, BALANCES, AND THE SEPARATION OF POWERS

The idea of a political constitution has its origins in the classical account of mixed government to be found in ancient Greek and Roman political thought.[18] The theory of mixed government originated from the classification of political systems on the basis of whether One, a Few, or Many ruled. According to this theory, the three basic types of polity—monarchy, aristocracy and democracy—were liable to degenerate into tyranny, oligarchy, and anarchy respectively. This corruption stemmed from the concentration of power in the hands of a single person or group, which created a temptation to its abuse in capricious and self-interested rule. The solution, which received its canonical expression in Book VI of Polybius's *Histories*, was to ensure moderation and proportion by combining or mixing various types.[19] As a result, the virtues of each form of government, namely a strong executive, the involvement of the better elements of society, and popular legitimacy, could be obtained without the corresponding vices.[20] As ancient Roman republican theorists of mixed government, most notably Cicero, remarked, the normative basis for this arrangement was the achievement of a form of freedom as non-domination that distinguished the 'free' citizen from a slave.[21] A slave is always subject to the whim and arbitrary rule of his or her master, who can treat them in whatever manner they wish without consulting their interests or views. By contrast, mixed

[18] M. Vile, *Constitutionalism and the Separation of Powers* (Oxford: Clarendon Press 1967) 2.

[19] Polybius, *Rise of the Roman Empire* (F. W. Walbank ed., I. Scott-Kilvert tr., Harmondsworth: Penguin 1979) Bk VI, chs 3, 4, 10.

[20] Polybius, *Rise*, Bk VI, chs 11–18.

[21] Philip Pettit, *Republicanism: A Theory of Freedom and Government* (2nd edn, Oxford: Oxford University Press 1999) 284–5.

government curbs arbitrary power by forcing the different sections of society to 'hear the other side' and engage with their concerns.

Three related constitutional mechanisms became associated with a mixed form of government. First, the conception of the dispersal of power. Second, the notion of checks and balances on power. Third, and developed somewhat later, was the thesis of the separation of powers. Many analyses of these mechanisms, especially those focused on the last, tend to conflate the three.[22] This tendency was fostered by Montesquieu's combination of the second and third in particular within his canonical account of the English constitution in Book 11, chapter 6 of the *Spirit of the Laws*, and compounded by James Madison when he added the first idea to the mix in his defence of the federal scheme of the US constitution in *The Federalist 47*. All three serve a parallel purpose, that of reducing the possibility of arbitrary exercises of power, and can be combined. However, as Jeremy Waldron has noted, they do so in different ways that should be kept analytically distinct.[23]

The dispersal of power need not involve either checking and balancing or the separation of different functions of governance, merely that not all power is held in the same hands. A federal system disperses power in this sense, for example. Such a dispersal might be regarded as serving the need to ensure that governance reflects local conditions and preferences, and so does not involve the arbitrary imposition of uniform rules and regulations on a diverse and heterogeneous political community. Yet, all the relevant powers might be unified in the hands of a single local authority and be neither separated nor checked. As Madison noted in *The Federalist 51*, a federal dispersal of power can provide a new dimension to a system of mixed government. However, it is not a requirement of the doctrine.

That proves important in the British context. Although the UK is a plurinational state, it has resisted moves towards such a dispersal of power. Rather, it developed through the incorporation of Wales, Scotland, and Ireland into the governance structure of the British state and granting these component parts representation in the sovereign British Parliament. True, the powers of local relative to central government have played an important, if neglected, part in the English, and later British, constitution from the middle ages onwards, and fed dissatisfaction with Charles I. However, within the UK, the devolution of authority to make certain specified decisions from the central to the local level has tended to be conceived as an administrative convenience rather than a form of dispersed power that extends mixed government to the sharing of sovereign authority between the nations of the UK. That remains the case even with the re-establishment of parliaments in Scotland, Wales, and Northern Ireland. For example, the decision to leave the European Union (EU) was ultimately a matter for the British Parliament, with the

[22] Jeremy Waldron, *Political Political Theory: Essays on Institutions* (Cambridge, MA: Harvard University Press 2016) 49.

[23] Waldron, *Political Political Theory*, 49–53.

devolved governments having little say in the process outside the largely consultative (and erratically convened) Joint Ministerial Committee EU.

In the UK, mixed government has been more associated with the second and third ideas of checks and balances and the separation of powers. The idea of checks and balances was crucial to the original formulation of mixed government, the crux of which involved different social groups governing concurrently, yet not only predated but also was independent from the latter idea. As Wilfried Nippel has remarked, Polybius's conception of mixed government did not involve 'normative ideas of a necessary differentiation of governmental functions'.[24] Its prime purpose was to ensure that the exercise of political power reflected the 'natural' balance of the different social classes and interests within the political 'body', and to provide mechanisms whereby each could check the other. Although the Polybian version of the argument came to predominate, it diverged in important respects from the Aristotelian account. Aristotle had regarded kingship as the best form, and democracy as a corruption of what he called Polity. However, he thought the ideal was almost impossible to obtain, and was highly likely to degenerate into tyranny, which was the worst possible option. Consequently, he advocated Polity as the most generalizable form of government. This consisted of a mixture of two corrupt forms—democracy and oligarchy. Unlike Polybius, Aristotle had not considered that different political bodies should represent different groups and he had thought that citizens should be directly involved in government. His aim had been to employ devices, such as a combination of election and lot, to ensure a social mixture amongst the political officers. Whereas Polybius conceived mixed government as a balance of classes, therefore, Aristotle had interpreted it as meaning a mingling of them. He had believed that whilst democracy and oligarchy undermined the common interest by placing government exclusively in the hands of either those without means or those with them respectively, a Polity resulted when those with moderate wealth predominated and tempered the conflict between rich and poor.[25]

The importance of balancing social power was given especial emphasis by Machiavelli, whose *Discorsi* can in many respects be read as a radical version of the Polybian argument, obtained via an Aristotelian appreciation of an active citizenry. Continuing the organic imagery of the ancients, he observed that all political bodies contain two classes, the nobles (*grandi*) and the people (*popolo*), whose 'humours' (*umori*) or desires conflict. He contended that the prime advantage of the Roman 'mixed constitution' admired by Polybius was the balance it achieved amongst these two humours by dividing power between the respective classes.

[24] Wilfried Nippel, 'Ancient and Modern Republicanism: Mixed Constitution and "Ephors"' in Biancamaria Fontana (ed.), *The Invention of the Modern Republic* (Cambridge: Cambridge University Press 1994) 9.

[25] Aristotle, *The Politics* (T. A. Sinclair tr., rev. edn, Harmondsworth: Penguin 1981) Bk III, ch. 7.

Indeed, he claimed that their discord, far from being destructive, had actively promoted 'all the laws made in favour of liberty'.[26] The republic had only collapsed when the economic struggle finally subverted this political balance and the patricians overthrew it in order to recover the privileges taken away from them by the Gracchi's attempt to enforce the Agrarian Law.[27]

Machiavelli's analysis involved a sociological insight that linked the relative merits of different political institutions or *ordini* to the social conditions—what he called the *materia*—of the polity in which they operated. 'Good laws' and 'good customs' were interdependent, and only 'extreme force', which had dangers of its own, could create the second through the imposition of the first.[28] He related the process of corruption and the attendant Polybian cycle of constitutional change, which ultimately affected even mixed governments, to changes in society at large.[29] Differences in manners and the degree of equality between citizens were particularly important in this regard. Thus, republics were more suited to egalitarian societies in which there was a general concern for the common good amongst the citizenry, whilst principalities were more appropriate to conditions of social inequality.[30] Machiavelli disputed classic fears of the inconstancy and unreliability of the multitude. He believed that the greater equality of republics made the people more prudent and law-abiding, and caused them to identify their personal interests more closely with the common welfare. In particular, there was a greater preparedness to bear arms and hence no need for mercenaries. These features rendered republican governments more stable and secure than principalities, in which the temptation to abuse one's power was greater.[31]

This Machiavellian sociological understanding of the role of the balance of power proves central to the operation of a political constitution. To achieve the requisite procedural legitimacy, the organization and operation of a political constitution needs to be tied to the character of the political society to which it applies—such as the pattern of social cleavages, the degree of economic development, and so forth that determine the political community's material constitution. The aim of this congruence between the political and the material constitution is to ensure the various groups and interests within society gain sufficient influence and control to be accorded equal concern and respect in the formulation of collective policies. It would prove crucial to ways the political constitution in the nineteenth and twentieth centuries came to encompass the representative institutions of mass democracy in response to the demand for universal suffrage.

[26] Niccolò Machiavelli, 'Discorsi' in Niccolò Machiavelli, *Il Principle e Discorsi* (S. Bertelli ed., Milan: Feltrinelli 1960) Bk 1, ch. 4.

[27] Machiavelli, 'Discorsi', Bk 1, ch. 37.

[28] Machiavelli, 'Discorsi', Bk 1, ch. 17.

[29] Machiavelli, 'Discorsi', Bk 1, chs 16–18.

[30] Machiavelli, 'Discorsi', Bk 1, ch. 55.

[31] Machiavelli, 'Discorsi', Bk 1, ch. 58; Bk 2, ch. 2.

The republican interpretation of mixed government as involving a balance of social groups first entered English constitutional discourse in Charles I's Answer to Parliament's Nineteen Propositions of 1642, where it served to characterize the parliamentary system as combining King, Lords, and Commons. It may seem paradoxical that it was royalists who introduced the view that monarchical power should be limited by the nobility and the people as part of a balanced constitution.[32] Yet, the move was forced on them by the insistence of the Nineteen Propositions on the need for the king's ministers and judicial appointees to be approved by and responsible to Parliament. It offered a way of insisting that the king also played a necessary and legitimate role and possessed appropriate entitlements within a scheme of parliamentary governance. The Answer's authors maintained that 'the experience and wisdom of your ancestors' had 'moulded' a mixture 'as to give to this kingdom (as far as humane prudence can contrive) the conveniences of all three, without the inconveniences of anyone, as long as the balance hangs even between the three estates',[33] and warned how to disturb this hard won balance risked unleashing the 'vices' of 'tyranny... faction and division [and] tumults, violence and licentiousness' to which monarchy, aristocracy, and democracy respectively were prone.[34] Meanwhile, although the Answer drew on the writings of Sir Edward Coke to assert the 'immemorial' character of this arrangement, this move also reveals how the ascription to Coke and his followers of a common law constitutionalism,[35] whereby a distant fundamental law grounded and constrained the authority of king and Parliament alike, goes too far. Not only had common lawyers granted the ancient status of Parliament's ability to enact law, but also statute had proved more effective than judicial 'discovered' law to bind the king to a petition of right.[36] In the Answer, the ancient constitution now became the product of an immemorial constitutive political act, wherein sovereignty and the right of law-making was constituted within the king in Parliament. Common law thereby became subordinated to parliamentary sovereignty as the embodiment of an ancient political constitution.[37]

However, this proved a dangerous argument to employ. Not only did it undermine the absolute authority of the king by suggesting that power was shared, as Robert Filmer pointed out,[38] it was also open to the radical Machiavellian

[32] Vile, *Constitutionalism*, 36–40.

[33] 'The King's Answer to the Nineteen Propositions, 18 June 1642' in J. P. Kenyon (ed.), *The Stuart Constitution: Documents and Commentary* (Cambridge: Cambridge University Press 1966) 22.

[34] 'King's Answer', 21.

[35] J. G. A. Pocock, *The Ancient Constitution and the Feudal Law* (2nd edn, Cambridge: Cambridge University Press 1987) 49–50, 234.

[36] Glenn Burgess, *The Politics of the Ancient Constitution: An Introduction to English Political Thought 1603–1642* (London: Macmillan 1992) ch. 8.

[37] Corinne C. Weston, 'England: Ancient Constitution and Common Law' in J. H. Burns (ed.), *The Cambridge History of Political Thought 1450–1700* (Cambridge: Cambridge University Press 1991) 388–90, 397–8.

[38] Robert Filmer, 'The Anarchy of a Limited or Mixed Monarchy' in Robert Filmer, *Patriarcha and Other Political Writings* (J. Somerville ed., Cambridge: Cambridge University Press 1991).

argument of James Harrington.[39] Harrington claimed that the mixed constitution was unstable precisely because it no longer reflected a social balance. The undermining of the feudal system and the gradual transferral of property, and with it military and political power, to the commons meant that the only stable political system was a republic in which property and military responsibilities were shared amongst them alone, rather than with the king and aristocracy.[40] Harrington's consequent advocacy of economic and institutional 'superstructures' capable of inducing civic virtue within a single social group proved important,[41] as we shall see, when it came to elaborating a democratic version of the separation of powers.

Unfortunately, Cromwell failed to institute the Harringtonian republic. Nevertheless, the problem of controlling government in a society without distinctions of rank remained. It was these circumstances that helped to crystallize the essential elements behind the idea of the separation of powers: namely, the notion that different agencies should perform distinct functions and the belief that the judicial branch especially should be independent. Lack of space prohibits an account of this history here.[42] Suffice it to say, that the struggle between king and Parliament, the experience of the Long Parliament, and the setting up of the Protectorate, all served in different ways to raise the issues of the respective roles, limits, and relations of legislature and executive. On the one hand, it emerged that large assemblies were inefficient for the implementation of laws and policy. On the other hand, it became apparent that legislative functions should not be entrusted to those executing or judging violations of the law if legislation was to be made in the common interest, administered impartially, and officials held to account. A separation of legislative and executive powers appeared justified on both counts.

This doctrine was a commonplace, therefore, by the time of the restoration and John Locke's seminal analysis of the 'powers of government' in the *Second Treatise*.[43] However, Locke elaborated the doctrine in ways that were to be crucial to political constitutionalism. First, Locke noted that legislation was more likely to be in the public interest, apply equally to all, and treat all those subject to it with equal concern and respect, if it was made on an equal basis by an assembly of those—or their representatives—who would have to live under these laws. Second, this mechanism will be undermined if legislators can control the application of the law and be able to exempt themselves or their supporters from it—hence the need to separate the legislative from the executive branch. Third, while an executive branch was required for general legislation to be efficiently and effectively

[39] J. G. A. Pocock, *The Machiavellian Moment: Florentine Political Thought and the Atlantic Republican Tradition* (Princeton, NJ: Princeton University Press 1975) 15–42.

[40] James Harrington, *Political Works* (J. G. A. Pocock ed., Cambridge: Cambridge University Press 1977) 163–5.

[41] Harrington, *Political Works*, 171–4.

[42] Vile, *Constitutionalism*, 37–52.

[43] John Locke, *Two Treatises of Government* (Cambridge: Cambridge University Press 1988) II, paras 143–4.

administered, transposed into policies, and applied to particular cases, to avoid arbitrary, discretionary rule that branch had to operate under the law. As a result, the legislative branch could be regarded as the 'supreme power'; since it set down the 'positive laws' and 'common rule' that are to be executed. Moreover, though the judiciary tends to be treated as an aspect of the executive branch in Locke's account, a key aspect of his conception of political society was that the executors of the law were not judges in their own case as to whether they had implemented the law or not: that possibility was the very definition of a tyrannous form of arbitrary rule. Finally, the exception was the 'federative power' of peace and war and international treaty-making and negotiations, that Locke contended could not be law-governed given the need for flexibility and dispatch to deal with unforeseeable situations. However, although this federative power was most appropriately held by the executive branch it needed to be separated from the executive power proper.

As Waldron notes,[44] the separation of powers operates here as a mode of articulated governance that operates in the service of the rule of law as a curb on arbitrary rule. However, although an independent judiciary plays an important role in this account, the rule of law is not the rule of constitutional law or of judges as its interpreters, as in legal constitutionalism, but the rule of legislation and the legislature, the primacy of which binds the judiciary as it does the executive. This account of the rule of law as involving the primacy of legislation, and hence of the legislature, with executive action needing to be authorized by duly made law and responsible to the legislature—sometimes indirectly via the judiciary, became the hall mark of political constitutionalism. However, to achieve this result, the separation of powers needed to be assimilated to a view of the English constitution as a model of the 'balance' to be achieved in mixed monarchy. While hinted at in Locke, it only became established doctrine with the constitutional settlement expressed in the Bill of Rights of 1689 that affirmed not only the Protestant character of the English state but also established a constitutional monarchy by asserting the absolute legislative authority of free and regular parliaments, including the power to abolish royal prerogatives by Act of Parliament.

3. MONTESQUIEU TO DICEY: FROM THE BALANCED CONSTITUTION TO 'PARLIAMENTARY GOVERNMENT'

This settlement attained its canonical expression in Montesquieu's account of the English constitution in the *Spirit of the Laws* of 1748. Montesquieu began by enunciating some of the basic premises of constitutional government. Political liberty, he asserted, differed from self-defeating licence by requiring acceptance of

[44] Waldron, *Political*, 57.

the rule of law.[45] However, law and liberty went together 'only when there is no abuse of power'. Since 'all experience proves that every man with power is led to abuse it', all power must be kept within bounds by so framing the constitution 'that power checks [*arrete*] power'.[46] His innovation lay in modifying the idea of functional separation so that it operates as a check.

Montesquieu's initial description of the separation of powers followed the Lockean distinction between legislative and executive, the latter being further subdivided into internal and external affairs. However, he immediately restated the doctrine, introducing this time a third 'power of judging'.[47] Although not the first to do so, this tripartite division only gained wide currency with Montesquieu. The vast majority of earlier writers had classified judicial power under the domestic duties of the executive, though they did argue that those who decided civil and criminal cases ought not to exercise other executive functions. He then drew not only the standard conclusion that uniting the executive and legislative endangered liberty by allowing a monarch or senate to make 'tyrannical laws in order to execute them in a tyrannical way', but also argued that an even greater danger of oppression followed if the judicial power was united to either of the other two, or worse still all three came together in the same person or body. His reasoning was that whilst the legislature was concerned solely with declaring 'the general will of the state' and the executive with 'nothing more than the execution of that general will', only the judiciary applied the laws to particular persons. Consequently, the true definition of despotism was the uniting of this power with the other two.

Montesquieu did not believe that formal separation alone would allow each to check the others. Criticizing the Venetian republic, he observed that although the legislative, executive, and judicial powers were divided between the Supreme Council, the '*pregardi*' and the '*quarantia*' respectively, 'all these tribunals are formed from magistrates who belong to the same social estate, which virtually turns them into one and the same power'. A material and procedural basis had to be given to the distinction, therefore.

Mixed government partially resolved this difficulty, since making the executive an hereditary monarch ensured its separation from the legislature. Departing, as he often did, from the reality of the English situation, he argued against ministers being taken from the legislature on the grounds that in this case 'the two powers would be united' and 'there would no longer be any liberty'. This arrangement also served the efficiency aspect of the separation of power, 'because this part of government, which almost always requires rapid action, is better administered by one person than many'. However, mixed government added an additional dimension

45 C.-L. De S Montesquieu, *De l'esprit des lois*, 2 vols (Paris: Garnier-Flammarion 1979) I, Bk XI, ch. 3.

46 Montesquieu, *De l'esprit*, I, Bk XI, ch. 4.

47 Montesquieu, *De l'esprit*, I, Bk XI, ch. 6, from which all the quotes that follow also come.

by dividing the legislature between two assemblies—the one consisting of the nobles and the other of the representatives of the people. Separate representation for the nobility was warranted by the need to protect their distinct interests and views stemming from the advantages of 'birth, riches or honours'. But bicameralism also operated as part of a checking mechanism. Montesquieu advocated that both the executive and the upper chamber should be able to check the power of the legislature by having the right of veto. Likewise, he believed that the legislature should have the power to investigate how the executive officers had carried out the law and impeach them if found corrupt. But he thought the monarch ought to be distinguished from his 'evil counsellors' in this respect, otherwise his independence would be jeopardized. These suggestions partially undermined a pure separation, since they gave the executive a negative share in legislation. However, they helped strengthen the weaker parts of the constitution against the growing strength of the legislature, whose wider and logically prior role of law-making made it the most powerful body and so the most in need of restraining from going beyond its remit.

Montesquieu's most novel argument in this regard was his reworking of the republican thesis that the best way of ensuring that legislation reflected the common interest was to have it made by the people. In a 'free state', he affirmed, 'every man who is considered a free citizen ought to be governed by himself. Hence the people as an estate ought to have the legislative power'. However, this republican point did not lead to advocacy of republican forms of government. He criticized ancient direct democracy for confusing the power of the people with its liberty. Such radical participation subverted the distinction between legislative and executive powers. Besides being unworkable in large states, even in small ones it involved many people in decisions they were 'unfit' to make. Representative democracy remedied these defects by introducing checks into the democratic process. It involved selecting only the more capable citizens and reducing those involved in debating public business to manageable proportions. It exploited the fact that people were better able to choose suitable candidates and, if necessary, reject them, than to propose laws. As Harrington had noticed, this division between proposers and resolvers could offer a perfect procedural guarantee of fairness.[48] Organizing constituencies geographically rather than according to estates, thereby removing the case for mandation, provided a further check against class-based legislation. Finally, in Book 19, chapter 27, Montesquieu introduced a related social foundation to the constitution in the customs of a free people. The habit of saying and thinking what one liked, led citizens to divide into parties supporting either the legislature or the executive. Self-interest motivated those favoured by the executive to support it, those with nothing to hope for to attack it. The effect of liberty, he

[48] Harrington, *Political Works*, 172, 174.

contended, was for citizens always to favour the weaker side. The jealousy of the people and their representatives in the legislature was in this respect the surest way to check the executive.

The fusion of the separation of powers and mixed government produced a socially and politically balanced and mutually checking constitution.[49] Although such an arrangement might lead to 'inaction', he claimed the 'necessary movement of things' forced the various parts to work together. The system served to distil the public interest out of certain disparate private ones, and to gain the advantage of the better elements in society in its enactment as law. Note, the judicial power remained hard to assimilate to this scheme, since it added a potential fourth department within the theory of mixed government. As we saw, Montesquieu believed this power would be especially dangerous if linked to either of the other two. He thought its independence was best achieved through the jury system and lay magistrates so that it did not become attached to any estate or profession. This lack of a social base or permanent cadre rendered it the weakest power. It became 'invisible' having 'in a sense, no force', at least in the political sense.

The influence of Locke notwithstanding, Montequieu's view of the constitution remained essentially organic rather than contractual. He emphasized mixed government and the balancing of the various parts of the body politic. He did not treat the constitution as a compact between the people that established government. As Thomas Paine remarked in his *Rights of Man* of 1791,[50] it was this conception of a constitution as a popular contract that lay behind the 'modern' legal model of a constitution of the United States, as a codified and comprehensive fundamental law that was antecedent to government.

By contrast, the British constitution continued to be conceived in ancient terms as a form of governing. The two main constitutional texts of the eighteenth and nineteenth centuries, Blackstone's *Commentaries of the Laws of England* (1765–69) and A. V. Dicey's *Lectures on the Law of the Constitution* (1885), both remain within Montesquieu's framework. They consider the British constitution a form of mixed government—that of Crown-in-Parliament—that combines the advantages of a system of checks and balances and the separation of powers that taken together ensure the rule of law conceived as the primacy of legislation. As Dicey summarized it, 'the sovereignty of Parliament, as contrasted with other forms of sovereign power, favours the supremacy of law' because 'the commands of Parliament . . . can be uttered only through the combined actions of its three constituent parts', with the need for an accommodation between monarch, Lords, and Commons providing a series of checks of balances. Meanwhile, the need to rule through law made by a sovereign Parliament 'constantly hampers . . . the action of the executive'

[49] Montesquieu, *De l'esprit*, I, Bk XI, ch. 6.
[50] Thomas Paine, 'Rights of Man Part 1'' in Thomas Paine, *Political Writings* (B. Kuklick ed., Cambridge: Cambridge University Press 1989) 78–92.

so that 'the government can escape only by obtaining from Parliament the discretionary authority which is denied to the Crown by the law of the land'.[51]

An important upshot of this approach was that 'the constitution is the result of the ordinary law of the land', so that 'the law of the constitution ... [is] not the source but the consequence of the rights of individuals'.[52] Dicey's argument has been dismissed as an 'outburst of Anglo-Saxon parochialism'.[53] Yet, the most glaring weakness is that the endorsement of the mixed constitution in the seminal legal texts of the period had little or no basis in reality, as political analysts of the actual working of the constitution had long pointed out. Three related aspects of this reality had preoccupied eighteenth-century political analysts of the constitution:[54] first, the 'influence' of the Crown in elections and the Commons through what was known as 'Old Corruption'; second, the role of parties that could not be understood either in the classical or Machiavellian terms of a struggle between different classes or branches of the legislature, but cut across both; and, finally, the primacy of the Commons, predominantly through its control over supply but also via the associated convention of the need for ministers to command a parliamentary majority and the effective disuse of the royal veto, and which had buttressed its independence through the Septennial Act. The distinction between 'Court' and 'Country' parties offered no real help in this regard, given that they could not be regarded as the 'grandi' or nobles and the 'plebs' respectively. Even if the latter liked to portray themselves as representing the people, they were hardly of, and only very imperfectly elected by, the people, while the former was if anything the king's rather than aristocracy's party. Indeed, the two groups were not so much what David Hume came to term 'parties of interest', as 'parties of affection' and to some degree 'of principle', more accurately associated with the alternative terms of Whigs and Tories.[55]

The intellectual task confronting contemporary observers of this reality was how to assimilate it to the mixed constitution. One solution was to suggest that all three elements—Crown, aristocracy, and commons—were present within the House of Commons and existed in balance there. As Hume argued, this involved a justification of the Crown's influence over the Commons via the members of the executive and its supporters, which he saw as having the salutary effect of transforming parties of principle and affection—both of which he regarded as prone to factionalism and irrationality, and as such sources of instability -into parties of interest, which tended to be more constant and rational.[56] Others observed

[51] A. V. Dicey, *Introduction to the Study of the Law of the Constitution* (8th edn, London: MacMillan 1915) Part II, ch. 13, 402, 405.

[52] Dicey, *Introduction*, Part II, ch. 4, 198–9.

[53] Judith Shklar, 'Political Theory and the Rule of Law' in A. C. Hutchinson and P. Monahan (eds), *The Rule of Law: Ideal or Ideology* (Toronto: University of Toronto Press 1987) 5.

[54] J. A. W. Gunn, 'Influence, Parties and the Constitution: Changing Attitudes, 1783–1832' (1974) 17(2) *Historical Journal* 301–28.

[55] David Hume, *Essays Moral, Political and Literary* (E. F. Miller ed., Indianapolis: Liberty Fund 1987), Part 1, Essays 7 and 8.

[56] Hume, *Essays*, Part 1, Essay 6.

that the aristocracy also operated as a distinct influence within the lower house, through the presence of their retainers. Meanwhile, the commons proper was represented by those elected without and in opposition to influence. In this way, the Commons became the arena in which the contest between the three estates took place. Hume viewed this transformation as an adaptation of the mixed constitution to a commercial age. The institutionalization of balance based on interests placed virtue in stable political arrangements rather than in the uncertain disposition of particular individuals, such as the monarch, and so supported a regular system of justice that upheld property rights and contract, the necessary prerequisites of a commercial republic.

Unsurprisingly, this defence of influence came under increasing attack from those denied office by such means, notably the radicals and the Whig politician Charles James Fox, who became a champion of electoral reform.[57] Throughout the eighteenth century no administration ever lost an election—ministries fell largely because they lost the support of the king, who managed the composition of the Commons to comply with his choice of ministers and whose prerogative to choose them went largely unchallenged. Only two resigned due to a failure to win a vote in the Commons. That became increasingly untenable with the mishandling of the American War of Independence and the questioning of the established order posed by the French Revolution. Yet the prospect of reform, supported by both Foxite Whigs and radicals such as Paine and Jeremy Bentham, albeit from divergent perspectives, raised a different threat to the balance of the constitution—that of democracy. Indeed, Bentham's Constitutional Code can be regarded as a radical democratic form of political constitutionalism designed to incentivize the alignment of the interests of an 'omnicompetent' elected legislature and, via them, the executive, with the promotion of the interests of the people as a whole, conceived in utilitarian terms as the securing of the greatest happiness of the greatest number.[58] However, the main concern of his contemporaries centred precisely on the growing encroachment of popular sovereignty on parliamentary sovereignty and its distinctive balance between commons, lords, and monarch.

The early and mid-nineteenth-century debate thereby came to focus on defending parliamentary sovereignty without in the process succumbing to either popular sovereignty or monarchical sovereignty through the use of influence and the royal prerogative.[59] The solution was seen in making the authority of the executive, as organized in the Cabinet, dependent on Parliament, without making Parliament dependent on the people. This argument found its defining statement

[57] Gunn, 'Influence', 310–11.

[58] Frederick Rosen, *Jeremy Bentham and Representative Democracy: A Study of the Constitutional Code* (Oxford: Clarendon Press 1983) and Philip Schofield, 'Jeremy Bentham' in Dennis J. Galligan (ed), *Constitutions and the Classics. Patterns of Constitutional Thought from Fortescue to Bentham* (Oxford: Oxford University Press 2014) 231–249.

[59] Angus Hawkins, '"Parliamentary Government" and Victorian Political Parties c 1830–1880' (1989) 104 *English Historical Review* 638–69, at 645, 660.

in Earl Grey's essay 'Parliamentary Government Considered with Reference to Reform of Parliament' (1858), and was adopted by contemporary constitutional authorities, such as Sir Thomas Erskine May's *Constitutional History of England* (1861–63).[60] Again parties (largely absent from Bentham's proposal[61]) played a crucial role. As May noted, that 'a form of government so composite, and combining so many conflicting forces, has generally been maintained in harmonious action, is mainly due to the organization of parties'.[62] Parties offered a degree of cohesion that could discipline individual MPs both in and out of office. To the extent they formed groups bound by shared ideals, they became a constraint on corruption via the royal prerogative. But at the same time they needed to be sufficiently loose not to rest on an electoral mandate, so that a ministry could fall without necessitating dissolution. It is this version of party that lies behind Burke's famous defence of representation as trusteeship based on Parliament offering a virtual representation of the national interest.[63] Parties in this account were parliamentary groups under aristocratic leadership not electoral organizations responsive to popular demands, which represented the interests within the country without giving them a direct voice. As a result, a mix between people, aristocracy, and monarch continued, with the new balance that encapsulated this mix being that between the competing parties of government and opposition.[64]

This doctrine of 'parliamentary government' underlies Dicey's famous account of parliamentary sovereignty outlined above. Yet, by the 1880s, parliamentary government had largely given way to the two-party system. If the 1832 Reform Act had been an attempt to maintain this arrangement in the face of demands for electoral reform, the reforms of 1867 and 1884 promoted the shift towards parties that were much more akin to electoral machines.[65] In a political analysis of *The English Constitution* of 1867, Walter Bagehot had already questioned the continued relevance of the mixed constitution. Bagehot made a key distinction between the 'dignified' and the 'efficient' elements of the constitution which he deployed to call into question the reality of both checks and balances and the separation of powers within the British system of government, and with it the existence of the rule of law. If the monarchy and the doctrine of the Crown-in-Parliament formed the 'dignified' parts of the constitution, which gave it a certain mystique and popular legitimacy, the 'efficient' parts 'by which it, in fact, works and rules' involved 'the nearly complete fusion of the legislative and executive powers' in the hands of the

[60] Hawkins, '"Parliamentary Government"', 657, 661.

[61] Rosen, *Jeremy Bentham and Representative Democracy*, 177–78.

[62] Thomas Erskine May, *The Constitutional History of England Since the Accession of George III*, 2 vols (vol. II, Boston: Crosby and Nicols 1863) ch. VIII, 17.

[63] Edmund Burke, 'Speech to the Electors of Bristol' in I. Hampshire-Monk (ed.), *The Political Philosophy of Edmund Burke* (Harlow: Longman 1987) 108–11.

[64] Hawkins, '"Parliamentary Government"', 647.

[65] Angus Hawkins, *Victorian Political Culture: 'Habits of Heart and Mind'* (Oxford: Oxford University Press 2015) ch. 10.

Queen's ministers through the government's control of a parliamentary majority. Moreover, after 1886 governments possessed office as a result of winning a parliamentary majority in elections. Bagehot, like Dicey, was an unenthusiastic democrat and worried that without the 'dignified' façade, the result would produce the 'democratic despotism' or 'unmoderated democracy' that many adherents of parliamentary government and the mixed constitution feared would result from the fusing of parliamentary with popular sovereignty.[66]

Yet, as Montesquieu had hinted, representative democracy had the potential to offer a new and 'efficient' mechanism of checks and balances through electoral competition between parties reflecting contrasting interests and ideologies. That shift had begun in 1841, when Sir Robert Peel's Tories returned more members to the Commons than the governing Liberals and, for that reason, were invited by Queen Victoria to replace them and form a government. This period also saw the term Her Majesty's Loyal Opposition enter common usage,[67] signalling a new electorally based parliamentary balance between the government and a government in waiting. The 1880s completed this process with the ideological consolidation of the Liberal Party post the Home Rule crisis and the Liberal and Conservative Parties full transformation into electoral machines, thereby finishing the process begun in the 1860s towards the modern two-party system.[68] The Parliament Act of 1911 finally brought the end to the remaining 'effective' elements of the mixed constitution by removing the veto of both the Lords and the monarch on the Commons and the will of an elected government. Occasioned by the House of Lords rejection of the Liberal administration's 'People's Budget', introducing both a super tax on the wealthy and death duties to fund its social reforms and pensions, and the king's refusal to appoint new Liberal Peers to overcome the Lords' opposition, it led to two elections in 1910 that confirmed the government's authority. Consequently, the legislative authority of the Commons was now tightly linked to its being an elected chamber where the government of the day commanded a majority of MPs. Over the ensuing thirty years, the two-party system—during which Labour was eventually to supplant the Liberals—effectively became the new political constitution.

4. REPRESENTATIVE DEMOCRACY AND PARTY COMPETITION: TOWARDS A NEW BALANCE OF POWER

The balance of the mixed constitution involved an explicit check against popular majorities. The 'majority' was simply that social class that involved the 'most'

[66] A. L. Lowell, *The Government of England*, 2 vols (vol. 1, London: Macmillan 1908) 447.

[67] The first use, as a quip, was by Sir John Cam Hobhouse in 1826, Waldron, *Political Political Theory*, 103.

[68] Hawkins, *Victorian Political Culture*, 325–8.

people, but their interests had at best to be weighed and balanced against those of the few—the aristocracy—and the one—the monarch. Although it proved flexible enough to adapt to changes in the social and economic material constitution, it involved an explicit bias towards upholding the prevailing class divisions, even if these had altered with the passage from a landed to a commercial society. As such, it had a tendency towards preserving the existing balance of society.

The gradual extension of the suffrage to encompass the whole adult population by 1928 meant that the majority now referred to a majority of the population as a whole. Political equality on the basis of one person one vote brought to the centre of politics what became known as the 'social question'. It was also associated with an expansion of the social and economic role of the state. A modern economy involved not only greater regulation but also the provision of a more extensive infrastructure, all of which required higher taxation and public borrowing. The displacement of the Liberal Party by a Labour Party rooted in the Trade Union movement may not have been inevitable, but the need to make a credible appeal to the working population was.[69]

As both Max Weber and Joseph Schumpeter noted, among other mainly foreign observers of the evolution of party systems,[70] electoral party competition promotes a dynamic balance, akin in certain respects to market competition among firms and entrepreneurs. As a result, the character of parties also changed. Organized mass parties to some degree preserved elite rule, but encouraged leading politicians to develop certain campaigning skills that enabled them to recruit a following. Building a majority now involved cross-party alliances of interest that were tied to competing ideational conceptions of the national interest. Although these could have—and largely came to possess—a class basis, as favouring the interests of capital or labour, the need to fish for votes more broadly meant that parties also built support around an ideological claim that policies favouring such interests were either more just and/or more beneficial to all. As a result, the balance came to be between competing programmes for government that encompassed, but were not simply defined by, competing affective or interest groups.

Reinforced by the mass mobilization and high taxation required to fight two world wars, these trends led Britain, in common with the rest of Western Europe, to be transformed from a liberal to a social democracy over the first half of the twentieth century. It was in this context that the contemporary debate arose over Britain's anomalous political constitution and proposals came forward that it adopt a 'modern' legal constitution.[71] Despite the new circumstances, these critiques reflected earlier worries that democracy undermined parliamentary government

[69] Hawkins, *Victorian Political Culture*, ch. 10.

[70] Max Weber, 'The Profession and Vocation of Politics' in Max Weber, *Political Writings* (P. Lassman and R. Speirs eds, R. Speirs tr., Cambridge: Cambridge University Press 1994) 309–69; J. A. Schumpeter, *Capitalism, Socialism and Democracy* (London: Routledge 1976) chs 21 and 22.

[71] Leslie Scarman, *English Law: The New Dimension* (London: Stevens and Sons 1974).

by empowering an executive that was unrepresentative of the people as a whole. Echoing Bagehot, Lowell and the literature of the 1860s–1880s bemoaning the decline of 'parliamentary government' and the triumph of the philosophic radicals' agenda of Bentham and the Mills, critics argued that MPs who owed their legitimacy to being members of a popularly elected party were mere lobby fodder, voting as directed by the party leadership. The efficient part of the constitution was the Cabinet, itself emasculated by secrecy and collective responsibility, and possibly just the prime minister, with the legislature but a dignified rubber stamp of an ever growing and more intrusive body of legislation.[72] The supposed result was what Lord Hailsham famously termed 'an elective dictatorship', whereby 'a bare majority in a single chamber' can 'assert its will over a whole people whatever that will may be'. Indicating the immediate and particular ideological motivation underlying this apparently general constitutional concern, he continued: 'It will end in a rigid economic plan, and I believe a siege economy, a curbed and subservient judiciary and a regulated press. It will impose uniformity on the whole nation in the interest of what it claims to be social justice'.[73]

As with his nineteenth-century forebears, Hailsham's view traded on regarding electoral competition as lacking balance, and involving the victory of a purely sectoral interest. He ignored how even in two-party systems a majority party is usually a coalition of different interests and ideological views that may fail to vote consistently along government lines. Nor did he note the parliamentary scrutiny of ministers and legislation performed by opposition parties, an aspect of Parliament likewise passed over by Bagehot. His remarks on the danger to the judiciary and a free press notwithstanding, his account contained no mention of the class and political biases prevalent in media ownership or membership of the judiciary.

Meanwhile, his solution was a revamped version of the mixed constitution, designed to 'so rearrange the balance of forces within the separate organs of the constitution as to make dominance by any one of them impossible'.[74] This new constitutional arrangement was to include a proportionately elected second chamber and a federal structure involving devolution to Scotland, Wales, Northern Ireland, and the English regions. Such counter-majoritarian arrangements can have a pronounced anti-egalitarian bias in giving extra weight to certain sectoral interests and favouring the status quo by making any change dependent on a super-majority or even consensus. However, this was Hailsham's explicit intention. 'Fundamental changes', he affirmed, 'ought only to be imposed, if at all, in the light of an unmistakeable national consensus'.[75] Indeed, not content with so diffusing power as to

[72] R. H. S. Crossman, 'Introduction' to Walter Bagehot, *The English Constitution* (Glasgow: Collins 1963).

[73] Lord Hailsham, *The Dilemma of Democracy: Diagnosis and Prescription* (Glasgow: Collins 1978) 9–10.

[74] Hailsham, *The Dilemma*, 68.

[75] Hailsham, *The Dilemma*, 21–2.

make such change politically unlikely, he sought to render it legally impossible by entrenching a doctrine of 'limited government or freedom under law' through a Bill of Rights that would guard against both 'equality' and 'the common good' and 'offer protections against the oppressiveness of unions and corporations' by upholding those entitlements of individuals and minorities that reflect 'the instructed conscience of the commonality'.[76]

Hailsham's thesis met with a spirited counter-blast from J. A. G. Griffith in his Chorley Lecture of 1978 entitled 'The Political Constitution'. Griffith sought to defend the modern democratic constitution. At the heart of his defence was the claim that the constitutional doctrine of equilibrium in defence of the 'general conscience of mankind' hid the genuine conflicts and disagreements that animated politics. In Benthamite manner, he viewed talk of natural or human rights as metaphysical nonsense. They were simply political claims that reflected the political prejudices of those making them.[77] Asking courts to decide difficult policy questions with reference to necessarily abstract concepts of rights involved not the rule of law so much as the rule of judges and their political views. The only legitimate way to resolve differences over rights was through an explicitly political process—one where those making such decisions where political actors who were responsible and accountable to the people who would be subject to them.[78]

Griffith contended this did not entail any disrespect for law or the judiciary. On the contrary, it involved upholding the proper role of both. Griffith insisted that 'only an outlaw' would regard a regular system of law upheld by an independent judiciary, which applied equally to all—including the government of the day—as undesirable.[79] However, rights became more certain in their judicial application through being incorporated into concrete legislation embodying a determinate and democratically authorized political policy choice aimed at addressing a specific issue or set of issues. Invoking a democratic version of Dicey's view of the rule of law, he argued that democratically elected governments could rightfully and non-arbitrarily enact such legislation so long as it met the two key conditions imposed by the British political constitution: that they did not infringe existing legal entitlements of individuals unless expressly authorized to do so by statute, and that any change to the law or their powers under it obtained the assent of a democratically elected Parliament. That did not mean he thought the current political process by any means perfect. He argued for a more open and accessible system of government, with greater scope for debate. However, he contended the aim had to be to improve not diminish the democratic qualities of governance by further legally constraining democracy through a written constitution.[80]

76 Hailsham, *The Dilemma*, 9–10, 13.
77 Griffith, 'Political Constitution', 17.
78 Griffith, 'Political Constitution', 16–19.
79 Griffith, 'Political Constitution', 15.
80 Griffith, 'Political Constitution', 15–17.

Ironically, by the time Griffith's lecture was published, a Conservative administration under Mrs Thatcher had been elected which was to use the very powers Hailsham, her new Lord Chancellor, had decried to promote changes he found congenial but others would regard every bit as fundamental an attack on the existing social consensus as those he had feared from Labour. Far from diffusing power, she used her parliamentary majority—achieved with never more than 43.9 per cent of the popular vote—to centralize it, curtailing the independence of local authorities in the process. She also weakened considerably the rights of labour to organize and strike through the Trade Union Act of 1984 and the Employment Act of 1988, and oversaw a significant increase in inequality.[81]

Griffith had noted how the contemporaneous constitutional proposals of Liberals and Progressives, such as Lord Scarman and Ronald Dworkin, had been remarkably similar in their details and philosophical basis, if not their political motivation, to the now shelved plans of Lord Hailsham.[82] Unsurprisingly, the ensuing eighteen years of Conservative rule made these plans increasingly attractive to a Labour party that feared the terms of the British political constitution might condemn them to permanent opposition.[83] Public law networks, such as the Venice Commission, also promoted legal constitutionalism not only for new democracies in Central and Eastern Europe and elsewhere, but also within established democracies such as the Nordic and Commonwealth countries, that like the UK had strong political constitutional traditions, and influenced movements such as Charter 88 within the UK. Tony Blair's first Labour administration in 1997 was to see the introduction of the Human Rights Act (HRA) in 1998, the creation of a Supreme Court, a strengthening of local government in London and other metropolitan areas, and considerable devolution to Scotland, Wales, and Northern Ireland. Meanwhile, the impact of the European Convention of Human Rights (ECHR), which, for example, curbed the use of certain procedures to interrogate terrorist suspects in Northern Ireland under the Thatcher administration, and of European Community law post the *Factortame* litigation, were held to have fashioned a European legal constitutional constraint on the sovereignty of Parliament.

These moves were not without their critics, who revived and developed many elements of Griffith's earlier argument. Labour lawyers, such as Keith Ewing,[84] documented the mixed judicial record—including that of the European Court of Human Rights (ECtHR)—in defending the rights of workers, whistleblowers, and asylum seekers against executive actions based on reason of state. Waldron argued

[81] Sandra Fredman, 'The New Rights: Labour Law and Ideology in the Thatcher Years' (1992) 12 *Oxford Journal of Legal Studies* 24–44.

[82] Griffith, 'Political Constitution', 9, 10–12.

[83] Anthony Lester et al. (eds), *A British Bill of Rights* (London: IPPR 1990); Ronald Dworkin, *A Bill of Rights for Britain* (London: Chatto 1990).

[84] Keith Ewing, *Bonfire of the Liberties: New Labour, Human Rights, and the Rule of Law* (Oxford: Oxford University Press 2010).

how a democratic vote on the basis of majority rule offered a fair mechanism for resolving disagreements about rights,[85] and defended the dignity of legislation as a more legitimate and deliberative way of deciding rights issues than judicial review. Adam Tomkins drew on the writings of Quentin Skinner to relate the historical origins of parliamentary sovereignty in the seventeenth century to a distinctively republican conception of liberty as non-domination rooted, as we saw, in the ancient idea of mixed government. He contrasted this republican argument with the liberal view of liberty as non-interference he associated with the doctrine of limited government informing many legal constitutionalist proposals, such as Hailsham's.[86] Finally, I developed a number of these strands in my own neo-republican account of political constitutionalism,[87] stressing in particular the relationship between non-domination and political equality, and noting the role of party competition as involving a dynamic new form of checks and balances promotive of certain constitutional values, such as equality under law and minority rights.

Despite these criticisms, it might be argued that Labour's constitutional reforms had moved Britain decisively towards a legal constitution. In particular, a number of judges, most explicitly and programmatically Sir John Laws, but also implicitly in key judgments by Lords Hoffmann in *R. v. Home Secretary, ex parte Simms* [2000], and Steyn in *Jackson v. Attorney-General* [2005] among others, argued that legality and rights, rather than parliamentary sovereignty, formed the cornerstone of Britain's 'common law constitution'. Contra Dicey, they claimed the law was the source not the consequence of our rights. Of course, this was not a new claim, and it might be objected the role of the common law has been conspicuous by its absence throughout this account. Yet, not only does the political constitution play a distinct and autonomous role, which rests on foundations independent of the common law and retains a capacity to shape its judicial interpretation, but also the Thatcher period gives the lie to claims that the common law has ever contained rights comparable to those found in modern Bills of Rights. Instead, these rights derive from the HRA, which has the status of an ordinary statute and institutionalizes a system of 'weak' review where Parliament has the last word.[88] As such, the recent prominence of rights in British legal culture reflects a democratic version of Dicey's dictum of how the exercise of our political rights can give rise to legal rights. Indeed, this was Lord Bingham's argument in *A. v. Secretary of State for the Home Department (Belmarsh Prison)* [2004].

Meanwhile, as I argue in Chapters 5 and 11, if one conceives both the Council of Europe, within which the ECHR operates, and the EU as associations of democratic states, that are under the mutual control of the democratically elected

[85] Waldron, *Law and Disagreement*, Part III.
[86] Tomkins, *Our Republican*.
[87] Bellamy, *Political Constitutionalism*.
[88] Bellamy, 'Political Constitutionalism and the Human Rights Act'.

representatives of their constituent states, then far from undercutting parliamentary sovereignty, these arrangements can be seen as mechanisms for maintaining it in the circumstances of an interconnected and globalizing world.[89] After all, that the UK's withdrawal from the EU was possible, underscores the degree to which Parliament remained sovereign.

5. WHITHER THE POLITICAL CONSTITUTION?

An increasingly important and vocal section of the Conservative Party has argued that not only EU law but also the ECHR, the HRA, and the UK Supreme Court place illegitimate legal constitutional constraints on parliamentary sovereignty. As Home Secretary, Theresa May argued for withdrawal from the ECHR (if not, pre-referendum, from the EU) and the scrapping of the HRA. Many of these supposed constraints related to executive powers to arrest and detain without trial or to deport alleged terrorist suspects (e.g. *Othman (Abu Qatada) v. the United Kingdom* [2012]). Parliamentary sovereignty was more directly involved in the *Hirst* case concerning prisoners' voting rights, where Parliament explicitly took the view that citizens forfeited such a right when committing any crime that merited a jail sentence, a position the European Court viewed as disproportionate. Yet other complaints, such as those of Jonathan Sumption,[90] seem aimed more broadly at a rights culture that turns issues of individual morality and responsibility into litigable matters requiring ever-greater state regulation.

These new Conservative critiques contrast with Hailsham's earlier argument, which had viewed rights-based judicial review as defending limited government. Now, judges are criticized, on the one hand, for threatening legitimate government action to protect citizens by favouring the terrorist and criminal against their potential or actual victims; and, on the other hand, for promoting a 'nanny state' that is over-protective by treating issues of health and safety and individual morality as matters of fundamental rights.

These criticisms seem as much a complaint about liberal judges as a concern with the encroachment of an emergent legal on the political constitution. Sumption's conception of politics resembles the 'parliamentary government' of the mid-Victorian era, with its invocation of Burke's understanding of the role of MPs. Moreover, he seems happy for judges to uphold classic liberal

[89] See Richard Bellamy, 'The Democratic Legitimacy of International Human Rights Conventions: Political Constitutionalism and the ECHR' (2014) 25 *European Journal of International Law* 1019–42 (revised as Chapter 5); Richard Bellamy, *A Republican Europe of States: Cosmopolitanism, Intergovernmentalism and Democracy in the EU* (Cambridge: Cambridge University Press 2019), summarized here as Chapter 11.

[90] Jonathan Sumption, *Trials of the State: Law and the Decline of Politics* (London: Profile Books 2019).

rights to property and freedom of contract should a Labour Party committed to 'social justice' ever come to power.[91] A similar conviction animates those Conservatives who consider repeal of the HRA would return the judiciary to the Thatcher era, when they upheld the allegedly 'traditional' British liberties of the common law.

Meanwhile, representative democracy and the related case for parliamentary sovereignty have also come under criticism. Parties have become transformed increasingly into governing cartels of professional politicians.[92] These parties may compete for office on technocratic grounds of competence and responsibility but not on democratic grounds of partisan ideologies and responsiveness to the electorate. As a result, the political constitution has taken on many of the characteristics of 'parliamentary government', with parties representing little beyond their respective prospective office holders. As in other democracies, dissatisfaction with parliamentary politics has fed into populism, which in the UK as elsewhere in Europe became closely linked to Euroscepticism. However, in the UK, senior members of the governing Conservative Party, including former ministers, proved willing to deploy these criticisms of party 'elites' to support a referendum on EU membership, which was eventually held in June 2016.

The ambiguities of recent Conservative defences of the political constitution became apparent in the aftermath of the referendum result. The Conservatives had made the EU a core issue in the 2001 and 2005 elections, with largely disastrous results. However, it had grown in salience following the financial crisis of 2008, with a referendum seen by a vocal section of the Conservative Party, and a much smaller section of the Labour Party, as a way of appealing beyond the party cartels within Parliament. The direct appeal to popular sovereignty suggests a new form of political constitutionalism—popular constitutionalism.[93] Yet, the appeal to the British 'people' had become increasingly problematic in the UK as a result of devolution—itself legitimized through the popular constitutionalist mechanism of a referendum and reflecting dissatisfaction in Scotland particularly with representation at Westminster. In the event, only popular majorities in England and Wales supported leaving the EU, with Scotland and Northern Ireland, together with Greater London, voting to remain. However, Leave won overall by 51.9 per cent to 48.1 per cent on a 73 per cent turnout.[94]

[91] Richard Bellamy, 'The Limits of Lord Sumption: Limited Legal Constitutionalism and the Political Form of the ECHR' in N. W. Barber, Richard Ekins ,and Paul Yowell (eds), *Lord Sumption and the Limits of the Law* (Oxford: Hart Publishing 2016) 193–212.

[92] Peter Mair, *Ruling the Void: The Hollowing out of Western Democracy* (London: Verso 2013).

[93] For a general defence of popular constitutionalism, see Bruce Ackerman, *Revolutionary Constitutions* (Cambridge, MA: Harvard University Press 2019). I criticize such approaches in my *Political Constitutionalism*, 129–41.

[94] I discuss the vexed issue of the legitimacy of the EU referendum in Chapter 10, which incorporates some elements of Richard Bellamy, 'Was the Brexit Referendum Legitimate, and Would a Second One Be So?' (2019) 18(1) *European Political Science* 126–33.

The result placed the prevailing parliamentary form of the political constitution under great strain given a majority of MPs had favoured remaining in the EU. Though technically advisory, few MPs felt the vote could be ignored. However, the terms of leaving remained deeply contested between the advocates of various 'soft' and 'hard' Brexits. With no deal commanding a parliamentary majority, both May and then Johnson attempted to push one through by appealing to a popular majority. This provoked legal moves to defend parliamentary sovereignty. In two key judgments (*Miller 1* and *2*) involving May's and Johnson's first administrations respectively, the Supreme Court insisted that the British constitution rested on parliamentary sovereignty. Some have seen these judgments as proof that a common law constitution underlies the political constitution.

This view links to an important objection, explored in Chapter 6, that contends that the authority of Parliament to rule must rest itself on some extra-political and ultimately legally recognized norm akin to what the English philosopher of law H. L. A. Hart termed a 'rule of recognition' or the Austrian jurist Hans Kelsen the legal and political system's 'basic norm'.[95] If so, that would suggest that the UK does have a legal constitution, albeit one that consists of a partly conventional and unwritten common law framework of political rules about the making of collective decisions and the exercise of executive power by virtue of the sovereignty of Parliament.[96] However, the political account takes its cue from Thomas Hobbes in regarding all norms of law and morality, including human rights, as only possible through the creation of a sovereign political order that can uphold and define them in impartial ways.[97] The reasons urging us to do so are prudential and rational rather than moral or legal.[98] On this account, the right of Parliament to rule was established in the seventeenth century through the consummate political act of a civil war and the beheading of King Charles I, the prior claimant to sovereign power. Since then, Parliament has gradually altered its own constitutive rules under pressure from citizens either claiming or exercising their political rights. On this reasoning, *Miller 1* can be seen as upholding a politically established norm that governments act with the consent of Parliament, unless they have gained explicit parliamentary assent to do otherwise—most notably by calling an election,

[95] H. L. A. Hart, *The Concept of Law* (2nd edn, Oxford: Clarendon Press 1994) 94–5; Hans Kelsen, *Introduction to the Problems of Legal Theory* (Oxford: Clarendon Press 1992) 54–5.

[96] T. R. S. Allan, *Law, Liberty, and Justice: The Foundations of British Constitutionalism* (Oxford: Clarendon Press 1993).

[97] Thomas Hobbes, *Leviathan* (Richard Tuck ed., Cambridge: Cambridge University Press 1991) 90. See too Bernard Williams, 'Realism and Moralism in Political Theory' in Bernard Williams, *In the Beginning was the Deed* (Princeton, NJ: Princeton University Press 2005) 1–17; Richard Bellamy, 'Turtles All The Way Down? Is the Political Constitutionalist Appeal to Disagreement Self-Defeating? A Reply to Cormac Mac Amhlaigh' (2016) 14 *International Journal of Constitutional Law (I-Con)* 204–16 (reproduced here in revised form as Chapter 6).

[98] Quentin Skinner, 'The Context of Hobbes's Theory of Political Obligation' in M. Cranston and R. Peters (eds), *Hobbes and Rousseau: A Collection of Critical Essays* (New York: Doubleday 1972) 109–42.

as May did in 2017. *Miller 2* is more complex, yet could be viewed as articulating the political limits to prorogue within a democratic political constitution. Fittingly, it returns us to our starting point of 1642, echoing Charles I's acceptance in the Answer that sovereignty, and hence prerogative power, lay not with the king or his ministers but with the king-in-Parliament, as ordained by an ancient political constitutive act as 'immemorial' as the common law, which it grounds.

In fact, the tribulations of the Johnson government came mainly from the difficulties posed by parliamentary procedure and the Fixed Term Parliament Act rather than the courts. Having won a large parliamentary majority in the 2019 election, the main constraint on his and his government's future action came not from the judiciary but from the electoral challenge of opposition parties and his growing unpopularity with voters on account of his participation in, and lying about, illegal parties during lockdown in number 10, as well as multiple other instances of self-serving mendacity within and outside Parliament and the flouting of the Ministerial Code by himself and others in his Cabinet. As he became ever more an electoral liability, his own backbenchers turned against him and forced him out in July 2022. Nevertheless, many commentators believe his actions and those of his successors as Leader of the Conservative Party mark a decisive deformation of the norms underlying the UK's political constitution. Their actions have rendered it open to a populist takeover analogous to, albeit by several orders of magnitude milder than, President Trump's subversion of the legal constitution of the United States.[99]

6. PLAN OF THE REST OF THE BOOK

This introduction has sketched three main versions of the political constitution within the UK—the mixed constitution, parliamentary government, and representative democracy. Each of these three versions has proved able to accommodate governments of very different ideological leanings and both adapt to, and partly shape, changing social and economic cleavages and conflicts. Legal constitutions are sometimes portrayed as standing outside and constraining politics, and by implication the social, economic, and ideational conflicts that give rise to political activity. In practice, they either reflect one side in these conflicts (usually the hitherto hegemonic side, that now faces electoral defeat) or not infrequently succumb to them (the average lifespan of a legal constitution is seventeen years).[100] By contrast,

[99] David Sanders, 'One Man's Damage: The Consequences of Boris Johnson's Assault on the British Political System' (2023) 94(2) *The Political Quarterly* 166–74. See too Jeff King, 'From Constitutional Crisis to Poisoned Chalice: A letter from London', VerfBlog (28 June 2024) <https://verfassungsblog.de/from-constitutional-crisis-to-poisoned-chalice/> DOI: 10.59704/8163652a51cb5c78.

[100] Zachary Elkins, Tom Ginsburg, and James Melton, *The Endurance of National Constitutions* (Cambridge: Cambridge University Press 2009).

political constitution operates by creating a self-enforcing equilibrium between the disagreements and clashes of different parties and groups by generating different kinds of checks and balances. However, such equilibriums need not be egalitarian, and historically have not been so. The contemporary challenge is to retain the democratic credentials of political constitutionalism at a time of increased social inequality and global interconnectedness, and a growing disaffection with politics in general and political parties in particular. The result is a system that frequently appears closer to 'parliamentary government' than representative democracy, a shift that has fed populism and raised the prospect of the populist deformation of the political constitution.

The first Part, that follows this introduction, consists of three chapters that offer a democratic defence and restatement of the three main claims for a political constitutionalism. In all three cases, I associate this defence with the republican notion of freedom as non-domination. The first claim, elaborated in Chapter 1, is that citizenship of a democratic state offers the basis for rights—the 'right to have rights' as Hannah Arendt put it,[101] albeit one that is compatible with 'weak review' by courts. The second claim, defended in Chapter 2, contends that the 'rule of law', even in the formal 'juristic' sense, presupposes that the making and administration of law be governed by a democratic process. The third claim, made in Chapter 3, develops the underlying account of the constitutional qualities of democracy as a system of checks and balances grounded in political equality, whereby citizens and their representatives must 'hear the other side'. It contends that proportional representation (PR) electoral systems, on the one side, and strong forms of local government, on the other, provide key components of a political constitutional system.

The next three Parts explore academic and real-world challenges to each of these claims respectively. Part 2 looks at objections to the democratic account of rights offered in Chapter 1. Two chapters consider whether even a statutory bill of rights, such as the UK HRA examined in Chapter 4, or international conventions of human rights, such as the ECHR examined in Chapter 5, involve empowering courts in ways that displace political with legal constitutionalism. That claim has been made by critics of political constitutionalism and certain of its defenders alike: the first to suggest its failings and implausibility,[102] the second to legitimize on democratic grounds both the repeal or 'updating' of the HRA—unfulfilled manifesto commitments of the Conservative Party in 2015 and 2019—and withdrawal from the ECHR—advocated by successive Conservative Home Secretaries from Theresa May onwards, and recently floated as a possibility by Kemi Badenoch, the current leader of the party.[103] By contrast, I shall argue both prove compatible with

[101] Hannah Arendt, *The Origins of Totalitarianism* (rev. edn, New York: Harcourt 1973) 267.
[102] Aileen Kavanagh, *Constitutional Review Under the U.K. Human Rights Act* (Cambridge: Cambridge University Press 2009).
[103] The Policy Exchange Judicial Power Project has been a prime source of critiques of the latter sort, e.g. Richard Ekins, 'Human Rights and the Rule of Law', Policy Exchange, 17 April 2024.

and supportive of political constitutionalism by offering modes of 'weak review'. Neither undermines parliamentary sovereignty, the cornerstone of a political constitution. Rather, they offer ways of supporting the democratic 'right to have rights' that it entails by extending and deepening legislative and executive attentiveness to rights considerations, both domestically and internationally.

Part 3 discusses two contrasting challenges to the democratic account of the rule of law offered in Chapter 2. The first challenge, examined in Chapter 6, suggests that politics cannot go all the way down without running into the issue of an infinite regress. Ultimately, politics requires a legal constitutional basis. The second challenge, the subject of Chapter 7, considers courts as a complementary and, in some respects, even a superior, democratic forum to electoral politics, thereby overcoming the democratic objections to judicial review. Again, I question both of these critiques. The first overlooks the need for political authority as a basis for law, the second underestimates the role played by political authorization and accountability in ensuring whoever possesses the sovereign authority to make and interpret law—be it the legislature or courts—treats those subject to their rule with equal concern and respect.

Part 4 turns to the populist challenge to the very democratic foundations of political constitutionalism as outlined in Chapter 3. Many have argued that legal constitutionalism provides the best and main resource to resist such democratic backsliding.[104] However, as other commentators have observed, populist regimes have also recruited certain formal aspects of legal constitutionalism to entrench their regimes and provide them with a sham legitimacy.[105] Meanwhile, if some commentators have contended that political constitutionalism has abetted populist critiques of legal constitutional constraints, others have criticized it for being too focused on representative democracy, thereby fuelling populist critiques of elitism.[106] They argue a genuinely political form of constitutionalism requires more popular participation in constitutional questions through referendums and similar mechanisms. Chapter 8 distinguishes populism from democracy and popular from political constitutionalism. I argue that a political constitutionalism focused on preventing arbitrary rule may have better resources for countering populism than a legal constitutionalism focused on limiting government. However, as Chapter 9 suggests, popular participation in debating constitutional reforms through referendums may provide one such check on arbitrary rule. Drawing lessons from the Brexit experience, referendums can supplement but need not supplant representative democracy and need (and should) not replace parliamentary with popular sovereignty.

[104] András Sajó and Renáta Uitz, *The Constitution of Freedom: An Introduction to Legal Constitutionalism* (Oxford: Oxford University Press 2017).

[105] Kim Lane Scheppele, 'Autocratic Legalism' (2018) 85 *University of Chicago Law Review* 545–83.

[106] Goldoni and McCorkindale, 'Why We (Still) need a Revolution'.

Finally, Chapter 10 continues the Brexit theme and returns to a question raised in Chapter 5: namely, can political constitutionalism remain plausible or desirable in an increasingly interdependent world confronting global problems? Once again, the negative view seems to be held by two otherwise opposed camps. On the one hand, lie those who contend that democracy can only be preserved if states 'take back control' by withdrawing from international agreements and being prepared to play fast and loose with the international rule of law.[107] On the other hand, lie those who regard such an ambition as undesirable as it is impossible and contend that sovereign authority should pass to a regional or global constitution overseen by a supranational court, with the democratic credentials of such a regime resting with a regional or global Parliament of some description.[108] Against both these views, I suggest that what have been termed '*demoi*-cratic' arrangements are possible that entail mutually respectful agreements among democratic states, with the legal system under their joint and several control. Moreover, I argue such arrangements enable rather than disable parliamentary sovereignty. As I noted in Chapter 5, they are central to the operation of the Council of Europe and the ECHR, and as I note here are also essential to the legitimacy and functioning of the EU. Such *demo*i-cratic forms of regional and global political constitutionalism also provide the best route to avoid the degeneration of established democracies into regimes characterized by xenophobic populism, while offering a voice to developing states seeking to construct a more equitable economic and political world order.[109]

[107] e.g. Richard Tuck, *The Left Case for Brexit: Reflections on the Current Crisis* (Cambridge: Polity Press 2020).

[108] e.g. Luigi Ferrajoli, *La democrazia attraverso i diritti. Il costituzionalismo garantista come modello teorico e come progetto politico* (Roma-Bari: Laterza 2013) chs 4 and 5; Jürgen Habermas, *The Divided West* (Ciaran Cronin tr. and ed., Cambridge: Polity Press 2006) ch. 8.

[109] The post-colonial schemes of regional cooperation and governance described by Adom Getachew can be seen as similar demoi-cratic constitutional mechanisms for avoiding the international domination of developing by developed states to the political constitutionalist account I offer in chapter 10 of the EU. See Adom Getachew, *Worldmaking after Empire: The Rise and Fall of National Self-Determination* (Princeton, NJ: Princeton University Press 2019).

PART 1
POLITICAL CONSTITUTIONALISM AS DEMOCRACY

1
Rights as Democracy

1. INTRODUCTION

Rights are often seen as political constitutionalism's Achilles heel. Even friendly critics worry that the tendency to privilege democracy risks undermining respect for individual rights, and consequently advocate a stronger role for rights-based judicial review.[1] Here, I want to take a different tack and suggest that rights imply democracy rather than being a constraint upon it. By that I do not mean, as some have argued, that rights are implied by democracy—that all rights can be seen as somehow inherent components of a democratic process.[2] Some, such as the right to vote, obviously are, but others, such as the right not to be tortured, have no inherent link to the democratic process—or do so only very indirectly.[3] Rather, I wish to argue that rights claims can only be justified in democratic terms—as claims made under conditions of political equality. This understanding of rights is quite different to the deontological account standardly offered by legal constitutional theories of a liberal hue that hark back to the natural rights tradition. That account sits with a view of liberty as non-interference, which sees its main object as the restriction of law and government. By contrast, the democratic account of rights I associate with political constitutionalism belongs to the republican view of freedom as non-domination. Here, rights reflect the common avowable interests of citizens and are political both in origin and in execution. On this account, the liberal view of a right against democracy appears both unjustifiable and incoherent.

The argument proceeds as follows. I start by showing how the very nature of a rights claim implies a democratic process in which citizens have the status of political equals when formulating collective decisions that are to apply equally to all. I then relate this democratic argument for rights to the republican conception of liberty as non-domination, rejecting along the way the liberal account of rights as trumps and its origins in a view of freedom as non-interference. Finally, I explore how this association of rights and democracy exists not simply at an ideal level but needs to be actualized within a real democratic process of a kind akin to the systems of actually existing democracies, with their combination of one person one

[1] e.g. Tom Hickey, 'The Republican Core of the Case for Judicial Review' (2019) 17(1) *International Journal of Constitutional Law* 288, 316 <https://doi.org/10.1093/icon/moz007>.

[2] e.g. Jürgen Habermas, *Between Facts and Norms: Contributions to a Discourse Theory of Law and Democracy* (William Rehg tr., Cambridge: Polity Press 1996).

[3] Peter Jones, *Rights* (Houndmills: Macmillan 1994) 173–4.

Defending the Political Constitution. Richard Bellamy, Oxford University Press. © Richard Bellamy 2026.
DOI: 10.1093/9780191826986.003.0002

vote, majority rule, and regular elections between competitive parties. Moreover, the normative and logical status of rights as intrinsically democratic in their mode of justification and application greatly circumscribes the legitimacy of using judicial and other non- or counter-majoritarian mechanisms to uphold rights against democracy.[4]

2. RIGHTS, POLITICAL EQUALITY, AND DEMOCRACY

Rights theorists working within the mainstream liberal tradition typically distinguish human and natural from institutional rights on the grounds that the former are in some sense prior to politics.[5] That is to say, they are either moral entitlements that human beings could and ought to be granted even in a putative state of nature, such as freedom from physical assault, or—more demandingly—they encompass those basic interests of human beings that all political communities should seek to secure not just for their members but also for non-members. In other words, such rights should either exist outside of any polity, or be realized within and upheld by all polities. As such, they define the boundaries, foundations, and, to some extent, the goals of politics.[6]

So conceived, rights readily appear as constraints on democracy. Rights can be viewed as 'trumping' those political decisions that curtail or fail to promote them. Yet, their apparent status as somehow prior to and above politics proves hard to sustain. Rights are sometimes presented as a two-term relation, whereby x has a right to some y. That gives rights a somewhat peremptory-sounding character. However, rights are always a three-term relation, whereby x asks some z to recognize and respect his or her claim to y, with attendant costs and benefits to z who will wish x to likewise recognize either his or her similar claim to y, or to some other good such as v. That is true even of a Hohfeldian 'liberty-right', whereby all that is being asked of others is that they have 'no right' to prevent its exercise.[7] For such forbearance may itself be controversial, as in certain instances of someone exercising a liberty-right to do what might be commonly regarded as wrong.[8] Therefore, x and z need to agree on rights and their respective correlative duties, or lack of them, in given situations. It is this need for a collective agreement on which rights we possess, when and where, what their implications may be in a given case, how they interact with other rights, and which policies and procedures might be most suited

[4] Richard Bellamy, *Political Constitutionalism: A Republican Defence of the Constitutionality of Democracy* (Cambridge: Cambridge University Press 2007).

[5] Jones, *Rights*, 73.

[6] Jones, *Rights*, 75–81.

[7] See Jones, *Rights*, 12–14, 17–22 for a discussion of Hohfeld's classification of rights and of liberty-rights in particular.

[8] Jeremy Waldron, 'A Right to do Wrong' (1981) 92 *Ethics* 21–39.

to realizing them, that places rights within what Albert Weale and Jeremy Waldron have called the 'circumstances of politics'.[9] For, these are all matters on which we may reasonably disagree yet need a common decision, producing the need for a political mechanism of some kind to resolve our disputes.

Theorists of natural and human rights have tended to assume away such disagreements. They have sought to ground their case for at least a set of basic rights on their 'self-evident' character as dictates of reason, divine law, or essential elements of human well-being.[10] Yet, self-evidence 'is not a very promising foundation for rights'.[11] What leads us to identify specific features of human beings or human sociability as 'natural', 'basic', or 'divinely ordained' depends ultimately on the moral theories we hold for which the specified capacities prove important. The upshot is that appeals to human nature and other supposedly 'objective' and 'universal' foundations of rights reflect rival ontological claims for which no generally agreed epistemology exists with the capacity to mediate between them. Even where there is agreement on the rather abstract set of general rights found in International Human Rights Conventions or domestic Bills of Rights, there can be disagreement about what they involve in practice with regard to a given case.[12] These disagreements need not reflect self-interest or bad faith—though on occasion they clearly do so, as in the case of regimes whose reluctance to recognize rights results from their oppression of their subject populations. Rather, disagreements—such as one finds in most democratic countries—may simply issue from what Rawls has called 'the burdens of judgment . . . the many hazards involved in the correct (and conscientious) exercise of our powers of reason and judgment in the ordinary course of political life'.[13] On Rawls's account, these burdens range from the different life experiences people bring to the assessment of a situation, to the multiple normative considerations likely to be involved and the difficulties of relating them to the often complex empirical evidence. Although he believed these 'burdens' only applied to conceptions of the good, they clearly also produce different understandings of the right. People may reasonably hold differing views not only of the sources and substance of rights, but also their subjects and scope, and how they might best be secured.[14] Thus, Nozickian libertarians, Ricardian socialists, Rawlsean social democrats, and Burkean conservatives all offer different accounts of the origins and extent of property rights and their relationship to other rights, which are expressed to different degrees, albeit usually in a less abstruse or

[9] Albert Weale, *Democracy* (2nd edn, Basingstoke: Palgrave 2007) 12–18; Jeremy Waldron, *Law and Disagreement* (Oxford: Clarendon Press 1999) 107–13.

[10] Jones, *Rights*, 96–7.

[11] Jones, *Rights*, 97.

[12] Jones, *Rights*, 224–5.

[13] John Rawls, *Political Liberalism* (New York: Columbia University Press 1993) 55–6.

[14] Richard Bellamy, 'Constitutive Citizenship vs. Constitutional Rights: Republican Reflections on the EU Charter and the Human Rights Act' in Tom Campbell, K. D. Ewing, and Adam Tomkins (eds), *Sceptical Essays on Human Rights* (Oxford: Oxford University Press 2001) 15–39.

sophisticated manner, in the everyday political debates of all mature democracies. At the level of principle, these disputes have not proved any more resolvable in the seminar rooms of philosophy departments than they have among policy-makers and citizens.

As I remarked above, such reasonable, good faith, ontological and epistemological disagreements about the nature of rights mean that the determination of which rights we have and how they should be upheld requires a political process. However, not any kind of process will do if it is to be consistent with both the very idea of rights, as something possessed and claimable by all, and the reasonableness of these disagreements about them. The argument that best fits these two criteria would appear to be something like the fairness argument for democracy. According to this view, which I develop more fully in Chapter 3, if the interests of individuals are equally affected by the overall decisions of the community to which they belong, and we follow J. S. Mill in regarding each individual as the best guardian of his or her own interest, then fairness dictates that they should all be able to play an equal part in the political process that makes those decisions.[15] On the one hand, decisions about rights are ones in which those affected will have an equal stake over the long term and taking into account the full range of decisions. Consequently, we need a process that will treat all as political equals in reaching mutually acceptable agreements, such as a system of majoritarian decision-making on the basis of equal votes offers. On the other hand, majoritarian voting per se is not tied to any of the arguments—voters can vote for any position and for any reason. As such, it delivers a fair and neutral process for deciding which position can claim the most public support as being in the collective interest.[16]

Conceived in this manner, the choice of democracy is not purely pragmatic. It follows from the very idea of rights and certain structural features of any claim to a right and the disagreements that will surround it. First, though there are many different arguments for human rights, it is an intrinsic feature of all of them that since rights attach to human beings as such they apply equally to all. Second, and relatedly, although rights connect to individuals, we have seen how they have a collective dimension. A right is not claimed solely for the individual in question but as a right that can be held and upheld equally by all other individuals—hence the need for a process to collectively agree on the right. Moreover, for the right to be collectively held and upheld requires not just each individual doing his or her bit according to some commonly agreed norm, but also common, publicly provided, structures—at a minimum a legal system and the means for law enforcement, such as a police force, courts, prisons. So secured, rights function in many ways like that which Raz has called an inherent public good:[17] that is, they promote common

[15] Jones, *Rights*, 180.
[16] Kenneth O. May, 'A Set of Independent, Necessary and Sufficient Conditions for Simple Majority Decision' (1952) 20(4) *Econometrica* 680–4.
[17] Joseph Raz, *The Morality of Freedom* (Oxford: Clarendon Press 1986) 198–9.

benefits that we must collectively produce through our attitudes to others and in which we can all equally share—a point to which I return below. Finally, we have noted how rights also operate as claims against those in authority. They imply that certain things should not be done or should not be denied to any individual.

These three aspects of rights point towards a core claim that underpins all rights claims: namely, the claim by each individual to be treated as a political equal who owes and deserves equal concern and respect to and from every other individual in the shared arrangements that frame their social life, a claim that must also be acknowledged by the authorities charged with administering these arrangements. The intimate link between democracy and rights arises from this core claim. For, democracy offers the only forum where different rights claims can be made and the collective structures necessary for their realization can be provided in a way that is consistent with rights claimants recognizing their fellow citizens, with their potentially rival claims, as deserving of equal concern and respect, and ensuring that the public authorities are responsive to their collective disagreements and deliberations about rights. Democracy offers a means for making decisions in which all meet as political equals to make reciprocal claims on each other when framing common policies, and can hold governments to account when they fail to reflect their preferences. In this way, the democratic process grants what Hannah Arendt termed the 'right to have rights'.[18] I am not thereby implying that all rights are intrinsic to democracy. As I noted above, not all rights relate to the democratic process. What I am arguing is that all rights involve a democratic form of justification—they imply a spirit of political equality to be accorded equal concern and respect that can only be achieved through a democratic process.

3. RIGHTS AND INDIVIDUAL LIBERTY: LIBERAL AND REPUBLICAN PERSPECTIVES

Seeing rights as somehow intrinsically democratic might be thought to subvert their 'traditional political purpose', that of telling 'those who wield political power what they may and may not do'.[19] However, that perception arises from aligning that 'traditional' understanding of the function of rights with the liberal conception of liberty as non-interference. By contrast, I shall argue that when that purpose is linked to the republican conception of liberty as non-domination—a view that more accurately accords with the nature of rights claims as delineated above—then democracy emerges as a necessary, even if not always sufficient, condition for its realization.

[18] Hannah Arendt, *The Origins of Totalitarianism* (revised edn, New York: Harcourt 1973) 267.
[19] Jones, *Rights*, 222.

3.1. Liberalism, Rights, and Freedom as Non-Interference

The liberal notion of freedom as non-interference seems to capture what many see as the central aspect of rights: namely, that there are certain things nobody should be allowed to do to another individual, such as torture, or prevent them from doing, such as exercising their freedom of speech. Given such rights only require the forbearance of others, they ought to be compossible—able to be held by all others—by their very nature, and so be non-negotiable because not requiring negotiation. Not all rights may be of this kind, but those that are offer some of the most important safeguards for individuals. On this account, there is no role for democracy to play in their formulation or maintenance—as noted above, they may even need to be exercised against democratic decisions.

Rights to non-interference seem to be the best candidates for being in some sense pre- and possibly anti-political. Indeed, all law becomes inimical to rights in being a form of interference, albeit potentially necessary to render them secure. This approach offers the paradigm of the view of rights as trumps that are held by individuals against the collectivity. Such rights seek to drive a wedge between the right and any notion of the common good, offering pre-conditions for each and every individual to pursue his or her own good in their own way. Yet, even rights of this form cannot be isolated from the 'circumstances of politics'. For they will not be immune from disputes as to their definition; from conflicts between the uses of these rights by different people as well as with other rights; or from the need for the intervention of public laws and collective structures to realize them. All these issues prove political in the broad sense noted above. For, they require a collective decision over the content and scope of these rights that will rest on value judgements concerning their purpose and nature—the public good or goods they serve—that allow for reasonable disagreement.

Thus, there may be agreement that no one should be tortured and all authorities and individuals should simply refrain from doing so, but interpretative disputes nevertheless exist as to whether certain punishments shade into torture or not—think of the arguments in the United States over whether the death penalty is per se 'cruel and unusual' or only certain methods for delivering it. It might be countered that though the practical meaning and implementation of this right are political, the right itself is not—it is a moral right that attaches to individuals as something one simply should not do to any person—hence the aforementioned agreement that torture is wrong. As I noted above, though, the moral force of even the most basic human rights does not follow from our humanity per se but the moral theory we hold, and people can and do have different views about the morality of torture, not all of which are rights-based. These differences will always prove relevant because the circumstances in which even a right such as this one arises is always political to the extent that the claim is made against other persons and so requires political and legal institutions whereby the basis, subjects, and scope of that claim can be collectively agreed upon and reliably enforced. There is no right of the individual as such, but only of the social individual within a political and legal context.[20] Indeed, the historical origins of a right not to be tortured lie not in an absolutist view that this right ought to be upheld whatever the consequences, but because it was regarded as ineffective as a means for extracting evidence and corrupting of those who employed it. It was the general utility of torture as a means for upholding the rights of the public, rather than the right of an individual regardless of its impact on the public, that led to its abolition.[21] A political agreement on the public meaning and the good served by this right, as well as the best means to uphold it, are neither additional to, nor potentially at odds with, the nature of such a right: they are essential to its definition and justification.

Similar debates arise in the case of free speech and whether incitement or libel count as speech. Here, though, there is the additional issue of how a right, the exercise of which appears to involve simply forbearance, can nonetheless clash with its similar exercise by others. We regard rights as important not simply for a single individual but for all individuals. If a right to free speech is to be collectively exercised, we will need rules of order ensuring we do not always all speak at once so that nobody can be heard above the cacophony, and there may be uses of that right that subvert other rights of individuals, as is the case with slander, hate speech, or the leaking of official secrets. Finally, such conflicts also mean that though many rights may appear simply to depend on an absence of interference, making them available to all will require intervention by public authorities to facilitate their use and guard against their abuse or subversion. It might be argued that we should simply seek to interfere as little as possible with the right in question so as to maximize its availability to all. Yet, what counts as interference is normatively laden,[22] as are the choices of what arrangements might maximally enhance a right in given circumstances. Some will regard certain omissions as well as acts as forms of interference, for example, or see threats and intimidation as potentially as inhibiting as physical force, others will not. Likewise, some might see an equal right as requiring no more than an equal chance to exercise it, such as might be achieved by a lottery, others that it be exercisable to an equal extent—with both views proving highly contestable even in their own terms, especially when it comes to establishing them in practice.

In collectively evaluating the nature and limits of rights and providing common means for their realization, as we have seen is necessary, the right comes to fall within, rather being separate from and potentially opposed to and 'trumping', the

[20] Richard Bellamy, 'Dirty Hands and White Gloves: Liberal Ideals and Real Politics' (2010) 9 *European Journal of Political Theory* 412–30, at 416–20.

[21] Cesare Beccaria, *On Crimes and Punishments* ([1764], Richard Bellamy ed., Cambridge: Cambridge University Press 1995).

[22] Onora O'Neill, 'The Most Extensive Liberty' (1979/1980) 80 *Proceedings of the Aristotelian Society* 45–59.

common or public good. For, the rights that will be viewed as commanding the equal concern and respect of all citizens will be those that correspond to their commonly avowable interests and that therefore provide an equal benefit to all. Indeed, not to align rights with the public good in this way has the perverse effect of making rights seem like the privileges of particular individuals rather than the universal entitlements of all citizens—an aristocratic rather than a democratic view. As Raz has noted with regard to free speech,[23] issues such as libel and slander make it implausible to see free speech as the right of each and every individual to say whatever he or she wants, regardless of its more general effects on the rights of others. It also seems odd to suggest that we have an interest in this right for our own personal use as individuals in order to vent our frustrations in monologues delivered in front of the bathroom mirror—satisfying though this may be on occasion. It is also the case that few of us are likely to be opinion-formers or whistleblowers either. So, we do not necessarily have a personal interest in exercising this right ourselves. Rather, we all have an equal interest in the benefits of free debate and criticism of public policy by the comparatively small group of people with the time and expertise to do so—politicians, journalists, those with specialist knowledge in a given area, and so on—and in the possibility to join that group being equally open to all, including ourselves should we feel motivated to do so. An equal right to free speech is thus instrumental to securing a public good rather than distinct from any such good. Hence, the common rules and structures that we favour for regulating free speech are those that we believe best serve that public purpose—for, these are the rights all should and could have. Once such structures are in place, their role is to provide an equal and common benefit for all rather than a privilege for an individual indiscriminately to berate his or her neighbours or business rivals out of spite or for personal profit.

3.2. Republicanism, Rights, and Freedom as Non-Domination

Rights, then, cannot be removed from politics. Instead, we need a form of politics that is consistent with their character. As we saw at the end of the first section, rights involve a core claim to be treated with equal concern and respect—both by one's fellow citizens in the shared arrangements that coordinate social life, and by the public authorities empowered to oversee them. Consequently, a political process for collectively claiming and deciding on rights will need to possess three key features. First, it must show equal respect for the different views of individuals as rights bearers. Second, it should also demonstrate equal concern for their capacity to employ their rights on the same terms as others. As such, it will need to be doubly collective—a process that involves all the public on an equal basis

[23] Joseph Raz, *Ethics in the Public Domain* (Oxford: Clarendon Press 1994) 54.

and promotes those rights and conceptions of rights that best reflect commonly avowed interests. Third, it will have to answer to the 'traditional purpose' of rights as means for holding power to account and marking its limits.

Unlike the classic liberal view of freedom as non-interference, the republican notion of non-domination captures this core claim underlying rights by offering a normative basis for these three requirements of a justified rights-generating political process. On this account, freedom and rights belong not to an asocial agent outside all social and institutional arrangements and able to do what he or she wants because of the lack of interference with or by others, but rather is a civic achievement of socially situated individuals whose relations are regulated by law. What gives these legal arrangements their liberty-preserving quality lies in their being formulated by free and equal citizens who are not bound to any master but rather negotiate their collective arrangements together as political equals in order to arrive at policies that serve their common good, rather than the partial and potentially dominating interests of particular powerful individuals or factions. The rights that arise from these arrangements still reflect the ways in which citizens tell those in power what they may or may not do. Yet, citizens achieve that 'traditional purpose' by claiming their rights through laws that apply equally to all—including their rulers—and which they ultimately control through a democratic process that shows each of them equal concern and respect as autonomous individuals.

Freedom as non-domination is not inimical to politics and law in the same way as freedom as non-interference.[24] Its aim is to achieve freedom from the arbitrary rule of a master rather than freedom from any rule. Rights play a part in that achievement, but they are the rights of citizens not the natural rights of human beings that could be held either outside of any society, or as members of any society. Rather, they result from the laws that citizens give themselves as equal members of a polity.

The view of rights as existing outside and potentially against politics, and hence able to trump a democratic process, overlooks how rights are claims made by citizens on fellow citizens within a social and political setting. Two key errors flow from this oversight. First, it ignores the fact, explored above, that the rights claims of one individual impact on those of other individuals. As we have seen, rights do not attach to human beings as such within a putative state of nature. They belong to, and reflect, a given social context and the public goods it provides for those who exist within and support it. An individual claiming a right is not the only person possessing trumps. All those he or she is claiming against possess trumps too. The trumping metaphor ceases to be useful in this context. At best, one can argue that there are some especially weighty claims that individuals may have that need to be weighed in the balance with the similarly weighty claims of other individuals.

[24] Philip Pettit, *Republicanism: A Theory of Freedom and Government* (Oxford: Oxford University Press 1997) ch. 2.

Second, these trumps have already been played in the democratic process, where we decide what rights the legal system should enshrine within the relevant legislation.[25] Legislators, and indirectly those who have elected them, can all express their views on rights in framing legislation, and seek to have their most basic interests and core views protected. All effectively play their trumps, but only on the same terms as everyone else. Therefore, in making a claim against a democratic decision, the rights claimer is illegitimately attempting to play his or her cards again, and in the process is failing to treat his or her fellow citizens with the equal concern and respect rights demand.

What, though, do we do in the case of those who do not have access to any of the relevant democratic institutions—who either live in non-democratic states or outside a given democratic state, be it as a stateless person or as a citizen of a different state—yet have a claim against the democratic decisions of a state that has adversely affected them? Surely, human rights claims often arise in their most powerful and urgent forms precisely in such situations, where either no democratic redress is available or democratic processes have ignored the interests of those excluded from them. Indeed, many established democratic systems have excluded certain members of the political community in the past—women, those without property, ethnic minorities, among other groups—and many continue to do so. All of this is undeniable. And yet, the claims such groups make can be seen primarily as claims for inclusion within the democratic community—to be treated as political equals.

Far from overlooking the claims of the excluded, the republican account has decided advantages over the liberal in this regard. For the liberal view can be used by the privileged to mandate such exclusions to prevent unjustified interferences with their entitlements—be it the property rights of the rich or the sovereignty of wealthy states. By contrast, the republican view mandates inclusion as a political equal within the decision-making processes of those powerful bodies capable of exercising domination over our lives. These may be public bodies—the state or its agencies—or private bodies, such as large corporations or financial institutions.[26] The liberal language of human or natural rights leaves the unprivileged outside the city walls, as mere petitioners for redress by the privileged within, who may deploy these self-same rights to deny any civic responsibility for these others. The republican approach brings all rights claimants within the city walls, giving them access to the political mechanisms required to offer them redress. Yet that brings the obligations as well as the privileges of citizenship—not least the duty to take the rights

[25] Waldron, *Law and Disagreement*, 12.

[26] As I note in Chapter 2, Chiara Cordelli's Kantian inspired democratic critique of the privatization of public services can be related to precisely this kind of republican argument. See Chiara Cordelli, *The Privatized State* (Princeton: Princeton University Press 2020) esp. ch. 2. The same can be said of Elizabeth Anderson's argument for workplace democracy in her *Private Government: How Employers Rule Our Lives (and Why We Don't Talk about It)* (Princeton: Princeton University Press 2019).

claims of others as seriously as they take their own. Unsurprisingly, the evidence shows that rights will only be reliably upheld where the democratic mechanisms exist for them to be claimed in this way, and that rights are just as reliably ignored and infringed where such mechanisms are absent.[27] It is to the specific virtues of actually existing democracy that we now turn.

4. RIGHTS AND DEMOCRACY: REAL AND IDEAL

A number of theorists have acknowledged the democratic character of rights in framing their accounts in terms of an idealized democratic process—be it the rights that must be presupposed by free and equal dialogue or discourse with another, or that would be agreed to, or could not be reasonably rejected in, circumstances where all participants are equally situated with regard to each other and none has power over another. This democratic argument for rights has been most explicitly stated by Jürgen Habermas.[28] Yet a parallel argument also informs John Rawls's *Political Liberalism*, where he characterizes his first principle of justice as reflecting an agreement between idealized citizens of a liberal democratic state as the necessary conditions for them to co-exist as political equals.[29] However, this idealized democratic argument for the foundations of rights does not necessarily entail a practical commitment to use real democratic systems to uphold them. First, both Habermas and Rawls seek to distinguish constitutional from normal politics, regarding the more general and public debate they associate with the one as legitimately constraining and providing the norms underlying the other.[30] Second, both see constitutional courts as exemplifying a more ideal form of democratic discourse than real democratic processes. Habermas argues that courts can review democratic decisions on procedural grounds to ensure they have issued from a duly democratic process,[31] while Rawls maintains they may review them on substantive grounds as well to ensure that certain non-democratic rights have not been infringed, thereby removing certain rights from politics altogether.[32] Finally, and as a corollary of this last point, both see litigation as a form of democratic participation.

This section challenges and qualifies all three of these ideal arguments, setting the scene for a more detailed discussion of the real-world democratic qualities

[27] Thomas Christiano, 'An Instrumental Argument for a Human Right to Democracy' (2011) 39(2) *Philosophy and Public Affairs* 142–76.

[28] e.g. Jürgen Habermas, *The Inclusion of the Other: Studies in Political Theory* (Ciaran Cronin and Pablo De Greiff eds, Cambridge: Polity Press 1998).

[29] John Rawls, *Political Liberalism* (New York: Columbia University Press 1993) 3.

[30] Habermas, *Between Facts and Norms*, 304, 486; Rawls, *Political Liberalism*, 232–3—for a critique, see Bellamy, *Political Constitutionalism*, ch. 3.

[31] Habermas, *Between Facts and Norms*, 263, 278–9.

[32] Rawls, *Political Liberalism*, 157, 161.

of courts in Chapter 7. I shall argue that idealized, court-based democracy is no substitute for real democracy. If political equality is necessary for all to be treated with equal concern and respect as both the claimers and the duty bearers of rights within the circumstances of politics, then no purely ideal account of democracy can substitute for real democratic practices and participation. Such ideal theories risk being entirely circular, construing the democratic process so that it favours their preferred view of rights. Nor can any abstract theory be so specific as to incorporate all the features that figure within actual contexts—not least the very diverse life experiences and concerns of those involved.

I shall start by outlining the constitutional qualities of normal democratic politics. The superiority of real democratic systems over courts lies in their providing a mechanism for identifying the legislative embodiment of rights most likely to track the commonly avowed interests of citizens by treating them with equal concern and respect. It achieves that result through providing a means for citizens to reach agreements in conditions of political equality. On this account, so-called normal politics is constitutional politics, for it allows the ongoing legislative enactment of rights in the democratic terms required to justify and legitimately realize rights claims. I then turn to an examination of courts and argue that far from offering a more ideal version of this process, courts lack the fundamental democratic quality of allowing an equal input from all affected citizens—their 'right' to author their rights. Nor can their interpretation of a constitutional document that may at some stage have had democratic legitimation in a referendum be regarded as offering a democratic basis for their judgments, isolated as these are from the democratic views of the current citizenry. Meanwhile, the distinction between procedural and substantive review proves hard to sustain. Not only are the rights inherent to a democratic process as contentious as those that lie outside it, with the latter (as I noted) often more basic and important than the former, but also judgments on what counts as a due process turns to a considerable degree on views of the nature of an appropriate outcome. However, if the courts cannot provide a forum for what Pettit terms 'authorial' democracy,[33] they can provide a venue for what he calls 'editorial' or contestatory democracy for those groups that may not have had a voice in the democratic determination of the right. As I argue with regard to the UK Human Rights Act and the European Convention on Human Rights (ECHR) in Chapters 4 and 5 respectively, litigation can play a democratic role here. However, as I contend in Chapter 7, such 'editorial' democracy is necessarily weaker than, and subordinate to, 'authorial' democracy—it offers the basis for a weak form of judicial review that can be overridden by the legislature.

[33] Philip Pettit, 'Democracy: Electoral and Contestatory' in Ian Shapiro and Stephen Macedo (eds), *Designing Democratic Institutions* (New York: New York University Press 2000) 105–44.

4.1. The Authorial Merits of Real Democracy

Democratic systems have undeniable defects and, though they can be improved, must always be expected to fall short of the ideal. However, much the same can be said of any human institution—including courts. So, in advocating courts as correctives for the mistakes of democratically elected and accountable executives and legislatures, it is necessary to bear in mind the mistakes that they will also make. The key question has to be whether courts possess practical and normative qualities that render them more likely to uphold rights, and to do so in more justified ways than democratic systems might do. In posing this question, I do not wish to deny that courts and democratic mechanisms have various complementary qualities, with each being best supplemented by the other—a point I return to below. However, their complementarity per se is not at issue here. Rather, the central point is which should have constitutional supremacy in defining whether rights have been upheld or not. Political systems, such as those of the United States or Germany, which have strong rights-based judicial review, hand over that decision to a supreme or constitutional court which can disapply laws they believe infringe rights. But many other systems—such as those in the UK and Nordic countries like Finland and Norway—have traditionally had far weaker forms of judicial review and give more power on these matters to legislatures and special parliamentary committees. In what follows, I shall argue that the use of these legislative as opposed to judicial mechanisms for rights protection can be justified not just on pragmatic grounds but also for normative reasons to do with the democratic character of rights. For, these normative arguments can never be embodied as fully in judicial practices as they are in legislative ones.

As I have argued elsewhere, and develop further in Chapter 3, the key constitutional quality of actually existing democratic systems arises from their combining majority rule with a dynamic form of the balance of power that results from electoral competition between parties.[34] This combination allows such systems to meet the requirement for political equality demanded of a republican notion of freedom as non-domination, thereby allowing rights to be considered in ways consistent with equal concern and respect, on the one side, and the blocking of arbitrary uses of power by those in government, on the other. Majority rule offers a fair decision-making procedure for resolving disagreements that gives all involved an equal voice, thereby satisfying the need for equal respect. Electoral competition in societies typified by cross-cutting cleavages, and where the main policy differences can be plotted on a left–right continuum, obliges voters indirectly—and politicians vying for power directly—to 'hear the other side', thereby meeting the requirement for equal concern. For, to build a majority, parties—or coalitions of parties—must

[34] Bellamy, *Political Constitutionalism*, ch. 6.

bring together the preferences of as many different groupings among the electorate as possible. The result is that the rival party blocs tend to converge on the median voter, which usually represents the Condorcet winner on a pair wise comparison of the various policy preferences of the electorate as a whole.[35] As research on the relationship of party manifestos to government policies has shown, within democracies that have these characteristics, there is a reasonably high correlation between the electoral campaign and the legislative programme of the successful parties.[36] Moreover, governments in such systems inevitably operate under the shadow of the coming election, and so remain accountable to shifts in electoral opinion. They have an ever-present incentive to formulate polices that are non-arbitrary because they track public interests—those that will coincide with respecting the views of most citizens and addressing their common concerns as far as possible.

As I argue at greater length in Chapter 3, in this scenario, the prospects of any tyranny of the majority are low.[37] Those who lose consistently will be groups at the extremes of the political spectrum, who have failed to modify their views sufficiently to be able to link up with other sections of the electorate. It is not that their rights have been denied, for they have had the right to express their views on which rights ought to be available and in what ways.[38] Their opinions about rights and the interests that lie behind them have been treated on an equal basis to everyone else's. However, they have not managed to convince their fellow citizens that their view of rights would treat all those affected by its implementation with equal concern and respect. And that failure largely results from not heeding the equally important rights claims of a sufficient number of their fellow citizens, so that the costs and benefits of any collective policy on rights can be shown to be fairly shared by all.[39]

This argument will not satisfy a rights theorist who holds that rights attach to individuals outside of any social or political arrangements and should be respected regardless of their costs to others. However, the previous section showed this position to be self-defeating, since it involves a violation of rights itself. The justification of any rights claim needs to be on the grounds that it offers an equal

[35] Peter C. Ordeshook, *Game Theory and Political Theory* (Cambridge: Cambridge University Press 1986) 245–57.

[36] Hans-Dieter Klingermann, Richard I. Hofferbert, and Ian Budge, *Parties, Policies and Democracy* (Boulder: Westview Press 1994).

[37] Anthony McGann, 'The Tyranny of the Supermajority: How Majority Rule Protects Minorities' (2004) 16(1) *Journal of Theoretical Politics* 53–77.

[38] Mark Tushnet, *Taking the Constitution Away from the Courts* (Princeton: Princeton University Press 1999) 159.

[39] As reported by Jose Antonio Cheibub, Fernando Limongi, Adam Przeworski, and Ye Wang, 'Anti-majoritarianism and Democracy: Effects of Judicial Review on Rights, Economic Growth, and Inequality '(4 September 2024), <http://dx.doi.org/10.2139/ssrn.5069081>, with their statistical analysis of rights protection showing 'nothing to indicate that judicial review is necessary to protect rights from majority encroachments'(at 12). Indeed, 'if anything, rights are more fully observed when majorities rule unconstrained by judicial review' (10). As they also note, the one set of rights that do get assiduously protected by courts, namely individual property rights, mean that 'the effect of judicial review is to perpetuate the inequality of income and wealth' (20).

recognition of the mutual rights claims of those others who will have the correlative duty to uphold it. Given disagreement about rights, the best available way of mediating between rival claims is via a fair process in which each person's views are treated on a par with everyone else's and there is encouragement for all to accommodate the preferences of everyone else so far as they can. As we saw, such a process can be regarded as reflecting the democratic spirit that lies at the heart of any reasonable rights claim. It also provides a means for realizing freedom as non-domination. For, it attempts to allow only those interferences that track common avowable interests—that is, those interests that can be avowed politically as showing those involved in a shared social scheme equal concern and respect through functioning as a public good in the sense mentioned earlier. What I have now argued—and develop in detail in Chapter 3—is that actual democratic systems can offer a realistic approximation to such a rights-promoting process.

4.2. Courts as Unreal Democracy

Nevertheless, there will certainly be occasions when democratic mechanisms—either inadvertently or otherwise—do not treat all interests equitably or accommodate certain key concerns sufficiently. Certain persons affected by collective decisions may be excluded from the decision-making process altogether, or be ignored by others due to prejudice or because they are too small and dispersed a group to have any hope of being able to organize themselves so as to be electorally significant. Electorates may also act myopically or be misinformed. In any democratic system there is also the possibility that certain constituencies may prove to have disproportionate influence or others none at all, with the result that electoral decisions may register false positives or false negatives. In these situations, many have thought courts might offer a legitimate safeguard against democratic failures—not least because their processes can claim a certain democratic legitimacy of their own.

Two related claims are made in this regard. First, it is claimed that courts—especially constitutional courts—employ a form of public reasoning and deliberation that is more truly democratic than a standard electoral process. Judges are not only trained to apply the law impartially, so that it applies equally to all, but also are bound to justify their arguments in terms of constitutional rights norms that themselves reflect the upshot of an ideal democratic process—the norms—roughly speaking the main liberal civil and political and even certain socio-economic rights—that anyone who accepted democracy would regard as necessary to secure participation as an equal within the public sphere broadly construed. The judiciary's independence from electoral pressures means they are less swayed by the need to pander to popular prejudices. Instead, they can ask whether legislation could be regarded as consistent with a publicly justified reading of these rights.

As I noted, this argument may be interpreted in either a substantive manner, as relating to the outcome of democratic decisions,[40] or in a procedural manner, with regard to the processes by which democratic decisions are made.[41] Second, it is held that litigation is itself a form of participation. In particular, it allows legislation to be contested on the basis that it fails to meet the standards of equity and fairness inherent to democracy by giving those unable to get an adequate hearing in the regular political process a chance to voice their concerns.[42]

As I will argue at greater length in Chapter 7, both these claims that courts offer a better and more ideal democratic forum for the authorship of rights than real democracy can be challenged. For a start, we have seen that constitutional rights norms can be subject to reasonable disagreements, especially when applied to particular cases. Given that the decisions of multimember courts are often made on the basis of a majority vote, the judiciary can clearly disagree as much as the rest of the population. Yet, their disagreements need not be representative of, or responsive to, the electorate as a whole. That might be no bad thing if we had grounds for regarding their disagreements as somehow resulting from more 'rights-responsive' reasons to those of the general public. But it is not obvious why that should be the case. The fact that they refer to rights in their reasoning does not of itself necessarily mean that their views of them are especially conscientious, better informed, or less biased than other people's. In fact, they may well be less so than politicians who, precisely because they need to engage with the views of the electorate, have to be aware of the impact of a particular way of interpreting and implementing rights on the lives and interests of those they represent. Each citizen's views may be partial, but the nature of the electoral contest makes politicians' views rather less so as they have to appeal across the board. By contrast, the danger is that the views of the judiciary are simply arbitrary from the public's perspective—they are merely the views of those individuals on the bench.

It will be objected that judicial reasoning is constrained by precedent and law. However, neither of these constraints per se can be regarded as necessarily producing a more objectively correct view of rights. If there were a clear methodology for arriving at the right answer on moral questions, then there would no longer be such disagreement about these issues—but no agreed method exists. At best, we have rival methods, each of which tends to exist in a circular relation to the view it wishes to promote. Meanwhile, not only is precedent a notoriously weak constraint—especially when dealing with hard or novel cases of the kinds that typically give rise to judicial review, but also it—and legal reasoning more

[40] Rawls, *Political Liberalism*, Lecture IV; Ronald Dworkin, *Freedom's Law: The Moral Reading of the American Constitution* (Oxford: Oxford University Press 1996) Introduction.

[41] John Hart Ely, *Democracy and Distrust: A Theory of Judicial Review* (Cambridge, MA: Harvard University Press 1980); Habermas, *Between Facts and Norms*, ch. 6.

[42] Aileen Kavanagh, 'Participation and Judicial Review: A Reply to Jeremy Waldron' (2003) 22 *Law and Philosophy* 451–86.

generally—may, insofar as they do apply, be inappropriate constraints. If courts are tied by precedent, then that implies a status quo bias that hinders those cases that might rightly challenge previous decisions. Likewise, the only parties and considerations a court can take into account are those that have legal standing in the case at hand. But when deciding public policy, it is often necessary to consider the knock-on effects for a wide range of seemingly unrelated policies. Moreover, not all the relevant moral issues involved need be best articulated in terms of rights. Indeed, exclusive focus on the way a right has been legally defined may subvert a full discussion of the question at hand. Think of the distorting effect of arguments about the right to free speech that focus on whether a given form of expression can be characterized as 'speech' or not.

Some theorists have argued that these difficulties can be overcome by a procedural approach to judicial review.[43] As Habermas puts it, 'a constitutional court guided by a proceduralist understanding of the constitution does not have to draw on its legitimation credit'—it can leave the substance of rights to a democratic process and confine its views to simply adjudicating on whether democratic decisions respect the 'logic of argumentation'.[44] Yet, he defines valid procedures in terms of 'the communicative presuppositions that allow the better arguments to come into play in various forms of deliberation'.[45] A 'consistent proceduralist understanding of the constitution relies on the intrinsically rational character of a democratic process that grounds the presumption of rational outcomes'.[46] In other words, the test for judging the rationality and appropriateness of a given democratic procedure rests on whether it produces rational outcomes. This argument simply undermines the procedural–substantive distinction. As with other rights, rights related to the democratic process need to be claimed and reformed within existing, normal democratic politics. For example, it is through such mechanisms that workers and women gained the right to vote in the UK, that forms of proportional representation were introduced in New Zealand and in the UK for regional and European elections, and so on. Compare these dramatic and progressive changes to the blocking of similar measures in the United States by successive judgments of the Supreme Court.[47]

What about the potential of litigation as an additional forum for democratic participation and contestation? Partly for related reasons, it may fail or be worse in this respect too. Litigation will only be possible for those parties that the court views as having a case in law. As a result, it is a restricted forum, the terms of which are controlled by the court. As we saw, these controls may be such as to hinder rather than facilitate new or hitherto excluded voices getting heard. Then there

[43] Ely, *Democracy and Distrust*.
[44] Habermas, *Between Facts and Norms*, 279.
[45] Habermas, *Between Facts and Norms*, 278–9.
[46] Habermas, *Between Facts and Norms*, 285.
[47] For details, see Bellamy, *Political Constitutionalism*, 107–29.

are the resource problems of going to court. Access to justice is costly and time-consuming, and cases can take years to be heard. That can often favour those with deep pockets. Given that all citizens start with an equal vote, there is the danger that courts enable illegitimate double counting, with those who cannot muster sufficient popular support to win in politics, shopping in an alternative forum that is less open and hence more favourable to the position of privileged minorities or sectional interests.

As a result of these defects, courts, like legislatures, can register false negatives and positives as well as legislatures.[48] But this practical weakness is not entirely symmetrical to that found in political processes. Though those who get to court may be treated equally with regard to the law, by contrast to the political system they cannot claim their rights to equal concern and respect on their own terms as political equals. The terms whereby they gain access to the law are always the law's, and in these sorts of cases the tribunal they must address is not one of their peers but the judiciary, who are set above them as those who determine the state of the law on the case in question. The difficulty lies in the fact that the very constraints needed to give individuals a fair trial under the law by impartial judges can also make courts inappropriate forums for considering the public good aspects of rights and ensuring that they show equal concern and respect to all those not represented within them. The insistence on legality, on the one side, and independence from extraneous influences, on the other, aims to ensure judges make decisions—as far as possible—free from personal bias, financial inducements, or fear of reprisals from those sympathetic to one or other of the parties. Yet, the common good aspects of rights may involve considerations beyond the law in question and require a responsiveness to the consequences for the public at large. Courts engaged in rights-based review typically deal with such questions under the heading of 'proportionality'. Yet, unlike legislatures, they lack the feedback mechanisms likely to ensure such judgments are well-informed. Governments have to respond to the votes of millions of citizens and their assorted needs by presenting them with a programme of government, and they have both the opposition and several hundred representatives seeking re-election from their diverse constituencies to remind them of that fact. For good reasons, courts are isolated from such pressures.

4.3. Courts and Editorial Democracy

It will be pointed out that not all litigants in human rights cases are tobacco companies contesting restrictions on advertising in the name of free speech, or film

[48] Richard Bellamy, 'The Republic of Reasons: Public Reasoning, Depoliticisation and Non-Domination' in Samantha Besson and José Luis Martí (eds), *Legal Republicanism: National and International Perspectives* (Oxford: Oxford University Press 2009) 102–20.

stars protecting their ability to sell their wedding photos to the highest bidder in the name of privacy. There are also asylum seekers, prisoners, the mentally ill, immigrants, and other unpopular or isolated minority groups, with limited, if any, access to the democratic sphere. Even if not all deserving cases get to court and not all those that do are decided well, there is at least the prospect that some of those individuals whose rights might otherwise go unregarded will get a hearing. For these cases, courts can offer a legitimate avenue of contestatory democracy. While the constraints typical of courts make them a poor authorial forum, they prove well suited as supports for an editorial forum. Courts seek in their own proceedings to ensure that litigants are treated impartially with regard to the settled norms of the law. In doing so, they apply notions of equity and procedural fairness. As a result, they are highly attuned to adjudicating on the issue of whether a given party to a dispute has received an adequate hearing or if the norms governing a case have been interpreted impartially and applied even-handedly to all parties. In cases where a litigant, such as an asylum seeker or a prisoner, can show that his or her position has failed to be treated equitably in any of these ways, then contestation of the authorial decision seems legitimate with the courts an appropriate forum. The issue then becomes how strong can such contestation be before it merges into a less legitimate form of authorial democracy?

Some accounts of editorial democracy, such as Pettit's—at least in certain formulations—see a written constitution and bill of rights as offering the authorial basis for such editorial contestation.[49] However, that overlooks the fact that the legislative branch may have claimed to have paid as much attention to these documents as the judicial, and merely sought to reinterpret them so that they accorded more truly with the current views and interests of people with regard to certain issues. If a court is allowed, as under strong contestatory review, to strike down legislation or to offer its own reading of its fit with constitutional norms, then it is in effect usurping the authorial function of electoral democracy. By contrast, a weak form of contestation allows courts merely to question the compatibility on the fairness grounds outlined above and to force a reconsideration by the legislature. As I note in Chapter 4, the British Human Rights Act can, in many respects, be read in such terms as a form of 'weak' contestatory judicial review. Under this scheme, the rights enumerated in the Act remain an ordinary piece of legislation that the electoral branch can alter if it deems that necessary. However, in the meantime the legislature is obligated to ensure its current legislation is compatible with such rights norms and to highlight explicitly when it seeks, for reasons it deems legitimate, to depart from them. Yet, courts can dispute with regard to a given case whether the legislature has considered all the potential impacts on individual rights sufficiently

[49] Philip Pettit, 'Republican Freedom and Contestatory Democratization' in Ian Shapiro and Casiano Hacker-Cordón (eds), *Democracy's Value* (Cambridge: Cambridge University Press 1999); Pettit, 'Democracy: Electoral and Contestatory'.

thoroughly and ask it to reconsider—though how and when they do so remains the prerogative of the authorial branch of democracy. Here democracy—real democracy—remains the authorial foundation for rights, with the courts offering a supplementary function as an editorial alarm bell.

5. CONCLUSION

Liberal accounts of rights view them as distinct from, and potentially constraints upon, politics. They are means for preventing illegitimate interferences with individual liberty. Democracy offers at best the most appropriate mechanism for upholding them. But that is only because of the empirical flaws of the alternatives and of our reasoning about rights, not due to the very nature of rights themselves. By contrast, I have argued that rights involve an implicit appeal to democratic forms of reasoning. Moreover, this inherently democratic character of rights follows from the republican view of liberty as non-domination. Nevertheless, this view can still capture 'the traditional political purpose of natural or human or fundamental rights' if this is seen as defending against arbitrary rule rather than any rule at all. Nor is this account simply an ideal view of the relations between rights and democracy, that itself has only a pragmatic relation to actually existing democratic processes. The only justifiable authorial foundation of rights must be some form of ongoing democratic decision-making that allows rights to be claimed under conditions of political equality. At best, as I develop in Chapter 7, courts provide the basis for a weak form of 'editorial' or 'contestatory' democracy, that draws attention to neglected or otherwise unheard voices. However, the only legitimate final say on rights rests with the people themselves, among whom the benefits and burdens of rights must equally fall as commonly avowed goods that serve their shared interests.

Of course, it is undeniable that many failings may and do bedevil actually existing democratic systems as mechanisms for achieving a civic condition of non-domination, in which rights may be claimed and sustained on an equitable basis. I raise some of these problems and suggest potential solutions in Chapter 3. However, before doing so I want to turn in the next chapter to another core claim of political constitutionalism—namely, that the rule of law also rests on a particular non-dominating form of the rule of persons that can likewise be identified with democracy.

2

The Rule of Law as the Democratic Rule of Persons

1. INTRODUCTION

One of the more (consciously) provocative arguments of *Political Constitutionalism* was the claim that 'the rule of law simply is the democratic rule of persons'.[1] That claim can be regarded as contentious in at least three senses that are relevant here. First, it appears to run counter to the whole notion of the rule of law as an alternative to, and constraint upon, the rule of persons. Second, it seems at odds with the concern to treat the rule of law as having a distinctive value, with attributes that cohere in a logical and consistent way around the nature of law. As a result, it risks falling into the trap of becoming an ideological repository for whatever the user of the term considers desirable or convenient—a tendency that infamously led Judith Shklar to deride the idea as no more than a 'bit of ruling-class chatter'.[2] Finally, it confronts the view that the rule of law both provides the basis for, and is potentially threatened by, democracy.[3] On this account, democracy is often assumed to be grounded in, and limited by, certain constitutional rules that courts have a duty to uphold. Without such legal protection, so this argument goes, a democratic majority could—and often would—subvert these rules in various self-serving ways.

The first part of this chapter (Sections 2–6) seeks to overcome all three of these objections. Taking each in turn, I shall argue that the democratic rule of persons proves both intrinsically and instrumentally essential to laws and the legal system possessing the formal, substantive, and procedural qualities associated with the rule of law (Sections 2–3). In particular, it enables laws to rule in ways that respect the values commonly associated with the rule of law: namely, respect for the dignity of all those subject to it, not least through constraining the ability of any

[1] Richard Bellamy, *Political Constitutionalism: A Republican Defence of the Constitutionality of Democracy* (Cambridge: Cambridge University Press 2007) 83. In a review article devoted to the book, David Dyzenhaus went so far as to call it a 'startling claim': 'How Hobbes Met the "Hobbes Challenge"' (2009) 72(3) *Modern Law Review* 491.

[2] Judith Shklar, 'Political Theory and the Rule of Law' in A. C. Hutchinson and P. Monahan (eds), *The Rule of Law: Ideal or Ideology* (Toronto: Carswell 1987) 1.

[3] e.g. John Hart Ely, *Democracy and Distrust: A Theory of Judicial Review* (Cambridge, MA: Harvard University Press 1980); Jürgen Habermas, *Between Facts and Norms: Contributions to a Discourse Theory of Law and Democracy* (William Rehg tr., Cambridge: Polity Press 1996); Rosalind Dixon, *Responsive Judicial Review: Democracy and Dysfunction in the Modern Age* (Oxford: Oxford University Press 2023).

Defending the Political Constitution. Richard Bellamy, Oxford University Press. © Richard Bellamy 2026.
DOI: 10.1093/9780191826986.003.0003

person or persons to dominate others through possessing the capacity to subject them to their arbitrary will (Section 4). Indeed, I shall claim that these normative goals of the rule of law can only be achieved through the democratic rule of persons (Section 5). As such, one can regard the rule of persons as both possessing the procedural qualities associated with the rule of law and as being a necessary condition for the attendant formal and substantive qualities of law to arise and obtain (Section 6). The second part of the chapter (Sections 7 and 8) then deploys this analysis to defend a system of parliamentary sovereignty as embodying such a democratic account of the rule of law. Drawing on A. V. Dicey (Section 7), I argue this arrangement proves consistent with both a formal and a more substantive account of the rule of law (Section 8).

2. THE HOBBES CHALLENGE: THE RULE OF PERSONS AS A CONDITION OF THE RULE OF LAW

The rule of law has typically been associated with laws possessing certain formal and, in some accounts, substantive features. However, commentators have also insisted that it has a procedural dimension relating to how laws are made, interpreted, and administered. One reason for that move stems from the fact that it proves hard to conceive how the rule of law can be achieved without the rule of persons. After all, as Jeremy Waldron has remarked, law 'can no more rule us by itself, than a cannon can dominate us without an iron-monger to cast it and an artilleryman to load and fire it'.[4]

Some theorists of law have tried to get around this problem by suggesting that law emerges spontaneously in the form of conventions to coordinate behaviour among persons.[5] Such conventions can be seen as part of the 'common sense' or reason of human beings, or even as a divinely ordained natural law, that reflect certain universal moral and prudential norms essential to any human association. However, social coordination proves notoriously vulnerable to numerous dilemmas of public choice, whereby people act in apparently instrumentally rational ways that prove self-defeating. Self-interest and partiality, passion, as well as the limitations of practical reasoning can all generate conflict and inconsistency. Likewise, identifying God and interpreting God's words can be a source of bitter disagreements. Indeed, even when the meaning of natural or human laws is agreed, their individual and relative bearing on particular situations may not be—producing another source of controversy. Complex cases tend to produce a

[4] Jeremy Waldron, 'The Rule of Law' in *The Stanford Encyclopaedia of Philosophy* (Edward N. Zalta ed., summer edn, 2020) <https://plato.stanford.edu/archives/sum2020/entries/rule-of-law/> 8.

[5] F. A. Hayek, *Law, Legislation and Liberty* (vol. 1, London: Routledge 1973) ch. 2.

high degree of indeterminacy as to what the most relevant moral and evidential considerations are, and which rules apply and how.[6]

To overcome such disagreements and dilemmas, and the conflicts of reasons, ideals, interests, and perspectives that underlie them, prompts what I termed Hobbes's challenge to the very idea of the rule of law.[7] Namely, that for law to rule requires a sovereign authority, that in Hobbes's view would necessarily be outside the law and indivisible, and so capable of imposing law equally and impartially on all. Given 'all Laws, written and unwritten have need of Interpretation',[8] any attempt to place the law above the sovereign would simply lead to an infinite regress. For, to set the law above the sovereign is in effect to set up another power with the power to judge and enforce these laws 'which is to make a new Sovereign' leading to the need of 'for the same reason a third, to punish the second; and so continually without end, to the Confusion, and Dissolution of the Common-wealth'.[9] That will be as true of laws of nature as of any human laws—for these laws can only be appealed to equally by all to the extent they are interpreted and applied by a common sovereign. In an important sense, they have no meaning or application absent such an authority. Instead, there will simply be a range of conflicting claims by different individuals, in which (if any) those of the strongest will prevail. Might will be right.

The Hobbes challenge led early legal positivists to consider law as nothing but the will or commands of the sovereign. As Hobbes put it: 'law' is but 'the word of him, that by right hath command over others'.[10] Yet, that claim poses two related questions. First, there is the question of whether the sovereign's commands will have the qualities—formal, substantive, and procedural—associated with law as opposed to being simply arbitrary acts of will. Second, and in certain respects most importantly, there is the question of whether one can establish if the sovereign does command 'by right' without invoking what H. L. A. Hart called 'secondary' rules of recognition indicating that the sovereign is legally authorized to decide what the law is.[11] I shall tackle the first question in the next two sections and the second in those that follow. However, as we shall see, the two questions are ultimately related. The right to rule turns out to be intimately connected to such an authority inherently ruling in a manner consistent with the properties commonly associated with the rule of law, with democracy answering the requirements of both.

[6] John Rawls, *Political Liberalism* (New York: Columbia University Press 1993) 55–6.

[7] Bellamy, *Political Constitutionalism*, 55.

[8] Thomas Hobbes, *Leviathan* (Richard Tuck ed., Cambridge: Cambridge University Press 1991) 143.

[9] Hobbes, *Leviathan*, 169.

[10] Hobbes, *Leviathan*, 80.

[11] H. L. A. Hart, *The Concept of Law* (2nd edn, Oxford: Clarendon Press 1994) 94–5.

3. THE RULE OF LAW AND LEGALISM

Law tends to be distinguished from a simple command or directive by virtue of various formal properties, such as Lon Fuller's list of eight formal principles that comprise what he termed the 'inner morality of law'.[12] Fuller's list consisted of generality; publicity; prospectivity; intelligibility; consistency; practicability; relative stability (not too frequently changeable); and congruence with official behaviour. Margaret Radin 'boils down' Fuller's list to two: that 'first, there must be rules; second, those rules must be capable of being followed'.[13] The first three aspects of Raz's list overlap with Fuller's list of eight, and he likewise claims they reflect a single idea 'that the law should be capable of being followed'.[14]

As Raz notes, these formal qualities of law have an important but limited virtue. To the extent the rule of persons takes the form of ruling by laws of these kinds, that rule will be more consistent and less arbitrary than ad hoc decision-making. The various criteria seek to ensure that the rules are made and operate with a certain impartiality, regularity, and durability, and are intelligible to, and knowable by, those subject to them—albeit in certain areas with the support of an expert in the field. They are not simply made up on the spur of the moment and applied retrospectively in order to persecute or help a particular person or group of persons. From the point of view of the ruled, a political system characterized by legality of this kind will be more predictable and constant, allowing those who are subject to such laws to plan. As such, rule by law can be regarded as respecting at least some core aspects of an individual's 'dignity as a responsible agent';[15] reflecting the human capacity for autonomous rational agency.[16]

Yet, important though these benefits are, five caveats are in order. First, although even tyrannical regimes have an incentive to rule through law because of the efficiency and efficacy advantages it offers compared to ruling by a steady series of arbitrary decrees, they have no incentive to do so consistently—a point developed in the next section. Indeed, even when they do so, the constraints of rule by law are minimal. Second, that is because the formal qualities associated with law do not in and of themselves address all aspects of human dignity—they do not, for example, guarantee a right to education or subsistence. Third, and worse, these qualities can be satisfied by laws that allow for various affronts to dignity, say by providing rules for the use of torture, or by formalizing certain iniquitous types of racial or

[12] Lon Fuller, *The Morality of Law* (New Haven: Yale University Press 1969) 39. Similar lists are adopted by John Finnis, *Natural Law and Natural Rights* (Oxford: Clarendon Press 1980) 270–1; John Rawls, *A Theory of Justice* (Cambridge, MA: Harvard University Press 1971) 236–9; Joseph Raz, 'The Rule of Law and its Virtue' in Joseph Raz, *The Authority of Law: Essays on Law and Morality* (Oxford: Clarendon Press 1979) 214–18.

[13] Margaret Radin, 'Reconsidering the Rule of Law' (1989) 69 *Boston University Law Review* 785.

[14] Raz, 'The Rule of Law', 218.

[15] Fuller, *The Morality of Law*, 162.

[16] Raz, 'The Rule of Law', 221; Finnis, *Natural Law*, 273.

gender discrimination. After all, the policy of segregation in the southern states of the United States was formally enacted and implemented through the medium of law by duly authorized authorities.

Fourth, the degree to which law can or ought to possess such formal qualities is also limited. For example, Timothy Endicott has remarked how vagueness is an ineliminable quality of law yet one that undermines many of the supposed formal features of law.[17] For example, he notes how Article 6 of the European Convention on Human Rights (ECHR) provides a right to trial on criminal charges 'within a reasonable time', and a right to be informed 'promptly' of charges, and a right to 'adequate' time to prepare a defence. These vague standards could be replaced with precise time limits, but these would be likely to prove arbitrary given the time to gather evidence and so forth will differ from case to case, depending on the type and circumstances of the crime. Yet such vagueness leads to a lack of clarity that may introduce some unpredictability and inconsistency into the application of the law, and fail to adequately constrain the potential for arbitrary rulings on the part of courts.

Likewise, retrospective legislation could be defensible in certain cases, such as the prosecution of crimes against humanity that were legal at the time they were committed yet morally repugnant.[18] Laws of this kind have been passed in many countries to prosecute former Nazis implicated in the Holocaust. Similarly, trials involving terrorist groups or organized crime have led to the creation of bodies such as the Special Criminal Court in Ireland. This court operates with three judges but no jury, so as to avoid issues of jury intimidation and allow evidence from the secret services to be admissible.

Cases of this last kind might be deemed regrettable and controversial exceptions to the rule of law. Yet, surely, it is in precisely such instances that one would want reassurance that these measures were not just justifiable but also lawful in some demanding sense. Meanwhile, as the examples of vagueness indicate, there is a general issue as to when the standard formal qualities associated with the rule of law are applicable or whether they are even necessary desiderata of law. At what point, for example, do we regard any change of the law as being in conflict with the requirement for stability? And is the rule of law somehow undermined by any area of life where law fails to rule? The rule of law qua an account of legalism seems not only a limited virtue but an ideal of limited use.

Fifth, and finally, it will be objected that rule by law is not the same as the rule of law, in that the persons with the right to rule are not themselves under the law. Of course, such an ideal may be impossible—as suggested above. However, to some

[17] Timothy Endicott, 'The Impossibility of the Rule of Law' (1999) 19 *Oxford Journal of Legal Studies* 3–5.

[18] Jeffrey Goldsworthy, *Parliamentary Sovereignty: Contemporary Debates* (Cambridge: Cambridge University Press 2010) 65–6.

extent this objection will not be entirely correct. Those tasked with implementing the law by whatever person or body that has the right to rule, can be required to do so by them according to certain legal rules. Indeed, if the laws they implement are to retain their integrity as possessing the qualities of law, then arguably they will need to perform their duties in a law-like way, according to certain procedures.

This last point suggests we need to pay as much attention to the process of ruling by law as to the formal or substantive qualities of law itself when thinking about the rule of law. This procedural dimension of the rule of law plays a key role in Fuller's eighth principle, which he claimed encompassed 'most of the elements of "procedural due process"',[19] and figures as principles 3 (regarding the making of law) and 4–8 (regarding its application) of Raz's list. Waldron offers the following set of procedural principles as necessary for the rule of law:

a. a hearing by an impartial and independent tribunal that is required to administer existing legal norms on the basis of the formal presentation of evidence and argument;
b. a right to representation by counsel at such a hearing
c. a right to be present, to confront and question witnesses, and to make legal argument about the bearing of the evidence and the various legal norms relevant to the case; and
d. a right to hear reasons from the tribunal when it reaches its decision, which are responsive to the evidence and arguments presented before it.[20]

To these one might add Raz's third principle that 'the making of particular laws (particular legal orders) should be guided by open, stable, clear, and general rules'.[21] Such principles are necessary to structure the legal process so it operates in a general, impartial, and rule-like way, that is consistent with the nature of law as possessing a certain form. They ensure that not only are laws to be distinguished from arbitrary commands by a ruler, but also that this curb on arbitrariness carries over to the way laws are interpreted and applied, and to a degree—explored further below—are made. As Raz puts it, they are:

> designed to ensure that the legal machinery of enforcing the law should not deprive it of its ability to guide through distorted enforcement and that it shall be capable of supervising conformity to the rule of law and provide effective remedies in cases of deviation from it.[22]

[19] Fuller, *The Morality of Law*, 81.
[20] Waldron, 'The Rule of Law', 10—adapting W. Tashima, 'The War on Terror and the Rule of Law' (2008) 15 *Asian American Law Journal* 264, though see too Raz, 'The Rule of Law', 216–17.
[21] Raz, 'The Rule of Law', 215.
[22] Raz, 'The Rule of Law', 218.

In what follows, I wish to suggest that these principles of the legal process are more important for the rule of law than the formal qualities associated with the nature of law. For, if individuals are to be able to plan and make choices in the light of certain laws, however they might be framed, then they need to be assured that they will be deployed in the spirit in which they are formulated.

Lying behind these principles are certain institutional recommendations designed to realize them, such as the balance of powers and the independence of the judiciary. In what follows, I shall suggest that one way of understanding these procedural and related institutional desiderata is as indicating how the rule of law is tied to a particular form of the rule of persons. Indeed, that pertains as much to the making as to the interpretation and application of the law, and ultimately reveals a dependency of the rule of law on the democratic rule of persons as its condition.

4. TYRANNY AND THE RULE OF LAW: LOCKE'S RIPOSTE TO HOBBES

In his classic essay on 'The Rule of Law and its Virtue', Joseph Raz remarks how:

> A non-democratic legal system, based on the denial of human rights, on extensive poverty, on racial segregation, sexual inequalities, and religious persecution may, in principle, conform to the requirements of the rule of law better than any of the legal systems of the more enlightened Western democracies. This does not mean that it will be better than those Western democracies. It will be an immeasurably worse legal system, but it will excel in one respect: in its conformity to the rule of law.[23]

Raz's point is that the rule of law, which he interprets in the formal terms discussed above, 'is just one of the virtues which a legal system may possess and by which it is to be judged'. It should not be confused with the many other substantive qualities we might regard as desirable—such as its upholding rights and justice. That does not mean that the formal attributes he associates with law do not themselves promote certain substantive values. As we have seen, he considered them to serve—at least in part—the dignity of individuals as autonomous rational agents through curbing, to some degree—if not by any means entirely, the arbitrariness of those possessing the right to rule. However, he insisted that the rule of law per se should be considered a distinctive and limited virtue of law and the legal system as such.

[23] Raz, 'The Rule of Law', 211.

Does the argument that the rule of law is in an important sense the democratic rule of persons make a similar logical error to the view he criticizes, in that it attempts to incorporate certain substantive values into the definition of the rule of law itself? Does it, in Matthew Kramer's terms, conflate the 'juristic' conception of the 'rule of law' (lower case) qua 'the realization of the necessary and sufficient conditions for the existence of a legal system' with the 'liberal democratic' conception of the 'Rule of Law' (upper case) qua 'moral-political ideal', committed to the 'dignity and equality of individuals'.[24] I don't think so. I shall argue that it avoids this mistake through being instead a quality of the processes of law making and implementation that are necessary for the law to have the formal features Raz (and Kramer) associates with even the juristic conception of the rule of law.

One way of grasping why that may be the case is to consider Raz's counter assertion, cited above, that a non-democratic system might serve the rule of law as well as, if not better than, a democracy—albeit in the service of less admirable purposes. That suggests the rule of law has simply an instrumental function of ensuring that a ruler's policies—however heinous they may be—can be effectively and efficiently pursued. Yet, such instrumental reasoning proves insufficient to ensure that such laws will be consistently applied and abided by. As soon as a law becomes inconvenient to such a non-democratic ruler or their minions, they will be liable to ignore it. As John Finnis remarks:

> A tyranny devoted to pernicious ends has no self-sufficient reason to submit itself to the discipline of operating consistently through the demanding processes of law, granted that the rational point of such self-discipline is the very value of reciprocity, fairness, and respect for persons which the tyrant, ex hypothesis, holds in contempt.[25]

Of course, even an evil regime will need to comply to some degree with the formal features of the rule of law if it is to have anything resembling a legal system. And if it is to endure as a regime for any period of time, then it will need such a system to coordinate everyday social and economic life as well as to achieve its wicked purposes. In this respect, Nigel Simmonds goes too far in likening a regime such as Hitler's to a gang of robbers that rules via a reign of terror alone.[26] After all, the Nazis needed to coordinate the activities of millions of people for twelve years, including fighting a modern war and perpetrating a horrifically efficient genocide.

[24] Matthew Kramer, *Objectivity and the Rule of Law, Debates* (Cambridge: Cambridge University Press 2007) 102, 143.

[25] Finnis, *Natural Law*, 273.

[26] Nigel Simmonds, *Central Issues in Jurisprudence* (London: Sweet and Maxwell 1986) 119, 123; see the critique in Matthew Kramer, *In Defence of Legal Positivism* (Oxford: Oxford University Press 1999) 65–6.

Yet, it is also true that such regimes and those that serve them will place little value on the rule of law apart from its instrumental qualities, with many involved in its administration adhering to legal rules for purely prudential reasons—not least, fear of the consequences of not doing so. As a result, such regimes tend to be characterized by widespread corruption and partiality towards members of the regime, and various kinds of arbitrary decision-making—be it to pursue feuds with rivals, settle petty grievances, or simply to satisfy a whim. As a result, those subject to such a legal system will never be able to count on its regular and impartial operations or consider the law as superior to its enforcer. Of course, some instances of circumventing the application of the law of an evil regime may well be morally preferable to applying it, even if done for immoral reasons—say, if a venal Nazi official accepts a bribe from a Jewish family that allows them to escape persecution.[27] However, the argument here is not to deny that a heinous regime can deploy the formal qualities of law for monstrous purposes. Indeed, to some degree they need to do so to accomplish them. Rather, this fact exemplifies the core contention of this chapter that law itself never rules—it derives its qualities from the quality of the processes determining the rule of persons that make and implement those laws. The nature of tyrannical rule, though, is such that law always risks having the quality of being an arbitrary command. As a result, while an evil tyranny may find the rule of law in the formal sense useful and even necessary to the pursuit of its nefarious ends, such a regime will never 'excel' in its 'conformity to the rule of law'. It will always ditch legality when it becomes inconvenient to the wishes or whims of the tyrant. Its essence will be as a system of arbitrary rule, free from the constraints of any form of due process. To adopt Kramer's terminology, the claim is that ultimately even lower case rule of law depends on democratic processes that embody certain democratic features associated with upper case Rule of Law.

Hobbes tried to get around this sort of critique by suggesting that not only was social peace and the very possibility of law, justice, property ownership, industry, and culture unachievable without submission to a sovereign power capable of enforcing the authoritative resolution of conflicting rights,[28] so that life under the sovereign would always be preferable to life in the state of nature and

[27] See Kramer, *In Defence*, 56–8, who deploys this sort of argument as part of his critique of those, such as Fuller and Simmonds, who seek to defend the inherent morality of legality as such. While I agree with this critique, Kramer goes too far in his turn in considering a totalitarian system to be one that will deploy juristic legality even more strictly than a liberal democracy. He sees this development as reflecting the growing need for such regimes to submit their subject populations to a stifling system of surveillance to ensure their compliance. Yet such a system is likely to require and encourage the use of ever more instances of personal and arbitrary rule. For example, the STASI in East Germany ended up employing one informer per 6.5 citizens—basically a system of direct personal rule (John O. Koehler, *Stasi: The Untold Story of the East German Secret Police* (Boulder, CO: Westview Press 1999) 7–8). As Kramer himself notes, the Stalinist terror indicates the degree of arbitrariness into which such a system of paranoid direct surveillance can descend (*In Defence*, 70 n. 32).

[28] Hobbes, *Leviathan*, ch. 13: 62.

the attendant civil war,[29] but also that the interest of the sovereign lay in fostering rather than weakening the vigour and prosperity of their subjects—after all, their own power rested on a healthy tax base to fund their armies and activities.[30] Sadly, the behaviour of dictatorial rulers suggests otherwise,[31] as Stalin's Great Purge of 1936–38, the Great Chinese Famine of 1959–61 created by Mao Zedong's misguided economic plans, and Hitler's genocidal policies and ruinous wars, all amply demonstrate. Meanwhile, if the instrumental reasons for a sovereign to govern via common rules and abide by them cannot be counted on, then neither can those of the sovereign's subjects to obey him or her. As Locke famously remarked, to believe otherwise would be 'to think that men are so foolish, that they take care to avoid what mischiefs may be done them by pole-cats, or foxes; but are content, nay, think it safety, to be devoured by lions'.[32]

If the instrumental argument for adopting the rule of law fails, the Hobbes challenge becomes all the more challenging—for what might induce any rulers wielding sovereign power to abide by the rule of law given that they are *ipso facto* above the law by virtue of being its source? One approach has been to thicken the notion of the rule of law by infusing it with substantive content in the form of rights. Yet that approach not only risks confusing the rule of law with the rule of good law, the avoidance of which even one of the main defenders of this approach acknowledges has 'logical force',[33] but also leaves the source of these values and the legitimacy of upholding some rather than others, or of interpreting them in one way rather than another, unaddressed. In other words, it falls prey to the original Hobbes challenge. Meanwhile, that dilemma cannot be avoided by treating such requirements as instances of natural law or an emergent customary law, as we saw Hayek advocated.[34] After all, common law systems claim to develop in this way yet are notoriously opaque and unpredictable, being inherently retroactive with a tendency towards reflecting little more than the ad hoc arbitrary rule of what Bentham called 'Judge & Co'.[35] Instead, I take a different tack by focusing on the right to rule and the process of legislation and adjudication.

[29] Hobbes, *Leviathan*, chs 13: 62, 18: 94.

[30] Hobbes, *Leviathan*, ch. 18: 94.

[31] Frank Dikötter, *How to be a Dictator: The Cult of Personality in the Twentieth Century* (London, New York: Bloomsbury 2019).

[32] John Locke, *Two Treatises of Government* (Peter Laslett ed., Cambridge: Cambridge University Press 1988) Second Treatise, ch. VII, sec. 93:328.

[33] Tom Bingham, *The Rule of Law* (London: Penguin) 67.

[34] Hayek, *Law, Legislation, and Liberty*, vol. 1.

[35] Jeremy Bentham, *A Comment on the Commentaries; and A Fragment on Government* (J. H. Burns and H. L. A. Hart eds, London: Athlone Press 1977); Gerald Postema, *Bentham and the Common Law Tradition* (Oxford: Clarendon Press 1986) 267–301; Waldron, 'The Rule of Law', 8.

5. THE CHALLENGE OF WILLIAMS AND ROUSSEAU TO HOBBES: SOVEREIGNTY AND THE RIGHT TO RULE

The Hobbes challenge arises from the need to address what Bernard Williams termed the 'first political question'.[36] Hobbes's imagined state of nature reflects the conditions that comprise what, following Albert Weale and Jeremy Waldron, I referred to as the 'circumstances of politics' in Chapter 1.[37] As I remarked there, these circumstances arise from what John Rawls called 'the burdens of judgment . . . the many hazards involved in the correct (and conscientious) exercise of our powers of reason and judgement in the ordinary course of political life'.[38] These limitations in our practical reasoning result in a situation in which individuals reasonably disagree as to the nature and substance of their rights and duties vis-à-vis others. The 'circumstances of politics' appear when unavoidable interactions among individuals mean that, despite these disagreements, they need to reach a collective agreement on what their respective rights and duties are. Hobbes's insight was that in order to escape the possibility of constant clashes between conflicting rights claims (the 'war of all against all'), individuals would need to subject themselves to a ruler possessing the capacity to decide for all.

To have that capacity, such a ruler must possess the attributes of sovereignty: namely, finality, supremacy, and comprehensiveness, in which possession of the first attribute depends on the ruler also possessing the second and third attributes.[39] To be able to decide an issue, an authority must have the final word with respect to the divisions among the individuals subject to it. Yet, for that to be the case, such an authority must also be supreme vis-à-vis alternative sources of authority and have a comprehensive jurisdiction over the activities of those under its sway.[40] Sovereignty so conceived forms a precondition for providing a response to 'the first political question', for without it, the Hobbes challenge persists and the designated political authority will not be able to have the final word in any dispute.

The creation of a political authority comes first in Williams's terms because a response to this question 'is the condition of solving, indeed posing, any others'.[41] As Hobbes had noted, there can be no rightful claims of rights unless these are authoritatively established through law. Otherwise, there will simply be the clash of conflicting assertions of rights, none of which can be authoritatively and stably

[36] Bernard Williams, 'Realism and Moralism in Political Theory' in Bernard Williams, *In the Beginning was the Deed* (Princeton, NJ: Princeton University Press 2005) 3.

[37] Albert Weale, *Democracy* (2nd edn, Basingstoke: Palgrave 2007) 12–18; Jeremy Waldron, *Law and Disagreement* (Oxford: Clarendon Press 1999) 107–13.

[38] Rawls, *Political Liberalism*, 55–6.

[39] F. H. Hinsley, *Sovereignty* (2nd edn, Cambridge: Cambridge University Press 1986) 1, 26.

[40] Richard Bellamy, *A Republican Europe of States: Cosmopolitanism, Intergovernmentalism and Democracy in the EU* (Cambridge: Cambridge University Press 2019) 74.

[41] Williams, 'Realism and Moralism', 3.

settled in a manner consistent with the rule of law. At best, certain individuals can impose their view on others, but such impositions will be arbitrary acts of will in which might is right.

Suppose particular individual claims could be regarded as objectively justified? Surely the imposition of such claims could not be regarded as arbitrary and hence as illegitimate? And if this was the case, would it not be legitimate to empower an individual or individuals capable of making such objectively justified claims as benevolent dictators, possessing the right to rule over other individuals who lack such knowledge?[42] Given the Rawlsian 'burdens of judgment', the possibility that any individuals could possess such an objective view must be regarded as doubtful. At the very least, it will always be open to potential reasonable contestation by others given what Rawls called 'the fact of pluralism'—the plurality of conflicting reasonable perspectives stemming from factors such as: the complex nature of much factual information and uncertainty over its bearing on any case; disagreement about the weighting of values; the vagueness of people's concepts; the different backgrounds and experiences of different people; and the variety of normative considerations involved in any issue, and the difficulty of making an overall assessment of their relative weight.[43] To mention just one of the difficulties such a claim encounters, even if individuals could overcome partiality in the sense of being self-interested, their thinking cannot avoid being partial in the sense of incompleteness with regard to knowledge and understanding of the material circumstances and value judgements of other individuals, raising the risk that they might overlook certain valid concerns of these others. But alongside such instrumental worries as to the likelihood such an enlightened despot could exist, there is the intrinsic objection that to impose even a just resolution fails to treat those subjected to it as equal autonomous reasoners.[44] In other words, it fails with regard to that virtue that Raz considered was possessed by even the most formal view of the rule of law: namely, respect for the dignity of individuals as autonomous reasoners.[45] As we shall see, this is a crucial consideration to which I return in the sections below.

Does Hobbes's solution fare any better? Williams's analysis suggests it does not, because to count as a response to the first political question any proposed

[42] Alon Harel, 'The Kantian Case against Democracy' (2023) 26 *Critical Review of International Social and Political Philosophy* 246.

[43] Rawls, *Political Liberalism*, 56–7; Richard Bellamy, *Liberalism and Pluralism: Towards a Politics of Compromise* (London: Routledge 1999) 7–8.

[44] Chiara Cordelli, *The Privatized State* (Princeton, NJ: Princeton University Press 2020) 63.

[45] It might be argued that I am conflating cognitive with ethical autonomy here—after all, even in a malevolent tyranny a citizen can reason as to whether compliance is the most rational course of action or not. Indeed, the regime rests on their reasoning that it is. However, I have argued that the nature of such regimes is precisely to undermine such instrumental calculations. That said, I am arguing that a regular system of law can only be established by meeting the BLD, and that entails a system of rule compatible with ethical autonomy.

answer must meet what he calls the Basic Legitimacy Demand (BLD).[46] Unfortunately, Williams was rather imprecise as to what that demand entails, in part because he considered it to have been met in different ways in different historical settings. At the most abstract level, however, he contends that for an authority to count as legitimately 'political' it cannot simply consist of the imposition of an arbitrary will. If an authority rules by virtue of its superior coercive power alone, it does not resolve the dilemmas of the state of nature and create a 'political' state but rather continues those dilemmas, in the manner implied by the quote from Locke earlier. It will simply enhance the capacity of an individual to impose his or her judgement on others. As we saw, while a tyrant may have instrumental reasons to govern in conformity with certain formal features of the rule of law, at least when that is possible and appropriate, these are contingent on doing so being in his or her interest. Consequently, a tyrant's rule cannot be regarded as inherently tied to a form of the rule of law that recognizes the dignity of the ruled.[47]

To provide a legitimate response to the first political question, therefore, the right to rule must be of a kind consistent with those subject to it retaining their dignity as equal autonomous reasoners. As a number of recent commentators have remarked, both Rousseau and Kant can be regarded as broadly accepting Hobbes's argument for the necessity of a sovereign ruler to provide the basis for the rightful claiming of rights and the establishment of the rule of law.[48] However, they considered this solution as raising a dilemma of its own: namely, whether it was possible to combine such sovereign authority with the freedom and equality of those subject to it. As Rousseau put it, the challenge was 'to find a form of association which will defend and protect with the whole common force the person and goods of each associate, and in which each, while uniting himself with all, may still obey himself alone, and remain as free as before'.[49] It is to how the rule of law might meet Rousseau's challenge that we now turn.

[46] Williams, 'Realism and Moralism', 5.

[47] Dyzenhaus, 'How Hobbes Met the "Hobbes Challenge"', 492–3, suggests that Hobbes proposes just this solution by regarding the sovereign's authority as inherently bound by the laws of nature, in ways that he considered should be evident to all. However, this solution begs the original question to which Hobbes was seeking to respond and makes Hobbes sound like Locke—a 'surprising claim' indeed.

[48] Cordelli, *The Privatized State*, ch. 2; Katrin Flikschuh, 'Reason, Right, and Revolution: Kant and Locke' (2008) 36(4) *Philosophy and Public Affairs* 275–404; Frederik Neuhouser, 'Rousseau's Critique of Economic Inequality' (2013) 41 *Philosophy and Public Affairs* 193–225; Arthur Ripstein, *Force and Freedom: Kant's Legal and Political Philosophy* (Cambridge, MA: Harvard University Press 2009); Anna Stilz, *Liberal Loyalty: Freedom, Obligation, and the State* (Princeton, NJ: Princeton University Press 2009); Anna Stilz, *Territorial Sovereignty: A Philosophical Exploration* (Oxford: Oxford University Press 2019) 93–101.

[49] Jean Jacques Rousseau, *The Social Contract and Other Later Political Writings* (Victor Gourevitch ed., Cambridge: Cambridge University Press 1997) 49–50.

6. MEETING ROUSSEAU'S CHALLENGE: KANTIAN DEMOCRACY AND THE RULE OF LAW

The crux of Rousseau's challenge lies in the need to combine the necessity for a sovereign authority with an account of freedom that highlights the dimension of non-domination. On Rousseau's (and, following him, Kant's) account, a non-dominating form of rule is intimately linked to sovereignty and both requires and makes possible the rule of law. Each of these three elements—non-domination, sovereignty, and the rule of law—entails the other two to be realized. What renders the conjoining of these three elements possible is a democratic process that involves showing equal respect and concern to all participants and that, as such, itself possesses the formal qualities of the rule of law. Let's take each element in turn.

6.1. Non-Domination

According to the republican account of non-domination adopted in this book—to which both Rousseau and Kant can broadly be aligned—the concern with domination derives from a view of human beings as moral equals, each entitled to act on their own autonomous choices on the same basis to everyone else. Following Philip Pettit, non-domination so conceived can be defined as the absence of alien, non-deliberative control.[50] Deliberative control, whereby others seek to persuade you via reasons you can accept or not, respects one's equal status as an independent reasoner and so involves no domination. By contrast, an agent or agency exercises non-deliberative control over your choices when they influence them either directly, be it through coercive interference or, more subtly, by manipulation or deception, or indirectly, without actual interference, through your simply fearing or anticipating their capacity to interfere and inhibiting your actions as a result of invigilation or monitoring, in ways that may lead to self-censorship or self-ingratiation. On the republican account, domination of both the interfering and the inhibiting kind results from a relationship of actual or potential mastery of one agent or agency by another. It derives from a situation in which one is no longer an equal and independent chooser.

[50] Philip Pettit, 'A Republican Law of Peoples' (2010) 9 *European Journal of Political Theory* 73–5; Philip Pettit, *On the People's Terms: A Republican Theory and Model of Democracy* (Cambridge: Cambridge University Press 2012) ch. 1.

6.2. Sovereignty

Herein lies the link that a number of republicans sought to establish between non-domination and sovereignty. If domination arises from being subject to a master, then individuals will only be non-dominated to the extent they are free from mastery as a result of possessing sovereignty, which we saw by definition entails having no superior.[51]

Establishing a situation in which each individual possesses sovereignty poses a dilemma, as both Rousseau and Kant fully appreciated. If individuals could live entirely independently of one another, as self-sufficient units, without any interaction, then each could be sovereign over his or her choices and domain. Likewise, if all acknowledged the sovereignty of a given conception of justice, then cooperation between individuals could be based on voluntary agreements that acknowledged their respective rights. However, given that social interaction proves both necessary and unavoidable, while the partiality of all individuals to their own interests and perspectives makes disagreements about justice inevitable, then—following Hobbes[52]—these authors argued that the need arose for a sovereign political authority capable of determining and enforcing collectively binding rules of social conduct. Without such an authority, then—again drawing on Hobbes[53]—they contended each individual ran the risk of being dominated by, or themselves dominating, every other individual they came into contact with.

Deploying the terminology I used earlier, this tradition of republicanism entirely concurred, therefore, with the view that we encounter the 'circumstances of justice' within the 'circumstances of politics'. Indeed, in the manner of Williams's Hobbesian realism discussed above, Rousseau and Kant took the further step of suggesting that there can be no justice outside of politics. In a situation where individuals unilaterally decide whether others have infringed their rights or they have infringed the rights of others, then—unless they all happen to agree on what is right—none has a duty to respect the view of rights held by others. They also cannot rightfully impose their view of justice on anyone else without similarly denying their moral equality as an equally authoritative judge of what justice demands. Therefore, sovereign authority becomes a precondition of justice because only such an authority can deliver a decisive and common process of adjudication capable of reliably and stably establishing objective duties on all. It provides this possibility precisely through being supreme and comprehensive, and thereby offering the prospect of replacing the unilateral will and subjective judgement of particular individuals with a non-unilateral will.

[51] Rousseau, *The Social Contract*, 51–4; Immanuel Kant, 'Introduction to the Doctrine of Right' in Immanuel Kant, *Practical Philosophy* (Mary Gregor ed., Cambridge: Cambridge University Press 1996) 393–4.

[52] Hobbes, *Leviathan*, ch. 13.

[53] Hobbes, *Leviathan*, ch. 17.

6.3. The Rule of Law

A sovereign political authority offers the prospect of a form of rule by law that meets some of the formal features of the rule of law and could establish the rights of individuals on an equal basis to each other in ways consistent with a reasonable conception of justice. However, as we saw, *could* need not mean *would*. For, the danger with this proposal lies in such a sovereign power also offering an unrivalled prospect for domination through becoming itself the instrument of a particular will, a worry raised once more by Hobbes and his account of sovereign power, with its apparent rejection of republican fears regarding domination.[54] Indeed, that danger seems inherent to the Hobbesian account.

Could this danger be overcome if the Hobbesian sovereign could be so constrained that its rule was that of an impersonal, non-lateral will, rather than of an agent's or agency's unilateral will? After all, the rule of law is sometimes characterized in such terms—as reflecting, say, an objective and universal account of justice of a kind all could and should accept through its being the product of a form of public reason on which all reasonable views could converge.[55] The rights of individuals under such a scheme would be those they are entitled to under the law, with those that administer it being simply the servants of the law. On this account, neither the law itself nor its interpreters or implementors can be regarded as either the product of, or of imposing, a private unilateral will. The legal system simply operates so as to produce a rightful condition of a kind all could and should agree to as just.

However, it seems hard to conceive how this proposal could avoid the difficulties associated with an enlightened despot discussed earlier.[56] Given the 'burdens of judgment' arising from the 'fact of pluralism', the Hobbes challenge seems inescapable and with it the problem that both the conception of justice embodied in the law and its interpreters cannot avoid subjecting those governed in this way to a unilateral will.[57] On the one hand, the attempt to ground public laws as objectively necessitated by some universal form of impartial reason none could reasonably reject seems doomed to failure. The 'circumstances of politics' arise precisely because no epistemology exists to objectively ground rival ontological claims. On the other hand, even if one could argue that among liberal and even some non-liberal societies a consensus on the importance of certain basic rights now exists, as evidenced by their adherence to certain international human rights conventions, these and other related principles are too indeterminate to settle in an unequivocal way how

[54] Hobbes, *Leviathan*, ch. 21.

[55] e.g. Alon Harel and Adam Shinar, 'Two Concepts of Constitutional Legitimacy' (2023) 12 *Global Constitutionalism* 81–2.

[56] On this point, see Chiara Cordelli, 'Kantian Democracy and Administrative Legitimacy: A Reply to My Critics' (2023) 26 *Critical Review of International Social and Political Philosophy* 268–9.

[57] Cordelli, *The Privatized State*, 63.

they might be best instantiated. After all, as I noted in Chapter 1, even liberal political philosophers disagree about such issues as the balance between freedom of speech and individual privacy or the nature of property rights.

If the aim is the establishment of a society of equals, none of whom dominates others, then basing the rule of law on a hypothetically shared non-unilateral will seems a non-starter. It seems impossible for such an account not to lead to those so ruled being dominated by the arbitrary will of another. The alternative, explored below, is for the laws that define the fundamental rights and duties of individuals to be the products of a system that embodies an omnilateral will in which each decides the same thing for all.[58]

6.4. Democracy

As is well known, Rousseau considered the only way to meet his challenge was by locating sovereignty in the people's democratically constructed general will.[59] As Kant, drawing on Rousseau, put it: 'only the concurring and united will of all, insofar as each decides the same thing for all, and all for each, and so only the general united will of the people, can be legislative'.[60] Indeed, he considered that: 'If a public law is so constituted that a whole people could not possibly give its consent to it . . . it is unjust'.[61] However, Kant can be interpreted as suggesting that this condition can be met through the political system meeting the hypothetical constraints of 'an original contract'. After all, Kant regards the 'original contract' as 'an idea of reason'.[62] Yet, as we saw, a purely hypothetical argument would deny the moral agency of those subject to the legal and political system. Instead, for reasons I elaborate further in Chapter 3, we need to see this system, if not every decision emanating from it, as expressing 'an omnilateral will as an *actual* popular will'.[63] Therefore, what follows extrapolates from the Kantian argument to suggest that to meet this criterion requires a non-dominating form of democracy involving a sovereign process that complies with certain formal procedural requirements of the rule of law.

As we have seen, the attraction of a sovereign political authority rests on its providing a solution to the problem of individuals being dominated by the

58 Rousseau, *The Social Contract*, 66–8; Kant, 'The Doctrine of Right' in Kant, *Practical Philosophy*, 457–8; Stilz, *Liberal Loyalty*, 38–56; Stilz, *Territorial Sovereignty*, 93–104; Cordelli, *The Privatized State*, 63.

59 Stilz, *Liberal Loyalty*, ch. 3.

60 Kant, 'Doctrine of Right', 457.

61 Immanuel Kant, 'On the Common Saying: That May Be Correct in Theory, but It Is of No Use in Practice' (hereafter *TP*) in Immanuel Kant, *Practical Philosophy* (Mary Gregor ed., Cambridge: Cambridge University Press 1999) 297.

62 Kant, *TP*, 296–7.

63 Stilz, *Territorial Sovereignty*, 94.

partial judgements and particular unilateral wills of others. Any single individual—however well-intentioned and selfless—will have a partial perspective, in the sense of being inevitably limited in their ability to comprehend or even be aware of all other peoples' situations, interests, and views, and likely—even unwittingly—to favour their own interests and point of view. Yet that means overcoming partiality cannot be achieved by deferring to arbitration by some self-styled impartial third party or parties. So conceived, a sovereign authority would be part of the problem rather than its solution, for it could not avoid acting arbitrarily towards those subject to it. Democracy proposes a solution to this difficulty by placing sovereign authority in an impartial mechanism that offers a public means for showing equal concern and respect to the views and interests of all citizens in determining collective policies. Such a mechanism aims to allow citizens to agree despite their disagreements by providing a way of making decisions all can accept as legitimate even when they dissent from a given decision.[64]

A democratic procedure consisting of majority rule based on one person one vote formally meets this requirement in being anonymous, neutral, and positively responsive.[65] These qualities render it both 'content-independent' and fair. It is content-independent in not being biased to any particular outcome and fair in providing every individual voter with an equal hearing, regardless of who they are or what they think. As such, it offers a form of public decision-making in which citizens can regard themselves as possessing an equal status, whereby all have a duty to recognize the right of everyone else to be treated with equal concern and respect.

One can regard democracy as possessing certain of the core procedural features of the rule of law that were outlined above with regard to the application of the law, only in this case they relate to the processes involved in making the law. For example, democracy operates impartially and independently, giving everyone an equal hearing, acknowledges a right to representation and, through the processes of authorization and accountability of representatives explored in Chapter 3, a right to express preferences and hear reasons. These qualities mean that acceptance of the decisions of a democratic process does not entail being ruled by the unilateral will of another, given the process operates neutrally and involves all as equal judges.

Nevertheless, such a formal mechanism offers only a necessary but not a sufficient condition to avoid domination. If a majority vote reflects the 'will of all' rather than a 'general will', then, as Rousseau noted, the possibility arises of certain groups dominating others because each will have voted with the sole objective of

[64] Thomas Christiano, *The Constitution of Equality: Democratic Authority and its Limits* (Oxford: Oxford University Press 2008) ch. 6.

[65] Kenneth O. May, 'A Set of Independent, Necessary and Sufficient Conditions for Simple Majority Decision' (1952) 20 *Econometrica* 680–4.

furthering their partial interests and perspective.[66] For example, a consistent minority could be subject to the arbitrary will of a majority if the majority's partial interests can be furthered through the exploitation of the minority and the suppression of their views. The formal features of the rule of law enter here. To avoid this possibility, in ways explored more fully in Chapter 3, a democratic process must also incentivize citizens to justify their collective decisions to each other on the basis of commonly avowable reasons that acknowledge the entitlement of all citizens to be treated with equal concern and respect. Though many policies will benefit particular groups, they must do so for general reasons that are acknowledged as applying equally to all and that promote a shareable public interest. Therefore, democratic legitimacy will depend to some degree on whether those belonging to the citizenry relate to each other in ways that render such an equal and public process possible and appropriate.[67] Put another way, democratic arrangements must be capable of reflecting the omnilateral will of those concerned to associate in a self-determining political community.[68]

For reasons examined in Chapter 3, two types of relations prove especially important in defining a *demos* among whom a democratic process for collective decision-making will be legitimate. First, there needs to be a high degree of interdependence between the members of a community and their most important interests must be more or less equally tied up in it, and be so over a long period of time—sufficient for them to care about the impact of current decisions for future generations.[69] Interdependence stimulates cross-cutting cleavages that make interest groups less factionalized, ease trade-offs, and diminish the possibility of consistent winners and losers. A rough equality of stake in the overall package of collective decisions gives citizens an equal interest in ensuring the basic structures of social cooperation are fair and equitable. It frames a commitment to promoting and sustaining investment in certain public goods that are conducive to their different projects, including collective schemes of social insurance and the maintenance of fair democratic procedures for deliberating on the public good. If some have less of a stake in these collective decisions than others, then it would not be legitimate for them to have an equal say because their interest in them will be partial by definition. They will be more inclined to underfund policies supporting a common good in which they do not share and to promote policies that support their sectional interests.

Second, and relatedly, citizens need to conceive themselves as a public and be able to act as such.[70] Such a self-conception gains support from a shared public

[66] Rousseau, *The Social Contract*, 60.
[67] Rawls, *The Law of Peoples*, 23–4.
[68] Stilz, *Territorial Sovereignty*, 94.
[69] Thomas Christiano, 'Democratic Legitimacy and International Institutions' in Samantha Besson and John Tasioulas (eds), *The Philosophy of International Law* (Oxford: Oxford University Press 2010) 130–2.
[70] David Miller, 'Democracy's Domain' (2009) 37 *Philosophy and Public Affairs* 212.

culture and sphere, themselves the product of a shared history, language, and customs that create a feeling of like-mindedness and the sense of participating in a collective project. A shared public culture provides a source of agreement on the kind of issues that can be raised and the values that can be appealed to, making it less likely interlocutors will view each other's points as mere personal opinions and interests that do not need to be addressed and responded to, thereby aiding compromise through focusing on common principles and priorities. A shared public sphere involving common media, discourse, and language or languages allows citizens to address each other as a public and encourages politicians to do so by offering common forums through which to communicate with each other. Otherwise, the danger is that politicians could simply play different groups off each other, saying different and even contradictory things to each group. Nor will citizens be forced to hear the other side. There will be no incentive to develop only commonly avowable policies and principles that address shareable values and interests or mutually acceptable compromises. Such incentives oblige those seeking special privileges, such as a religious group seeking an exemption from certain common policies or a business asking for a tax break, to frame their demand in terms of a general principle or benefit applicable to the whole community and not just them. Again, the risk is that, otherwise, society will become divided into discrete and insular publics, with distinct views and interests on key issues. As a result, the possibility of partial decision-making favouring only given sectorial groups increases, as does the potential for persistent minorities.

A democratic process that operates subject to these conditions proves non-dominating. As I outlined above, mastery of a kind that leads to domination arises from an imbalance of power, dependency, and arbitrariness.[71] If A has more power than B, then A can reliably alter B's choices but not vice versa. In this scheme, all have an equal power in making collective decisions and none can reliably control another. If B is dependent on A, then the cost to B of defying A may be prohibitively high. However, under this arrangement all are equally subject to, and have an equal stake in, collective rules and goods that are under their free and equal control. As Rousseau observed, 'each, by giving himself to all, gives himself to no one'.[72] There is mutual but not personal dependence. Finally, arbitrariness exists if A can will what B chooses according to A's partial judgement and interests, without consulting those of B. Here, though, collective rules must consult the commonly avowable judgements and interests of those subject to them.

Clearly, actually existing democratic systems operate with varying degrees of success in meeting these conditions and at best are 'nearly democratic' in the specified senses. To some degree, this variation depends on specific details of their

[71] Frank Lovett, *A General Theory of Domination and Justice* (Oxford: Oxford University Press 2010) 119–20.
[72] Rousseau, *The Social Contract*, 50.

political and social arrangements, such as the electoral system, which I will consider in Chapter 3. However, they will also be affected by the way sovereignty is arranged. Historically, state sovereignty has provided the context within which democratic mechanisms have been able to emerge within states.[73] How has state sovereignty helped give democratic decision-making these qualities?

First, as we saw, supremacy and comprehensiveness supply a precondition for all policies being made by and applying equally to all. Unless a single authority has ultimate responsibility for the totality of social relations and is under the control of all subject to them, then collective decisions will not be those of and for the collectivity. They will reflect partial interests and perspectives. Second, these attributes of sovereignty arise from a sovereign *ruling agent or agency* being located within a territorial *polity* with its own system of governance or *regime* and people or *demos*.[74] These four features interact in a variety of ways with sovereignty being the product of their interaction. As a result, citizens become part of a polity-wide system of political and legal cooperation and share a public sphere. They provide the context within which citizens can live under the rule of law without it being a source of domination. They achieve this through engaging in a collective practice of defining and upholding laws that provide a fair scheme of rights through being responsive to their omnilateral will through a democratic process.

Note that for such a democratic arrangement to reflect an omnilateral will does not entail it produces universal consent to either specific laws or the promotion of shared substantive values, both of which would be impossible to meet.[75] Rather, it involves the weaker condition of embodying equal respect for the views of the governed by virtue of the existence of a plausibly democratic system that gives citizens equal participation in decision-making.[76] Nevertheless, to meet even this weaker condition, it will not be sufficient that democratic processes merely involve the public. Rather, they must do so on a basis that can be publicly acknowledged by at least the vast majority of those to whom they apply as broadly fair and appropriate, not least in demonstrably giving equal consideration to their views and interests in framing collective policies. No matter how far such procedures may conform to abstract democratic principles in theory, their legitimacy will be impugned to the extent their operation is perceived in practice to reflect unduly the values of a subsection of the political community, such as the ruling elite, and of responding disproportionately to their sectional interests.[77]

[73] Quentin Skinner, 'The Sovereign State: A Genealogy' in Hent Kalmo and Quentin Skinner (eds), *Sovereignty in Fragments: The Past, Present and Future of a Contested Concept* (Cambridge: Cambridge University Press 2010) 26–46.

[74] Michel Troper, 'The Survival of Sovereignty' in Kalmo and Skinner (eds), *Sovereignty in Fragments*, 132–50, at 137–9.

[75] John Simmons, *Moral Principles and Political Obligations* (Princeton, NJ: Princeton University Press 1979).

[76] Allen Buchanan, 'Political Legitimacy and Democracy' (2002) 112(4) *Ethics* 689–719.

[77] Christiano, *The Constitution of Equality*.

Consequently, such democratic institutions do not involve the people themselves being sovereign. It is not citizens but the system—the ruling agencies—most particularly the legislature and executive—and its agents—the people's elected representatives—that possess sovereign legislative and administrative authority. However, their legitimacy depends on them being representative of the people they rule, through being authorized and accountable to them through a democratic process that treats all those subject to its collective decisions as of equal status and worth. To the extent the democratic and legislative process credibly meets such criteria, it can be regarded as a sovereign decision that nevertheless overcomes both the Hobbes and the Rousseau challenges. Such a process makes possible the rule of laws that are not simply products of an arbitrary and unilateral will. Rather, the laws can be regarded as representative of an omnilateral will that issues from a process that recognizes the free and equal judgement of all.

It might be asked why individuals should accept this process as authoritative. After all, they may disagree with the collective decision. How is that not submitting to the will of another? The answer lies in the non-dominating characteristics of the democratic process. If we consider it wrong to violate an individual's autonomous judgements, then we should feel morally obligated to accept an authority that renders the exercise of our own autonomous judgement consistent with the similar exercise by others, without giving rise to the prospect of being dominated by the arbitrary will of another. As I have already remarked, a democratic process itself is not controlled by any particular will, nor is it partial to any particular position. Rather, its decisions are ones in which we all actively participate, albeit indirectly through our elected representatives. Acceptance of democratic decisions differs in this important respect from acceptance of the decisions of a putatively impartial and benevolent Hobbesian sovereign, who administers a legal system granting all equal rights. Such an arrangement would involve following a will other than our own. By contrast, the democratic process is one that precisely combines the exercise of our own judgement in combination with the equal exercise of their judgement by everyone else.

Moreover, the outcomes of that process cannot be regarded as under the control of the will of any one person—it is equally responsive to our respective wills but impartial and neutral with regard to them all. As Pettit has put it, it meets what he calls the 'eyeball' and the 'tough luck' tests.[78] That is, it treats all involved in it as equals, with those decisions that go against us being not predetermined and to be accepted on the grounds that within a pluralist society not everything is likely to go your way. To the extent the process possesses these qualities, therefore, we have reasons to accept its decisions not because the decision is 'right' or even 'the will

[78] Pettit, *On the People's Terms*, 84–5, 177.

of the majority', but on the grounds that it is a process that respects our mutual autonomy and is apt to treat us with equal respect and concern.[79]

Of course, actually existing democracies may fail to meet these criteria through either unintended or intentionally created (and self-serving) biases in the process. As I shall argue in Chapter 3, the focus of a political constitutionalism must lie in ensuring that the democratic system possesses the constitutional qualities associated with a balance of power that ensures collective decisions are deliberative in character and give all sides an equal hearing. Law must be perceivable as the people's law. Yet that is necessarily an ongoing and agonistic process.

6.5. The Rule of Law and the Rule of Courts

So far, I have argued that the rule of law is best seen as the rule by legislation emanating from a due democratic process. Only a suitable democratic process can instantiate a rightful condition among individuals—one that recognizes their equality as autonomous agents—and give rise to laws that may legitimately rule them all. However, legislatures may make the laws but officials and especially courts will apply them. Given the need for interpretation by the courts when applying laws to cases, does that not inevitably raise the Hobbesian challenge in the form of the arbitrary rule of judges?

As I indicated above and in Chapter 1, and will explore more fully in the remaining sections of this chapter as well as in Chapters 4, 5, and 7, that challenge would be raised in the case of 'strong form' judicial review of legislation for conformity with the terms of the higher law of a codified constitution. Such a review power would be contrary to the rule of law as conceived here, for it would entail citizens being subject to the unilateral will of judges. Here my concern is whether the challenge arises even in the everyday judicial application, as opposed to the review, of legislation.

Ethical positivists suggest that legislatures should draft law in sufficiently clear and detailed ways as to render a very strict application of the law to specific cases possible.[80] However, we have seen that a degree of indeterminacy in the law is inevitable and justifiable. Moreover, as I noted in *Political Constitutionalism*, even the plainest language will not eradicate all 'linguistic' ambiguity.[81] Nor can judges avoid

[79] As Chiara Cordelli notes, the authority of the democratic process can be assimilated to Raz's service account, whereby it offers 'a second-order exclusionary and content-independent reason for action': Cordelli, *The Privatized State*, 67. However, as Waldron notes, majority rule actually goes beyond Raz's account by building in respect for people's differing judgements. Jeremy Waldron, *Law and Disagreement* (Oxford: Clarendon Press 1999) ch. 5.

[80] Tom Campbell, *The Legal Theory of Ethical Positivism* (Aldershot: Dartmouth 1996) 129–48.

[81] Bellamy, *Political Constitutionalism*, 83–4.

interpretative arguments relating to the systemic properties of the law—as when they ponder under which rule a given case might fall. There will also be instances when the mechanical application of the law appears to produce unjust or dysfunctional outcomes.[82] Of course, the legislature can stipulate rules for the interpretation of rules, but these too will not be complete. Nor can appeals to legislative intent overcome the dilemma, for they likewise will be subject to interpretation. Not only is the history of any act usually unclear and the imputing of intent to a collective agent notoriously difficult, but also the self-same linguistic ambiguities, problems of systemic coherence, and unforeseen injustices and disutilities will reappear in a new guise as judges seek to ascribe to legislatures an intention to use words in given ways, to see the law as cohering with other laws in a given fashion, and so on.

Thus, the issue cannot be to outlaw judicial interpretation altogether, but to see if a form of judging exists that is consistent with the circumstances of politics and the primacy of democratic legislation. As I observe in Chapter 7, we can consider certain of the procedural qualities typically viewed as desirable in courts as reflecting a democratic ethos. The norm that all should be considered as equal before the law has a clear democratic provenance. But so does the insistence on judicial independence and impartiality, which are intimately related to it. If legislation passed by one government is to carry on being applied under the next, until such time as it is explicitly repealed or changed by a new legislature, then courts need to be independent for democratic reasons. That is, they cannot be too dependent on the arbitrary will of any given administration if all are to be treated equally. Likewise, with impartiality. It is important that the law not be seen as expressing either the personal interest of the judge or private ideological or ethical commitments. Here too, a democratic ethic is at work in directing judges to be disinterested and openminded,[83] so that they hear all sides of a case.

Legal constitutionalists tend to assume these two qualities require courts to be not only set apart from the legislature and executive but also placed above them—with a Supreme Court the locus of sovereign power, claiming that only then does law rule. Yet, independence so conceived may actually impair both impartiality and the rule of law if it allows judges to read the law in terms of their own concerns and opinions rather than in terms of the concerns and opinions of the people in whose name it was made.[84] In this regard, judicial decision-making requires a certain democratic humility. As I explore in Chapter 7, that may be more likely to result by providing a plural and inclusive system of judicial appointments and

[82] For these three broad categories of interpretative argument (linguistic, systemic, and justice and utility), see Neil MacCormick, 'Argumentation and Interpretation in Law' (1993) 6 *Ratio Juris* 16–29.
[83] Matthew Kramer, 'Impartiality' in Richard Bellamy and Jeff King (eds), *Cambridge Handbook of Constitutional Theory* (Cambridge: Cambridge University Press 2024).
[84] David Kosař and Samuel Spáč, 'Judicial Independence' in Richard Bellamy and Jeff King (eds), *Cambridge Handbook of Constitutional Theory* (Cambridge: Cambridge University Press 2024).

accountability than by insulating the judiciary from politics entirely.[85] Arguably, that democratic attitude informs the tendency of courts to employ analogical reasoning,[86] with extensive, and often excessive, deployment of precedents, so as to avoid any appearance of eccentricity or exception in their rulings. Such practices are also more likely to foster the rule of law desideratum of consistency in the application of the law, through its invocation of the doctrine of *stare decisis*.[87] After all, a supposed virtue of the rule of law is that people can rely on it when planning their lives. Such reliance gets subverted if settled precedents can be overturned on the whim of fluctuating majorities on the court.[88]

Of course, these constraints are weak and may be even weaker with apex courts against which there is no appeal. Here, though, an important democratic constraint comes in by limiting courts to so-called 'weak form review',[89] as was discussed in Chapter 1 and to which I return in Chapter 4. This practice places sovereignty firmly with the legislature—preventing courts from disapplying law and allowing adverse judicial decisions or interpretations to be overridden or responded to with new legislation. Yet, that move has been viewed at odds with the rule of law. It is to this argument that we now turn.

7. PARLIAMENTARY SOVEREIGNTY, COURTS, AND THE RULE OF LAW

The account given so far provides an argument for regarding the legislative sovereignty of a democratically elected Parliament as embodying the rule of law. And yet, it is commonly argued by legal scholars, political scientists, and judges that the opposite is true, and that the rule of law ideal is either incompatible with,[90] or, at the very least, potentially—if not necessarily—undermined by,[91] parliamentary sovereignty.

[85] D. M. Brinks and A. Blass, 'Rethinking Judicial Empowerment: The New Foundations of Constitutional Justice' (2017) 15(2) *International Journal of Constitutional Law* 296–331.

[86] Cass R. Sunstein, *Legal Reasoning and Political Conflict* (Oxford: Oxford University Press 1996) chs 2 and 3.

[87] Martin Shapiro, 'Toward a Theory of *Stare Decisis*' (1972) 1(1) *The Journal of Legal Studies* 125–34. See too Martin Shapiro and Alec Stone Sweet, *On Law, Politics and Judicialization* (Oxford: Oxford University Press 2002) ch. 2.

[88] As Jeremy Waldron noted in his Hart Lecture 2023 on 'The Crisis of Judicial Review', the overturning of the legitimate expectation, established by *Roe v. Wade*, 410 U.S. 113 (1973) and *Planned Parenthood v. Casey*, 505 U.S. 833 (1992), that abortion would be available was among the cruellest and most reprehensible features of *Dobbs v. Jackson Women's Health Organization*. Reversing these precedents involved something akin to a breaking of a promise with the American people.

[89] Mark Tushnet, 'Weak-form Judicial Review and "Core" Civil Liberties' (2006) 41 *Harvard Civil Rights-Civil Liberties Law Review* 1–22.

[90] T. R. S. Allan, *Law, Liberty and Justice: The Legal Foundations of British Constitutionalism* (Oxford: Clarendon Press 1993) 16; Sir John Laws, 'Law and Democracy' (1995) 72 *Public Law* 85, 88.

[91] e.g. Francis Jacobs, *The Sovereignty of Law: The European Way, The Hamlyn Lectures 2006* (Cambridge: Cambridge University Press 2007) 5; Vernon Bogdanor, 'The Sovereignty of Parliament

Why should that be the case? These critics consider that legal forms and/or substantive norms must bind Parliament to ensure legislation cannot be the product of an arbitrary will.[92] They see parliamentary sovereignty as analogous to rule by a Hobbesian tyrant. Consequently, they contend the sovereignty of a judicially protected higher law, such as a codified legal constitution provides, must frame the legislative and political process. They allege that because courts must adopt legal reasoning and operate in conformity to the relevant laws, their decision-making is constrained in ways that of a legislature is not. As a result, judicial decisions conform to both a formal and (in most of these accounts) a more substantive—rights-based—conception of the rule of law.

Yet, as we saw, however one interprets the rule of law, it's doubtful that such arrangements can avoid the Hobbes challenge. Advocates of legal sovereignty rarely acknowledge, let alone confront, that challenge. However, this failure gives rise to the very issues of arbitrary rule that they claim to avoid. As I elaborate below, as well as in later chapters (especially 4, 6, and 7), this critique does not in any way deny the vital role played by legal institutions in upholding certain formal and substantive features of the rule of law. On the contrary, as I acknowledged above, laws could not rule without being enforced in a consistent and equitable manner by the courts. However, for the reasons favouring democracy given in earlier sections of this chapter, I shall maintain such judicial activity must complement, and be ultimately subordinate to, legislative sovereignty.

7.1. Dicey on the Relation of Parliamentary Sovereignty to the Rule of Law

A. V. Dicey's *Law of the Constitution*, particularly ch. 13, 'On the relation of Parliamentary sovereignty to the rule of law', provides the natural place to start considering this complementarity of parliamentary sovereignty and courts in maintaining the rule of law.[93] Dicey's account of the rule of law seems, at first blush, to be court-centred. His three main characteristics of the rule of law depend on breaches of the law being (1) determined in the 'ordinary legal manner before the ordinary courts of the land',[94] with (2) all members of society, regardless of rank or position, being equally subject to 'ordinary law' and these 'ordinary tribunals' so

or the Rule of Law?', Magna Carta Lecture, 15 June 2006, 20, available at<http://royalholloway.org.uk/About/magna-carta/2006-lecture.pdf>.

[92] For a useful survey, on which I have drawn for this section, see Jeffrey Goldsworthy, *Parliamentary Sovereignty: Contemporary Debates*, (Cambridge: Cambridge University Press 2010) ch. 3.

[93] A. V. Dicey, *Introduction to the Study of the Law of the Constitution* (8th edn, London: MacMillan 1915).

[94] Dicey, *Introduction*, 183–4.

that no one is 'above the law',[95] and, apparently most challenging to parliamentary sovereignty, (3) that rights 'are with us the result of judicial decisions determining the rights of private persons in particular cases brought before the courts, so that the constitution can be regarded as 'judge-made' and part of 'the ordinary law of the land'.[96] Dicey conceded that parliamentary sovereignty and the rule of law so defined 'may appear to stand in opposition' or to be 'at best only counterbalancing forces', but contended 'this appearance is delusive'.[97]

Two sets of reasons motivated this contention, involving, as Mark Walters has noted, the reconciliation of his two core principles of legality and sovereignty.[98] First, Dicey characterized parliamentary sovereignty as legislative sovereignty only. Its commands are not the arbitrary decrees of a despotic monarch but can only be exercised through 'formal and deliberate legislation'. These formal and deliberative qualities arise from the legislative process itself, whereby 'the will of Parliament can only be expressed through an Act of Parliament'.[99] Second, as a result, Parliament does not exercise 'direct executive power'. Rather, the powers granted to the executive have to be legally authorized. Of course, that does not prevent Parliament granting wide discretionary powers to the executive. However, such powers will continue to be exercised under the law. Notwithstanding his notorious antipathy to administrative law as a distinct branch of law removed from the ordinary courts, Dicey nevertheless acknowledged its development in England as a result of the rise of the administrative state.[100]

Dicey regarded the need for Parliament to act through legislation, including with regard to its own processes and powers, on the one hand, and for statutory authorization of executive authority, on the other, as producing an inseparable connection between parliamentary sovereignty and legality. For it meant that Parliament and the executive ultimately operated under the law as interpreted by the courts. Moreover, he believed such interpretation to be guided by norms of consistency and coherence that meant that the executive and administration would have to act under the entire body of law. As a result, the ability of courts to prevent executive officers from acting in ways that could be deemed *ultra vires* was a considerable constraint.[101] Does that mean, though, that—following the logic of Hobbes's challenge—legal sovereignty has effectively passed to the courts? Dicey claims it does not. Courts must always enforce duly passed statutes over all other sources of law. So, although Parliament is under the very law it has passed as interpreted by

[95] Dicey, *Introduction*, 189, 198.
[96] Dicey, *Introduction*, 191–3.
[97] Dicey, *Introduction*, 402.
[98] Mark Walters, *A.V. Dicey and the Common Law Constitutional Tradition* (Cambridge: Cambridge University Press 2020) 165.
[99] Dicey, *Introduction*, 402–3.
[100] A. V. Dicey, 'The Development of Administrative Law in England' (1915) 31(2) *Law Quarterly Review* 152.
[101] Dicey, *Introduction*, 183–4.

the courts, it ultimately controls what the law is. As he concludes the chapter: 'By every path we come round to the same conclusion, that Parliamentary sovereignty has favoured the rule of law, and that the supremacy of the law of the land both calls forth the exertion of Parliamentary sovereignty, and leads to its being exercised in a spirit of legality'.[102]

Critics of parliamentary sovereignty tend not be satisfied with this solution because they claim Parliament could still act arbitrarily, even if the formalities of the legislative process were followed. However, Dicey offers a response in noting that though legislating may be a formal requirement, it is 'no mere matter of form'.[103] As I noted in the previous section, a democratic process can avoid being itself a form of arbitrary rule to the extent it has rule of law-like qualities that motivate equality of respect and concern towards those subject to its decisions. It achieves this result through encouraging inclusiveness and impartiality, notably through enshrining political equality among those with a stake in collective decisions in ways that establish the need to 'hear the other side' and to adopt commonly avowable reasons that address the public interest. As I remarked in the introduction, Dicey somewhat anachronistically considered such qualities could be attributed to Parliament as a result of its embodying the ancient notion of 'mixed government' by virtue of its three constituent parts of Crown, Lords, and Commons, and their need to act together.[104] However, as I also hinted there and will explore further in Chapter 3, the core idea of the notion of 'mixed government'—that of securing a balanced and non-dominating system of decision-making—can be met by the institutions and practices of representative democracy, such as competitive parties, bicameral legislatures, and so forth. Whatever the shortcomings of Dicey's characterization of the operations of Parliament, his key insight remains consistent with a political constitutionalist view of the rule of law: namely, that the rule of law rests primarily on the qualities of a sovereign political process of 'formal and deliberate legislation', and secondarily, if just as crucially, on the regular and consistent application of that legislation through the courts.

8. PARLIAMENTARY LEGISLATION AND THE FORMAL AND SUBSTANTIVE FEATURES OF LAW

How convincing is Dicey's argument? Can a sovereign democratic legislature, operating in tandem with an independent judiciary—that is nonetheless unable to appeal to any higher, constitutional, law as a constraint upon duly enacted legislation or legally taken decisions—be expected—as Dicey assumed—to respect both

[102] Dicey, *Introduction*, 409.
[103] Dicey, *Introduction*, 402–3.
[104] Dicey, *Introduction*, 402–3.

the formal and more substantive features typically associated with the rule of law? I believe it can.

8.1. Legislation and the Form of Law

The possession by legislation of something like Fuller's set of formal characteristics of 'law' is sometimes regarded as necessary for it to be compatible with the rule of law. Without these qualities, legislation will be equivalent to a set of commands aimed at particular persons rather than offering a set of rules that can be impartially applied by the courts and administration to the social interactions of all citizens.

There are weak and strong versions of this requirement. With regard to the weak version, no necessary or inherent conflict need obtain between legislative sovereignty and the resulting legislation possessing certain general qualities that facilitate its consistent application to individual cases by an independent judicial or administrative process.[105] Of course, such formal qualities may not only constitute a limited virtue but also be of limited applicability and value. As we saw, even tyrannous regimes will have instrumental reasons to want laws to be followable by those subject to them, and as such for there to be a degree of coherence among different laws, generality in their form, and regularity in their application by the courts. Such qualities will facilitate not only the daily life of citizens but also administrative efficiency and effectiveness, including the pursuit of some of the more malign policies of such regimes. Needless to say, a tyrannous regime will always be liable to act outside the law whenever it proves convenient to do so. However, for democratic regimes there is no inherent conflict between legislative sovereignty and subjecting the executive and legislature to judicial review to ensure they act in conformity with the duly enacted laws of the land. Indeed, as Dicey argued, one can regard the legal obligation to abide by duly enacted laws as a requirement of the integrity of a system of democratic legislation.

Strong formal theories go further, though, and seek to render any legislation that aims at a particular purpose involving specific persons as both arbitrary and pernicious. Certainly, legislation designed to criminalize the activities of given political opponents would fit this category. However, some theorists—most notably F. A. Hayek (and, on some accounts, also Dicey[106]), suggest that any rules that are not entirely general, abstract, and applicable equally to all would contravene the rule of law. Indeed, on Hayek's account, the rule of law comes close to meaning the opposite of the rule of legislation.[107] Hayek portrays legislation as the product of

[105] Goldsworthy, *Parliamentary Sovereignty*, 63–6.

[106] Ivor Jennings, *The Law and the Constitution* (London: University of London Press 1933) 256.

[107] F. A. Hayek, *Law, Legislation and Liberty*, vol. 1, *Rules and Order* (Chicago: University of Chicago Press 1973) 72–3, 124–44. In what follows I draw on the critiques of Hayek in Bellamy, *Liberalism and*

a managerial mentality that seeks to organize society according to some rational plan rather than allowing conventions to emerge spontaneously through the free interactions of individuals. As such, *pace* Dicey, Hayek considers legislation barely to differ from the decrees of a despotic monarch.

Now, it is certainly true that legislators do not set out to frame laws in formal terms per se. But that is because it would be nonsensical to do so. They devise laws with particular ends in mind. However, they then give them a certain form in order to obtain the law-like characteristics needed to promote these ends by moving officials and citizens consistently towards them, without the need for continuous commands—albeit, often with a certain vagueness necessarily thrown in as well. Such legislation largely emerges to provide people with security in circumstances where no such spontaneous conventions can otherwise be expected to emerge—or where those that do may prove inequitable.

Denying that such legislation might be necessary leads Hayek into absurdities. For example, he suggests that 'measures designed to control the access to different trades and occupations, the terms of sale, and the amounts to be produced and sold' require reference to particular goals and so 'involve arbitrary discrimination against persons' thereby contravening the rule of law as he conceives it.[108] Yet he immediately backtracks, admitting it is sensible to ensure doctors are suitably qualified before being allowed to practise, pilots pass eye tests, and even that sellers of firearms and poisons should be 'persons satisfying certain intellectual and moral qualities'.[109] In fact, most government regulations arise not as part of a rational plan but as responses to particular problems, being progressively modified through the trial and error mechanism Hayek approves.

Hayek's critique is particularly aimed at legislation related to redistribution and economic regulation. He suggests that such regulation involves arbitrary interferences with property rights and freedom of contract, and involve discriminating either in favour of or against particular classes of persons. Yet, formal equality of treatment can harm those whose particular capacities or circumstances mean they ought to be treated differently, and can legitimate practices that exploit these differences and entrench unjust inequalities. Consider, for instance, the feminist critique of equal opportunities law that embodies a covert male comparator test that overlooks structural factors that have relegated many women to low-paid casual employment.[110] Making one abstract general rule apply equally and universally to all simply denies the very social diversity and complexity that Hayek claims to

Pluralism, ch. 1 and Bellamy, *Political Constitutionalism*, 67–74. See too Jeremy Waldron, 'Legislation and the Rule of Law' (2007) 1(1) *Legisprudence* 91–123.

[108] F. A. Hayek, *The Constitution of Liberty* (London: Routledge 1960) 227–8.

[109] Hayek, *The Constitution of Liberty*, 228.

[110] Catharine MacKinnon, 'On Difference and Dominance' in Catharine MacKinnon, *Feminism Unmodified: Discourses on Life and Law* (Cambridge, MA: Harvard University Press 1989) 36.

champion, and with it the need to treat those who are not the same in different ways to those who are.

It is often forgotten that the then Quentin Hogg's (later ennobled as Lord Hailsham) famous critique of parliamentary sovereignty as giving rise to an 'elective dictatorship' was largely motivated by the neo-Hayekian claim that the record of the Labour administrations of the 1960s and 1970s revealed how, unchecked, future social democratic governments were destined to 'impose uniformity on the whole nation in the interest of what it claims to be social justice'.[111] Like Hayek, his proposed constitutional scheme was to render such measures unlikely by constraining legislation by so-called genuine law. Yet, the Hayekian model of formal rules would render the whole modern regulatory state, including environmental protections, minimum wage, health and safety legislation, restrictions on investment and profit taking, and so on, incompatible with the rule of law.[112] By contrast, a prime merit of the democratic approach to the rule of law is that it allows and promotes such legislation. For, a political system grounded in political equality will be apt to support the public structures and services needed to foster social equality.[113]

8.2. Legislation and the Substance of Law and the Legislative Process

Although legal philosophers tend to follow Raz in favouring formal and limited views of the rule of law,[114] practitioners—notably judges—habitually adopt more substantive, rights-based views.[115] Likewise, most of those who criticize parliamentary sovereignty on rule of law grounds do so on the basis of a substantive account.[116] Two broad concerns motivate rights-based criticisms of legislative sovereignty: one focused on democratic outputs and the other on democratic processes. These critics tend to emphasize one or other concern. In different ways,

[111] Lord Hailsham, *The Dilemma of Democracy: Diagnosis and Prescription* (Glasgow: Collins 1978) 9–10.

[112] As Keith Ewing has shown, this view was widely accepted by the British judiciary at the time. For example, Lord Denning criticized Labour's Trade Union Acts of 1974 and 1976 extending union freedom as the 'greatest threat to the rule of law'. Lord Denning, *What Next in the Law* (London: Butterworths 1982) 321; and although Lord Diplock considered (unlike Denning) that parliamentary sovereignty meant these Acts should nonetheless stand, he nonetheless agreed that this legislation 'was intrinsically repugnant to anyone who has spent his life in the practice of the law or the administration of justice' (*Express Newspapers Ltd v. McShane* [1980] ICR 43, at 57). See Keith Ewing, 'The Social Democratic Constitution' in Peter Cane and Harshan Kumarasingham (eds), *The Cambridge Constitutional History of the United Kingdom* (vol. 1, Cambridge: Cambridge University Press 2023) 188.

[113] Cordelli, *The Privatized State*.

[114] e.g., John Tasioulas, 'The Rule of Law' in John Tasioulas (ed.), *The Cambridge Companion to the Philosophy of Law* (Cambridge: Cambridge University Press 2020) 117–34.

[115] Bingham, *The Rule of Law*, 66–8.

[116] e.g. Jacobs, *The Sovereignty of Law*, 5; Bogdanor, 'The Sovereignty of Parliament or the Rule of Law?', 20.

both concerns are assumed to stem from certain inherent deficiencies in democracy rather than as amendable flaws in existing democratic practices. As such, these concerns cannot be addressed by reforms to the legislative process but rather require the legal sovereignty of an entrenched and judicially protected Bill of Rights to frame legislation.[117]

For those who stress the first concern, the whole purpose of constitutionalism consists of ensuring the 'rule of law' via 'a system that establishes legal rights that the dominant legislature does not have the power to override or compromise'.[118] On this account, of which Ronald Dworkin offers one of the more sophisticated and influential versions, democracy proves apt to sacrifice the rights of minorities because it favours the 'statistical' aggregation of preferences, thereby risking the 'tyranny of the majority'.[119] Yet that view ignores not only the deliberative qualities of both electoral and legislative processes, but also the way the very statistical aspects of democracy can exemplify equal concern and respect through treating all neutrally and impartially.[120] It also overlooks the extent to which individual rights have standardly been secured through legislative action.[121] Indeed, as was highlighted in Chapter 1, majoritarian democracy has more than a contingent link to human rights protection because in sharing power equally, at least in formal terms, it favours the promotion of public policies that promote the equal rights of voters.[122]

Dworkin advocates what he considers 'the most straightforward interpretation of American constitutional practice' whereby 'judges have final interpretive authority' and consider 'the Bill of Rights as a constitution of principle'.[123] He contrasts the principled deliberations of courts with the trading to maximize preference satisfaction of legislatures. As a result, he advocates 'strong form' rights review, whereby the US Supreme Court and similar bodies elsewhere, should be able to strike down legislation they consider to violate such a Bill. However, contrary to his mentor Learned Hand,[124] he denies that judges are thereby acting either as 'a bevy of Platonic Guardians' or on their own discretion and ideological opinions when making their judgments.[125] Rather, they look for answers proposed by the

[117] For a review, see Richard Bellamy, 'Bills of Rights' in Richard Bellamy and Jeff King (eds), *Cambridge Handbook of Constitutional Theory* (Cambridge: Cambridge University Press 2024).

[118] Ronald Dworkin, 'Constitutionalism and Democracy' (1995) 3 *European Journal of Philosophy* 2.

[119] Ronald Dworkin, *Freedom's Law: The Moral Reading of the American Constitution* (Cambridge, MA: Harvard University Press 1996) 21–6.

[120] Waldron, *Law and Disagreement*, 113–16.

[121] Grégoire Webber, Paul Yowell, Richard Ekins, Maris Köpcke, Bradley W. Miller, Francisco J. Urbina, *Legislated Rights: Securing Human Rights through Legislation* (Cambridge: Cambridge University Press 2018).

[122] Thomas Christiano, 'An Instrumental Argument for a Human Right to Democracy' (2011) 39 *Philosophy and Public Affairs* 142–76.

[123] Dworkin, *Freedom's Law*, 35.

[124] Billings Learned Hand, *The Bill of Rights* (Cambridge, MA: Harvard University Press 1958) 73.

[125] Ronald Dworkin, *A Matter of Principle* (Cambridge, MA: Harvard University Press 1985) 27; Dworkin, *Freedom's Law*, 22.

principles enshrined in constitutional law and 'anchored in history, practice and integrity'. As such, judges can be characterized simply as agents implementing the rule of law rather than as ruling personally. However, he concedes that 'we must not exaggerate the drag of that anchor. Very different, even contrary, conceptions of constitutional principle—of what treating men and women as equals really means, for example—will often fit language, precedent, and practice well enough to pass these tests'.[126] Yet, if 'personal moral conviction' ultimately proves more important than the 'craft of a judge' in deciding contentious issues of constitutional principle, then the case for assigning them to a judicial rather than a political process becomes ever more tenuous.

Dworkin acknowledged that many constitutional judgments require judges to address 'intractable, controversial, and profound questions of political morality that philosophers, statesmen, and citizens have debated for many centuries'. Why then should people and their representatives simply have to 'accept the deliverances of a majority of the justices', especially given he also accepted their 'insight into these great issues is not spectacularly special'?[127] Why should we regard a simple judicial majority as having greater authority than a legislative majority among a far greater number of representatives elected by, and accountable to, millions of citizens?[128]

Perhaps that might be justified if Dworkin was correct in his belief that the statistical majorities of legislatures were more prone to tyrannous decisions than the simple majorities typical of constitutional courts. However, the empirical evidence for such claims proves weak. In fact, there is no clear empirical correlation between the protection of minority rights and the existence of strong form rights-based judicial review grounded in an entrenched Bill of Rights.[129] Of course, that is not to say that legislatures never fall short in their attentiveness to rights considerations. However, the same holds for courts. Moreover, there are ways of improving such attentiveness that are compatible with legislative sovereignty. As was argued in Chapter 1 and is further developed in Chapter 4, a legislated Bill of Rights—such as the Human Rights Act—can serve to make rights review a core component of the legislative process that renders the legislature a 'forum of principle', in which democratic representation gives all concerned a part in debating moral questions and acknowledges their stake in any collective decision.[130] Meanwhile, 'weak form' review by the courts can draw the attention of legislators to individual cases where rights protection may fall short, either as a result of arbitrary executive or

[126] Dworkin, *Freedom's Law*, 11.

[127] Dworkin, *Freedom's Law*, 74.

[128] Jeremy Waldron, *Political Political Theory: Essays on Institutions* (Cambridge, MA: Harvard University Press 2016) 197, 237–9.

[129] Jeff King, 'The Democratic Case for a Written Constitution' (2019) 72 *Current Legal Problems*, 13 and n. 30.

[130] Waldron, *Law and Disagreement*, 289–91; Jeremy Waldron, 'Legislating with Integrity' (2003) 72(2) *Fordham Law Review* 388–94.

administrative decisions or shortcomings in the drafting of legislation. Likewise, the formal procedural qualities of courts ensure that democratically enacted laws and authorized decisions are implemented in consistent and lawful ways that ensure conformity to the rule of law. Yet, in both cases, the law is not disapplied as a result of an adverse judgment and the legislature ultimately has the power to ignore that ruling or to amend the legislation to meet the concerns raised by the court.

Note that this democratic critique of 'strong form' rights-based judicial review, of the kind advocated by Dworkin, would not be met by having the Bill of Rights enacted and entrenched through some extra-legislative democratic process, as some suggest.[131] Such constitutional principles are by their nature abstract and open to a broad range of interpretations,[132] thereby raising the Hobbes challenge and giving the court charged with upholding them a degree of arbitrary power to impose its unilateral will. By contrast, statutory Bills of Rights and 'weak form' judicial review place their interpretation within the democratic realm on an ongoing basis.

This arrangement might still be open to the second concern, relating to the rights implied by the democratic process itself. Jürgen Habermas puts forward a version of this view that might seem especially challenging to the argument advanced here.[133] He considers there to be an internal relation—which he terms the co-originality—between the rule of law and popular sovereignty.[134] While he accepts that 'the *democratic process* bears the entire burden of legitimation', he contends this process presupposes in its turn a substantive account of the 'system of rights that makes citizens' private and public equality possible'.[135] Indeed, the establishment of any democratic process necessarily brings into being the rights and duties on which its functioning depends. However, he goes beyond this logical entailment to argue that this system of rights can be given a transcendental justification in terms of the 'communicative presuppositions' necessary for 'the better arguments to come into play', on the one hand, and the 'procedures that secure fair bargaining conditions', on the other.[136]

On Habermas's account, the rule of law requires that the democratic process be consistent with these substantive universal preconditions of fair rational discourse.

[131] e.g. Bruce Ackerman, *We the People: Foundations* (Cambridge, MA: Harvard University Press 1991).

[132] Bellamy, *Liberalism and Pluralism*, ch. 7; Bellamy, *Political Constitutionalism*, ch. 1.

[133] John Hart Ely, *Democracy and Distrust: A Theory of Judicial Review* (Cambridge, MA: Harvard University Press 1980) proposes another influential version of the procedural view—see Bellamy, *Political Constitutionalism*, 107–20 for a critique, as well as Bellamy, 'Bills of Rights'. I think similar criticisms to those I make here of Habermas can also be made of Ely and others who adopt similar arguments, e.g. Rosalind Dixon, *Responsive Judicial Review: Democracy and Dysfunction in the Modern Age* (Oxford: Oxford University Press 2023). Habermas's account has the virtue of making the theoretical assumptions needed to sustain such views more explicit.

[134] Jürgen Habermas, *Between Facts and Norms: Contributions to a Discourse Theory of Law and Democracy* (Cambridge, MA: Harvard University Press 1996). See too Cordelli, *The Privatized State*, 68–71.

[135] Habermas, *Between Facts and Norms*, 263.

[136] Habermas, *Between Facts and Norms*, 278–9.

He suggests that, for pragmatic and principled reasons, a legislature should not be given a final say on whether it and the democratic process that elects it meet these criteria. To do so would make elected politicians 'judges in their own cause'. Rather, these democratic rights should be entrenched in a codified constitution and interpreted and enforced by a constitutional court. Yet, Habermas believes this to be a relatively uncontroversial role. By contrast with a Dworkin style form of rights-based review focused on outcomes, 'a constitutional Court guided by a proceduralist understanding of the constitution does not have to overdraw on its legitimation credit'.[137]

As I noted briefly in Chapter 1, Habermas's proposal seems subject to the very criticisms and problems he seeks to avoid. For a start, it is doubtful that the process–outcome distinction comes out cleanly. He packs a great deal into process rights—not only the standard civil and political rights, but also social rights to education, welfare, and a minimum standard of living. All good things. But that would allow courts to adjudicate on quite a lot of social and economic policy. These areas are not only controversial in themselves, but also their link to the political process can be questioned. For example, he surely is not implying that the poor and ill-educated ought not to be allowed to vote? Yet, is that not an implication of his view that certain social rights have to be guaranteed for the process to be legitimate and fair? Meanwhile, he links judgments about process to 'the logic of argumentation' and in particular its epistemic qualities in ensuring the 'best' arguments prevail. However, that criterion seems to entail judging on the basis of putative 'outcomes'.

Even if he could avoid basing judgments concerning process on their tendency to bring about his favoured outcomes, there is no reason to believe that judgments as to the fairness or justice of process rights will be any less controversial and less subject to the 'circumstances of politics' than judgments about rights linked to certain substantive outcomes. Even if broad universal agreement could be reached at an abstract level on some civil and political rights, such as those found in international conventions, how they can best be met in particular circumstances is likely to be subject to reasonable disagreement. It is doubtful that courts can claim to be more impartial and above the fray than legislatures on such matters. For example, I doubt Habermas agrees with how the US Supreme Court decided either *Bush v. Gore*, 531 U.S. 98 (2000) or *Citizens United v. Federal Election Commission*, 558 U.S. 310 (2010). Even decisions that are less clearly partisan in character can be controversial on empirical and normative grounds. Take the German Federal Constitutional Court abolishing minimal thresholds (3% in this case) for parties to gain representation in the European Parliament.[138] Some will agree with the Court's view that such thresholds are undemocratic in denying a voice to even small groups of citizens and can only be justified when, as in domestic elections

[137] Habermas, *Between Facts and Norms*, 279.

[138] BVerfG, Judgment of the Second Senate of 26 February 2014 – 2 BvE 2/13 -, paras 1–30.

where they upheld such thresholds continuing, countervailing considerations regarding government stability prevail. Others, though, may feel that the absence of thresholds risks giving the extreme views of quite small groups a disproportionate voice in decisions where their support might be pivotal. Like all citizens, judges will have both a stake in any decision and, with the best will in the world, a partial view of how any judgment on such rights will impact people. Unlike a democratic system, they will lack information stemming from often millions of voters as to their views and experience on the topic. Like the legislature, they will also need to rule on their own competence to decide the issue and their decision may well be made with an eye to its implications for their own power. For example, they may be overly cautious so as to avoid entering into territory they deem to be too controversial.

None of the above is to deny that a legislature can be motivated to gerrymander electoral rules in favour of the prevailing majority. But *can* need not mean *will*. As Anthony King observed, few codified and entrenched constitutions provide 'for one of the most significant features of any constitutional order: the country's electoral system'.[139] Even if they did, they could contain nothing as detailed as say the UK Representation of the People Act. So, much of the heavy lifting would need to be done by legislatures. Quite how best to realize 'fair' and 'good' democratic decision-making is also often highly context-dependent. For example, the UK has employed a wide variety of voting systems for elections to different levels of government—including First Past the Post for the House of Commons, the Supplementary Vote previously used for mayoral elections up to 2023, the Additional Member System for elections to the Scottish Parliament and the London Assembly, a closed Proportional List system for the Welsh Assembly from 2026—a system used in England, Wales, and Scotland for elections to the European Parliament from 1999 to 2019, and the Single Transferable Vote used for the Northern Ireland Assembly and local authorities in Scotland. All of these electoral systems can be justified or criticized on various grounds. It is hard to see how courts could avoid controversy. Meanwhile, there are democratic mechanisms—some explored in Chapters 8 and especially 9—that can counteract self-serving measures by a given legislative majority. For example, a Parliament could enact a constitutional reform bill whereby, as in Denmark, changes to constitutional statutes require a parliamentary majority either side of a general election and approval by a popular referendum.[140] Indeed, arguably a convention in the UK already exists for such changes to be put to a referendum. Of course, no mechanism is foolproof. The claim is merely that the rule of law both requires and can be consistent with a democratic mechanism, even with regard to democracy itself.

[139] Anthony King, *The British Constitution* (Oxford: Oxford University Press 2009) 7.

[140] See Dennis Thompson, 'Why Representative Democracy Requires Referendums' in James Gardner (ed.), *Comparative Electoral Law* (Cheltenham: Elgar 2022) 193–211.

9. CONCLUSION

This chapter has defended a view of the rule of law focused on the democratic rule of persons within a sovereign representative legislature. Such a view is compatible with the role of independent and impartial courts in applying the law. But the legislature always lies upstream from the courts, which on this account would be restricted to weak review at best. This arrangement provides a solution to the Hobbes challenge consistent with the avoidance of domination by an arbitrary will—a core concern of most accounts of the rule of law. It arises from the democratic process itself possessing constitutional qualities associated with the way it institutionalizes political equality among those subject to collective decisions that they have a role in making. It is to the institutional features of such a democratic form of political constitutionalism that we now turn.

3

Checks and Balances as Democracy

Political Equality and Majority Rule in the Democratic Mixed Constitution

1. INTRODUCTION

The discussion of rights and the rule of law in Chapters 1 and 2 respectively turned on the need for both to be defined and enacted in ways consistent with a certain conception of the moral equality of those concerned. This conception involves two elements.[1] On the one hand, it denies notions of ascribed status based on birth or social identity. There are no natural slaves or aristocrats. On the other hand, it sees all individuals as equal moral agents, entitled to engage in autonomous, self-directed action in pursuit of their own conception of the good. As we saw, both these elements shape in their turn the 'circumstances of politics' and give rise to a moral requirement for political equality. The autonomous actions and judgements of different individuals give rise to a plurality of valuable ways of life and conceptions of the good, producing both social and ideational conflicts and disagreements as to how they can be justly resolved. Consequently, individuals make diverse and often incompatible claims against each other. This situation generates in turn the need for a sovereign political authority capable of determining a unitary scheme of rights and laws that is binding on all, notwithstanding people's distinctive and often antagonistic perspectives and interests. However, for this authority to be legitimate, it must be consistent with the aforementioned two aspects of moral equality. As such, it must eschew hierarchical relationships with regard to those under it, on the one hand, and avoid imposing a set of rights and laws unilaterally on individuals, on the other. A failure to meet these two conditions risks placing those subjected to such an authority under the dominating and potentially oppressive, exploitative, or demeaning arbitrary will of another person or group of persons.

The previous two chapters argued that these two conditions require that collective decisions, including those regarding basic rights, be made according to a process capable of showing equal respect and concern to all those involved—and that such a process entails giving those with an equal stake in a collective decision

[1] This conception of moral and political equality draws on Elizabeth Anderson, 'What Is the Point of Equality?' (1999) 109(2) *Ethics*, esp. 312–14.

Defending the Political Constitution. Richard Bellamy, Oxford University Press.
DOI: 10.1093/9780191826986.003.0004

equal control over how it is made. I have claimed that a democratic system of regular free and fair elections based on one person one vote and majority rule formally meets these requirements. It can avoid the asymmetric power relations that produce domination by upholding the equal status of all citizens as free persons, entitled to have their views and interests given equal consideration in the making and implementing of the laws and policies that shape their lives. However, actual democratic systems are habitually criticized for falling short of this democratic ideal. A legal constitution is often seen as necessary to rectify these shortcomings—not least to uphold the rights of minorities against tyrannous majorities or the undermining or distortion of the democratic process by elites. This chapter seeks to show how democratic processes and institutions have the resources to address these concerns themselves, without recourse to the judicial remedies typically associated with a codified and entrenched legal constitution with the status of higher law.

The traditional liberal legal constitutional worries regarding democracy have been two-fold and can be neatly labelled 'legislative tyranny' and 'executive tyranny'. Both are seen as potential pathologies of majority rule, that legal constitutionalists claim require the counter-majoritarian oversight of a constitutional court to be avoided.[2] The first may arise if the legislative majority can pass discriminatory laws that fail to treat all citizens with equal respect and concern. Such legislation might reflect or pander to popular prejudices, or be undertaken to skew the democratic process to favour the incumbent government. For example, Republican-controlled state legislatures in the United States have engaged in each of these types of discrimination, as have populist regimes in Hungary and Poland. The second may arise if an elected government can act in arbitrary ways analogous to forms of personal rule. For example, this charge has frequently been levelled at the Westminster system, where a parliamentary majority has been said to allow the executive to operate as an 'elective dictatorship'. It is also a potential problem for Presidential systems, such as that of the United States, that accord a directly elected President wide-ranging executive powers.

I shall argue that democratic mechanisms—notably, regular elections involving multiparty competition, devolution to local authorities, and proportional representation (also referred to as PR)—can offer appropriate responses to both these

[2] As Adam Przeworski, *Crises of Democracy* (Cambridge: Cambridge University Press 2019) 5–6 has noted, drawing on Anthony McGann, *The Logic of Democracy: Reconciling Equality, Deliberation, and Minority Protection* (Ann Arbor, MI: University of Michigan Press 2006), there are empirical and logical reasons for doubting this claim. As democratic systems which have neither the separation of powers nor strong rights-based constitutional review, such as the UK and Sweden, indicate, party competition can provide majorities with incentives to restrain themselves from violating minority rights. Indeed, the tendency towards rights violations may even be encouraged in the case of governments protected by counter-majoritarian institutions. That said, I shall argue these concerns can be further reduced by enhancing the competitive and collaborative qualities of the political system in ways that require the building of more complex majorities.

issues. They provide a system of democratic checks and balances that encourage politicians and citizens to hear—and to some degree harken to—the other side, thereby promoting democratic equality of respect, concern, and control. Moreover, such mechanisms should not be viewed as super- or counter-majoritarian constraints on or corrections to majority rule, as some have argued,[3] so much as ways of better realizing rule by the majority.

These democratic arrangements support both the 'positive', or empowering, and the 'negative', or constraining, aspects of constitutionalism.[4] On the one hand, they allow citizens to participate on equal terms in political decision-making, albeit indirectly through their representatives, and encourage deliberation on collective decisions that considers their disparate desires for, concerns about, and valuations of, various policy options. On the other hand, they offer citizens an equal chance to sanction and remove politicians who fail to promote their interests—be it through incompetence, a lack of responsiveness, bad luck, self-interest, or changes in public preferences. Moreover, in a political system involving the devolution of certain competences to local government, citizens exercise their democratic powers in different and competing jurisdictions, which can likewise check and balance each other. A political system involving such provisions offers a political constitutional alternative to a legal constitutionalism involving strong form, rights-based judicial review. Of course, as I emphasized in Chapter 2, political constitutionalism values a legal system capable of applying the law in a consistent and formally equitable manner. However, that need not involve empowering judges as the supreme arbiters of a codified constitution. Juristocratic constitutionalism, as De Tocqueville (approvingly) observed, is an 'aristocratic' rather than a democratic notion[5] that displaces equality with hierarchy and, as I remarked in Chapter 2 and explore further in Chapter 7, risks undermining the rule of law and subjecting citizens to an arbitrary judicial will. The aim here is to indicate how the supremacy of a parliament of suitably authorized and accountable elected representatives can incorporate democratic checks and balances and so be conceived as providing a political constitutional alternative that guards against the problems that motivate the liberal advocacy of legal constitutionalism.

The argument unfolds in two main stages. Stage one occupies Sections 2 and 3 of this chapter. I begin by recapping the basic argument for a democratic system of majority rule provided in Chapters 1 and 2. As I noted in Chapter 2, the neo-Kantian account of legitimate political authority, which requires a political system that is non-dominating through being compatible with the omnilateral will of

[3] e.g. Arash Abizadeh, 'Counter-Majoritarian Democracy: Persistent Minorities, Federalism, and the Power of Numbers' (2021a) 115(3) *American Political Science Review* 746; Aileen Kavanagh, *The Collaborative Constitution* (Cambridge: Cambridge University Press 2024) 42–3.

[4] N. W. Barber, *The Principles of Constitutionalism* (Oxford: Oxford University Press 2018) 2–9.

[5] Alex de Tocqueville, *Democracy in America* (Eduardo Nolla ed., James T. Schleifer tr., vol. 1, Indianapolis: Liberty Fund 2012) ch. 8.

those subject to it, entails some form of democracy. Indeed, I shall argue that a democratic process of collective self-determination is implied in the very way Kant conceives of the hypothetical contract establishing a sovereign political authority in the first place. However, while political legitimacy requires broad if not unanimous agreement on the system of decision-making, within modern large-scale and pluralist societies one cannot assume either a similar level of agreement on the many collective laws and policies that must be decided within such a system or the direct involvement of every citizen in making these decisions. Contemporary democratic systems are necessarily majoritarian and representative. Consequently, the claim must be that such systems can offer a non-dominating form of decision-making that embodies political equality of a sufficient quality to meet the Kantian requirement. To defend this claim, I respond to two sets of principled objections to such a system. The first set objects to the very idea of political equality on epistemic and levelling down grounds. The second set contends that lottocracy and consensus would realize political equality better than electing representatives and deciding on the basis of majority rule.

Stage two takes up Sections 4, 5, and 6 and addresses the worries raised by the prospect of legislative and executive tyranny. In essence, these worries turn on how far a system of representative, majoritarian democracy can realize political equality in practice as well as in principle. I suggest that goal can be achieved by so configuring democratic institutions that they constitute a system of checks and balances on the model of the ancient idea of mixed government, updated for an egalitarian society that nonetheless contains a plurality of different interests and perspectives.

The core of such a democratic system is regular, free, and fair elections between competing parties, in which voters have a reasonable chance of removing incumbent governments and politicians in favour of opposition candidates offering alternative programmes.[6] Nevertheless, even within a working democracy possessing these qualities, worries over legislative and executive tyranny can arise as a result of two versions of what I call the proportionality problem. The first version arises if not all those given an equal vote have an equal stake in a decision, the second version when voters confront more than a pairwise choice. The first suggests there may need to be a distribution of decision-making authorities within a polity to ensure that decisions are taken among those with an equal stake in them. A distinction between various local levels of government, on the one hand, and central government, on the other, seeks to address this issue. The second suggests the need for a form of proportional representation that translates the horizontal equality

[6] Przeworski, *Crises of Democracy*, 5 calls this an 'electoralist' or 'minimalist' view of democracy, which he notes is shared by Joseph A. Schumpeter, *Capitalism, Socialism and Democracy* (London: Routledge 1976) and Norberto Bobbio, *The Future of Democracy: A Defence of the Rules of the Game* (R. Bellamy ed., Cambridge: Polity Press 1987) among others.

provided by each person having an equal vote in an election into vertical equality in the equal influence each voter can exert on the governmental and legislative agenda. Addressing each of these issues mitigates the risk of legislative tyranny in ways consistent with a 'complex' rather than a 'simple' form of majority rule.[7] At the same time, they provide the basis of a democratic parliamentary system that guards against executive tyranny. In other words, balancing centre and periphery, on the one side, and different minorities when constructing a majority—as PR encourages—on the other, has both the positive result of promoting deliberation among a wide range of voices across a political community and the negative result of checking legislative and executive majority tyranny. As a result, these mechanisms serve to enhance the positive and negative constitutional qualities of a democratic system of checks and balances.

2. DEMOCRATIC EQUALITY AND MAJORITY RULE

As Elizabeth Anderson has remarked, democratic equality is a relational view of equality. As such, it:

> regards two people as equal when each accepts the obligation to justify their actions by principles acceptable to the other, and in which they take mutual consultation, reciprocation, and recognition for granted.[8]

As she goes on to specify, such a conception of equality fits the traditional goal of a social contract that seeks to determine what should and can be collectively willed.[9] As I shall argue below, this understanding of a social contract provides a bridge to a theory of democracy and beyond that to political constitutionalism. For, on this account, a legitimate political association will be one in which the rules and principles governing its members' social relations emerge from collective decision processes that involve these same members determining these rules and principles for themselves on equal terms with each other.[10]

Jeremy Waldron has noted how, from the perspective of the Kantian understanding of democracy put forward in Chapter 2,[11] the idea of an original contract

[7] I take this term from Steffen Ganghof, *Beyond Presidentialism and Parliamentarism: Democratic Design and the Separation of Powers* (Oxford: Oxford University Press 2021) 6–7, but deploy it in a broader sense than him.

[8] Anderson, 'What Is the Point of Equality?', 313.

[9] Anderson, 'What Is the Point of Equality?', 314.

[10] See Albert Weale, *Democratic Justice and the Social Contract* (Oxford: Oxford University Press 2013) 5–7.

[11] Jeremy Waldron, 'Citizenship and Dignity' (3 January 2013). NYU School of Law, Public Law Research Paper No. 12-74. Available at SSRN: <https://ssrn.com/abstract = 2196079> or <http://dx.doi.org/10.2139/ssrn.2196079> 4–7.

provides a link between human dignity and the status of citizenship.[12] For a start, it entails viewing the members of a political community as if they were its co-framers. That involves not only the 'passive' notion that the public laws of the community should be regarded as capable of achieving their consent, but also that they possess the 'active' capacity to make those laws as well as to follow them. Kant characterizes moral agency as akin to political agency in involving the status of 'a law-giving member of the kingdom of ends'.[13] Indeed, he considers 'the dignity of humanity consists in just this capacity to give universal law, though with the condition of being subject to this very law-giving'.[14] As was argued in Chapter 2, one can go further and note how the very possibility of morality and of holding rights depends on the civic condition, whereby one obtains 'the right of rights': that is, the ability to rightfully claim rights against others through an authoritative political process.

A political community conceived in this way is something that citizens create and sustain together. As such, it must not only ensure equality of concern to its members through public laws that treat all as equals, but also equal respect to them as individuals capable of voting for and making such laws.[15] Indeed, the latter is the condition for the former. To achieve that result, collective deliberation regarding the rules and structures governing our common social life must be non-dominating, so that no one is at the mercy of the arbitrary will of others. In other words, equal concern and respect turn on a system of political equality that gives all those with an equal stake in a given system of rules and structures an equal say over their content.

Kant views the idea of an original contract as a hypothetical test of gauging whether a political system could meet this criterion by asking whether it could be conceivable as issuing from 'the united will of a whole people'. Yet, although he portrays this test as 'an idea of reason', he noted 'its undoubted practical reality'.[16] For, a political system that failed actually to attract the shared assent of the vast majority of its members would lack the legitimate authority necessary to make and enforce law without resorting to the domination and oppression of most of its citizenry.[17] However, that a political system can possess such near universal support does not mean that each and every law and policy will do so—on the contrary, as I noted above, that would be at odds with the conflicts associated with the pluralism of reasonable conceptions of the good that lie behind the circumstances of politics.

[12] Immanuel Kant, 'On the Common Saying: That May Be Correct in Theory, But It Is of No Use in Practice' (hereafter *TP*) in Immanuel Kant, *Practical Philosophy* (Mary Gregor ed., Cambridge: Cambridge University Press 1999) 296–7.

[13] Immanuel Kant, 'Groundwork of the Metaphysics of Morals' (hereafter *GW*) in Kant, *Practical Philosophy* (Mary Gregor ed.) 83.

[14] Kant, *GW*, 89.

[15] Kant, *TP*, 297.

[16] Kant, *TP*, 296–7.

[17] Anna Stilz, *Territorial Sovereignty: A Philosophical Exploration* (Oxford: Oxford University Press 2019) 94–5.

Rather, it will be necessary to establish a form of rule that can be assented to by all even if most of the laws and policies that are decided on in this way may not be. As Albert Weale has noted, one of the attractions of social contract theory lies in its making this procedural turn. It displaces conflict about the substance of collective decisions onto broad consensus on a procedure for making these decisions that people have reason to agree to.[18] And the core of such an acceptable process will be that it motivates those making decisions to relate to each other as equals.

One way of institutionalizing such relations is to ensure all are rulers and ruled in turn, actively engaged in both making and abiding by common laws so that there is no group with 'the hereditary privilege of *ruling rank*'.[19] That points to some version of democracy broadly conceived.[20] In contemporary societies, democracy has taken the form of one person one vote and majority rule within regular competitive party elections to elect the legislature and executive, and a real possibility of alternation between the parties in government.

As I noted in Chapters 1 and 2, a simple majority procedure of this kind has a *prima facie* claim to operate as an anonymous and neutral mechanism that leads to the equal weighing of people's views.[21] It is anonymous in that all votes count equally regardless of who casts them. It is neutral in that it is not biased towards the alternatives under consideration, and so treats the preferred options of voters equally. As such, it proves an egalitarian procedure that grants participants equal control over collective decisions, albeit indirectly via their elected representatives, in a way that shows them equal respect as moral agents entitled to be treated with equal concern with regard to the pursuit of their fundamental interests. As we shall see, matters become more complicated—and majority rule more indeterminate—once more than two alternatives are involved.[22] In Section 6.2 of this chapter, I shall argue that more complex ways of calculating the majority are available that preserve the egalitarian qualities of this simple model based on a dichotomous choice.

Nevertheless, in a heterogeneous society, even the fairest and most inclusive forms of majoritarianism will still entail some minorities being ruled in ways that conflict with their values and interests, at least some of the time.[23] To this extent, though the promise of democracy is that it provides a process that treats all voters as equal autonomous reasoners, it cannot be envisaged as a system of self-government.[24] Inevitably, it involves heteronomy. As Lars Vinx has argued, a

[18] Weale, *Democratic Justice and the Social Contract*, 6–7.
[19] Kant, *TP*, 297.
[20] Stilz, *Territorial Sovereignty*, 128.
[21] Thomas Christiano, 'Political Equality' in J. Chapman and A. Wertheimer (eds), *Majorities and Minorities NOMOS XXXIII* (New York: New York University Press 1990) 153–7; Albert Weale, 'Three Types of Majority Rule' (2019) 90 *Political Quarterly* 64–6.
[22] Christiano, 'Political Equality', 157–70; Weale, 'Three Types of Majority Rule', 67.
[23] Przeworski, *Crises of Democracy*, 198.
[24] Though I agree with Przeworski's view that democracy inevitably involves heteronomy—and can disappoint on that account—I think he is wrong to consider that a betrayal (albeit inescapable) of its

crucial component of the democratic contract, therefore, is that we agree to defer to the rule of others on the condition that there are regular elections that are sufficiently free and fair as to give us an equal chance to win them and rule ourselves in the future.[25] Consequently, there can be no democratic mandate to abolish or undermine democracy,[26] as certain populists claim—a point to which I return in Chapter 8. Meanwhile, I shall suggest in Section 6 that both local government and PR provide not only for more complex forms of majority rule but also strengthen the 'equal chance' of all citizens to rule (if indirectly) as well as be ruled.

Summarizing the above, we can see the democratic contract as involving three mutually supportive kinds of political equality. First, it aims at aggregative equality in which all those with an equal stake in a decision are given an equal say. Second, it entails adversarial equality, in which each voter has an equal chance over time of having a government that broadly aligns with at least some of their core preferences. Finally, both of these forms of political equality encourage deliberative equality of the relational kind described by Anderson, which involves an obligation of mutual reason giving. As we shall see in Sections 4, 5, and 6, a system of complex majorities provides a means for achieving all three forms of political equality through establishing a system of checks and balances that also work against legislative and executive tyranny.

3. OBJECTIONS TO THE VERY IDEA OF DEMOCRATIC EQUALITY AND MAJORITY RULE

Before turning to the defence of a model of electoral representative democracy that can meet the terms of the democratic contract, it is important to address the criticisms and alternatives of those who object to either the substantive norms or the procedural forms of this conception of democracy. On the one hand, epistocrats and those troubled by the prospect of levelling down raise concerns about the very idea of political equality. The first suggest that political decision-making should reflect the inequalities in people's expertise with regard to various policies. The second maintain that only direct democracy can deliver equal control over legislation, and that this is clearly impractical. On the other hand, lottocrats and advocates of consensus consider sortition and unanimous decision-making as more egalitarian than electoral democracy or majority rule. What follows explores each of these critiques in order.

central claim to offer a system of self-government: *Crises of Democracy*, 198. The promise of democracy lies in its egalitarian procedural qualities.

[25] Lars Vinx, 'Democratic Equality and Militant Democracy' (2020) 27 *Constellations* 690.
[26] Vinx, 'Democratic Equality and Militant Democracy', 691.

3.1. Epistocracy

A key critique comes from those who dispute both the intrinsic and instrumental importance of giving all members of a political community who reach a minimal level of competency—standardly associated with a modest age requirement and basic mental functioning—equal political rights to vote, to run for and hold office, to express opinions, and other entitlements standardly associated with democratic citizenship. These critics note that individuals differ greatly in their powers of reasoning and how informed they are about various issues. We have rigorous tests for competency for professions such as medical doctors, pilots, accountants, and lawyers, so why not for the policy-makers responsible for key decisions relating to different areas of public life? Would it not be possible for a group of suitably qualified and well-disposed technocratic enlightened despots to govern wisely and justly in ways that equally advance the interests of all those subject to their benevolent rule?[27]

This technocratic critique assumes that the public interest can be rationally discoverable quite separately from what people may believe it to be. To cite a Platonic metaphor long associated with this form of thinking, governing is a skill akin to that of a captain, with rulers requiring an equivalent training and knowledge to safely steer the ship of state and prevent it foundering on the rocks or capsizing in a storm. Yet, this sort of argument seriously under describes the character of statecraft.[28]

It is true that we all rely on the advice and skill of experts to make crucial decisions in many areas of our lives, both as individuals and collectively. However, even in those areas where expertise is relatively uncontroversial, so that experts and policies can be accredited according to generally acceptable public norms, we consider it reasonable for individuals to be allowed to choose their expert and decline their advice.

For a start, scientific knowledge in many areas can be incomplete, uncertain, and imprecise, so that qualified scientific experts may nevertheless disagree. For example, this incompleteness, uncertainty, and imprecision holds for many medical conditions, leading doctors to diverge in their diagnoses and treatments.[29] For these reasons, we think it not unreasonable for people to ask for a second opinion. Democratic challenges to ambiguities and inexactitudes in expert reasoning

[27] e.g. J. Brennan, *Against Democracy* (Princeton, NJ: Princeton University Press 2016). See too the outline of this critique offered in Robert A. Dahl, *Democracy and its Critics* (New Haven, CT: Yale University Press 1989) ch. 4.

[28] The following critique draws on Dahl, *Democracy and its Critics*, ch. 5; Robert A. Dahl, *Democracy* (New Haven, CT: Yale University Press 1998) 69–74 and Thomas Christiano, 'The Basis of Political Equality' in Elizabeth Edenberg and Michael Hannon (eds), *Political Epistemology* (Oxford: Oxford University Press 2021).

[29] Zeynep Pamnuk, *Politics and Expertise: How to Use Science in a Democratic Society* (Princeton, NJ: Princeton University Press 2021) 3.

provide an important way to avoid a consensus emerging that results more from 'group think' than evidence and logic.[30] It also points to the need for citizens and their representatives to assume responsibility for examining expert claims and the assumptions and values that underlie them.[31]

Even when expert knowledge is more certain, a key role remains for individual moral choice. Public health systems may only fund us to consult qualified doctors about our illnesses and to follow medically approved treatments, say, but we generally try and exercise some choice over which doctors we see and whether or not to follow their recommendations. Such leeway is regarded as an inherent feature of human dignity, whereby the importance of our being judges of our fundamental interests and what is valuable in our lives far outweighs any differences that may exist between us in our capacity to produce or appreciate different values. Indeed, it is unclear whether one could even make evaluative comparisons between these kinds of differences. For example, we respect that someone should have the choice not to submit to a certain cancer treatment because they view the cure as worse than the disease. Even if that treatment has a high chance of success, that would not make their choice 'worse' than that of someone who chose to undergo the treatment—it is simply their choice to make.

Of course, collective political decisions involve choosing for others as well as ourselves—albeit, in a democracy, on equal terms to each other. However, there is considerably more disagreement in politics than in medicine about both the values to be promoted and the appropriate ways to do so.[32] There is no epistemic warrant for our rival ontological claims about the good society in the manner that medical science can often (if not always) underpin particular claims about human health. Such moral and political disagreement creates an epistemic problem for epistocracy.

As we have noted, human beings have different interests and value a variety of ends, many of which conflict either contingently or inherently. Moreover, they disagree as to how these conflicts might be resolved. That renders problematic any notion of a rationally discoverable, objective, public interest. For example, should a local community give extra funding to schools, swimming pools, or parks? There are trade-offs here, and how they are settled will reflect people's different priorities and conceptions of the good. It is debatable that balancing these conflicting ends is a purely technical matter. Technocrats would need to commit to a rather strict (and highly contentious) form of perfectionism to escape such disagreements.

Meanwhile, modern societies are not only pluralist and complex, so that their members hold diverse and often conflicting views and interests, but also open. Such openness means they develop in unexpected and unpredictable ways, be it

30 Pamnuk, *Politics and Expertise*, 10–11.

31 Pamnuk, *Politics and Expertise*, 12–13.

32 Dahl, *Democracy and its Critics*, 66; Christiano, 'The Basis of Political Equality', 116.

because of the human capacity for conceptual innovation or due to changing needs and preferences, and the unanticipated impacts of human activity. Most public policies are subject to numerous unknown and often unforeseeable variables that make their effects a matter of informed guess work at best, thereby allowing for considerable empirical disagreement even among experts—as when economists dispute the pros and cons of raising or lowering interest rates at any given time. Here too, there can be differences over the normative evaluation of empirical evidence, both because of the complicated nature of the empirical data itself and the variety of normative considerations likely to be involved, each possessing a different force.[33]

Last, but far from least, expertise does not necessarily equate with impartiality or incorruptibility.[34] True, partiality can result as much from our limited and imperfect knowledge and the resulting cognitive biases and fallibility, as from selfishness or the natural tendency to attend to our own interests and those of people like us, among other human frailties. However, like all other citizens, the skilled and well trained will have a comparatively restricted range of personal experiences and be specialists only in certain fields of knowledge, so that their perspectives will also inevitably be incomplete and partial. Nor can they be counted on to be virtuous and dedicated to the public rather than their own good, or that of those with a similar outlook and economic interests to themselves.

The historical record largely confirms these shortcomings of epistocracy. As Thomas Christiano has observed,[35] hierarchical rule grounded on epistemic claims has been the norm rather than the exception throughout most of human history. However, whether in the past or the present, those excluded from an equal share of power by virtue of its concentration in a particular ruling group have generally had their interests marginalized at best and at worst disregarded and actively suppressed. Moreover, this upshot has been the same whether the society is feudal, capitalist, or communist in character.

Democracy seeks to overcome these epistemic and partiality problems by giving citizens the possibility to advance their own interests on an equal basis to each other despite their disagreements as to which policies might be in their collective interest. As a result, the democratic process can motivate politicians to not only take expertise into account—or risk ruling so incompetently they lose the next election—but also pay attention to the views and interests of their fellow citizens and respond to their concerns.

This critique of epistocracy, therefore, does not entail rejecting expertise and denying it should inform policy-making. It merely means that, given the aforementioned limitations of expertise, experts should be 'on tap' rather than 'on top',[36]

[33] Dahl, *Democracy and its Critics*, 69–76; Rawls, *Political Liberalism*, 55–7.
[34] Dahl, *Democracy and its Critics*, 76.
[35] Christiano, 'The Basis of Political Equality', 117–18; see too Dahl, *Democracy and its Critics*, 77–9.
[36] Dahl, *Democracy* 71.

and responsive to, and controlled by, the views and interests of those they serve through a process that accords them equal control. The relationship of voters to representatives is sometimes described as involving a division of labour between the electorate, who set the ends of policy, and the executive and legislature, who provide the means.[37] To return to the Platonic metaphor, that makes it sound as if voters are like passengers who determine their destination and select between rival captains and ships offering to take them there. However, the ends–means division is too clear-cut.[38] As we saw, there may be uncertainty and expert disagreement with regard to means. Consequently, there is likely to be a range of means to achieve any agreed end, each involving different costs and benefits for different sections of the community and raising a range of moral questions that people can, and almost certainly will, legitimately pose and answer in contrasting ways. The desirability, feasibility, and acceptability of pursuing certain ends or adopting particular means all raise various ethical and practical issues, that citizens may reasonably view and weigh in diverse ways. As a result, democratic elections need to promote a debate about ends *and* means, in which the range of people's concerns surrounding both, on the one side, and expert opinion on the advantages and disadvantages of different options, on the other, get broadly aired and weighed. In Section 4, I shall discuss how one can characterize party competition in free and fair elections as a system of democratic checks and balances. Here, I wish to focus on how this democratic process overcomes the informational and motivational shortcomings of epistocracy, without necessarily generating parallel flaws among citizens of its own.

The need for representatives to be authorized by, and accountable to, those they represent can be regarded as a dynamic and interactive relationship in which each shapes and responds to the views of the other.[39] Such mutual responsiveness can help overcome the epistemic weaknesses of rulers and ruled alike. Discussions of the epistemic features of democracy tend to focus on its capacity to produce 'right answers' in ways associated with either the Condorcet jury theorem or the wisdom of crowds. However, related to both—and perhaps of greater importance—is the role a democratic system plays as an information-gathering mechanism. It offers a means to draw on the dispersed knowledge of millions of citizens, providing insights into how collective policies can impact very differently situated individuals with diverse needs and goals. As such, it offers a way of informing governments as to the concerns of the governed as a whole and providing feedback on the effects of their decisions. It thereby helps to overcome the inevitably imperfect and biased perspectives we all possess as individuals. Meanwhile, the need to offer plausible ways of meeting popular concerns—ways that can survive public criticism by their

[37] Christiano, *Constitution of Equality*, 104.
[38] Pamnuk, *Politics and Expertise*, 12.
[39] I. M. Young, *Inclusion and Democracy* (Oxford: Oxford University Press 2000) 129.

opponents and the media and be capable of delivering when put into practice—gives politicians inducements to consult with experts as to the feasibility of their proposals. Their deployment of expert opinion, in its turn, feeds into and informs public debate.

As we noted, the epistemic partiality and group think of politicians and experts alike is apt to be linked to self- and group-interest. Competition for power and subjecting rulers to the democratic control of the ruled incentivizes politicians to at least appear to be listening to ordinary citizens and addressing their collective interests. At the same time, the process can broaden the horizon of citizens themselves. Epistocrats tend to deploy an economic theory of democracy to suggest citizens are themselves motivated by self-interest and lack the incentives to become fully informed or even to vote on collective issues over which they have minimal influence.[40] However, representative democracy involves the organization of representatives and represented into party groups that share enough in common for the former to be able to coherently represent the latter. In general, that commonality is not generated by a mere coincidence of shared individual interests in a particular set of particular policies, but rather is linked to a more general ideological perspective concerning the most just way to organize society and the policies that serve the common good. Participation in a collective enterprise to achieve desirable goals helps to motivate and facilitate acting—if only by voting—and becoming informed.[41] After all, when making many everyday decisions, such as buying a car or choosing a career, people benefit from 'free information' from regular social interactions and further information from trusted intermediaries with similar priorities to our own. Friends, opinion leaders, and especially parties provide similar cues in this respect, indicating candidates and a platform likely to be grounded in reasoning and aims we share.

Of course, no democratic system is without faults. Disillusionment with actually existing democracies, if not the democratic ideal, has grown in recent years, and been accompanied by democratic backsliding by populist regimes. I explore some of these challenges in Chapter 8 of this book. For all its flaws, though, democracy outperforms autocracy—even of an epistocratic kind. As the impact of the rise of universal suffrage and its relation to higher economic growth and greater welfare in the twentieth century vividly illustrates, the worst off do better economically and socially through being included in the franchise.[42] And the logic of that being so is clear: namely, that equal concern and respect for all citizens goes hand in

[40] e.g. C. Achen and L. Bartels, *Democracy for Realists: Why Elections Do Not Produce Responsive Government* (Princeton, NJ: Princeton University Press 2017) ch. 2; Brennan, *Against Democracy*, ch. 2.

[41] Christiano, 'The Basis of Political Equality', 125–7.

[42] Christiano, 'The Basis of Political Equality', 119, cites Wright's study (in G. Wright, *Sharing the Prize: The Economics of the Civil Rights Revolution in the American South* (Cambridge, MA: Harvard University Press 2013)) of the economic impact on Afro Americans of the Voting Rights Act of 1965 as a potent example of this effect.

hand with their possessing an equal chance to influence the political agenda and remove and replace those who fail to address their ideals and interests.

3.2. Levelling Down

The extension of the argument from political equality to a form of representative democracy to meet the epistocracy objection might be vulnerable in its turn to the levelling down objection. According to this view, if we take the intrinsic value of democracy seriously, as according people equal control over collective decisions in recognition of their equal dignity and status, then we should prefer a direct democratic system to a representative one. That would be true even if direct democracy proves instrumentally less effective than representative democracy, so that citizens' fundamental interests are promoted to a lesser degree as a result.[43]

A number of responses can be made to this objection.[44] As we noted above, the intrinsic argument rests in part on the instrumental, for the intrinsic worth of democracy lies in its being a means to the end of distributing the resources needed to pursue our fundamental interests on an equal basis. Moreover, the egalitarian distribution of these resources matters because more of them is better than less. If it was the case that above a certain base line we would be indifferent to having more, then the appropriate distributive scheme would be to ensure all reached that base line. If I have had my fill of cake, I have no reason to complain at someone else having more cake than me. As Christiano notes, Pareto superior inequalities are to be preferred to Pareto inferior inequalities, therefore, even if such a scenario remains unjust through not being equal.

That said, as Christiano also points out, direct democracy is likely to create more inequalities than representative democracy, as well as being inefficient. Representative democracy involves a division of labour, whereby citizens authorize politicians to implement policies that accord with their ideals and interests and can hold them to account should these measures fail to do so. As long as regular elections ensure their evolving views are fairly represented in the legislature and executive, then the conditions of political equality are satisfied. By contrast, direct democracy would place a huge burden on citizens, most of whom would lack the time and resources to become informed and deliberate about a vast number of complex topics. In this context, participation would be likely to be much more unequal, favouring those able and willing to devote themselves to politics. After all, it was such egalitarian considerations that led to MPs being paid in the first place. As a result, direct democracy risks being both Pareto inferior and more inegalitarian than representative democracy.

[43] David Estlund, 'Political Quality' (2000) 17 *Social Philosophy and Policy* 127–60.

[44] What follows draws on Christiano, *Constitution of Equality*, 104–6.

The levelling down objection is often extended to suggest that representative democracy is also counter-majoritarian. These critics raise two issues in this regard.[45] First, as is the case with any two-tier system, representation is likely to incur a majority deficit. That is, the number of voters within a constituency who disagree with the decision are likely to be greater than those who agree, thereby producing inequalities of *a priori* voting power among the electorate.[46] Second, again like other two-tier systems involving more than one sub-unit, it risks violating the anonymity criterion. This criterion is a basic requirement of equality in voting, whereby an outcome depends solely on the numbers of voters supporting each of the options rather than who those voters are. However, suppose in a polity of three constituencies there are two that have voted for the red party and one that has voted for the blue party, with the red party having a majority of thirty in constituency A and the blue party a majority of sixty in constituency B.[47] If thirty-one voters in both A and B switch their preferences—with thirty-one changing from red to blue in A and thirty-one from blue to red in B, then the government of the polity will switch from red to blue. Yet that result violates anonymity (and, in the process, political equality), whereby outcomes should not change when equal numbers of voters of opposed preferences switch their votes.

Both these problems certainly apply to representative systems based on single-member constituencies elected according to a plurality rule, such as those for the UK Parliament or US Congress. Yet, as Christiano has pointed out, both can be alleviated by a form of proportional representation which ensures the majority in the legislature reflects the majority among voters.[48] Such systems also reduce the extent to which representatives are likely to act as trustees rather than as delegates. As I shall argue in Section 6.2, proportional representation is more likely to produce parties and candidates aligned to manifestos that reflect the policy preferences of their voters.

3.3. Lottocracy and Consensus

Some of those criticizing the majoritarian and egalitarian credentials of representative democracy do so to suggest that we should regard the democratic goal of political equality as being better achieved through non-electoral mechanisms, such as sortition and consensus. They claim these mechanisms are more egalitarian forms of equal control than electoral democracy and majority rule respectively. Yet, both proved flawed from a democratic perspective committed to political equality.

[45] Abizadeh, 'Counter-Majoritarian Democracy', 746.
[46] I take the term and definition from Abizadeh, 'Counter-Majoritarian Democracy', 744.
[47] I have adapted this example from Thomas Christiano, *The Rule of the Many: Fundamental Issues in Democratic Theory* (Boulder, CO: Westview Press 1996) 225–6, 233–4.
[48] Christiano, *The Rule of the Many*, 232–3.

These flaws parallel the worries I have raised with regard to epistocracy and the levelling down objection. I will discuss each in turn.

3.3.1. Lottocracy

Lottocracy has been seen as a way of giving everyone an equal chance to rule. From classical antiquity up to the eighteenth century, sortition rivalled election as the main form of democracy. Its contemporary advocates argue that random selection and regular rotation in office provides a more appropriate and effective way of giving everyone an equal chance to shape the political agenda and make decisions than the equal opportunity to stand for office or the indirect influence of an equal vote for representatives.[49] Of course, the likelihood of being chosen may be remote in a large society.[50] An individual may be no more likely to serve in a lottocracy than they would be in an electoral democracy. For example, the UK currently has some 47 million registered voters divided among 650 constituencies, giving the average citizen a roughly one in 70,000 chance of selection every five years or so. Given these odds, the equal chance to rule per se seems rather a risky deal. As Christiano has remarked, one would hardly regard a welfare system that entitled all citizens (and restricted them to) a single free weekly national lottery ticket that gave them all an equal chance of being a millionaire as an egalitarian form of social redistribution just because everyone had an equal chance of winning the benefits lottery.[51]

A better argument, though, holds that a lottocracy offers a more equitable way of choosing political representatives that will give rise to a legislative body that is more likely to make decisions that give equal weight to the views and interests of citizens.[52] The claim here is that random selection avoids the voter bias and the influence of those with wealth, connections, and other forms of power that bedevil selection and election as a candidate in an electoral democracy. Consequently, sortition will likely result in representatives from all walks of life and lead to greater diversity. Indeed, when combined with stratified sampling, whereby representatives are selected in proportion to their possessing certain socially salient features found in society as a whole, such as gender, age, and ethnicity—an assembly chosen in this way is likely to be more representative of society as a whole—at least in its make-up—than an elected assembly.[53] As such, it can offer indicative rather than

[49] Alexander A. Guerrero, 'Against Elections: The Lottocratic Alternative' (2014) 42(2) *Philosophy and Public Affairs* 135–78; Hélène Landemore, *Open Democracy: Reinventing Popular Rule for the Twenty-First Century* (Princeton, NJ: Princeton University Press 2020); Gil Delannoi, Oliver Dowlen, and Peter Stone, *The Lottery as a Democratic Institution* (Dublin: Policy Institute 2013); Peter Stone, *The Luck of the Draw* (Oxford: Oxford University Press 2011); and Arash Abizadeh, 'Representation, Bicameralism, Political Equality, and Sortition: Reconstituting the Second Chamber as a Randomly Selected Assembly', (2021b) 19(3) *Perspectives on Politics* 791–806.

[50] Christiano, *Constitution of Equality*, 108.

[51] Christiano, *Constitution of Equality*, 109–10.

[52] Abizadeh, 'Representation, Bicameralism, Political Equality, and Sortition', 798.

[53] Abizadeh, 'Representation, Bicameralism, Political Equality, and Sortition', 800.

responsive representation.[54] That is, a randomly selected legislature will be apt to reason like citizens as a whole.

Yet, that cannot be counted on. For example, the sampling criteria may pick out and weight features that are of no or less significance than others for citizens so far as their political choices are concerned. The selected representatives may even act on their own idiosyncratic views or do the bare minimum to draw a salary. In either case, there will be little that can be done about it. Citizens will be bystanders to the deliberation—they will lack any instruments to motivate representatives to respond to their preferences. These failings relate to the most important flaw of lottocractic schemes: namely, that sortition downplays the political agency all citizens may exercise in the authorizing their representatives and holding them to account.[55] Choosing who should represent you is itself subject to negotiation and deliberation, forcing party managers to screen candidates for qualities and views likely to play well with voters. The prospect of being held to account and sanctioned for poor performance incentivizes representatives to consider how their decisions will be received—both at the next election and in the future. While any system of representation involves inequality between the representatives and the represented, these processes narrow that gap. By contrast, lottocracy both weakens the agency of citizens and reduces the incentives of representatives.

This weakness is likely to exacerbate some of the very problems proponents of lottocracy associate with electoral democracy and claim it can overcome. Part of the lottocratic case rests on the empirical claim that representative democracy is elitist and favours the views and interests of elites.[56] However, that view has been around as long as mass democracy, and, like the epistocratic view examined above, rests on dubious empirical assumptions regarding the collective rationality and knowledge and the susceptibility to manipulation of the general population.[57] That is not to deny that oligarchical tendencies can and do exist that lead politicians to be overly responsive to the interests of the wealthy—not least due to the influence of money in elections and their economic power more generally.[58] But these tendencies need not be considered as inherent to electoral democracy per se. To a large extent, they reflect what O'Neill and White term 'the associational

[54] Philip Pettit, 'Representation, Responsive and Indicative' (2010) 17(3) *Constellations* 426–34.

[55] Christiano, *Constitution of Equality*, 110–11; Abizadeh, 'Representation, Bicameralism, Political Equality, and Sortition', 798.

[56] Abizadeh, 'Representation, Bicameralism, Political Equality, and Sortition', 795–7.

[57] Richard Bellamy, 'The Advent of the Masses and the Making of the Modern Theory of Democracy' in T. Ball and Richard Bellamy (eds), *The Cambridge History of Twentieth Century Political Thought* (Cambridge: Cambridge University Press 2003) 70–103.

[58] e.g. Larry M. Bartels, *Unequal Democracy: The Political Economy of the New Gilded Age* (Princeton, NJ: Princeton University Press 2008); Martin Gilens and Benjamin I. Page, 'Testing Theories of American Politics: Elites, Interest Groups, and Average Citizens' (2014) 12(3) *Perspectives on Politics* 564–81, though see Omar S. Bashir, 'Testing Inferences about American Politics: A Review of the "Oligarchy" Result' (2015) 2(4) *Research & Politics* 1–7.

environment' within which they operate,[59] elements of which can be changed. Campaign finance laws can be made stricter, and workers better informed and organized through trade unions so as to more effectively contest the influence of big business and finance.[60] Moreover, similar biases to those found in electoral systems can also enter a lottocratic arrangement. The wealthy and better educated may be more able and willing to serve—having the resources and competence to do so—and exert greater influence in deliberations. Non-professional politicians may be more susceptible to lobbying and the influence of conspiracy theorists and the like due to a lack of general information.

The unpredictability of sortition and the regular rotation of representatives also works against consistency in law- and policy-making and long-term planning.[61] Each selection will bring a new set of representatives who may hold quite different views to their predecessors and successors. As a result, whatever agreements they make are likely to be transient. That may undermine one of the chief virtues of the rule of law—the managing of expectations and the provision of a stable framework within which citizens can plan. It can also hinder the tackling of persistent problems that require planning and investment over time—such as the mitigation of and adaptation to climate change. A feature of parties is the way they unite representatives around a programme of policies animated by a certain ideology or set of principles. It encourages politicians to see themselves as acting for others to achieve a certain vision of society through a set of short- and longer-term policies. Meanwhile, citizens have agency in both informing that vision and voting and campaigning for or against it.

3.3.2. Consensus

Similar problems arise with consensus as a decision rule rather than the majority principle. As we saw, an appropriate test for the legitimacy of the legal and political system as a whole is to ask whether it could issue from an omnilateral will. Why would such a real test not be suitable for every policy decision? Surely, insisting on unanimity for collective decisions offers the best safeguard against majority tyranny and ensures popular decisions are genuinely in the interest of all.[62]

For a start, this proposal overlooks what occasions the need for an authoritative political system in the first place—namely, the presence of reasonable disagreement about collective policies. The demand for consensus amounts to a form of anarchy long criticized as impossible to realize by R. P. Wolf.[63] Followed to its

[59] Martin O'Neill and Stuart White, 'Trade Unions and Political Equality' in Hugh Collins, Gillian Lester, and Virginia Mantouvalou (eds), *Philosophical Foundations of Labour Law* (Oxford: Oxford University Press 2018) 252.

[60] O'Neill and White, 'Trade Unions and Political Equality', 252–68.

[61] J. White, *In the Long Run: The Future as a Political Idea* (London: Profile Books 2024) 196–7.

[62] J. M. Buchanan and G. Tullock, *The Calculus of Consent* (Ann Arbor, MI: University of Michigan Press 1962) 90.

[63] R. P. Wolff, *In Defence of Anarchism* (New York: Harper & Row 1970).

logical conclusion, this argument would require agreement on the political agenda and the options to vote on as well agreement on one of those options. Meanwhile, the transaction costs of attempting to reach unanimity, were that even possible, seem prohibitive. Apart from other difficulties, they would likely increase the opportunities for different groups to hold out for bribes and other advantages, thereby increasing so-called 'pork barrel' political manoeuvres.[64]

Moreover, it cannot be regarded as egalitarian. Consensus or super majority rules involve a status quo bias. Votes to stick to what exists carry more weight, since one person or a small group of people can hold out against change. As a result, their single or handful of votes carry as much weight as the far larger mass of votes aligned against them. Of course, it may be argued that consensus thereby offers protection for discrete and isolated minorities, whose views and interests might otherwise be ignored at best or at worst suppressed. Yet it also offers protection of the unjust privileges of wealthy and powerful minorities against justified challenges on egalitarian grounds of a poor and less powerful majority—as in John Calhoun's proposal for a system of concurrent majorities to protect the slave-owning interests of the southern states of the United States.[65] Democracy and majority rule are precisely about overcoming those imbalances that lead to domination and oppression. How far that may be achieved without giving rise to arbitrary rule by the majority is nonetheless an issue that needs to be taken seriously and to which we now turn.

4. CHECKS AND BALANCES VS. THE SEPARATION OF POWERS

The last two sections have defended the very idea of political equality and its embodiment in a regular democratic electoral process involving one person one vote and majority rule. As we saw, such a scheme appeals on intrinsic and instrumental grounds as a fair way of resolving disagreements over collective decisions in ways that treat all involved equally and impartially. However, as I noted, its procedural fairness has been widely criticized as insufficient to avoid either the empowerment of governments able to act in arbitrary ways (executive tyranny), or the passing of laws that suppress minority rights (legislative tyranny). Liberal legal constitutionalists have standardly appealed to the separation of powers as a mechanism for dealing with these alleged failings. On the one hand, separating the executive from the legislative branch was considered a way of ensuring the first could be checked by the second, thereby reducing the likelihood of the government having

[64] Weale, *Democracy*, 158–60.

[65] J. C. Calhoun, 'A Disquisition on Government' (1851) in *Union and Liberty: The Political Philosophy of John C. Calhoun* (Ross M. Lence ed., Indianapolis, IN: Liberty Fund 1992) 3–78.

a guaranteed majority, as tends to be the case with parliamentary systems. On the other hand, and even more importantly, a separate judicial branch was supposed to ensure the independence of the judiciary and its capacity to override legislation that infringes constitutional rights and norms. This section briefly calls into question the plausibility of this approach—outlining criticisms with regard to courts that are developed further in later chapters of the book, especially Chapter 7. That sets the scene in the next two sections of this chapter for an argument that a system of complex majoritarianism can be seen as a contemporary form of the ancient notion of mixed government, based on different groups within a polity checking and balancing each other so that all are motivated to 'hear the other side' (*audi alteram partem*) and address their views and interests. As I argued in the Introduction to this book, mixed government can be regarded as providing the historical template of a political conception of the constitution. In its democratic form, it also aligns with the democratic contract by supporting aggregative, adversarial, and deliberative equality.

The separation of powers evolved as providing an alternative mechanism to the mixed constitution for protecting against arbitrary rule. This doctrine replaced the distinction between classes central to the ancient system of mixed government based on balancing the different interests of monarchy, aristocracy, and the common people, with a functional distinction between legislative, executive, and judicial acts. It advocated the division of government into three corresponding agencies, which should remain distinct, with no overlap amongst the personnel who staffed them.[66] The aim was to ensure that those who formulate the laws are distinct from those entrusted with their interpretation, application, and enforcement. In this way, those who make the laws would themselves be made subject to them. As a result, the legislature would have an incentive to avoid self-interested legislation and to frame it in general terms, so as to be equally applicable to all. These rules then guide the decisions of the executive and judiciary, who, because they are similarly under the law, also have good reason to act in an impartial manner.[67]

This arrangement was supposed to overcome both executive and legislative tyranny by securing the mutual accountability of each of the branches of government. However, it suffers from a number of notorious and related problems, of which three are particularly important. First, there is the conceptual and practical difficulty of distinguishing the different functions.[68] When judges, for example, adjudicate on which rules do or do not apply in particular cases, they also often end up setting precedents that, in effect, constitute new rules. Similarly, officials frequently have to create rules in the course of implementing a given law, that in turn come

[66] Maurice Vile, *Constitutionalism and the Separation of Powers* (Oxford: Clarendon Press 1967) 13–18.

[67] W. B. Gwyn, *The Meaning of the Separation of Powers: an Analysis of the Doctrine from its Origin to the Adoption of the United States Constitution* (The Hague: Martinus Nijhoff 1965) 127–8.

[68] Vile, *Constitutionalism*, 318–21.

to take on a life of their own. The executive may also be legally empowered to take decisions in exceptional or emergency situations requiring a quick response, with such decrees having the effect of laws. Legislators, too, are inevitably concerned with how the laws they frame will be interpreted and applied to specific cases. Thus, each branch of government will find itself engaged in all three activities to some degree or another. The more complex the activities of government, the more interrelated they are likely to become.

Second, to the extent such functional separation is possible, its ability to limit the power of those controlling the various agencies will be undermined if all represent similar groups or interests. For example, if the judicial branch is dominated by appointees who share the ideological convictions of both the executive and the legislature, then all three functions will be effectively held in the same hands, even if the personnel are nominally different. In such circumstances, neither branch will be separated in more than the most formal sense and will fail to either check or balance the others.

Third, and most importantly, the separation of powers fails to provide incentives that ensure these agents serve their principals—the citizens.[69] This functional separation involves a vertical division of power. In consequence, each functional part can either increase its political rents or shirk its responsibilities and displace the costs for poor decisions on to the others. Indeed, to the extent each separate branch of government retains autonomy over its own separate functional sphere, it remains able to act arbitrarily on matters within its competence. As I shall detail in Chapter 7, this possibility is particularly present in the case of the judicial branch, for which almost no mechanism usually exists for rendering it accountable for its decisions—a circumstance intimately linked to its functional separation and independence. For example, it may enhance its power through the recognition of new sets of rights, without having to bear any responsibility for the impact of its decisions on other social policies or potential increases in taxation. Much the same can be said of the executive. In presidential systems, which place executive power in a single person who has a direct democratic mandate and cannot be dismissed for political failings by any democratic body—be it the legislature or their nominal political party—the separation of powers gives rise to a form of what Steffen Ganghof calls 'executive personalism'.[70] As he notes, executive personalism is 'a historical overhang from monarchy'. Yet, by contrast to the mixed constitution, it lacks adequate checking by the other branches. For within their allotted sphere, such presidents (like constitutional courts in their sphere) may act as they will—their only incentive is not to perform so badly that they delegitimize or break the system, or at least their role within it.

[69] G. Brennan and A. Hamlin, 'A Revisionist View of the Separation of Powers' (1994) 6(3) *Journal of Theoretical Politics* 351–2.

[70] Ganghof, *Beyond Presidentialism*, 1–2.

As a result of these three weaknesses, the separation of powers provides no compelling reason of itself for the different functions of government to 'hear the other side'—be that each other, or the people they are supposed to serve. Instead they create potential forms of executive and judicial tyranny.[71] As I shall argue in Sections 5 and especially 6 that follow, within a parliamentary regime, the electoral system, on the one side, and local government and federal or quasi federal arrangements, on the other, provide the basis for a contemporary mixed constitution involving a democratic system of checks and balances.

Two features of this democratic mixed constitution need to be stressed. First, it is a horizontal distribution of power. It involves either rival aspirants for power, as in competing parties, or rival centres of power, as in competing governments at the local or regional levels. Second, and most importantly, it offers a link between principal and agent that renders the legislature and the executive both responsive and inclusive with regard to the citizenry. For the rival power seekers or centres must recruit the support of a majority of the people to govern. Because the nature of pluralism within modern dynamic societies is such as to ensure majorities consist of coalitions of minorities, there will always be the opportunity for rivals to bid for each other's supporters.[72] In this respect, as Madison noted, the operation of the political system follows that of the market—both are mechanisms for 'supplying, by opposite and rival interests, the defect of better motives'.[73] As Madison had learnt from Hume, the new connotations of 'balance' appeared nowhere more evident than in the economy and the dynamic equilibrium of the 'balance of trade'.[74] However, the American appreciated how just as the competition for profit drives rival producers and providers to supply the wants of customers at an optimal price, so the competition for power operates in an analogous way and encourages politicians to reduce their political rents in order to supply benefits to citizens without unduly raising taxes or imposing other costs upon them, such as reducing their liberties. Balance so conceived supports deliberative equality by offering incentives for the different parties to 'hear the other side' and build winning electoral coalitions that are missing in the old, segmental, account of balance. It also supports adversarial equality and losers' consent, as—in the context of regular elections—it provides a mechanism for removing the incumbent government and replacing it with an alternative, giving voters an equal chance over time of being rulers and ruled in turn. However, I shall argue that for this balance to be achieved while avoiding either executive or legislative tyranny, it must involve a 'complex' majoritarianism that is sensitive to what I call the proportionality problem and thereby

[71] For a fuller discussion of these points, see Bellamy, *Political Constitutionalism*, 203–5.

[72] Dahl, *Democracy and its Critics*, chs 15, 17, and 18.

[73] Alexander Hamilton, James Madison, and John Jay, *The Federalist* (Terence Ball ed., Cambridge: Cambridge University Press 2003), The Federalist No. 51, 252.

[74] Wootton, 'Liberty, Metaphor, and Mechanism', 19.

realizes aggregative equality. It is to the source and definition of this problem that I now turn.

5. SIMPLE MAJORITARIANISM AND THE PROPORTIONALITY PROBLEM

In this section, I shall argue that the criticisms standardly levelled against majority rule relate to a system of 'simple' majoritarianism. This system can lead to one or both instances of what I shall call the proportionality problem. The first instance arises when individuals are not represented in proportion to the stake they have in a given collective decision, the second when they are not represented in proportion to the number of voters supporting a given option. As I shall explain below, each of these instances involves a failure to satisfy the terms of the democratic contract as outlined earlier. The next section details how both instances of this problem can be addressed by more 'complex' models of majoritarianism that prove not only more genuinely majoritarian but also more consistent with political equality, as well as less likely to give rise to tyrannous rule. Here, I explain the distinction between simple and complex majoritarianism and note how the first is neither truly majoritarian nor egalitarian—not least when associated with the two instances of the proportionality problem.

5.1. Simple and Complex Majoritarianism

In making the distinction between 'simple' and 'complex' majoritarianism, I adopt the terminology, if not all of the reasoning and evaluation of their respective merits, of Steffen Ganghof.[75] Like Ganghof, I consider a basic concept of democracy to be majority rule. Consequently, democracy cannot be realized in counter-majoritarian systems, such as those grounded in consensus.[76] I also agree with him that different conceptions of majoritarian democracy are possible.[77] These reflect different institutional arrangements that cash out the relevant democratic principles in contrasting ways that can be compared on the basis of how far they realize these principles in different social circumstances. In other words, and I see this as his crucial argument for my purposes, the normative attractiveness of a democratic system relates not just to its instrumental and/or intrinsic qualities as a way of realizing political equality, but also to its processual qualities for those participating

[75] Ganghof, *Beyond Presidentialism*, 69–70.
[76] Ganghof, *Beyond Presidentialism*, 67.
[77] Ganghof, *Beyond Presidentialism*, ch. 4.

in it and the ways it functions in practice through various democratic institutions, such as electoral systems, parties, and parliamentary chambers.[78]

Simple majoritarianism proves inadequate for reasons related to this last point. Abstracting and idealizing for the moment from actual electoral systems, this conception forms part of a political system that seeks to present voters with a limited, ideally a binary, choice between parties, that compete against each other for the people's vote to win a majority. Within parliamentary systems, this electoral arrangement typically involves winning a majority (or, more likely, a plurality) in sufficient single-member constituencies of equivalent size so as to win a majority of seats in parliament.[79] As we shall see, such simple majoritarianism cannot meet the terms of the democratic contract.

Simple majoritarianism has seemed strongest in offering a clear form of 'adversarial equality'. For example, Ganghof regards this approach as being 'simple' in simplifying the cognitive demands on voters by presenting them with a straightforward choice.[80] He also believes it enhances the clarity of political responsibility, since the single party/presidential candidate attracting an electoral majority or plurality in a majority of constituencies will form the government, thereby making it easier for voters to hold politicians to account. As I shall detail below, I depart from Ganghof in considering these latter attributes to be less firmly associated with simple majority systems and more common features of complex majority systems than he—like many others—allows.

However, the core simplicity (and chief weakness) of this type of majoritarianism results from its underlying assumption that voters' preferences can be aligned along a single dimension—traditionally from left to right.[81] If true, then aggregative and deliberative equality would be satisfied. Competition along a single dimension can be regarded as likely to lead parties to converge on that set of policies with most appeal to the median voter,[82] which will generally prove to be the Condorcet winner—that is, the package of policies likely to beat all others under majority rule when placed in a pairwise comparison with alternatives.[83] However, this need to be responsive to the median voter—and, in the process, to respond equally to all voters and align with those policies with majority support—depends on the winning party having to gain the backing of near or over 50 per cent of the electorate to win a majority of seats in parliament (or to elect the president).[84] That necessity, though, can be undermined in various ways.

[78] Ganghof, *Beyond Presidentialism*, 53.

[79] In presidential and semi-presidential systems, it will also entail a similar electoral process to select the president.

[80] Ganghof, *Beyond Presidentialism*, 69.

[81] Weale, 'Three Types of Majority Rule', 67.

[82] M. D. McDonald, S. M. Mendes, and I. Budge, 'What Are Elections For? Conferring the Median Mandate' (2004) 34 *British Journal of Political Science* 1–26.

[83] Peter C. Ordeshook, *Game Theory and Political Theory* (Cambridge: Cambridge University Press 1986) 245–57.

[84] Weale, 'Three Types of Majority Rule', 66.

The two ways I wish to highlight here are arguably the most important, both of which involve an instance of the proportionality problem. The first arises from the possibility that simple majoritarianism leads to over centralization and a failure to accommodate local and regional differences. The second concerns simple majoritarianism's failure to adequately reflect the multidimensional character of contemporary politics. The first instance means that not all voters may have an equal stake in a collective decision. The second instance may result in their lacking an equal say. If both hold, then simple majoritarianism will fail to provide for either 'aggregative equality' for elections to Parliament or, as a result, 'deliberative equality' within the legislature. Both failures may lead to legislative or executive majority tyranny. The next section outlines each of these instances of the proportionality problem in turn, while the section that follows indicates how a complex form of majoritarianism can address them in ways that both satisfy the democratic contract and institute forms of checks and balances that can address the concerns over majority tyranny.

5.2. Two Instances of the Proportionality Problem

The first way simple majoritarianism proves problematic relates to the other major enduring cleavage of modern democratic systems (alongside the left–right divide): that between centre and periphery. This cleavage reflects, on the one hand, certain territorially based cultural and ethnic minorities within the polity, such as the French Québécois in Canada, and, on the other hand, various socio-economic policies that are most effectively, efficiently, and equitably decided at the local level. Both of these factors drive calls for the devolution of power from the centre to the periphery. Essentially, they reflect the presence of a number of distinct demoi within a polity, that involve a sub-group of citizens who have an equal stake in a subset of collective decisions that are distinct from those decisions that relate to the common interests of all citizens. This circumstance calls for a form of complex majoritarianism that accommodates the fact that the majority in each of these sub-units of the polity may be for a different set of policies. When the majority at the centre unduly interferes in the decisions of one of these peripheral majorities, it risks creating a proportionality problem whereby this simple central majority acts disproportionally by giving an equal say to those living in different parts of the polity who lack an equal stake in the decisions of another part.[85]

The second main way the underlying assumption of simple majoritarianism has been undermined relates to the fragmentation of political opinion so as to disrupt the assumption of a dominant left–right cleavage. This development has resulted

[85] Harry Brighouse and Marc Fleurbaey, 'Democracy and Proportionality' (2010) 18(2) *Journal of Political Philosophy* 137–75.

from changing social and cultural norms and values associated with broader economic, technological, and societal transformations. These changes raise issues in areas such as gender equality, religious belief, environmental protection, the nature of work, and individual autonomy and self-fulfilment that can often cut across traditional left–right divisions and divide those otherwise aligned in left–right terms.[86] They may even produce new allegiances and alliances that supplant the traditional left–right alignments, such as the GAL (Green, Alternative, Libertarian)–TAN (Traditional-Authoritarian-Nationalist) cleavage proposed by some political scientists.[87] As a result, the simple choice between two main parties of the left and right will struggle to encapsulate the range of available options.

The standard way to confront this latter problem in a manner consistent with simple majoritarianism is through substituting a plurality for a majority vote—that is, awarding the constituency to the candidate with the most votes in an electoral competition between three or more candidates. However, that can mean that the party winning the most constituencies can obtain a huge legislative majority without achieving a majority among the electorate, as political systems that employ this method, such as the UK or the United States, readily illustrate.[88] This possibility gives rise to the second proportionality problem. For example, at the 2024 UK General Election, Labour won 63 per cent of the parliamentary seats (411 out of a possible 650) with only 33.7 per cent of the popular vote on an electoral turnout of 59.9 per cent. While this result was the least proportional in British electoral history, a high degree of disproportionality between electoral and legislative majorities has been the norm rather than the exception in recent UK elections. For example, Mrs Thatcher's Conservative Party legislative majorities of 1979, 1983, and 1987 were achieved with between 42 and 44 per cent of the popular vote, while Tony Blair's Labour Party electoral victories of 1997, 2001, and 2005 achieved even greater legislative majorities with a popular vote of only 43, 40, and 35 per cent respectively.

As I noted in the discussion of 'levelling down', a wide disproportionality between electoral and legislative majorities raises concerns because it undermines political equality among voters—the legislative and, in parliamentary systems, government agenda will be responsive to electoral minorities rather than majorities.[89] When Lord Hailsham famously decried the tendency of the Westminster system to produce an 'elective dictatorship', therefore, the underlying problem was not the tyranny of a democratic majority but the tyranny of a minority elected by a plurality.

[86] Ronald Inglehart, *Cultural Evolution: People's Motivations Are Changing, and Reshaping the World* (Cambridge: Cambridge University Press 2018).

[87] R. Dalton, *Political Realignment: Economics, Culture, and Electoral Change* (Oxford: Oxford University Press 2018).

[88] Weale, 'Three Types of Majority Rule', 69.

[89] Weale, 'Three Types of Majority Rule', 70.

As with the proportionality problem created by the centre–periphery cleavage, so with that created by the multiplying of options, the answer lies with a system allowing for a more complex majority. The simple majoritarianism associated with a plurality system like that of the UK makes it difficult for third parties to emerge and challenge the established two main parties. Their vote will be spread too thinly to win a plurality—although their presence will mean that the victorious party becomes less likely to win an electoral majority. The exceptions are parties, such as the minority nationality parties, whose support is territorially concentrated—and, in fact, the success of third parties has tended to depend on their ability to appeal to local issues in a limited number of constituencies, as has traditionally been the case in the UK with the Liberal Democrats and more recently with the Greens. By and large, though, third parties will remain too small to have a significant influence on national politics. For example, the Scottish National Party (SNP) may have won 95 per cent of the Scottish seats in Westminster at the 2015 general election, but in a parliament of 650 MPs, fifty-six seats proved insufficient to ensure, for example, that the First Minister of Scotland was consulted on the terms governing Britain's exit from the European Union (EU) following the 2016 referendum, when 62 per cent of those voting in Scotland had voted to remain. By contrast, proportional representation allows for a much wider range of parties that can reflect the diversity of voter preferences and provide them with an equal weighting in the composition of the legislature and government and align them more closely to majority opinion among the electorate. True, territorially concentrated minority parties, such as the SNP, will remain minorities in national politics, but may well be able to exert greater influence as part of a coalition.

6. COMPLEX MAJORITARIANISM AND DEMOCRATIC CHECKS AND BALANCES

As we have seen, both proportionality problems are exacerbated by (indeed, they arise due to) simple majoritarianism. By contrast, a system of complex majoritarianism can address the first problem via the devolution of governmental power to local and regional authorities and the second by proportional representation systems and the formation of coalition governments. My claim will be that such systems sustain all three types of political equality required by the democratic contract and establish checks and balances that avoid (or at least decrease) the possibility of legislative and executive tyranny associated with simple majoritarianism. I shall argue that the democratic checks and balances created by these institutional arrangements can be regarded as both more legitimate and more effective than those associated with the separation of powers, earlier criticized in Section 4.

6.1. Equality of Stake and the Devolution of Power

Democracy offers a fair means for people to make collective decisions in ways that satisfy the condition of political equality given the limitations of human practical reasoning and the fact of pluralism, all of which give rise to reasonable disagreements. However, as I argued in Chapter 2, the legitimacy of granting individuals an equal say in these collective decisions depends on those involved forming a demos. As I observed there, citizens belong to a demos by virtue of being members of what Thomas Christiano calls a 'common world'.[90] Members of a common world are engaged in what John Rawls termed a scheme of social and political cooperation that implicates and supports all, or practically all, of their basic liberties and fundamental interests in multiple and comprehensive ways.[91] As such, involvement in a common world can be distinguished from membership of a partial association, such as a church, club, or economic enterprise, which engages only some of their members' interests, often to differing degrees.[92] By contrast, modern states broadly fit the common world criterion, providing a fairly encompassing legal and regulatory system that covers most social interactions, and a set of public services, including a system of health and education, welfare, and infrastructure—such as a transport system, all of which are supported either directly or indirectly through a state tax and financial system.[93] Democracy provides the means through which participants within such a common world can collectively shape its scope and functioning, and hence the mutual rights and obligations that membership entails. Two types of relations among its members make such democratic decision-making fair and possible. The first set of relations involves those given an equal say having an equal stake in this common world; the second that they share a public sphere whereby they can deliberate as to its extent and character in common. I shall discuss each in turn.

According to the stakeholder principle, all those with a roughly equal stake in the totality of decisions emanating from a given legal and political system, if not every one of them, should have an equal say in their making. The equal stakeholder criterion for involvement in the democratic process is less inclusive than the 'all affected principle' (AAP) and, while it overlaps with the 'all subjected principle' (ASP), is inherently as well as instrumentally linked to democracy. As Rainer Bauböck has observed,[94] the AAP and ASP look at democratic rights from a protective rather than a participatory perspective. They emphasize what Anna Stilz

[90] Christiano, *Constitution of Equality*, 78–83.

[91] John Rawls, *Just as Fairness: A Restatement* (Erin Kelly ed., Cambridge, MA: Belknap Press of Harvard University Press 2001) 5–6.

[92] Christiano, *Constitution of Equality*, 81.

[93] Christiano, *Constitution of Equality*, 80.

[94] Rainer Bauböck, 'Morphing the Demos into the Right Shape. Normative Principles for Enfranchising Resident Aliens and Expatriate Citizens' (2015) 22 *Democratization* 821–6.

calls the 'taker dimension' rather than the 'maker dimension' of political institutions.[95] By contrast, the stakeholder criterion emphasizes the maker dimension and the interest a people have in being authors of their common world. On this account, the claim to being a citizen of a given sovereign political community belongs to those who regard their freedom and rights as inherently linked to the collective self-government and flourishing of that polity over time.[96] This argument links citizenship rights to the performance of civic duties and a commitment to the political community and its members, including to future generations. On this view, inclusion in the citizenry or demos depends on participation in the production and shaping of the collective goods on which the rights of citizens depend and on performance of the obligations entailed by membership of a political community. That suggests that all permanent residents should be included in the citizenry, since they play a part in 'making' and sustaining the political community through abiding by and respecting its laws, being good neighbours and family members, working and paying taxes, and so forth.[97] By contrast, those who are only temporary 'takers', such as tourists briefly subject to the law of the country they are visiting, have a right to equal treatment under the law but not to an equal say in making that law.

The notion of an equal stake plays an important role in the justification for majority rule as being consistent with aggregative equality. On this account, if the basic liberties and fundamental interests of every individual in the polity are equally at stake in a collective decision and each individual is the best judge of his or her interests, then, in fairness, all these individuals are entitled to play an equal part in making the decision to ensure their interests are equally considered.[98] Therefore, a democratic system based on one person one vote assumes that all involved have a roughly equal stake in the overall package of decisions, if not in each and every one. If that was not the case, and a significant group had less of a stake in the generality of collective decisions than most others, an equal vote might lead to the underfunding of public services or the rejection of public regulations on which many people's well-being depends. Consequently, a democratic case exists for either so shaping the demos that all those involved do have a roughly equal stake, or in giving individuals a vote proportional to their stake, and thereby treating them fairly and with equal respect, if not literally equally in the sense of exactly the same.[99]

Demos-shaping to create an equal stake among citizens is fairly common within most democracies. For example, most states devolve certain public services to local

[95] Stilz, *Territorial Sovereignty*, 93–4.

[96] Bauböck, 'Morphing the Demos', 825.

[97] See A. Sangiovanni, 'Solidarity in the European Union' (2013) 33(2) *Oxford Journal of Legal Studies* 222.

[98] Christiano, *Constitution of Equality*, 81.

[99] Brighouse and Fleurbaey, 'Democracy and Proportionality'.

communities. States are generally heterogeneous: urban areas differ from rural areas, some regions have an ageing population and others a higher proportion of children and young people, and so on. The central state may have certain regulations that can be generally regarded as being in the equal interest of all, as when the positive and negative externalities of certain public goods can only be fully internalized at the state level. But there will be a reasonable case for allowing different regions and localities to exercise a degree of self-government over a number of issues. Demographic and socio-economic differences can make the spending priorities of one region legitimately different to another, at least on those matters that impact mainly local residents. A democratic system that allowed, say, urban areas to determine all the policies of rural areas (or vice versa) could be regarded as failing to take account of the unequal stakes citizens had in the relevant collective decisions, so that a disproportionate stake was given to some citizens.

The second set of a relations forming a demos enter here. A democratic system of one person one vote offers a formally impartial system that endeavours to integrate our multifarious points of view and so promote policies that reflect our various concerns and circumstances. Nevertheless, to do so, the process must incorporate incentives for us—or, more realistically, the decision-makers we elect—to go beyond a partial perspective and 'hear the other side' in ways that move policy-making towards an impartial consideration of what is in the public interest rather than simply responding to the private interests of various particular groups. In other words, democracy must incorporate deliberative as well as aggregative equality. To achieve this result, the process must involve a more substantive notion of impartiality, whereby policy-makers address the commonly avowable interests of citizens by appealing to reasons that are widely shared as suitable criteria for collective decision-making and justifying decisions in terms of their contribution to the common good.[100] As we saw above, for such appeals to be possible entails citizens having equal stakes in a common world. However, as I noted in Chapter 2, it also involves citizens sharing a sense of what count as public reasons, and the ability to reason in public—notions typically associated with the presence of a shared public sphere, involving a common language and media. Democratic systems that lack these public qualities are likely to allow politicians to play different groups off against each other. It also gives rise to the danger of consistent minorities, in which particular groups with distinctive cultural or other priorities are persistently excluded from collective decisions. We can see this danger as another instance of the proportionality problem.

Many states contain cultural and national minorities and grant them self-governing rights over certain issues to address this problem.[101] This solution

[100] David Miller, 'Democracy's Domain' (2009) 37 *Philosophy and Public Affairs* 201–28.

[101] Will Kymlicka, *Multicultural Citizenship: A Liberal Theory of Minority Rights* (Oxford: Oxford University Press 1995) 11–13.

provides another instance of demos-shaping and likewise involves the devolution of particular competences to certain territorially concentrated cultural or other minorities, as in Scotland or Catalonia. It overlaps with and—given that these territorial units can often be as large as (or even larger than) many states—usually includes devolution to different local authorities to ensure an equal stake. However, it also involves crafting the polity in ways that ensure that those involved in collective decision-making have an equal stake in a common world and can debate its extent and character in common.

For a democratic system to operate in an equitable and impartial manner within a heterogeneous polity requires a degree of institutional complexity with regard to different territorial levels of government and among different socio-economic and cultural groups. The result is to create a system of complex majoritarianism involving a number of interacting and overlapping demoi. Such a complex system both enhances aggregative and deliberative equality, as we have seen, while dispersing power in a way that supports adversarial equality and can potentially check executive and legislative tyranny. As such, it serves both the positive and negative aspects of constitutionalism noted in the introduction to this chapter.

Positively, it can enhance democracy by increasing the forums available to citizens to lobby and exert influence, with their vote counting for more at the smaller subnational levels. These levels are also more accessible to them and deal with day-to-day issues, such as rubbish collection, that pose fewer cognitive demands than many national policies and allow for a more direct assessment.[102] Negatively, multiple subnational levels of government can create checks and balances between both each other and between centre and periphery that can reduce the potential for domination at either level. For example, these subnational authorities can offer competing jurisdictions between which individuals and business can move—giving people the option, say, between liberal social policies, higher taxes yet greater investment in infrastructure and education, on the one side, and lower taxes, less investment, but tougher law and order policies, on the other.[103] Multiple self-governing jurisdictions also provide opportunities for experimentation and mutual learning as to the best way to tackle similar problems.

Checks and balance can also operate between centre and periphery in that parties that are in the opposition at the national level can be the governing party within a subnational authority.[104] On the one hand, such local administrations potentially provide representation that is more aligned to the majority preferences of their residents than at the national level and can offer an alternative to certain policies. As I note in Chapter 8, the most effective resistance to populist regimes

[102] Daniel Weinstock, 'Towards a Normative Theory of Federalism' (2001) 53 *International Social Science Journal* 76–7.

[103] Jacob T. Levy, 'Federalism, Liberalism and the Separation of Loyalties' (2007) 101(3) *American Political Science Review* 460–1.

[104] Weinstock, 'Towards a Normative Theory of Federalism', 76.

has often issued from opposition administrations in metropolitan areas. On the other hand, there are national policies in which all citizens have an equal stake that can legitimately constrain those pursued locally and can reflect the different preferences of a national majority. Meanwhile, within multinational societies the granting of self-government rights to territorially concentrated ethnic and cultural minorities can mitigate the risk of their becoming permanent minorities within the polity, whose distinctive preferences for certain language or religious policies are consistently neglected. Instead, it allows them to form a majority on at least certain issues that relate to a subset of their fundamental interests. Of course, devolution per se may not prevent domination—it may even permit it should it allow the majority group within the devolved unit to persecute in its turn a given minority, as was the case in Northern Ireland prior to the Good Friday Agreement of 1998, for example. For this reason, it is important to see the relationship between centre and periphery as involving mutual checks.

Although these arguments tend to be associated with the federalism literature,[105] such a system may or may not entail a fully-fledged federal structure. After all, the UK has no formal federal institutions, yet involves both functional and minority national self-governing territorial units possessing significant competences and democratic legitimacy. These subnational units include the Greater London and Greater Manchester Combined Authorities, both of which have directly elected mayors and (in London's case) a directly elected Assembly, and encompass thirty-two and ten metropolitan boroughs respectively, as well as the devolved administrations and directly elected parliaments of Scotland, Wales, and Northern Ireland, all of which also include various levels of local government. Indeed, as Jacob Levy has pointed out, many of the advantages standardly associated with federalism, such as Tiebout sorting and competitive federalism, can only function at levels below the standard federal unit.[106] Federal units such as California or Texas are larger than many countries and not easy for persons and companies to exit from—a difficulty increased in many multinational states in which moving to another federal unit may involve a change of language.

Standardly, federal systems also give subnational units a national voice in a second chamber. Arguably, that can help ensure national policies do not unduly encroach on their prerogatives and competences and are informed by local differences. However, such a chamber is only likely to be an effective check and balance if the party affiliations of its members and majority differ from that of the first chamber. Federal representation may also not serve other important functions commonly associated with a second chamber, such as the detailed scrutiny

[105] e.g. a summary of most of the points made above can be found in Andreas Follesdal, 'Federalism', *The Stanford Encyclopedia of Philosophy* (Edward N. Zalta and Uri Nodelman eds, Winter 2022 edn) <https://plato.stanford.edu/archives/win2022/entries/federalism/> Section 3.2 Reasons for preferring federal orders over a unitary state.

[106] Levy, 'Federalism, Liberalism and the Separation of Loyalties', 461–2.

of legislation for its coherence, legality, justifiability, and likely effectiveness. As I argue below, a more effective check may come from the first chamber reflecting a complex rather than a simple majority as a result of being elected via proportional representation. Such arrangements also provide a mechanism to protect the political interests of territorially dispersed minorities.

While legal constitutions generally include federal arrangements where they exist, they are largely silent with regard to local government. That silence can make such authorities vulnerable to encroachment from the centre. In his 2009 book exploring the British Constitution, Tony King traced the gradual disempowerment of local authorities by the Thatcher administrations to a point where he doubted they could still be deemed 'governments' in any meaningful sense, given that their funding and tasks were largely determined by the centre.[107] However, that cannot be said today of the devolved administrations of Scotland, Wales, and Northern Ireland, while in the intervening period since King's book was published, Metropolitan Authorities have also gained substantial powers. So, local authority competences can wax as well as wane. Much depends on how far the centre has to take the interests of the periphery into account. As I hinted above, and explore below, that may come from the legislature and government themselves reflecting a complex majority.

6.2. An Equal Say, Proportional Representation, and Compromise

As we have seen, a key component of the case for democracy rests on its giving those with an equal stake in a collective decision an equal say in its making. Simple majoritarianism involving a plurality electoral system can be regarded as meeting this standard in a formal sense by giving all voters an equal vote in regular elections. However, this formal account of political equality can be regarded as deficient in two respects.[108] First, it reduces the main electoral choices to two main parties (other parties may exist, but they tend to get squeezed out); and second, it restricts an equal say to an equal chance to cast a single vote. The first deficiency means that the available options fail to reflect the distribution of preferences among the electorate—as such, it fails to provide adequately for aggregative equality. The second proves compatible with huge disparities between the electoral and the legislative majority, thereby undermining the deliberative equality of the electorate's views when it comes to policy-making. Taken together, both undermine adversarial equality and allow governments to pursue policies and pass legislation that reflect the views and interests of a minority of those subject to them.

[107] Anthony King, *The British Constitution* (Oxford: Oxford University Press 2009) ch. 7.

[108] I have adopted and adapted the distinction between 'formal' and 'substantive' accounts of political equality within the democratic process found in Christiano, *The Rule of the Many*, 208–13.

To avoid these deficiencies requires a more substantive account of political equality that factors in both the representativeness of the options offered relative to what voters consider to be salient issues, and the degree to which the actions and decisions of the executive and the legislature align with the preferences of a majority of the electorate. The first consideration is needed to give voters an equal chance of supporting a party that reflects their views and interests, the second to secure the equal influence of voters over the measures and laws that get implemented. A system of PR to select the legislature addresses the first and to some extent the second of these points.[109] On the one hand, it lowers the threshold for electorally significant new parties to emerge that cater to the concerns and opinions of territorially dispersed minorities—and particularly those positions that cannot be neatly plotted on the left–right spectrum characteristic of the two traditional centre parties. On the other hand, PR electoral systems produce a legislature that is roughly proportional to the electoral choices made by voters. Not all systems are exactly proportional—minimal thresholds or the division into single or even multimember constituencies can all produce distortions in this regard—but all perform much better than the simple majority plurality system.

I discussed earlier the lottocratic use of stratified sampling to produce a legislature that operates more as a mirror of the electorate as a whole and ensures that all sections of society gain a legislative voice equal to their numerical size. There are also other mechanisms to ensure certain minorities get represented, such as the creation of majority–minority electoral districts in the United States. The difficulty with these devices, however, lies in the supposedly salient social cleavages—such as ethnicity, religion, language, level of education, and so on—being selected by others. Yet, as I noted with regard to similar schemes for sortition, these features may not be of political significance for many citizens themselves, who give greater weight to different issues. By contrast, an electoral system of proportional representation allows citizens themselves to determine which concerns they wish to inform political decision-making. As Christiano puts it, PR encapsulates a 'principle of voluntary proportionality',[110] whereby the legislature reflects the ideals and interests of citizens that they themselves have selected as politically salient in proportion to the number choosing them.

As such, PR issues in a doubly complex majority that preserves aggregative equality among citizens at the electoral stage and provides the basis for such equality at the legislative stage.[111] At the electoral stage, each citizen not only has a vote with equal numerical weight but also a roughly equal numerical influence on the range of party options available for them to vote for. At the legislative stage, the composition of the legislature reflects the numbers of voters supporting each of

[109] Weale, 'Three Types of Majority Rule', 70–1.
[110] Christiano, *Rule of the Many*, 219–24.
[111] McGann, *Logic of Democracy*, 41–3, 55–9.

those options. In a parliamentary system, the party(ies) commanding the legislative majority form(s) the government. Under PR, however, no single party is likely to command a majority on its own. Instead, either two or more different parties will need to form a coalition government with a stable majority for a shared programme, or one or occasionally more parties will need to operate as a minority government able to recruit support from a variable set of parties for different elements of their legislative programme. I shall argue below that multiparty competition at the electoral stage and the necessity for collaboration at the legislative and governmental stages provide democratic forms of checks and balances that both support adversarial and deliberative equality and offer protection to minorities. Before doing so, however, I want to address certain standard objections to PR.

As we have seen, a key supposed advantage of PR lies in its allowing for complex majorities involving more than two alternatives. However, all such systems are open to the social choice critique raised by Kenneth Arrow's Impossibility Theorem, whereby no aggregation rule in such circumstances can produce a determinate outcome while satisfying five seemingly reasonable normative conditions: Pareto optimality, non-dictatorship, independence of irrelevant alternatives, unlimited domain, and transitivity of preference orderings.[112] The best-known instance of the problem is that of majority cycles.[113] This possibility has led some theorists, notably William H. Riker, to argue that democratic decision-making is incoherent and arbitrary, with its inherent instability only overcome through elite manipulation, such as log-rolling and agenda-setting.[114] While Riker's claims have been questioned empirically as being less likely than he assumed,[115] the logical possibility of such outcomes remains. However, it is unclear that this finding need bother democratic theorists. The social choice critique arises from the assumption that the prime purpose of democracy is to aggregate preferences so as to maximize social utility. The critique derives from the dilemmas posed for this goal by any intransitivity of preference orderings. Yet, that assumes there is an entity called society with preferences of its own. By contrast, the argument here has been that the justification for, and legitimacy of, democracy rests on its fairness to individuals

[112] K. J. Arrow, *Social Choice and Individual Values* (2nd edn, New Haven, CT: Yale University Press 1963).

[113] The so-called Condorcet method for aggregating preferences involves a pairwise comparison of the preference rankings of the various options by each of the parties. However, that can produce a cycle, as in the example from Weale, *Democracy*, 137–9 given below, where w beats x, which in turn beats y, which in turn beats z, which then beats w.

Party A (40%): w x y z
Party B (20%): x z w y
Party C (20%): y z w x
Party D (20%): z x y w

[114] W. H. Riker, *Liberalism Against Populism: A Confrontation Between the Theory of Democracy and the Theory of Social Choice* (San Francisco, CA: Freeman and Co. 1982) 137, 239. For a careful outline of Riker's main arguments, see Gerry Mackie, *Democracy Defended* (Cambridge: Cambridge University Press 2003) 5–9 and ch. 2.

[115] Mackie, *Democracy Defended*, 18–19 and ch. 3.

through the equal distribution of decision-making power. It is the commitment to this goal that provides the backdrop to any aggregation, focusing concern on having equitable procedures for agenda-setting, deal-making, and debate (and thereby addressing Riker's objections regarding elite manipulation). The Arrovian problems per se are irrelevant from this perspective.[116] To the extent Condorcet cycles arise, then in candidate elections this result can be overcome by selecting the person who loses by the smallest margin(s) in one or more pairwise comparisons.

A more challenging objection relates to whether the tendency for PR systems to issue in coalition governments weakens the processes of democratic authorization and accountability so that, contrary to what I claimed above, equal votes will not translate into equal influence over the legislature and executive. The claim here is that because parties rarely obtain a majority under PR, voters can never know precisely what set of government policies they are authorizing or who to hold to account for the success or failures of any administration. Instead, parties and their representatives are given free rein to negotiate among themselves and will inevitably compromise their declared electoral programmes to enter government, betraying certain policy commitments in the process. Moreover, once in office, they will be able to claim any successes for themselves and blame all failures on their coalition partners.[117] As I noted above, Steffen Ganghof follows these critics in seeing simple majoritarianism as performing better in this respect.[118] However, this criticism suffers from a number of flaws.[119] For a start, even under simple majority systems, involving first past the post and single-member constituencies, increased support for third parties has occasioned the need for coalitions, as was the case in the UK in 2010. Second, parties do not act as freely as these critics suggest. In systems where coalitions are the norm, they tend to indicate in advance their preferred coalition partners and even more commonly make clear those potential partners they would find unacceptable. By and large, they will align themselves with those parties they find most ideologically congenial. Finally, coalition agreements are often put to the respective party memberships to accept or reject, and involve policy commitments that can be clearly traced to one or more of the coalition partners, for which they can be held responsible. Likewise, parties that concede a core electoral commitment are likely to be punished at the subsequent election.

[116] Elizabeth Anderson, 'Critical Notice of Amartya Sen, "Rationality and Freedom"' (2005) 114(2) *The Philosophical Review* 261–2, defending James Buchanan, 'Social Choice, Democracy and Free Markets' (1954) 62 *Journal of Political Economy* 114–23.

[117] For these criticisms see Anthony Downs, *An Economic Theory of Democracy* (New York: Harper and Row 1957) 156 and Maurice Duvenger, 'Which Is the Best Electoral System?' in Bernard Grofman and Arend Lijphart (eds), *Choosing an Electoral System* (New York: Praeger 1984) 33.

[118] Ganghof, *Beyond Presidentialism and Parliamentarism*, 70. See too Frances M. Rosenbluth and Ian Shapiro, *Responsible Parties: Saving Democracy from Itself* (New Haven, CT: Yale University Press 2018) 236.

[119] In what follows, I draw on Christiano, *Rule of the Many*, 232–8.

A related criticism points in the opposite direction. According to this critique, the notion of giving voters equal influence over the legislative and governmental agenda turns politicians into delegates and thereby undercuts their ability to deliberate or to compromise so as to achieve policies that are collectively agreeable and conducive to the common interest. Christiano has suggested that while representatives should be considered delegates as to aims, they can be regarded as trustees with regard to means, with deliberation limited to the latter.[120] However, as I remarked earlier, this distinction is too neat—parties might share a common desire for economic growth, for example, but differ considerably as to whether that is best achieved via state investment in public services and infrastructure or tax cuts for wealthy potential investors and entrepreneurs. Moreover, compromise will inevitably involve some mutual give and take with regard to both ends and means.

What connects representatives to their electorate in such negotiations will be a shared ideological vision rather than a given set of policy commitments. One can see that vision as being more fundamental, since it provides the principles and social and natural scientific reasoning that lies behind the advocacy of particular policies. Such a vision provides the basis for what Jane Mansbridge terms 'gyroscopic' representation,[121] whereby politicians are selected on the basis of possessing a certain moral compass that guides how they deliberate and act. That compass derives from a vision they share with their voters and, to the extent they remain faithful to it, they can be regarded as acting as they have been authorized to do. Such authorization is both more complete and more flexible than having an imperative mandate to enact certain policies. It is more complete in that it covers the unanticipated events and issues that governments inevitably face and for which there will be no already existing policy mandate. It is more flexible in allowing politicians to debate and negotiate with others in the spirit of the attitudes and views of those they represent, thereby giving them equal influence over collective decision-making in the legislature.

Of course, flexibility has its limits and can prove contentious. Indeed, some theorists have even suggested that a willingness to compromise necessarily involves a degree of hypocrisy from politicians.[122] Yet that goes too far and suggests that political integrity requires politicians to be inflexible dogmatists. Ideologies are rarely so closed that they cannot accommodate adaptations to changing circumstances.

[120] Christiano, *Rule of the Many*, 215–19.

[121] Jane Mansbridge, 'Rethinking Representation' (2003) 97 *American Political Science Review* 520–2. For the application of this account to compromise, see Richard Bellamy, 'Democracy, Compromise and the Representation Paradox: On Coalition Government and Political Integrity' (2012) 47(3) *Government and Opposition* 441–65.

[122] Judith Shklar, *Ordinary Vices* (Cambridge, MA: Harvard University Press 1984) 77; D. Tillyris, 'The Virtue of Vice: A Defense of Hypocrisy in Democratic Politics' (2016) 22(1) *Contemporary Politics* 12–15. For a critique, see Richard Bellamy and Sandra Kröger, 'Truthfulness, Pluralism and the Ethics of Democratic Representation' (2024) 27(3) *British Journal of Politics and International Relations* 1023–43.

Moreover, within systems in which coalitions and compromise are the norm, parties desiring a chance of holding office, or passing a measure they hold dear, will need to anticipate with whom and on what terms they would be willing to collaborate. As such, they will need to have a schedule of preferences and, as I noted, will tend to ally with those closest to them ideologically. Most importantly, as I also remarked, parties tend to rule out certain alliances as incompatible with their guiding values. Meanwhile, politicians will also be aware that if they stray too far from their electoral commitments, they risk being held to account and sanctioned come the next election.[123]

The ability of voters to influence both elections and legislatures is facilitated by parties rather than individuals being the key actors in democratic political processes.[124] For a start, parties reduce the informational and coordinational demands on voters. Without parties, voters will need to gather information on all the available individual candidates and work out how they might align with each other. Personal information about each of the candidates is also likely to prove more important. For example, some candidates may be more consistent in their views or more apt to change than others, some more or less competent on certain topics, some possess better negotiating skills than others, or be better at debating, and so on. Parties simplify the options voters need to choose from and impose a certain discipline on their candidates. As a result, voters do not need to research each and every candidate. They can take a cue from party affiliation as to whether or not a candidate chimes with their policy preferences and ideological convictions. Parties will also tend to have members with different skills and expertise, making them more apt to deliver on the range of issues supported by their electorate. Even in multiparty systems, parties will themselves be mini coalitions of like-minded politicians, and can coordinate alignments with compatible groups. Finally, voters can be more confident in a party's identity remaining consistent over time than they may be in the consistency of individual unaffiliated candidates. It will be harder for parties, and consequently their individual candidates, to change policies, values, or affiliates on a whim or for purely self-interested reasons. In sum, while the cognitive and coordinative demands on voters of a complex majoritarian PR system are greater than under a simple majoritarian plurality system, parties simplify some of this complexity and render it manageable for voters.

A multiparty system that represents the multidimensional political landscape in the manner of PR not only provides better representation of the preferences of voters, but also a more effective and equitable democratic system of checks and balances that ensures different voices are included and equally weighed in collective

[123] E. Beerbohm, 'The Ethics of Electioneering' (2016) 24(4) *Journal of Political Philosophy* 393.

[124] Christiano, *Rule of the Many*, 222–3; Russell Muirhead and Nancy Rosenblum, 'Political Liberalism vs. "the Great Game of Politics": The Politics of Political Liberalism' (2006) 4(1) *Perspectives on Politics* 102–3; Robert Goodin 'The Place of Parties', *Innovating Democracies:Democratic Theory and Practice After the Deliberative Turn* (Oxford: Oxford University Press 2008) ch. 10, 204–223.

decision-making. At the electoral stage, having more parties increases the degree of political competition. The testamentary and promissory claims made by candidates are likely to be subject to enhanced scrutiny and contestation from multiple perspectives. Claims that involve faulty reasoning or lack a plausible evidentiary basis are more likely to get called out as a result—though, of course, one cannot count on that actually happening any more than one can count on the defence or prosecution in an adversarial legal system to adequately challenge each other's claims.

It might be assumed that if PR is the right electoral voting system it should also be the most appropriate system for voting in the legislature. However, as Weale has shown, here it makes sense for collective parliamentary decisions to be made by majority rule. For, if PR preserves equality among voters when electing parties, majority rule in the legislature preserves equality among those parties.[125] As Weale observes, the combined consequences of issue-by-issue majority voting coincides with the Condorcet-winner,[126] as this procedure involves finding those alternatives that command majority support.[127] He observes how the Condorcet-winner 'both captures the idea of a majority converging around a compromise solution where there are divergent ideal preferences and it can be construed as the outcome of a procedure by which members of a political community take issues one by one'.[128] True, as we saw, cycles may emerge. However, Weale argues that so long as these are discrete, so that voter preferences on one issue do not depend on the outcome of a vote on another, then sequential voting is acceptable as a way of breaking the cycle.[129]

Weale favours a system of minority government, as in Denmark, where the governing party will need to build a different coalition for each issue, so that each and every piece of legislation can claim the support of a complex, Condorcet majority.[130] It might be objected that such governments tend to be more unstable and short-lived than coalition governments with a shared programme commanding majority support. However, the difference between forming a coalition and having a minority government may not be that great. After all, when parties negotiate a governing coalition they likewise will need to consider each individual part of their programme and weigh up what compromises will be necessary to win a sequence of majority votes.

Either way, one can regard this need to compromise around the true majority as involving a form of checks and balances at both the electoral and the legislative stages that foster adversarial and deliberative equality. Party competition, on

125 Weale, *Democratic Justice*, 172.
126 Technically known as 'the issue-median'.
127 Weale, *Democracy*, 135–6.
128 Weale, *Democracy*, 137.
129 Weale, *Democracy*, 146–7.
130 Weale, Three Types of Majority Rule', 72–4.

the one side, and the need to negotiate governing or legislative coalitions, on the other, will tend to steer parties away from ideological extremes with only minority support. The tendency of competing parties to converge on the median voter in systems of complex majoritarianism protects minorities. Because electoral and legislative majorities are built on electoral coalitions of minorities and are prone to cycling, a governing majority has an incentive not to rely on a minimal winning coalition. Instead, they will be best advised to build a broad-based programme that overlaps with elements of their main opponents. As a result, any given minority—especially one representing a cross-cutting cleavage—is likely not to be excluded from a majority coalition keen to retain its hold on power. By contrast, counter-majoritarian blocks on majority rule tend to favour concentrated over dispersed minorities, allowing extremes to exercise vetoes.[131] These dynamics have operated even in a simple majoritarian system, such as that of the UK, where, for example, legislation on equal opportunities with regard to issues of gender, race, and disability was passed with cross-party support from the mid-1960s onwards.[132]

Meanwhile, competition and coalition can constrain both executive and legislative tyranny. Even in the event of a Grand Coalition, encompassing the main centre parties, such has regularly occurred in Germany in recent years, there will always be an opposition capable of calling out the errors of the government and presenting alternatives. Meanwhile, complex majorities necessarily involve building coalitions of minorities that encourage a degree of inclusiveness and respect for minority rights and perspectives. It also means that, to some degree, all policies will be subject to potential opposition and hence require deliberation.

Ronald Dworkin has contended that 'the majoritarian process encourages compromises that may subordinate important issues of principle'.[133] He suggests this marks a major difference with the more principled approach typical of a supreme or constitutional court. Although he does not elaborate on this point in the cited text, elsewhere he has specified his objection to be to what he calls 'checkerboard compromises'.[134] His worry is that in a legislature in which representatives are divided on a contentious issue, then they might be tempted to adopt a policy that combines their preferences in an inconsistent and unprincipled way. His example is an abortion policy adopted by a legislature in which a third of the representatives would criminalize abortion and two-thirds would allow it. He

[131] A. J. McGann, 'The Tyranny of the Supermajority: How Majority Rule Protects Minorities' (2004) 16 *Journal of Theoretical Politics* 56, 71.

[132] e.g. in the UK, the Race Relations Act 1965, Sex Discrimination Act 1975, Disability Discrimination Act 1995, Civil Partnership Act 2004, and Marriage (Same Sex Couples) Act 2013 all arose as government initiatives rather than in response to litigation before domestic or international human rights courts. The (Abolition of Death Penalty) Act 1965 and the Abortion Act 1967, legalizing abortion, also both emerged from private members bills and were passed on a free vote.

[133] Ronald Dworkin, *Freedom's Law: The Moral Reading of the American Constitution* (Cambridge, MA: Harvard University Press 1996) 30.

[134] Ronald Dworkin, *Law's Empire* (Cambridge, MA: Harvard University Press 1986) 178–86.

conjectures they might resolve their disagreements via a law that forbids women born between January and April to have abortions but permits those born between May and December to do so. He contends that such a result might be deemed politically fair—it respects political equality and reflects the balance of opinion in the country—but leads to a law that lacks integrity by failing to cohere around a 'single' moral conception grounded in a community's shared principles with regard to which all are to be treated equally.[135]

There are a number of problems with Dworkin's argument. First, as we have seen, the very need for a political process to decide such matters arises from there being no agreed moral view on many core matters. Second, the objectionable nature of his fictitious example lies in its arbitrary unfairness to those born in the wrong months.[136] Imagine, though, that this was a matter that was devolved to a local jurisdiction, a third of which criminalized abortion while two-thirds did not, with federal law allowing women to move freely and easily from the former to the latter for the purpose of having an abortion. That would be a checkerboard solution of sorts, but one that would arguably be unobjectionable from Dworkin's point of view since legislation in each locality would respect the dominant moral view in that jurisdiction. Or say the legislature agreed on a policy that limited a woman to three abortions? This agreement would be a fair political compromise and arguably likewise a checkerboard solution but nonetheless one that was equal for all.[137]

Dworkin's criticism implies that constitutional courts never compromise. However, since they too generally decide by either a majority or consensus, judges also may need to compromise to reach a decision—most generally in one of two ways, both of which are arguably less principled than those typical of legislatures. On the one hand, they may do so by a process of trimming—seeking what Cass Sunstein calls 'incompletely theorised agreements'.[138] However, that can entail leaving to one side the principled issues that may divide them. On the other hand, they may seek a trade-off whereby a group of judges will demur to those judges who care most about issue y, which they care less about—even though they have opposed views, so long as they get their way on issue x, about which they care much more.[139] Both these cases involve making 'shallow' compromises, that avoid confronting the matter of principle—on which judges, like political representatives,

[135] Dworkin, *Law's Empire*, 179, 182, 184.

[136] Silas Wasserstrom, 'The Empire's New Clothes' (1986) 75(1) *Georgetown Law Journal* 251–2.

[137] I take this example from Wasserstrom, 'The Empire's New Clothes', 252.

[138] Cass Sunstein, *Legal Reasoning and Political Conflict* (Oxford: Oxford University Press 1996) ch. 2. What I call compromise as 'trimming' involves, for example, avoiding the principled issues that divide us politically and seeking to come to an agreement on a narrow point of law, such as a legal precedent we may accept for divergent reasons that all parties leave to one side. See Bellamy, *Liberalism and Pluralism*, 98–100.

[139] Compromise as 'trading' typically involves 'splitting the difference'—as in haggling over the price of a car. See Bellamy, *Liberalism and Pluralism*, 96–8.

may be apt to differ. In politics, though, such shallow compromises can be much harder to arrange—they involve far more people and issues, with the ability of politicians to make purely pragmatic trade-offs being constrained by party discipline and voter scrutiny. As a result, coalition partners will be drawn towards 'deep' compromises, involving a more principled willingness to 'hear the other side' and to engage positively with the views and interests of others.[140] One can see this positive, principled, stance towards compromise, born out of the acceptance of the fact pluralism, as the flip side to the common negative, but equally principled, stance, mentioned above, whereby the main centre and other parties, as in Germany and France, rule out collaboration with the far right on the grounds that their views are at odds with the principle of political equality that undergirds democracy.

Steffen Ganghof has suggested that the best mechanism for avoiding not only executive tyranny in particular but also legislative tyranny is by combining simple and complex majoritarianism within a system of semi-parliamentarism.[141] He argues that the lower chamber should be elected according to the former model and be able to pass a vote of no confidence that could remove an executive or government, while legislation should require the assent of a second chamber representing a complex majority produced through PR.[142] However, I have questioned whether a plurality system necessarily performs better than PR as a means for holding executives to account. Moreover, a second chamber might offer a better additional check through representing local and regional government, thereby reinforcing their voice at the centre. Meanwhile, the scrutiny function often associated with a second chamber could be strengthened through giving greater weight to parliamentary select committees possessing a cross-party and cross-chamber membership, that act as an alternative career path for more independent-minded MPs than a ministerial career, and allow them to develop expertise in an area of where they have an especial interest.[143] Nevertheless, as I noted at the start of this chapter, there is no uniquely best democratic system for realizing democratic ideals. Democratic institutions will always need to be tailored to local circumstances. Ganghoff's scheme could well appeal in the UK by keeping a plurality system (consisting of single member constituencies and first-past-the-post) for the House of Commons while allowing PR for an elected House of Lords, and would certainly be an improvement on the present arrangement.

Of course, like all human institutions, democratic systems—no matter how well designed—may fail and extremists come to power. Yet, as I discuss in Chapter 8, the same applies to entrenched legal constitutional systems, which

[140] For the shallow–deep compromise distinction and the importance of the latter in political negotiations, see Bellamy, 'Democracy, Compromise and the Representation Paradox', 448–55.

[141] Ganghof, *Beyond Presidentialism*, 36–7, 87.

[142] Ganghof, *Beyond Presidentialism*, 88–91.

[143] See Meghan Benton and Meg Russell, 'Assessing the Impact of Parliamentary Oversight Committees: The Select Committees in the British House of Commons' (2013) 66(4) *Parliamentary Affairs* 772–97.

populists have readily employed to entrench their position against democratic change. As Chapter 2 contended, and Chapter 6 develops further, politics comes first, with the functioning of the legal system being only as good as that of the political system.

7. CONCLUSION

A system of checks and balances based on complex majoritarianism supports the democratic account of rights and the rule of law outlined in Chapters 1 and 2. In the case of rights, laws become more equitable and attentive to rights the more pluralistic a society becomes, so that rulers have to engage with a broad range of roughly equal groups all possessing a degree of political leverage.[144] It is no accident that the most progressive periods of social reform in modern times have coincided with mass mobilization for war, when rulers had to convince citizens of the value of fighting for their country. In many countries, war also stimulated the extension of the franchise to workers and especially to women, who now became an acknowledged part of the domestic labour force. More generally, citizens are more likely to submit to an authority in which they regard themselves as having a part—however small that may be.

Likewise, with regard to the rule of law. Governments are more likely to accept the need to make their rule both predictable and equitable—the two qualities of law-like rule—when it depends on the voluntary compliance of diverse groups of their citizens.[145] As we saw in Chapter 2, people want predictability in the political rules so that they can act autonomously and plan ahead. However, politicians also value this quality because it allows them to govern increasingly complex societies in an efficient and regular manner. They cannot anticipate every situation and rule effectively using ad hoc measures. They too need a stable legal framework that can regulate the majority of social interactions. Apart from anything else, it means they can delegate the vast majority of mundane, everyday, decisions to various officials—including an independent judiciary—so that they can focus on the issues that interest them or are of most salience for people. Most importantly, as the competition for power becomes institutionalized, rulers acquire an interest in the rules of the political game being similarly predictable and stable.

Of course, citizens will never have absolutely equal influence over rulers, despite acquiring equal votes. The better organized and financed will always do better than the poor and disorganized, though the desire to avoid widespread popular unrest should never be discounted. Changes in agendas, problems, and resources

[144] S. Holmes, 'Lineages of the Rule of Law' in J. M. Maravall and A. Przeworski (eds), *Democracy and the Rule of Law* (Cambridge: Cambridge University Press 2003) 49.

[145] Holmes, 'Lineages of the Rule of Law', 30.

will favour different groups and alter the political balance between the socially and economically strong and weak. The key, though, must always be to multiply the groups with which power holders have to engage, forcing them to 'hear' and 'harken to' as many sides as possible. I have suggested that forms of complex majority offer a way of achieving such a mix in ways that enhance aggregative, adversarial, and deliberative equality in line with the terms of a democratic contract. As we have seen, these forms of equality are mutually reinforcing—the more inclusive aggregative equality is, the more competitive adversarial equality is likely to be, with both enhancing deliberative equality.

As I noted at the start, the aim of this chapter has not been to offer an institutional blueprint for all democracies but rather an argument for how institutionalizing the terms of the democratic contract offers an appropriate form of political constitutionalism. However, the mechanisms suggested here as most apt to realize these terms can be adapted and extended in various ways within different democracies. For example, the arguments favouring devolution could be just as well applied to workplace or economic democracy and support corporative arrangements. After all, workplaces differ in similar ways to localities, with employees having an equal stake in the decisions affecting the terms of their employment that those employed in other enterprises will lack and that vary in multiple ways according to the nature and location of the business.[146] As I noted above when discussing lottocracy, the empowerment of organized labour—which such an extension would reinforce—is arguably the most effective and legitimate way of overcoming the oligarchic challenge to democracy.

This chapter brings to a close the first part of this book and the restatement of the basic lineaments of a democratic conception of political constitutionalism. The next three parts deal with the challenges—both academic and practical—that arise for each of the three elements of this conception: from the turn to domestic and international conventions on rights; and the associated growing importance of juristocracy as a constraint on democracy; to the deformation of democracy created by rise of populism and the increased significance of technocratic non-majoritarian supranational regulatory bodies brought about by the increasing economic interdependence of democratic states due to globalization. I shall argue that a political constitutionalist response is possible to each of these. As I shall show, these developments can be brought under democratic control—and to some degree be part of—a system of democratic checks and balances compatible with the constitutional goals of reducing arbitrary rule and enhancing equality of concern and respect for all in ways that foster the democratic promotion of rights and the rule of law.

[146] See Robert A. Dahl, *A Preface to Economic Democracy* (Berkeley and Los Angeles, CA: University of California Press 1985); Elizabeth Anderson, *Private Government* (Princeton, NJ: Princeton University Press 2019).

PART 2

THE RIGHTS CHALLENGE— DEMOCRACY AS RIGHTS?

4

Domestic Bills of Rights

Political Constitutionalism and the Human Rights Act

1. INTRODUCTION

The UK has long presented scholars of constitutionalism with a puzzle.[1] Despite never having had an entrenched written constitution, it can claim to be the inspirer and originator of two key elements of modern legal constitutionalism: the separation of powers and a Bill of Rights. Book 11, chapter 6, of Montesquieu's *De l'Esprit des lois* (1748), which drew on English sources and took the English constitution as its model, is commonly regarded as the urtext of the former, while the 1689 Act Declaring the Rights and Liberties of the Subject and Settling the Succession of the Crown offered the template for the latter. Yet, as I reported in the Introduction, from more or less the same period, parliamentary sovereignty emerged as the distinctive constitutional feature of the UK—a characteristic that commentators from the late eighteenth century onwards have believed negated, or at least trumped, both of these attributes of a legal constitution. As Dicey, who became this doctrine's chief ideologist, famously and approvingly noted, there is 'in the English constitution an absence of those declarations or definitions of rights so dear to foreign constitutionalists'.[2] With the highest court then part of the House of Lords and the Lord Chancellor a member of the executive, judicial separation was also partial. True, some commentators—notably Tom Paine—considered these British peculiarities meant, effectively, that the UK had no constitution at all.[3] On this account, the paradigm of constitutionalism had passed from Britain to the United States. However, from Edmund Burke onwards, a host of defenders of the Westminster system have regarded it as offering a distinct and superior model of political constitutionalism, which protects British liberties far more effectively than the paper parchment of a legal constitution ever could.

[1] Some of the most salient features of the UK/British constitution derive from Scotland, Northern Ireland, and, most recently, Wales all possessing distinctive legal and political arrangements. However, the aspects discussed here can largely be captured by speaking of the United Kingdom as a whole, although certain commentators cited in this paragraph were writing before the Act of Union with Scotland of 1707 or incorrectly employ 'England' as a synonym for the United Kingdom.

[2] A. V. Dicey, *Introduction to the Study of the Law of the Constitution* (10th edn, London: Macmillan 1959).

[3] Thomas Paine, 'The Rights of Man, Part I' in B. Kucklick (ed.), *Political Writings* (Cambridge: Cambridge University Press 1989) 81, 131.

Defending the Political Constitution. Richard Bellamy, Oxford University Press. © Richard Bellamy 2026.
DOI: 10.1093/9780191826986.003.0006

Has this all changed with the Human Rights Act (HRA) and the subsequent creation of a Supreme Court separate from Parliament and the government, which was to some degree prompted by the new Act?[4] Passed in 1998, the HRA empowers courts to review legislation for compliance with the rights enshrined in the European Convention on Human Rights (ECHR)—albeit in what has been called a 'weak' form that does not allow courts to disapply the law, though it does require them either to interpret legislation in compliant ways or declare it incompatible.[5] Many scholars have regarded this development as the most significant of the various constitutional reforms carried out in the UK over the past decade.[6] However, the precise nature of that significance remains a matter for dispute. Some have regarded it as 'an unprecedented transfer of political power from the executive and legislature to the judiciary' that, for either good or ill, has undermined parliamentary sovereignty, the capstone of the UK's political constitution, and replaced it with a legal constitution.[7] Others, though, have seen it as either compatible with—even an extension of—the UK's political constitution[8] or, at least, as a typical British compromise between political and legal constitutionalism.[9] Meanwhile, a few—among them members of both these camps—have wondered, albeit for different reasons, whether any of it matters.[10] A number even maintain that, despite appearances, legal constitutionalism always has played a crucial and,

[4] There has also been a reduction of the responsibilities of the Lord Chancellor as a result of the Constitutional Reform Act of 2005.

[5] On 'weak' versus 'strong' judicial review, see Jeremy Waldron, 'The Core of the Case Against Judicial Review' (2006) 115 *Yale Law Journal* 1346–1406, at 1355–6, who assigns the HRA to the first. This term is also used by Mark Tushnet, 'Alternative Forms of Judicial Review' (2003) 101 *Michigan Law Review* 2781–2802. As we shall see, others dispute this distinction.

[6] The other, equally significant developments are devolution, membership of (followed by the departure from) the European Union (EU), and the changes to local government. So far, no scholar has adequately assessed all four and the interesting and complex ways they interrelate, though at least one scholar—Vernon Bogdanor, *The New British Constitution* (Oxford: Hart Publishing 2009) 62—has argued that the HRA can be seen as the 'cornerstone' of all these diverse developments, something most reviewers of his book have doubted. As I share this scepticism, apart from a few remarks on both the European Court of Human Rights (ECtHR) and the European Court of Justice (ECJ), I shall be restricting my analysis to the HRA.

[7] K. D. Ewing, 'The Human Rights Act and Parliamentary Democracy' (1999) 62 *Modern Law Review* 79–99. For a parallel view from a legal constitutionalist, see Bogdanor, *The New British Constitution*, ch. 3, and his approval of Lord Steyn's opinion (quoted at 64) that the HRA turned the UK into 'a true constitutional state' that 'made the judiciary the guardians of the ethical values of our bill of rights'.

[8] e.g. Waldron, 'The Core', and—from a rather different perspective—Alison Young, *Parliamentary Sovereignty and the Human Rights Act* (Oxford: Hart Publishing 2009).

[9] e.g. Stephen Gardbaum, 'The New Commonwealth Model of Constitutionalism' (2001) 49 *American Journal of Comparative Law* 707–60; Janet Hiebert, 'Parliamentary Bills of Rights: An Alternative Model' (2006) 69 *Modern Law Review* 7–28, though the latter is guarded as to whether it has been successful.

[10] e.g. K. D. Ewing, 'The Futility of the Human Rights Act' (2004) *Public Law* 829–52, from the political constitutionalist side, and David Dyzenhaus, 'Are Legislatures Good at Morality? Or Better at it than the Courts?' (2009) 7 *International Journal of Constitutional Law* 46–52, at 47–50, from the legal constitutionalist.

in many respects, ineliminable role within the British constitution. These developments simply formalize that fact.[11]

In what follows, I shall attempt to assess these various points of view. The assessment is not so much descriptive as analytical and normative. My aim is less to assess if current judicial practice suggests the HRA *is* compatible with a distinctly political conception of the constitution and more to explore if it *could* be so. Such an exercise seems worthwhile for the following reason: if such an account could not be given, then the political constitution would be dead—if, indeed, it had ever been alive, and could only be revived by repealing or considerably amending the HRA (something, as we shall see, that is dismissed as impossible by some, though advocated in various guises by the Conservative Party in its manifestos for the 2015, 2017, and 2019 elections). Like other proponents of political constitutionalism, I would find such a conclusion disturbing given that our objections to legal constitutionalism arise not from opposition to human rights but because we regard political means as offering securer safeguards for them. Consequently, it ought to be possible to reconcile political constitutionalism with something like the HRA's attempt to enumerate them in an ordinary statute and offer qualified protection by the courts.

I should note that some have seen the HRA, as well as parallel developments in other Commonwealth countries, as giving rise to a new model of constitutionalism that balances legal and political constitutionalism in a novel way while offering an alternative to both.[12] By contrast, I believe it is more accurate to say that just as different forms of legal constitutionalism give greater or lesser weight to the legislature and popular sovereignty when amending or deciding constitutional questions, so different forms of political constitutionalism have allowed greater or lesser degrees of judicial independence and discretion. Both kinds of constitutionalism allow for some balance, and there is nothing new in that.[13] The crux is where supremacy lies—with the legislature, as political constitutionalists desire, or the judiciary, as legal constitutionalists wish, and how far judges make judicial deference to Parliament a central feature of their role. On this account, therefore, the crucial test with regard to the HRA, from a political constitutionalist perspective,

[11] That will be the case for those who take either a Dworkinian or a natural law perspective on the nature of the judge's role; see, e.g., T. R. S. Allan, *Law, Liberty, and Justice: The Legal Foundations of British Constitutionalism* (Oxford: Clarendon Press 1993) and David Dyzenhaus, *The Constitution of Law: Legality in a Time of Emergency* (Cambridge: Cambridge University Press 2006). See too Allan's and Dyzenhaus's reviews of my book Richard Bellamy, *Political Constitutionalism: A Republican Defence of the Constitutionality of Democracy* (Cambridge: Cambridge University Press 2007) in T. R. S. Allan, 'Book Review' (2008) 67 *Cambridge Law Journal* 423–6, at 425–6 and David Dyzenhaus, 'How Hobbes Met the "Hobbes Challenge"' (2009) 72 *Modern Law Review* 488–506, at 490–1, 505–6.

[12] e.g. Gardbaum, 'The New Commonwealth Model'; Stephen Gardbaum, 'Reassessing the New Commonwealth Model of Constitutionalism' (2010) 8 *International Journal of Constitutional Law* 167–206.

[13] See Bellamy, *Political Constitutionalism*, 5–6, 10.

is whether or not it renders legislative supremacy redundant.[14] My central claim is that it need not do so, and remains consistent with the doctrine of parliamentary sovereignty whereby, in Dicey's words,[15] Parliament possesses 'the right to make or unmake any law whatever; and, further, that no person or body is recognised . . . as having a right to override or set aside the legislation of Parliament'.[16] Indeed, the HRA potentially buttresses the role of Parliament.

Two important clarifications need to be entered and underlined, at this point. Both are crucial to the analysis of the sections that follow and the assessment of whether the HRA and political constitutionalism are compatible. First, as noted above, although political constitutionalists are sometimes dubbed 'rights sceptics', none—so far as I am aware—deny that individuals possess rights (even if they offer different accounts of the moral and other sources of such rights).[17] Rather, they are sceptical about rights-based constitutional review by courts. In fact, as I argued in Chapter 1, their position is grounded in at least one right—what Waldron calls 'the right of rights'—that of participating as an equal claimer of rights in collective decision-making.[18] The argument is premised on the view that, among those who take rights and justice seriously, the very grounding theorists of a liberal or social democratic persuasion normally give for such rights—namely, that they support equal concern and respect for autonomous individuals—points towards prioritizing the individual's right to participate as an equal in collective decision-making about the shape of rights in their society.

Second, political constitutionalists do not deny that all legislation will be subject to an element of judicial review when applied by courts to particular cases. No law can be drawn up in such a detailed way that it anticipates all possible cases that might be decided with reference to it. Nor can judges avoid deploying what might

[14] For example, it is the belief that it does that leads Mark Tushnet, 'New Forms of Judicial Review and the Persistence of Rights- and Democracy-Based Worries' (2003) 38 *Wake Forest Law Review* 813–38, at 814, to conclude, sorrowfully, that the HRA and parallel developments elsewhere have simply withdrawn the Westminster model from sale, a view shared more positively by Bogdanor, *The New British Constitution*, among others.

[15] Dicey, *Introduction*, 39–40.

[16] Young, *Parliamentary Sovereignty*, offers a doctrinal analysis of parliamentary sovereignty that she believes renders it consistent with entrenchment of the HRA. As becomes clear in the second part of her book, this argument is then placed at the service of a 'dialogic' model of human rights review that places courts and the legislature on an equal basis. Whatever the merits of Young's reading of parliamentary sovereignty in its own terms, it is incompatible with the account of political constitutionalism given here which requires legislative supremacy. Therefore, in what follows I shall take parliamentary sovereignty as precluding such entrenchment.

[17] J. A. G. Griffith, 'The Political Constitution' (1979) 42 *Modern Law Review* 17, perhaps comes closest in dubbing rights simply 'political claims by individuals and groups'. However, he certainly believed that the claims of the relatively powerless in society deserved to be taken very seriously indeed and offered a more equal hearing than he thought likely by the judiciary.

[18] Jeremy Waldron, *Law and Disagreement* (Oxford: Clarendon Press 1999) ch. 11; Richard Bellamy, 'Constitutive Citizenship vs. Constitutional Rights: Republican Reflections on the EU Charter and the Human Rights Act' in Tom Campbell, K. D. Ewing, and Adam Tomkins (eds), *Sceptical Essays on Human Rights* (Oxford: Oxford University Press 2001) 15–39; Bellamy, *Political Constitutionalism*, ch. 4.

be regarded as principles of natural justice in their interpretation of how the law applies.[19] However, the decision as to whether legislation might be regarded per se as rights-compliant and how such compliance might best be achieved, ought, on their view, ultimately to rest with the legislature.

The argument progresses as follows. First, I contend the HRA brings 'rights home', strengthening, in certain respects, domestic rights instruments vis-à-vis the ECHR. Second, I argue that sections 19 and 4 of the Act retain and even enhance Parliament's scrutiny of rights and its sovereignty over the courts in defining and upholding them. Finally, I maintain that section 3, and rights-based judicial review more generally, can be assimilated to a system of weak review, whereby courts defer to the legislative 'scope' determined by Parliament and are restricted in their independent determinations to the judicial 'sphere' of the fair conduct of the case at hand. Such weak review has always been necessary. However, the HRA arguably reinforces judicial deference by giving it a stronger statutory basis.

2. THE HRA: FROM POLITICAL TO LEGAL CONSTITUTIONALISM?

What might be termed the basic case for regarding the HRA as an extension of political constitutionalism is, in formal terms, relatively straightforward. Indeed, most commentators—including those who believe it *de facto* marks a shift towards legal constitutionalism—accept that the drafters of the HRA went to considerable lengths to render the judicial protection of Convention rights compatible with the Diceyan view of parliamentary sovereignty, cited above,[20] which we have seen forms the key aspect of Britain's political constitution.

The Diceyan doctrine is usually identified with two main features: first, that Parliament can legislate in any way or area it pleases, including, if necessary, amending and repealing any existing legislation, and, second, that no other institution may disapply parliamentary legislation. At the simplest level, the HRA appears to meet the first criterion in being an ordinary piece of parliamentary legislation—it has no special, entrenched status—and, as such, can be revised or withdrawn on the basis of a parliamentary majority. Meanwhile, as we shall see, section 4 of the Act, which allows courts to issue a 'declaration of incompatibility' with Convention rights, has been drafted so as to maintain the second criterion.

[19] Perhaps the only theorist associated with the political constitutionalist camp who might disagree is Tom Campbell, *The Legal Theory of Ethical Positivism* (Aldershot: Dartmouth 1996), but see Bellamy, *Political Constitutionalism*, 83–8, for a comment on this view, and Jeremy Waldron, 'Judges as Moral Reasoners' (2009) 7 *International Journal of Constitutional Law* 2–24.

[20] See Nicholas Bamforth, *Understanding the Impact and Status of the Human Rights Act 1998 within English Law*, Global Law Working Paper 10/04 <http://www.law.nyu.edu/global/workingpapers/2004/ECM_DLV_015806> xxii, on the one side, and Aileen Kavanagh, *Constitutional Review Under the U.K. Human Rights Act* (Cambridge: Cambridge University Press 2009) 310–13, on the other.

For such declarations do not in themselves disapply the offending legislation—only Parliament can do that. Needless to say, though, many commentators have found the basic position a little too simple and formal. I shall begin by looking at the relationship between the HRA and the ECHR and the European Court of Human Rights (ECtHR) to see if it offers a strengthening of domestic control over rights congenial to a political constitutionalist. I then turn to the other main provisions of the HRA and explore how far a weak form of judicial review, which preserves legislative supremacy on rights questions, is plausible.

2.1. Bringing Rights Home? The HRA and the ECHR

Some have objected that repeal of the HRA would be tantamount to withdrawal from the ECHR.[21] However, although article 1 of the Convention requires contracting states to secure Convention rights within their jurisdictions, it does not specify how this might best be done. The primary domestic mechanism need not be judicial—and, indeed, was not in either the UK or several Nordic countries for over fifty years. Of course, it might be argued that the ECHR itself undermines the political constitutionalist position, with the HRA simply reinforcing that weakening—a position I dispute in Chapter 5. Here, it suffices to note that formally the Convention is an international agreement between sovereign states from which they can withdraw or could potentially seek to renegotiate, as has periodically occurred when adding protocols or changing the composition and workings of the ECtHR. This status has also allowed the UK not to sign up to all the protocols to the Convention and to hold reservations with regard to particular articles. Few would deny that withdrawal from the ECHR would have such grave consequences as to be unlikely—adversely affecting the UK's international standing and moral legitimacy. However, these constraints on parliamentary sovereignty are political not legal and leave the first criterion, identified above, intact.

The second criterion might seem trickier, given that the ECtHR can pass judgment on parliamentary legislation or administrative acts. True, there is a certain intergovernmental logic in the membership and organization of the ECtHR. The Court's decisions also provide for a margin of appreciation in the interpretation of rights, thereby conceding that while national governments and legislatures must all value Convention rights, their valuations of them may diverge to reflect local circumstances and traditions. Indeed, many clauses of the Convention allow the protection of individual rights to be balanced against other collective concerns such as public order, health, and security. States may even temporarily derogate from certain provisions when these countervailing considerations are deemed to make it

[21] Gavin Phillipson, 'Deference, Discretion and Democracy in the Human Rights Act Era' (2006) 60 *Current Legal Problems* 40–78, at 62.

necessary to do so. Though the ECtHR can rule that laws or executive actions that have the sanction of Parliament may breach the ECHR—and British governments have invariably complied with such rulings—unlike European Community (EC) law, the ECHR contains no principles of supremacy and direct effect and, unlike the European Court of Justice (ECJ), the ECtHR cannot instruct British courts to disapply rules of national law or interpret them in a particular way. The ECtHR can only award remedies against signatories as a matter of international, not domestic, law. It might be argued that, even pre-HRA, the courts had begun to cite the ECHR of their own accord and risk going beyond what was officially permitted.[22] However, the courts still deferred to Parliament's explicit repudiations: for example, in the *Joint Council for the Welfare of Immigrants* case, where the Court of Appeal's judgment was overruled by primary legislation the following day.[23] So the second criterion is also met.

Nevertheless, despite the compliance of the ECHR regime with parliamentary sovereignty, there is no denying that the growing number of cases against the UK brought before the ECtHR was felt to be an embarrassment that the HRA was designed, in part, to rectify. In this regard, many viewed the HRA as reinforcing political constitutionalism. The HRA would 'bring rights home' by offering domestic remedies that would reduce the need for recourse to the ECtHR.[24] The decisions of a domestic court would be both less embarrassing than adverse judgments by a foreign court and, most importantly, more in tune with the particular circumstances and traditions of the UK, including its political constitution. Certainly, there is good reason to believe that a national court will be more susceptible to indirect domestic democratic pressures than an international court is likely to be. Even if formally independent, national courts form part of the domestic political system. Their membership draws on the same broad political class from which national politicians emerge—a significant number of whom may even have practised law alongside them. Moreover, the selection of judges is subject to various forms of direct or indirect political control and influence. A far thicker public sphere exists at the national as compared with the international level. Consequently, domestic courts come under greater scrutiny by the media and a broad range of interest groups and, thus, are more aware of public opinion than international courts. As a result, they tend to feel more obliged than their international counterparts to legitimize themselves and gain acceptance for their decisions among the wider public. As research on the US Supreme Court indicates, courts follow the polls—or, at least, sustained national electoral trends.[25]

[22] *R. v. Secretary of State for the Home Department, ex p. Brind* [1991] 1 AC 696, 748 (Lord Bridge).

[23] *R. v. Secretary of State for Social Security, ex p. Joint Council for the Welfare of Immigrants* [1997] 1 WLR 275.

[24] White Paper, *Rights Brought Home: the Human Rights Bill*, cm.3782.

[25] See Robert A. Dahl, 'Decision-making in a Democracy: The Supreme Court as National Policymaker' (1957) 6 *Journal of Public Law* 279–95; W. Mishler and R. S. Sheehan, 'The Supreme

That said, the ECtHR continues to cast its shadow over the HRA. In particular, section 2(1) HRA requires domestic courts to 'take into account' any relevant Strasbourg jurisprudence relating to a judgment involving a Convention right. That could be quite a weak instruction, strictly applying only to cases where the UK was a party. In fact, the courts generally have accorded Strasbourg jurisprudence a binding status.[26] Arguably, that policy follows from the aim of avoiding litigation before the ECtHR. Moreover, domestic courts have deferred to Strasbourg as to the definition of what Convention rights require.[27] Since their role under the HRA is simply to ensure compliance with these rights, they have deemed it inappropriate to challenge or outstrip the ECtHR rulings on what an acceptable standard of observance involves. However, this has not meant that Parliament need treat ECtHR norms as a ceiling rather than a floor, even if domestic courts have done so. Judges have merely felt (and, *pace* certain legal constitutionalist commentators,[28] from a political constitutionalist position rightly so) that it is for Parliament rather than the courts to decide whether it wishes to elaborate legislation that goes beyond what the ECtHR deems necessary to protect rights. So, while the HRA does not weaken the necessity of the British Parliament to stay compliant with ECtHR decisions, the deference of domestic courts to Strasbourg also creates a potential brake on their judicial activism and has arguably encouraged them to develop a domestic deference principle giving Parliament leeway as to how it might secure a given right. Though some argue such deference hinders the development of a distinctive British human rights jurisprudence,[29] to a degree, that can reinforce political constitutionalism.

However, even where the new Supreme Court, like its predecessor, does not go beyond the UK's commitments under the ECHR, its role is to make that commitment more present and continuous. As we shall see, a key issue has been the recognition, in part mandated by a Strasbourg decision,[30] that proportionality rather than the looser norm of reasonableness now be applied when Convention rights are at stake.[31] Meanwhile, the Court has acknowledged that not all ECtHR jurisprudence necessarily applies to the UK, having been formulated with regard to cases involving circumstances that do not obtain in Britain, or is always sufficiently

Court as a Counter-majoritarian Institution? The Impact of Public Opinion on Supreme Court Decisions' (1993) 87 *American Political Science Review* 87–101.

[26] *R. v. Special Adjudicator, ex parte Ullah* [2004] UKHL 26.

[27] *R. v. Special Adjudicator, ex parte Ullah*, at 20.

[28] e.g. Jonathan Lewis, 'The European Ceiling on Human Rights' (2007) *Public Law* 720–47.

[29] e.g. Roger Masterman, 'Aspiration or Foundation? The Status of the Strasbourg Jurisprudence and the "Convention Rights" in Domestic law' in Helen Fenwick, Gavin Phillipson, and Roger Masterman (eds), *Judicial Reasoning Under the U.K. Human Rights Act* (Cambridge: Cambridge University Press 2007) 57–86.

[30] *Smith v. United Kingdom* (2000) 29 EHRR 493.

[31] *R. (Daly) v. Secretary of State for the Home Department* [2001] UKHL 27.

clear or well-reasoned that it can be followed.[32] There are also cases where there is, as yet, no relevant Strasbourg case law.

For the reasons noted above, it may still remain not just symbolically or formally but also, in many ways, substantively more in line with political constitutionalism for such judgments to be made by a domestic rather than an international court. Even in cases where the Court sees itself as doing no more than acting as Strasbourg would at one remove, it will be doing so as the agent of a UK political order and be subject to the pressures from Parliament and British public opinion from which, to a large extent, it derives its authority and legitimacy.[33] And when it acts in cases of a kind where Strasbourg either has yet to offer a view, or has done so in ways that seem unclear or inappropriate, the Court can provide an interpretation that corresponds to the British context, including those circumstances that reflect its distinctive political processes. For example, at least some law lords have stressed that the HRA does not 'authorize the judges to stand in the shoes of Parliament's delegates, who are decision makers'.[34] The possibility does exist, therefore, for the HRA to bring rights home in ways that could potentially strengthen political constitutionalism vis-à-vis the ECtHR. The crux is whether, in doing so, the HRA must necessarily weaken political constitutionalism in other ways and move the UK ineluctably towards a legal constitutionalism, as some claim has occurred.[35] Or can the Act be read more coherently as offering a way for bringing legal within political constitutionalism, as is generally thought its drafters intended?

2.2. Parliamentary Supremacy and Weak Review

The crucial provisions for assessing the respective roles of Parliament and the courts under the HRA are sections 3, 4, and 19 of the Act and the interplay between them. Section 19(1) requires the minister in charge of a Bill to make 'a statement of compatibility' before the second reading 'to the effect that in his view the provisions of the Bill are compatible with Convention rights' or explicitly to remark 'that although he is unable to make a statement of compatibility the government nevertheless wishes the House to proceed with the Bill'. Section 3(1) obliges the courts to read primary and subordinate legislation, whenever enacted, in a way that is compatible with Convention rights 'so far as it is possible to do so'. However, section 3(2) specifies 'this article does not affect the validity, continuing operation or enforcement of any incompatible' primary or subordinate legislation. In these cases, where both a provision is deemed incompatible and the primary

[32] *Kay v. Lambeth London Borough Council* [2006] UKHL 28, 44; *Brown v. Stott* [2003] 1 AC 733.
[33] e.g. Lord Hoffmann in *R. (Alconbury) v. Secretary of State for the Environment, Transport and the Regions* [2001] WLR 1389 [76], though compare the more cautious Lord Slynn at [26].
[34] *R. (Mahmood) v. Secretary of State for the Home Department* [2001] 1 WLR 840 [33].
[35] e.g. Kavanagh, *Constitutional Review*.

legislation concerned prevents the removal of any incompatibility, then—as I noted above—section 4 allows the highest relevant courts to 'make a declaration of incompatibility'.

However, such declarations of incompatibility do not strike down offending provisions, which remain in force, operable, and valid, and are not binding on the parties against whom they are made. The decision on whether to remedy the incompatibility by amending the legislation rests with the government and, ultimately, Parliament, although provision is made in section 10 for a fast-track legislative procedure to provide such remedial action. Let us explore each of these provisions in turn.

2.2.1. Sections 19 and 4: Upholding parliamentary supremacy?

On the surface, sections 19 and 4 might appear to be straightforward instruments of political constitutionalism. The first could be taken as offering the courts a clear indication that the legislation should be regarded as compatible; the second gives the last word on whether to revise legislation or not to Parliament.

However, once again matters are not clear-cut. With regard to section 19, courts initially paid little attention to these declarations of compatibility—in great part, for reasons a political constitutionalist ought to approve. By and large, courts have been wary of according too much weight to statements by ministers or others as to what they intend by any piece of legislation.[36] The standard case for paying attention to such statements is that the intentions of those who author a legislative text should be regarded as informing its authority. Yet, it is part of the political constitutionalist case that Parliament and its committees allow many voices to enter into the legislative process, with the result being the product of a dialogue among these voices and involving the mutual modification of many individual positions. Therefore, the authors of legislation are not individual members so much as the legislative body as a whole. Given that Parliament is not a coherent, unitary actor, it is doubtful that it makes any sense to speak of its intentions. At the very least, the only sensible way we can access those intentions is by paying attention to the plain meaning of the legislative text itself rather by attending to individual interventions in parliamentary debates.

A similar problem arises with the offering of reasons by legislatures. Legal constitutionalists sometimes contrast courts and legislators in this regard, and argue as if legislation is thereby unreasoned. Again, the reasoning occurs in the actual legislative process; the reasons of the legislature as a whole can only be those embodied in the legislation itself. After all, the reasoning of the individual members of the legislature may well have differed as to why the legislation represents an appropriate

[36] Although, since *Pepper v. Hart* [1993] AC 593, courts have accepted they can refer to the parliamentary record in Hansard as an aid to statutory construction, subsequent decisions have given ministerial statements less weight than the text itself. See *Wilson v. First Country Trust* [2003] 3 WLR 568.

reading of rights on this matter. Like multimember courts, their agreements are likely to be 'incompletely theorised',[37] the product of a convergence on a policy that may seem reasonable from a number of points of view.[38]

Some of these difficulties have been addressed potentially by the establishment of a Joint Committee on Human Rights (JCHR) two years after the HRA. The JCHR reports to both Houses on the compatibility question, taking evidence from ministers, government departments, non-governmental organizations (NGOs), and legal experts. It suggests amendments, where it deems them necessary, and has pushed the government towards outlining its views on points at issue in the explanatory notes published with every government Bill. These reports have ensured that rights considerations are raised in parliamentary debates and are often referred to in that context. As a result, it cannot be said that the rights enumerated in the HRA have received insufficient scrutiny in the framing of legislation. There are good grounds, then, for regarding the legislative text as embodying the legislature's considered view of the balance of rights with regard to any given policy. Legislation is not, as some have characterized it,[39] simply the product of the unprincipled trading and aggregation of interests to promote public utility regardless of its impact on rights. Rights and interests have both played a role in the legislative process.

Nevertheless, two problems remain in regarding this feature of legislation as rendering the HRA fully compliant with political constitutionalism. First, legal advisers play a crucial role in the JCHR's deliberations. Their advice consists largely of second-guessing the likely judgments of the courts, be they domestic or the ECtHR. In this way, as Alex Stone Sweet pithily put it, 'governing with judges' all too often 'means governing like judges'.[40] Yet, as we saw, a strong part of the political constitutionalist case lies in asserting the superiority of legislative over judicial decision-making with regard to the moral and political questions surrounding rights. To the extent Parliament feels constrained by legalistic reasoning in its rights deliberations, this alleged advantage of political over legal constitutionalism is diminished.[41] However, this point probably proves overstated. For example, the Communications Act 2003,[42] which banned political advertising in the broadcast media except for independently regulated election and referenda broadcasts by political parties and a limited number of other relevant organizations which had

[37] Cass Sunstein, *Legal Reasoning and Political Conflict* (Oxford: Oxford University Press 1996) 48–50.

[38] Waldron, *Law and Disagreement*, ch. 6.

[39] Ronald Dworkin, 'Introduction', *Freedom's Law: The Moral Reading of the American Constitution* (Cambridge, Mass.: Harvard University Press 1996).

[40] Alex Stone Sweet, *Governing with Judges: Constitutional Politics in Europe* (Oxford: Oxford University Press 2000).

[41] See Hiebert, 'Parliamentary Bills of Rights'; Danny Nicol, 'The Human Rights Act and the Politicians' (2004) 24 *Legal Studies* 451–79.

[42] Communications Act 2003 (UK), *c*. 21, ss 319–321.

been registered with the Electoral Commission, was the subject of two reports by the JCHR and was scrutinized by a specially appointed joint committee of both Houses of Parliament. As a result, Parliament believed that, although the legislation potentially breached article 10 ECHR concerning freedom of expression, it would proceed nonetheless as permitted under section 19. Indeed, it could be considered that Parliament's deliberation of the issue proved important in persuading the House of Lords to rule unanimously that courts should regard the law as compatible with article 10 ECHR in a subsequent case.[43] As Adam Tomkins has remarked, this example shows how Parliament can use the new procedures to influence the courts rather than the other way round, with the HRA promoting precisely the sort of legislative deliberation about rights that political constitutionalists advocate.[44]

Some commentators still feel, though, that a second and more intractable problem remains. For no matter how thorough and independent Parliament's deliberations of rights may be, its ability to control the judicial process remains limited. Resolving this question turns on how deferential the courts are—or can be made to be—to what Parliament decides on the rights question. Section 4 potentially supplies a solution in this respect, and has been regarded as the key provision in maintaining the political constitutionalist status quo. Thus, Jeremy Waldron regards the inability of courts to refuse to apply or moderate the application of a given law, notwithstanding their view that it is incompatible with human rights, as the hallmark of what he and others term 'weak judicial review'.[45] Waldron sees the UK as at the stronger end of a continuum[46]—given that judicial declarations of incompatibility can trigger a legislative process of remedial action—that puts New Zealand, where similar declarations have no such effect, at the weakest end. Canada, where courts can disapply the law but legislatures can pass laws with a 'notwithstanding' clause that insulates them from judicial scrutiny, occupies a middle position. It is true that the UK also occupies a roughly middle position since, under section 19, a minister can propose legislation he or she believes to be incompatible with Convention rights; nevertheless, this is a power that has been rarely employed so far.[47]

Section 4 was heralded as a core provision of the HRA. It was seen by many advocates of the measure as inaugurating a new model of judicial review that lay midway between political and legal constitutionalism.[48] However, others—both legal and political constitutionalists—have argued that, in practice, there is little

[43] *R. (Animal Defenders International) v. Secretary for Culture, Media and Sport* [2008] UKHL 15, esp. Lord Bingham at [7]–[21].

[44] Adam Tomkins, 'The Role of Courts in the Political Constitution' (2010) 60 *University of Toronto Law Journal* 1–22, at 5, 19.

[45] Waldron, 'The Core', 1355. See also Gardbaum, 'The New Commonwealth Model', 14.

[46] Waldron, 'The Core', 1356.

[47] As was discussed above, this mechanism was used in the Communications Act 2003.

[48] e.g. Gardbaum, 'The New Commonwealth Model'; Francesca Klug, 'The Human Rights Act—a "Third Way" or "Third Wave" Bill of Rights' (2001) 4 *European Human Rights Law Review* 361–72.

difference between weak and strong judicial review—indeed, that the former is a chimera.[49] They note that, so far, Parliament has always complied with such rulings and amended the offending legislation accordingly. The key point, though, is why. Four sets of reasons have been given, none of which is inherently incompatible with political constitutionalism.

The first is that Parliament has exercised its prerogative. That it does so only rarely is neither here nor there, it remains Parliament's to exercise.[50] Indeed, if one takes the highest-profile instance of a declaration of incompatibility, that of *Belmarsh Prison*,[51] Parliament can hardly be regarded as supinely accepting the Court's decision. Though it granted the Court's judgment that the current detention scheme involved unreasonable discrimination against non-UK citizens, it took several months to respond, adopting the new control-order scheme following one of the longest parliamentary debates ever. Meanwhile, the prisoners were only released once the new legislation was enacted so that they could be immediately rearrested. Rightly or wrongly, therefore, Parliament can hardly be viewed as conceding judicial supremacy.

A second reason is political culture—that any government would simply find it politically inexpedient to go against such a court ruling unless it were sure of overwhelming political support in doing so, as was the case, for example, when Roosevelt stood up to the Lochner-era reasoning of the US Supreme Court.[52] However, to the extent this argument holds—which, given the pre-election commitment of the Conservative Party to repeal the HRA, is perhaps highly disputable—this reasoning also is not per se incompatible with political constitutionalism. After all, political constitutionalists value responsiveness to public opinion, and if a lack of popular legitimacy explains Parliament's compliance rather than a binding constitutional measure that literally gives them no choice in law but to comply, then its deference to judicial declarations of incompatibility is in line with the political constitutionalist position.

A third reason holds that where such declarations have been issued, it is likely the ECtHR would have made a similar ruling. A failure to comply with a declaration of incompatibility would give *prima facie* weight to any appeal to Strasbourg and increase the likelihood of the case going against the government.[53] Though some have argued that, where there is no existing case law, the ECtHR might apply a wider margin of appreciation than the domestic court, this is not probable. As we

[49] e.g. David Dyzenhaus, 'The Incoherence of Constitutional Positivism' in Grant Huscroft (ed.), *Expounding the Constitution: Essays in Constitutional Theory* (Cambridge: Cambridge University Press 2008) 138–60; Kavanagh, *Constitutional Review*, 282–92, 417–18.

[50] Waldron, 'The Core', 1357; Jeffrey Goldsworthy, 'Judicial Review, Legislative Override, and Democracy' (2003) 38 *Wake Forest Law Review* 451–72, at 454–9.

[51] *A and others v. Secretary of State for the Home Department* [2004] UKHL 56, [2005] 2 WRL 87, HL.

[52] Mark Elliott, 'Parliamentary Sovereignty and the New Constitutional Order: Legislative Freedom, Political Reality and Convention' (2002) 22 *Legal Studies* 340–75, at 348.

[53] Kavanagh, *Constitutional Review*, 284–7.

saw, not only have the domestic courts been guided by ECtHR standards in their judgments but also the fact that the highest domestic court had ruled some piece of legislation contravened a Convention right would almost certainly be taken as evidence by the ECtHR that this was the case. Nevertheless, we have seen the ECHR regime per se is not incompatible with political constitutionalism.

More troubling from the political constitutionalist perspective, however, is the fourth reason, namely, that the Court has only issued declarations of incompatibility in those cases where the judges concerned felt certain the government would comply, while in other situations they have used their power of interpretation under section 3(1) to render legislation compatible with Convention rights.[54] Indeed, the use of section 3(1) has been seen by legal and political constitutionalists alike as the aspect of the HRA that poses the greatest potential challenge to parliamentary sovereignty. Many have argued that it largely undermines whatever powers may have been reserved to Parliament under sections 19 and especially 4.[55] Consequently, it proves crucial for the political constitutionalist case to defend a plausible account of judicial deference and weak review in the use of section 3.

2.2.2. Weak review and section 3: The judicial 'sphere' and deference to the 'scope' of legislation

There are three main concerns with the use of section 3 by the courts.[56] First, some have worried that the injunction that all subsequent as well as preceding legislation be read as Convention-compatible goes against the view that no Act of Parliament can bind later Parliaments, with later legislation involving an 'implied repeal' of any prior legislation with which it was inconsistent. Second, the ability of the judiciary to interpret legislation in a manner it feels is Convention-compatible has been seen as allowing it, effectively, to amend legislation in ways that are contrary to the clear intention of Parliament. Third, that as a result, use of section 3 makes sections 19 and 4 largely redundant.

With regard to the first concern—the doctrine of implied repeal—courts have always assumed that in the absence of an explicit repeal of, or challenge to, prior legislation, then it is reasonable to suppose that Parliament wished to legislate in a way that was compatible with existing law. As a result, they have interpreted all new laws 'so far as it is possible' as if that were so. Moreover, under the HRA, the declaration of compatibility under section 19 gives the courts explicit grounds for holding that view. Of course, where they find legislation to be incompatible, they now have to say so explicitly. It might be argued this requirement replaces an implied repeal with an explicit repeal.[57] Still, as we saw, such declarations do not of

[54] Kavanagh, *Constitutional Review*, 119.

[55] Kavanagh, *Constitutional Review*, 318–19, 332–6, 416–20.

[56] For contrasting accounts of these issues, see Bamforth, *Understanding the Impact*, and Kavanagh, *Constitutional Review*, ch. 11.

[57] David Feldman, 'The Human Rights Act 1998 and Constitutional Principles' (1999) 19 *Legal Studies* 165–206, at 178–80.

themselves disapply the law—that remains Parliament's prerogative. The Court must continue to apply the disputed legislative provisions, suggesting that, until such time as Parliament decrees otherwise, Convention rights do not apply in the area covered by the new legislation. As Nicholas Bamforth has argued, the HRA protection of Convention rights does not need to be repealed implicitly or explicitly in this case, because it is limited by the Act to those cases that do not fall within section 4 as incompatible with it.[58]

The second concern appears more problematic, for it involves the fear that section 3(1) will lead the courts to depart from the conventional meaning of the legislative text in ways that had previously been deemed inappropriate, thereby challenging the rights-based judgments of Parliament. Yet here, too, the departure from traditional forms of statutory interpretation may be less substantial than is assumed, with judicial discretion, in certain respects, reduced rather than increased. Some commentators make it seem that any failure not to follow the literal letter of the law must involve the undermining of legislative supremacy and, with it, political constitutionalism.[59] However, as I noted above, it has always been the case that statutory interpretation has involved courts in clarifying unclear or ambiguous terms, correcting drafting errors, and overcoming incoherent or unintelligible provisions that are irreconcilable with the rest of the statute. With the best will in the world, one cannot hope to eradicate all such linguistic problems. Nor can legislators be expected to foresee all the potential cases and circumstances to which their legislation may be applied. As a result, they often use terms such as 'reasonable' and employ general rules rather than specific standards with the intention of giving judges a degree of discretion that will enable them to tailor legislation to the peculiarities and particulars or special features of a given case. It would be impossible to rule out such discretion and replace it with a mechanical application of the law except in the crudest imaginable way, such as a two-strikes-and-you-are-out rule, that excludes drawing the various distinctions between cases that are generally seen as necessary to avoid unjust and dysfunctional outcomes.[60] Any attempt to overcome this problem by writing all these distinctions into the law, would inevitably give judges discretion to choose which ones applied. Even then, it would be hard to imagine that every eventuality could be anticipated.[61]

However, none of the above need mean that judicial discretion is totally unconstrained. Any type of constitutionalist must believe it possible, for one reason or another, that judges can be bound by law—at least in the sense that they feel an

[58] Bamforth, *Understanding the Impact*, xxxv–xxxvii.

[59] Dyzenhaus, 'The Incoherence', has a tendency to slip into this view. See also Dyzenhaus, 'How Hobbes Met the "Hobbes Challenge"'.

[60] Modified, in *R. v. Offen* [2001] 2 All ER 154, to apply only to offenders within the specified range of offences who were a danger to the public.

[61] Bellamy, *Political Constitutionalism*, 83–4, and Neil MacCormick, 'Argumentation and Interpretation in Law' (1993) 6 *Ratio Juris* 16–29.

obligation to justify what they do by reference to it. A political constitutionalist need only ask if it is possible to have a concept of law that conjoins Convention rights with parliamentary sovereignty in a coherent way that might constrain the sorts of legal reasons judges could offer for their decisions. In particular, can there be legal norms that prevent judges from simply interpreting the law so that it accords with an outcome they personally believe best realizes human rights in the case at hand?[62] I think a broadly legal-positivist view, of the democratic kind outlined in Chapter 2,[63] holds there can be.[64]

Both the HRA and the other pieces of legislation that are to be read alongside it have a common source that renders them legally valid—namely, Parliament. Therefore, the grounds of compatibility—or incompatibility—must be those stemming from this source within the legislation itself. Under section 19, Parliament will have supplied only a limited set of reasons for regarding a given piece of legislation as Convention-compatible, or possibly none at all, and it is to these that the judge must defer. I shall call this a limitation of interpretative 'scope'. Alongside it, is a limitation of the interpretative 'sphere' that is related to the activity of judging itself. Judges have a legally constituted role. They are not armchair moral philosophers but sit in courts constituted by certain rules and procedures that they have a duty to oversee in order to ensure a trial is conducted fairly and provides justice for the litigant. These include such formal rule-of-law notions as treating like cases alike, acting impartially, ensuring all sides have an equal chance to present their case, and so on. A political constitutionalist holds that it is appropriate for Parliament to decide general substantive issues of rights and to offer legislative resolutions of the disagreements that attend them. However, that function is compatible with regarding courts as entitled to ensure that the procedures for passing the law were duly followed and that the judicial process remains fair when it comes to applying such rights in practice. The due process, particularly in the court room, is their domain, where they can legitimately claim more expertise and authority than Parliament.[65]

Naturally, there are discretionary elements in deciding how the law applies. My point is simply that such discretion need not be arbitrary but may be legally sanctioned and deployed with regard to a certain set of moral principles—those enumerated in the HRA—and in conformity with the rationale of existing law (its 'scope') and the norms of the judicial role (as applying to the 'sphere' of the court

[62] Obviously, saying that, on this account of law, judges would not be legally justified in deciding cases solely in this way is different to saying that it prevents them from doing so in reality or denying that, on occasion, they might be morally bound to do so.

[63] See too Jeremy Waldron, 'Can There Be a Democratic Jurisprudence?' (2008–09) 58 *Emory Law Journal* 675–712.

[64] Natural law lawyers, Dworkinian 'interpretative constructivists', and, though I think with less reason, legal realists will not find this account congenial, but theirs are not the only games in town. It suffices for my purposes to argue that a coherent account could be offered.

[65] See Tomkins, 'The Role of Courts', 6.

and related procedural issues). Such deployment comes with a legal duty to say when these options cease to be at all plausible because further reasons are needed to resolve the case in a rights-compatible fashion. To the extent this legal guidance has its source in Parliament, it will not be the case that section 3(1) HRA undermines the very notion of parliamentary sovereignty by offering a distinct moral test for the existence of law.[66] Indeed, as Sandra Fredman has suggested,[67] the HRA arguably strengthens Parliament in this regard because it directs judges to be guided in their decisions not by vague, permissive social sources of morality—such as notions of 'natural justice' or an apparently ever-expandable 'common law'—but by a specific and democratically enacted list of rights.

In fact, the Court has consistently argued that its post-HRA rights-based review of legislation has legitimacy because it accords with the express will of Parliament that it interpret the law with regard to these norms.[68] In itself, however, simply listing a certain set of rights will not be enough to constrain judicial discretion. For these rights still allow for pretty broad and widely differing interpretations, and it is the basic claim of political constitutionalists that a democratically elected legislature ought to be responsible, ultimately, for justifying which interpretation applies in legislation. The notions of scope and sphere enter here, offering crucial guidelines. The former constrains the allowable breadth of legislative interpretation to those purposes proposed by—or that can be plausibly attributed to—Parliament, the implications of which for rights are now spelled out under section 19; the latter, the domain where judicial independence holds sway.

By implication, these criteria also provide guidelines for addressing the third concern noted above. For, they can help determine when interpretation under section 3 should give way to a declaration of incompatibility under section 4; namely, on those occasions where the Court cannot render the law compatible with its reading of Convention rights, within the judicial sphere, without going beyond or altering the scope of the legislation, thereby trespassing on the legislative domain that properly belongs to Parliament. Crucially, this division of labour also relates to the application of the doctrine of proportionality, which is regarded as one of the main innovations introduced by the HRA. Whereas courts may legitimately question whether a measure that restricts an individual's rights within the judicial sphere is proportionate to the legislative goal to be achieved, they should avoid judging whether the legislative scope per se is proportionate in its effect on Convention rights in cases where precisely that issue has been determined by

[66] Note, I am adopting an exclusive rather than inclusive form of legal positivism here. I am not saying the incorporation of moral principles into the law makes them criteria of legal validity but, rather, that they are legally valid to the extent they have been incorporated into law by Parliament.

[67] Sandra Fredman, 'Scepticism under Scrutiny: Labour Law and Human Rights' in Campbell, Ewing, and Tomkins (eds), *Sceptical Essays*, 197–214.

[68] e.g. *International Transport Roth GmbH v. Secretary of State for the Home Department* [2002] 3 WLR 344, per Law L.J. at [71].

Parliament under section 19. At most, they should employ section 4 to request Parliament reconsider. That leaves the constitutional determination of rights where a political constitutionalist believes it properly resides—with the legislature. Indeed, even advocates of constitutional judicial review under the HRA appear to accept that the more a court's decision touches on matters of legislative scope, the greater its deference to the executive and legislature should be, allowing at the very least for a wider margin of appreciation as to what the upholding of rights might require.[69] For such judgments necessarily involve courts in determining the relative weight different interests and values contribute to the public good—a matter that, for the political constitutionalist, the limitations of the judicial sphere, not least their isolation from the public, however warranted for the impartial application of the law, makes them ill-suited to do.

To see how these criteria might work in practice, let us consider their implications for two leading cases under the HRA—*R v. A*[70] and *Ghaidan v. Mendoza*.[71] As I noted at the outset, my intention is not to show that these and other cases were decided in ways compatible with political constitutionalism but, rather, to ask if they could have been and, if so, what that would have involved. All three concerns were potentially at issue, with a number of commentators arguing that these cases reveal how the use of section 3(1) effectively undermines the apparent safeguard of parliamentary sovereignty provided by section 4.[72] By contrast, I shall argue the foregoing analysis suggests section 3 can be regarded as a justified use of judicial discretion within the Court's own sphere. However, *R v. A* also involved a challenge to the legislative scope of the law in question, albeit with attempts by certain members of the Court to argue otherwise, and so ought to have led, at most, to a declaration of incompatibility under section 4. Instead, *Ghaidan* can be read as being consistent with a reasonable understanding of Parliament's determination of the relevant law's scope when applied to this case and, as such, provides an example of the use of section 3 to address rights in the judicial sphere that is consistent with a political constitutionalist perspective.

In *R. v. A*, the legislative provision at issue was section 41 of the Youth Justice and Criminal Evidence Act of 1999 (YJCEA). Known as the 'rape shield' provision, it prohibited the admissibility of evidence regarding sexual history apart from certain narrowly defined exceptions. The intention was to overcome the much-criticized section 2 of the Sexual Offences (Amendment) Act of 1976, which had left the question of admissibility largely to the discretion of the trial judge, with the

[69] Kavanagh, *Constitutional Review*, 182–3—although Kavanagh adopts a 'contextual' approach that, in practice, allows courts to interfere with the scope of legislation whenever they feel the measure is disproportionate in its impact on rights (239)—effectively removing all limits to constitutional review other than 'prudence' and 'courtesy'.

[70] *R v. A (No 2)* [2002] 1 AC 45.

[71] *Ghaidan v. Mendoza* [2004] 3 WLR 113.

[72] Conor Gearty, 'Revisiting Section 3 (1) of the Human Rights Act' (2003) 119 *Law Quarterly Review* 551–3; Danny Nicol, 'Law and Politics After the Human Rights Act' (2006) *Public Law* 722–51.

perceived result that the position of complainants had frequently been prejudiced by irrelevant and humiliating evidence that had come to deter many women from even bringing rape cases. The point at issue in *R. v. A* was whether this provision breached the defendant's right to a fair trial under article 6 ECHR by blocking evidence of an alleged prior consensual sexual relationship.

The House of Lords ruled that, although *prima facie* it appeared that the statute offered a reading of the balance between the rights of complainants and defendants that was heavily weighted towards the former, it was allowed—indeed, incumbent on them 'in accordance with the will of Parliament'—to employ section 3(1) HRA to read section 41(3)(c) YJCEA in such a way as to include an 'implied provision' that evidence necessary to make the trial compatible with article 6 ECHR was admissible. However, this 'reading in' goes beyond the removal of a linguistic confusion or error of the kind adverted to above. As such, it appears to trespass on the scope of the legislation, given that there can be no doubt that Parliament had wished to block the use of the very kind of evidence the Court now sought to allow. That said, the heart of the case was a sphere of responsibility that could be regarded, rightfully, as that of the judiciary: the fair conduct of a trial. The difficulty lay in the Court's being unable to rectify its perception that an injustice might arise in this sphere without altering the scope of the legislation. True, the Court did attempt to justify its decision by arguing that the reading in was to give effect to what it believed was the main purpose of the legislation; namely, to ensure rape trials were not biased. The Court claimed this case had merely revealed that in these particular circumstances—either unanticipated or not fully considered by the legislature—the laudable desire to protect the rights of complainants, found in the express wording of the statute, had undermined its central implicit purpose by jeopardizing the equally compelling rights of defendants. Thus, it could be said the Court's argument was that its decision had the limited purpose of better realizing the legislature's intent or scope, and doing so in a sphere where it possessed a competence that had always been reserved to it and in terms that the legislature itself had ordained in the HRA. Certainly, it is significant that the Court felt it necessary to legitimize itself in this way. Still, even if purposive construction has long formed part of statutory interpretation,[73] many commentators feel—rightly in my view—that, in this case, the Court went too far and effectively changed the scope of the legislation.[74] Given the Court's justified worries with regard to its own sphere, it would have been better to issue a declaration of incompatibility. Indeed, those who defend the judgment, do so as part of a more general defence of strong forms of constitutional review.[75]

[73] Kavanagh, *Constitutional Review*, 102–3.

[74] e.g. Danny Nicol, 'Statutory Interpretation and Human Rights After Anderson' (2004) *Public Law* 274–82.

[75] e.g. Kavanagh, *Constitutional Review*, 20–2.

By contrast, *Ghaidan*, which became the leading case of HRA interpretative adjudication, arguably represents a weaker form of review. This case centred on whether paragraph 2(2) of the Rent Act 1977, which allowed a person who had lived with a tenant 'as his or her wife or husband' to be treated as the tenant's 'spouse' and, hence, to be entitled to a secure tenancy on the death of their partner, could be read as including same-sex couples. It was thought such a reading was required to avoid discrimination on impermissible grounds 'under Article 14 taken together with Article 8' ECHR. The Court decided that section 3(1) allowed it to do so, thereby overturning a ruling in a pre-HRA case, *Fitzpatrick*,[76] which had deemed the express wording of 'husband' and 'wife', to be gender-specific and so had ruled out homosexual couples. Again, at least one law lord argued that behind the explicit wording lay a more abstract legislative purpose of protecting the interests of people 'living together in a close and stable relationship', and it was this 'underlying thrust of the legislation' that made a rights compatible interpretation possible.[77] Others argued similarly, also apparently stepping back from Lord Steyn's more radical position in *R. v. A*, that a rights-compatible interpretation should (and in this case did) reflect the 'fundamental features of the legislative scheme' and 'go with the grain' of the law.[78] Given that Parliament itself had amended the 1977 Act in 1998 to make provision for unmarried heterosexual couples, thereby implying a change of legislative focus from official marriage to cohabitation, these arguments that the interpretation fell within the scope of the legislation seem well founded. Indeed, even *Fitzpatrick* might have been decided otherwise. After all, courts had departed from the express wording of statutes in other pre-HRA cases in order to reflect changes in social morality.[79] In *Ghaidan*, the passage of the Civil Partnership Bill through Parliament at the time, which would prevent future discrimination against same-sex couples, and the fact the government did not contest the case further reinforced the acceptability of seeing the judicial interpretation as compatible in scope with Parliament's underlying purpose. This approach conforms to a standard pattern within the HRA case law, whereby even if courts depart from the enacted intention of Parliament found in the express terms of a statute, they will refer to its unenacted legislative purpose and to the more general parliamentary intention that they use section 3(1) to make legislation Convention-compatible. As such, their interpretations remain consistent with political constitutionalism.[80]

[76] *Fitzpatrick v. Sterling Housing Association Ltd* [2001] 1 AC 27.

[77] Lord Nicholls in *Ghaidan*, at [35], [33].

[78] Lords Millett and Rodger in *Ghaidan*, at [67], [110], [111], [116]. *Nota bene*, Millett offered a dissenting opinion that s 4 should have been used because the express terms of the Act made a compatible interpretation impossible.

[79] e.g. *R. v. R* [1992] 1 AC 599, which expanded the law of rape to include husbands who raped their wives, and which hitherto had been explicitly excluded by the relevant statute.

[80] For a parallel account, see Jeffrey Goldsworthy, 'Parliamentary Sovereignty and Statutory Interpretation' in Rick Bigwood (ed.), *The Statute: Making and Meaning* (Wellington, NZ: LexisNexis 2004) 187–210.

It might be objected that, even so, *Ghaidan* involved sufficient creativity with regard to the reinterpretation of scope as to render a declaration of incompatibility more appropriate. The contrast with *Bellinger*—a case involving the recognition of a marriage by a transsexual woman as valid, where a declaration of incompatibility was issued—proves instructive in this regard.[81] Here, the government had accepted a recent ECtHR decision holding the UK to be in breach of articles 8 and 12 for denying legal recognition of gender reassignment;[82] it was already exploring the many issues to do with such recognition that went beyond the immediate case; and it had announced new legislation would be available, offering a remedy to the plaintiff. As a result, the interpretation by the Court was unnecessary in order to obtain justice for the litigant and would have preempted the work of the legislature. Invoking section 4 did little more than confirm the view that Parliament had already taken of the issue. Instead, in *Ghaidan*, interpretation was the only way to find justice for the litigant—whose partner, being dead, would not benefit from legislative change. So, there were strong reasons, relating to its sphere, for the Court to adopt the interpretative route. Moreover, it could do so, as we saw, by following existing legislative developments as to the law's scope. A parallel point emerges in *Re S*,[83] where the Court overrode a reading in by the Court of Appeal on the grounds that it went against a 'fundamental feature' of the legislation in question, in this case the implementation of care orders by local authorities under the Children Act 1989. Here, the Court of Appeal's interpretation can be viewed as going beyond both the judicial sphere as well as the law's scope by essentially proposing a wholly new procedure for dealing with care orders in contrast with that proposed by Parliament. The Court's reading in could be neither catered for within the existing terms of the Act nor related to its underlying purpose.

Of course, notions such as the 'sphere' and 'scope' of judicial decisions and legislation do not provide hard and fast rules. A number of judges have also felt uneasy about using section 3(1) to depart from what they see as the 'mandatory language used by Parliament' in order to attribute to it a 'presumed' intention.[84] However, to a degree, Parliament has always looked to the courts to use their discretion effectively to interpret legislation in ways that seem suited to the case and to extend or amend it to fill gaps or avoid injustices. Does that make the ritual deference to Parliament mere window dressing? Some arguments along these lines suggest that because courts are the end users of legislation and because the law cannot prescribe entirely how it should be applied, parliamentary sovereignty is a myth.[85] I do not believe that need be so. One may regard Parliament as the valid source of law in the UK but accept that judges have always had to employ a range of

[81] *Bellinger v. Bellinger* [2003] 2 AC 467.
[82] *Godwin v. United Kingdom* (2002) 35 EHRR 447.
[83] *Re S, Re W* [2002] 2 AC 291.
[84] e.g. *Secretary of State for the Home Department v. MB* [2007] UKHL 46, per Lord Bingham at [44].
[85] e.g. Dyzenhaus, 'The Incoherence'.

tools—logical, linguistic, and moral, among them—to make reasonable decisions. Some of these tools are needed to make sense of the law in a given case; others to indicate where the law fails to make sense and needs supplementing from other, less binding, sources, such as positive morality or the exercise of judicial moral and political judgment. What judges are doing in referring back to Parliament is recognizing the need to validate their views in a given way. They can distinguish good or bad laws from good or bad judgments about laws and, appropriately enough, see Parliament as the forum where, despite our disagreement about rights, we can seek to resolve them in authoritative ways. Having law-based criteria for determining the merits of law will naturally strengthen the confidence with which judges use them. Effectively that is what the HRA does by making the ECHR part of domestic law. Yet it is perfectly coherent for judges to say they acknowledge the force of Convention rights as legal standards because Parliament has authorized them to do so and to see Parliament as the ultimate arbitrator of whether or not they apply and—to the degree that is possible through general laws—of how they apply. So conceived, judicial interpretation post-HRA would be more solidly in line with parliamentary sovereignty than it was before.

3. CONCLUSION

The HRA contains a number of explicit provisions designed to protect parliamentary sovereignty and the UK's political constitution. Legal constitutionalists have argued not only that these provisions ought not to apply—that they are illegitimate and, in certain ways, unconstitutional—but also that they are implausible and impossible to operate in practice. My prime aim has not been to show that they do operate, so much as that they could and, for reasons defended more fully in Chapter 1, should do so. As I noted, legal constitutionalist critics of parliamentary sovereignty regard the court's deference to this doctrine with great scepticism—as either deluded or purely formal and possibly cynical.[86] It is sometimes assumed that political constitutionalists embrace a similar scepticism regarding notions of rights, the rule of law, or judicial impartiality. However, as I argued in Chapters 1 and 2, at its heart political constitutionalism can be regarded as providing a defence against just such scepticism.

On the one hand, political constitutionalism offers a way of identifying law and explaining its authority by associating its source with a democratically elected legislature.[87] On this account, the assurance we have that law reflects our interests and secures our rights, and that we therefore have good reason to obey it, comes from the fact that it is promulgated and debated by our representatives. Far from

[86] e.g. Kavanagh, *Constitutional Review*, 82, 336.
[87] See Waldron, 'Can There Be a Democratic Jurisprudence?', 696–7.

being sceptical of rights or law, political constitutionalists defend both. They merely regard the legislature as the most appropriate forum for seeing rights in the round and ensuring that their specification in legislation considers the full range of concerns necessary to promote the public interest. They also see the need for a large number of accountable representatives to agree on a settled law as a means for preventing arbitrary rule by any one person or group.

On the other hand, that does not involve any scepticism about courts—merely that legislation and adjudication involve different qualities. Judges have responsibility for, and expertise in, issues of fair process that form part of their sphere, and in assuring the law is appropriate to its scope or purpose with regard to a given litigant. These are issues that cannot be addressed fully at the legislative level, which is too remote from the peculiar circumstances that surround a particular case. However, by the same token, courts are by their very nature too narrow in focus and as forums to deal adequately with the issue of deciding a collective policy on rights that looks at the myriad ways different rights interact. They lack the informational and legitimacy advantages that come from decision-making by large numbers of representatives responsive to the views of millions of electors.

I have argued that the HRA should be read as reinforcing both these features of political constitutionalism. Section 19 and the processes that have developed around it reinforce the conscientiousness with which Parliament deliberates about rights. Section 3(1) reinforces the rights-based aspects of adjudication. However, courts also have the ability to reinforce further Parliament's responsibilities through section 4—using this provision both to signal when they feel Parliament might, in the light of a given case, be advised to think again, or to indicate where they believe the executive may have overstepped its authority and should be subjected to additional parliamentary scrutiny.

This division of labour accords with the reasoning Locke gave for moving from the state of nature to civil society and that lies at the heart of the 'separation of powers', which he first began to theorize. Namely, that civil society overcomes the disadvantages in the state of nature of the lack of a known and settled law 'allowed by common consent to be the Standard of Right and Wrong and the common measure to decide all controversies between them' and of 'a known and indifferent Judge, with Authority to determine all differences according to the established Law'.[88] Parliament provides the mechanism for establishing a settled law through common consent; the judiciary supplies an indifferent judge with regard to its application. By contrast, legal constitutionalists risk conflating rights, law, and legislation with judicial adjudication. Meanwhile, they offer no clear mechanism, of a kind equivalent to electoral accountability, to explain why we should not see their assurances that judges are not deciding in arbitrary ways, but according to

[88] John Locke, *Two Treatises of Government* (Peter Laslett ed., Cambridge: Cambridge University Press 1988) 350–1.

the higher constitutional law offered by rights, as anything but formal pieties. After all, judges disagree on what these rights require yet need not seek to reconcile their disagreements in ways that might obtain 'common consent', and the highest courts allow no challenge to their decisions. Rights-based constitutional review by courts thereby replaces the sovereignty of Parliament with the sovereignty of judicial monarchs, returning us to what Locke regarded as worse than the state of nature—a condition where the ruling power governs by 'extemporary Dictates and undetermined Resolutions', the 'unlimited Decrees of their sudden thoughts, or unrestrain'd, and till that moment unknown Wills'. In this way, scepticism about the possibility of a political constitution turns into scepticism about constitutionalism itself. And so, we come back to the opening apparent paradox, the resolution of which arises by virtue of the British constitution's remaining true to its history in successfully combining both the separation of powers and a Bill of Rights not in despite of but *because* of parliamentary sovereignty. Indeed, it is only by rendering courts a complement to a sovereign parliament in this way that the separation powers can avoid degenerating into a form of juristocracy that combines all power in the judiciary in the manner criticized in Chapter 3 and discussed and illustrated further in Chapter 7.

This analysis suggests that the aforementioned criticisms of successive Conservative Party leaders rest on misperceptions of the reasoning underlying many court judgments and false premises regarding the compatibility of the HRA with parliamentary sovereignty. For example, these two errors inform respectively Michael Howard's two contentions that the HRA at best fosters an 'avalanche of political correctness' and 'costly litigation',[89] at worst promotes judicial activism that hampers effective action against terrorism and illegal immigration.[90] Indeed, when a Conservative government commissioned an Independent Human Rights Act Review in 2020, the panel's subsequent report viewed these concerns as largely misplaced, with the HRA enjoying broad popular support despite persistent hostility in certain quarters. Unsurprisingly, perhaps, a core recommendation of the review was to improve civic education concerning the HRA to dispel various misconceptions regarding rights in general and the operation of the HRA in particular (an education, one is tempted to say, needed above all for a number of Conservative politicians and sections of the popular press).[91]

By and large, the review regarded the HRA as functioning in a manner consistent with parliamentary sovereignty, and as such with the interpretation given in this chapter. As it noted, 'neither section 3 nor section 4 adversely affect

[89] Michael Howard, 'Time to Liberate the Country from Human Rights Laws', Conservative Party website, 18 March 2005 <https://web.archive.org/web/20050607001928/https://www.conservatives.com/tile.do?def = news.story.page&obj_id = 120747#>.

[90] Michael Howard, 'Judges Must Bow to the Will of Parliament', *The Daily Telegraph*, 10 August 2005.

[91] The Independent Human Rights Act Review, Executive Summary, December 2021, paras 14(vi) and (vii), 15.

Parliament's constitutional power to enact legislation as it sees fit . . . [and] are clearly limited to a *statutory* review of legislation. Section 3, properly understood, confers an *interpretative* power—within the well-settled province of the Courts—not an amending power (the province of the legislature) . . . With regard to section 4 . . . *If* the Court makes a declaration of incompatibility, Parliament is not *obliged* to act on it'.[92] As a result, the panel saw no need for the government's proposed scrapping of the HRA and its replacement by a new Bill of Rights, merely some clarification (according with current practice) regarding the use of sections 2 and 3 in line with the arguments made above.[93] Though Dominic Raab, as Deputy Prime Minister and Minister for Justice, went forward with a Bill of Rights Bill nonetheless, the government withdrew this measure in 2023 following his resignation over allegations of bullying.

Notwithstanding this reversal of policy, the Conservative administration meanwhile adopted an arguably far more insidious approach to rights by disapplying or modifying the application of the HRA in four Acts of Parliament passed after 2021. Most notably, section 3 of the Safety of Rwanda (Asylum and Immigration) Act 2024 disapplies almost the whole of the HRA with regard to that Act, with section 2 requiring that 'every decision-maker'—be they a politician, an administrator, or a judicial or other tribunal—'must conclusively treat the Republic of Rwanda as a safe country' despite all evidence to the contrary, including a unanimous decision by the UK Supreme Court and the dissenting view of Parliament's International Treaty Commission.[94] In fact, so long as the Act remains in force not even the Prime Minister can block removal on the grounds that Rwanda is unsafe. Jeff King considers that this development 'exposes the very real limitation of the statutory protection of rights' and the related claim for it to be part of an alternative political form of constitutionalism.[95] I disagree. Much as the autocratic legalism of democratic backsliding regimes adopts the forms of a legal constitution without the constitutional substance,[96] so one can regard these moves as involving a deformation of the political constitution that likewise robs it of its constitutional qualities. As I have argued in both Chapter 1 and in this chapter, political constitutionalism does not entail rights scepticism. Rather, it involves taking rights seriously through the process of legislation and by rendering legislative and executive acts subject to contestation, with the final decision resting with Parliament. I have suggested that

[92] The Independent Human Rights Act Review, Executive Summary, paras 51 and 52. There was one dissenter regarding s 3, whose views are addressed in chapter 5, para 82 of the full report.

[93] The Independent Human Rights Act Review, Executive Summary, paras 20, 43, and 44.

[94] *R. (AAA) v Secretary of State of the Home Department* [2023] UKSC 42. See too the UNHCR Analysis of the Legality and Appropriateness of the Transfer of Asylum-Seekers under the UK–Rwanda arrangement: An Update, 15 January 2024.

[95] Jeff King, *From Constitutional Crisis to Poisoned Chalice: A Letter from London*, *VerfBlog*, 28 June 2024 <https://verfassungsblog.de/from-constitutional-crisis-to-poisoned-chalice/> 4, DOI: 10.59704/8163652a51cb5c78.

[96] Kim Lane Scheppele, 'Autocratic Legalism' (2018) 85 *University of Chicago Law Review* 545–83.

the HRA fosters such seriousness in various ways consistent with political constitutionalism. Yet, the measures of the outgoing Conservative governments have sought to remove any consideration of rights concerns from the legislative, judicial, or administrative process. Moreover, they do so on the spurious grounds that such a removal is required to maintain parliamentary sovereignty and the integrity of the democratic process. It might be argued that the remedy for such a failure lies with a legal constitution. Yet, as I remarked above, and detail in Chapters 7 and 8 in particular, legal constitutionalism has often supported and helped entrench democratic backsliding rather than constraining it. The most legitimate and effective response ultimately comes from augmenting rather than curtailing democracy, not least by uniting civic education with enhanced avenues for political participation along the lines proposed in Chapter 3 and discussed further in Chapters 8–10.

Much of the criticism of the HRA gets linked to its association with the ECHR and an undue deference to the jurisprudence of the ECtHR. For example, Raab's proposed new Bill was conceived as a distinctively 'British' Bill of Rights. That position arises from the belief that deferral to an international court necessarily impugns parliamentary sovereignty. I discussed this issue with regard to section 2 HRA above. On this issue too, the Independent Panel's view can be broadly aligned with the interpretation offered here: as they note, ECtHR decisions do not bind UK courts and in practice UK legislation and case law take precedence over ECtHR case law, though they suggested amending section 2 to make this precedence clearer.[97] However, there is a more general issue—central to the international rule of law—as to how far membership of any international legal system can be compatible with political constitutionalism. The belief that it is not proved central to arguments for withdrawal from the European Union (EU), discussed in Chapter 10. However, it is also key to the relationship to international human rights conventions in general and the ECHR in particular (and, one might add—though this tends to be glossed over by those opposed to membership of both the EU and adherence to the ECHR—all other international legal arrangements, such as the World Trade Organization (WTO)). It is to this issue that I now turn.

[97] The Independent Human Rights Act Review, Executive Summary, paras 18 and 20.

5

International Human Rights Conventions

Political Constitutionalism and the European Convention on Human Rights

1. INTRODUCTION: THE DEMOCRATIC LEGITIMACY OF INTERNATIONAL HUMAN RIGHTS CONVENTIONS

A prime purpose of international human rights conventions (IHRCs) is to encourage the signatory states to comply with a certain set of human rights standards. The international human rights courts (IHRCts) often charged with upholding these conventions, such as the European Court of Human Rights (ECtHR), increasingly claim the authority to oblige states to alter legislation in areas that have hitherto been regarded as exclusively domestic, such as the punishment of prisoners, membership of the armed forces, the nature of marriage, or the treatment of children by parents and schools, often overturning the judgments of domestic legislatures and constitutional courts in the process. Such decisions have been welcomed as enhancing both rights and, in a broader sense, democracy, in that they seek to advance equal concern and respect for the individuals and groups involved. Yet, they have also attracted growing criticism from a substantial number of legal and political actors, including judges, politicians, and academics, from within established democracies. These critics argue that IHRCts, such as the ECtHR, are not only less democratically legitimate than domestic legislative and judicial mechanisms for the promotion and protection of rights, but also risk undermining these domestic instruments.[1]

The objections to IHRCts voiced by these critics are normative rather than strictly legal. After all, all well-functioning democracies have signed up to at least some IHRCs, thereby incurring the resulting legal obligations. The issue is whether they *should* have done so, or—in the case of those who claim that the circumstances

[1] e.g. by Lord Hoffmann, at one time the second most senior judge in the UK, in 'The Universality of Human Rights', Judicial Studies Board Annual Lecture (19 March 2009) and, most recently, Lord Sumption, when a judge on the UK Supreme Court, in 'The Limits of Law', the 27th Sultan Azlan Shah Lecture, Kuala Lumpur (20 November 2013), reprinted in N. W. Barber, Richard Ekins, and Paul Yowell (eds), *Lord Sumption and the Limits of Law* (Oxford: Hart Publishing 2016) 15–26. Sumption subsequently developed his views in his Reith Lectures, published as Jonathan Sumption, *Trials of the State: Law and the Decline of Politics* (London: Profile Books 2019). For a similar view from the United States, see Jeremy A. Rabkin, *Law without Nations? Why Constitutional Government Requires Sovereign States* (Princeton, NJ: Princeton University Press 2005).

Defending the Political Constitution. Richard Bellamy, Oxford University Press. © Richard Bellamy 2026.
DOI: 10.1093/9780191826986.003.0007

that made it reasonable to do so in the past no longer obtain—should continue to remain parties to them. Four related democratic concerns underlie their criticisms.[2] The first objection arises from the fear that these arrangements undermine domestic democracy because they involve citizens being subject to an authority that is not exclusively accountable to them. Call this the 'exclusive democratic control' objection. The second holds these international arrangements suffer from a democratic deficit and are largely controlled by unaccountable 'liberal' elites, with their 'liberalism' attracting parallel, if distinct, criticisms from conservatives and socialists for allegedly privileging the interests of cultural and wealthy minorities respectively at the expense of the concerns of a majority of citizens. As a result, there is an absence of ongoing democratic control. This forms the 'global democratic deficit' objection. The third argues that the transfer of powers from the state to such bodies tends to lack appropriate democratic authorization in the first place, and that executives have abused their powers in using a treaty to alter the competences of domestic constitutional structures and the related democratic and legal processes. This comprises the 'constitutional transfer' objection. Finally, the fourth contends that IHRCs can add to the discretionary power of the judiciary. Two worries are involved here. On the one hand, it is felt that the terms of IHRCs are so vague and abstract, that both domestic judges and IHRCts can more or less choose when and in what ways to apply them to particular cases in potentially arbitrary ways. On the other hand, domestic judges may become inappropriately bound by IHRCt rulings made with regard to another jurisdiction that involves quite different circumstances. These reservations constitute the 'judicial discretion' objection.

These objections are not new. Andrew Moravcsik has shown how they figured prominently among the established European democracies at the time of the drafting of the European Convention on Human Rights (ECHR), making their initial support ambivalent at best.[3] Yet, far from disappearing or diminishing in significance as the influence of such bodies has grown, they continue to attract considerable and ever more vocal support.

These four concerns might be thought to reflect a distinctively political constitutionalist perspective that rules out adherence to any international legal convention that is subject to interpretation by a supranational court.[4] However, they have also been invoked from a legal constitutionalist perspective, including by courts in countries with a tradition of 'legal' constitutionalism, such as the United States and

[2] Allen Buchanan and Russell Powell, 'Survey Article: Constitutional Democracy and the Rule of International Law: Are they Compatible?' (2008) 16 *Journal of Political Philosophy* 326–49.

[3] Andrew Moravcsik, 'The Origins of Human Rights Regimes: Democratic Delegation in Postwar Europe' (2000) 54 *International Organisation* 217–52.

[4] In addition to the UK critics mentioned in Chapter 4, see the analysis of recent criticisms of such bodies in Nordic countries in Andreas Follesdal and Marlene Wind, 'Nordic Reluctance towards Judicial Review under Siege' (2009) 27 *Nordic Journal of Human Rights* 131–41.

Germany.[5] Paradoxically, at least some of these legal constitutionalist arguments—those stemming from what I have termed a 'limited' legal constitutionalist perspective, that are especially prevalent in the UK[6]—represent precisely the sort of neo-liberal position that many left-wing adherents of political constitutionalism associate with such international legal systems and that leads them to reject them.[7] Despite certain similarities with political constitutional positions, the argument of 'limited' legal constitutionalists centres mainly on the 'judicial discretion' objection. They complain the ECtHR's 'living instrument' doctrine allows for an expansive view of rights that undermines a libertarian understanding of individual autonomy and personal responsibility that they associate with truly fundamental rights.[8] Though they pay lip service to the 'exclusive democratic control' objection, that is not because they share the political constitutionalist's view of democracy as giving citizens equal control over government and legislation in ways that allow them to push for collective policies that equally advance their interests, thereby expanding social and economic rights. Indeed, they criticize that view too.[9] Rather, they seem to have a faith in people's attachment to a restricted set of negative individual liberties to non-interference, with their preferred limited reading of the ECHR reflecting a broad democratic consensus. By contrast, my main concern here will be to show that the more genuinely democratic concerns of the more left-leaning genuine political constitutionalists need not lead to negative conclusions regarding international legal regimes such as the EHRC, the focus of this chapter, or the European Union (EU), examined in Chapter 10.[10] In fact, an account of their rationale and operation can be given that not only satisfies the four objections but also largely accords with the nature of the ECHR and, as we shall see, with the EU. Consequently, those who invoke political constitutionalist reasoning to oppose such arrangements on democratic grounds, be it from the left or, rather more tendentiously, from the right, prove mistaken. Note, my focus here is not on

[5] e.g. Curtis Bradley and Jack Goldsmith, 'The Current Illegitimacy of International Human Rights' (1997) 66 *Fordham Law Review* 319–69.

[6] See Richard Bellamy, 'The Limits of Lord Sumption: Limited Legal Constitutionalism and the Political Form of the ECHR' in Barber, Ekins, and Yowell (eds), *Lord Sumption and the Limits of Law*, ch. 11, 193–212. An extended version of this article, that includes a discussion of his Reith Lectures, appeared in Italian as 'I limiti di Lord Sumption: Costituzionalismo giuridico limitato, Costituzionalismo politico e Convenzione Europea dei Diritti dell'Uomo' (2019) 3(3) *Rivista di Diritti Comparati* 3–40.

[7] See Martin Loughlin, *Against Constitutionalism* (Cambridge, MA: Harvard University Press 2022) 180–7, 190; Alexander Somak, *The Cosmopolitan Constitution* (Oxford: Oxford University Press 2014) 24, 237–4.

[8] e.g. Sumption, *Trials of the State*, 7–10; Noel Malcolm, *Human Rights and Political Wrongs* (London: Policy Exchange 2017) 69–72.

[9] e.g. Sumption, *Trials of the State*, 16, 19; Martin Loughlin's commentary in 'What Would John Griffen Have Made of Jonathan Sumption's Reith Lectures?' (2019) 90(4) *The Political Quarterly* 788 90.

[10] A representative selection of articles reflecting this critique can be found in the Policy Exchange Judicial Power Project publication: Richard Ekins and Graham Gee (eds), *Judicial Power and the Left* (London: Policy Exchange 2018), particularly Danny Nicol, 'The Left, Capitalism, and Judicial Power' and K. D. Ewing and John Hendy, 'The Politics of Labour Law in the European Court of Human Rights'.

the substantive content of particular judicial judgments but rather the democratic legitimacy of judges to make them. However, my view will be that to the extent IHRCts operate within a political constitutionalist framework, the more likely it will be that their reasoning will be aligned to egalitarian considerations—not least those with regard to upholding equal concern and respect between the different *demoi* of the states subject to their jurisdiction.

This political constitutionalist perspective yields a different understanding of the character of IHRCs to that associated with legal cosmopolitans.[11] They tend to dismiss the four objections and assume IHRCs must involve a form of legal constitutionalism in which strong rights-based judicial review by an IHRCt provides a justified and necessary constraint on both popular and state sovereignty.[12] As we shall see, though, IHRCs can be conceived in quite different terms as products of popular and state sovereignty that are necessarily and justifiably under the joint and equal control of sovereign democratic peoples as part of an international political constitution. Indeed, I shall argue that in the absence of a global *demos* and democratic system, which, even if possible, prove normatively problematic, such an international political constitution may be the only way to render not only political but also legal constitutionalism at the domestic level consistent with IHRCs and IHRCts. Such regimes create a system of checks and balances at the international level that mirrors that favoured by political constitutionalists at the domestic level.[13] They involve a *demoi*cratic[14] and constitutional pluralist[15] arrangement, that encourages mutual respect for the different legal and political systems of the states involved through mutual control of the supranational bodies and organizations through which they are regulated. In particular, as we shall see further in Chapter 10 when looking at the EU, they provide mechanisms for states to control their mutual relations in fair ways promotive of individual rights and to tackle collectively global problems, such as climate change, and transnational processes and organizations, such as financial markets, multinational corporations, and certain terrorist groups.

[11] e.g. Mattias Kumm, 'The Legitimacy of International Law: A Constitutionalist Framework of Analysis' (2004) 15 *European Journal of International Law* 907–31.

[12] Thomas Pogge, *World Poverty and Human Rights: Cosmopolitan Responsibilities and Reform* (Cambridge: Polity 2008) 53, 177; Allen Buchanan, *Justice, Legitimacy and Self-Determination: Moral Foundations for International Law* (Oxford: Oxford University Press 2003).

[13] Somak, *Cosmopolitan Constitution*, 3–6, 20–2 sees the 'cosmopolitan constitution' as a form of 'political constitutionalism redux', because he regards this arrangement as simply reflecting the actual balance of social and economic power in the contemporary world. As a result, such regimes become authoritarian mechanisms for the imposing a neo-liberal scheme of rights suited to the interests of global capitalism. By contrast, I advance this arrangement as a normative model, with the potential for the enabling the democratic control of the global economy.

[14] For the notion of *demoi*cracy see Kalypso Nicolaïdis, 'European *Demoi*cracy and its Crisis' (2013) 51 *Journal of Common Market Studies* 351–69.

[15] For a clear account of legal pluralism in general see N. W. Barber, *The Constitutional State* (Oxford: Oxford University Press 2010) ch. 9, with 164–70 discussing constitutional pluralism in the EU in particular.

The argument proceeds in four steps. As we saw in Chapters 1 and 4, although the political constitutionalism supports the 'exclusive democratic control' and 'judicial discretion' objections, it is nevertheless compatible at the domestic level with a legislative Bill of Rights and weak judicial review by an independent judiciary operating within politically dependent courts. To meet these two objections, therefore, an IHRC and associated IHRCt must possess similar qualities to their respective domestic counterparts and be likewise under the democratic control of those subject to them, either directly or via their elected representatives. To achieve this result, it appears necessary to respond to the 'global democratic deficit' and 'constitutional transfer' objections as well. Step one explores the suitability of a global democratic system as a means for achieving this result, and argues that while theoretically it could do so, it has practical and normative shortcomings. Step two offers an alternative route. It starts by suggesting why political constitutionalists might regard IHRCs and IHRCts as necessary to preserve rather than undermine exclusive democratic control in an interconnected world. I then show how all four objections could be met via an IHRC and IHRCt that are embedded within an international association of democratic states and under their equal ongoing democratic control. Step three shows how such a system largely accords with the EHRC. Step four concludes by suggesting a political constitutionalist approach to IHRCs involving weak review by IHRCts has few disadvantages and many advantages with regard to rights protection compared to a cosmopolitan legal constitutionalist position incorporating strong review.

2. A GLOBAL POLITICAL CONSTITUTION?

Political constitutionalists believe that the determination of any collective policy on rights must be under the equal control of those to whom they are to apply, at least indirectly via their elected representatives. Courts may play a part in ensuring that all interests have been equally considered, but the final say must rest with the democratic legislature and ultimately the people themselves. To be compatible with political constitutionalism, therefore, IHRCs and IHRCts must be: (1) products of and controlled by an international system of normal democracy grounded in and attuned to the domestic systems of the contracting states; (2) offer international versions of a legislative bill of rights; and (3) only involve the exercise of 'weak' review.

Consequently, the fourth, 'judicial discretion', objection to IHRCts can only be met by overcoming the first, 'exclusive democratic control', objection. Meeting these two objections at the international level would seem to require also meeting the second, global democratic deficit, objection, and the third, constitutional transfer, objection, by creating a global or, in the European and similar cases, a regional *demos* and a corresponding global or regional political and constitutional order, with which all *demoi* merge via a series of referenda.[16] Even supposing such a global democratic system was both feasible and desirable, its establishment would still pose a significant contingent barrier to the democratic legitimacy of IHRCts for the foreseeable future. Yet, the feasibility and desirability of such global or regional democratic systems can also be doubted, since they are unlikely to possess the constitutional qualities political and legal constitutionalists associate with democracy.

The political constitutionalist case rests on the democratic process being able to promote the collective interests of those involved in a public and equal way. Unless there is a shared public sphere and reasonably clear lines of authorization and accountability, on the one hand, and a roughly equal stake in the decisions being made and sufficient shared values and cross-cutting cleavages to overcome the problem of persistent minorities, on the other, neither of these qualities is likely to obtain.[17] A global *demos* will in all probability be too culturally and socially differentiated for either of these ontological prerequisites for fair democratic decision-making to exist.[18] Moreover, the homogenization needed to overcome these difficulties would itself involve a loss of value in denying those existing peoples, which do possess a shared political culture and history, the capacity to live according to their various different and not always compatible norms.

Many legal constitutionalists have similar reservations about such schemes. Some legal cosmopolitans have supposed it would be sufficient from a legal constitutionalist perspective to meet the third, constitutional transfer, objection and have a constitutional referendum transferring the requisite authority to an IHRCt.[19] Yet, as the German Federal Constitutional Court's Maastricht and Lisbon decisions indicate,[20] that would not satisfy all such legal constitutionalist concerns. In these judgments, the Court argued its legitimacy lay in representing a German *demos* that is capable of expressing itself through an associated national democratic system. As such, the Court could only hand over that responsibility to the Court of Justice of the European Union (CJEU) in circumstances where the CJEU was similarly responsible to a European *demos*. Only then would it be appropriate to ask the German people if they were prepared to join such an arrangement. Until that time it might be possible for a state to confer certain competences on an international body but the responsibility for ensuring it operated legitimately remained with the

[16] Jürgen Habermas, 'The Constitutionalization of International Law and the Legitimation Problems of a Constitution for World Society' (2008) 15 *Constellations* 444–55.

[17] Thomas Christiano, 'Democratic Legitimacy and International Institutions' in Samantha Besson and John Tasioulas (eds), *The Philosophy of International Law* (Oxford: Oxford University Press 2010) 119–37.

[18] David Miller, 'Democracy's Domain' (2009) 37 *Philosophy and Public Affairs* 201–28.

[19] Buchanan and Powell, 'Constitutional Democracy'.

[20] *Brunner v. European Union Treaty*, 12 October 1993, BVerfGE 89, 155 [1994]; *German Lisbon Decision*, 30 June 2009, BVerfG, 2 be 2/08.

relevant domestic institutions, not least the German Court itself.[21] Thus, it would appear that, for legal as well as political constitutionalists, the legitimacy of IHRCts will rest for the foreseeable future on their being placed under the *demoi*-cratic control of the various *demoi* that acknowledge their authority,[22] at least indirectly via their democratically authorized and accountable political and legal representatives. It remains to be seen how, if at all, this can be achieved.

3. INTERNATIONAL COURTS AND A *DEMOI*CRATIC ASSOCIATION OF DEMOCRATIC STATES

The last section indicated that for political and many legal constitutionalists a democratically legitimate system of international human rights protection will need to be subject to ongoing democratic political control through the ordinary legislative process. Such control must apply to the content of the IHRC, the running of the legal system charged with its interpretation, and to the competences and—in the ultimate instance—to the decisions of the IHRCt. The challenge, addressed in this section, is to see whether that is possible without assuming a regional or global *demos* and democratic system that might exercise that control.

The first, exclusive democratic control, objection provides a key barrier in this regard. It suggests that the only democratically legitimate international order would be a world of separate and independent democratic states. However, this picture of autarkic democratic states is unrealistic given the current reality of interdependence, a condition on which a great deal of our economic well-being depends. In these circumstances, decisions in one state can have important consequences for those in another state, undermining exclusive democratic control. Creating international regimes, such as IHRCs, is one way to respond to this situation. In certain respects, they involve a weakening of exclusive democratic control. But in other respects, as I shall show, these regimes can be conceived in ways that seek to bolster it and to render it as compatible with an interconnected world as possible.

Three issues might motivate democratic states to establish IHRCs and IHRCts. All three stem from a commitment to upholding the 'right of rights' of peoples (and hence of their citizens) to live under democratic regimes. First, states may support such mechanisms as ways of promoting democratization. The move to judicialization generally occurs when hegemonic elites fear their political

[21] *German Lisbon Decision*, [301]. I appreciate these judgments are controversial, and the Court's bark proved louder than its bite given it affirmed the German constitution's openness to international law. Here, it suffices to note legal constitutionalists could raise this objection. See Peter Lindseth, *Power and Legitimacy: Reconciling Europe and the Nations State* (Oxford: Oxford University Press 2010) 24.

[22] For the notion of *demoi*cracy see Kalypso Nicolaïdis, 'European *Demoi*cracy and its Crisis' (2013) 51 *Journal of Common Market Studies* 351–69.

opponents may overturn their policies.[23] The governments of new democracies can rationally see such international commitments as helping to lock in the domestic status quo against their non-democratic opponents. Mature democracies may doubt the utility or legitimacy of such arrangements for themselves but regard them as helpful for less established democracies. Support for this function can be regarded as a corollary of the political constitutionalist belief that rights are best protected through democracy and because of the threat that non- or unstable democratic regimes may pose to democracies.[24]

Second, even if all states are democratic, democratic states have an incentive to ensure that their ability to operate in a democratic manner is not undermined by the decisions of other states, democratic or otherwise. Therefore, they have reason to create institutions to guarantee democracies treat each other with equal concern and respect.[25] Examples include trade negotiations, particularly concerning the exploitation of another country's natural resources, and the promotion of global public goods such as combating climate change and protecting the environment more generally. These arguments also extend to establishing mechanisms to ensure trans- and multinational corporations and organizations respect democratic standards and decision-making.

Both the first and second issues can also be related to protecting the stateless and those seeking entry to democratic states. On the one hand, such persons lack access to the democratic process and, since democratic states are committed to spreading democracy, the reasoning underlying the first issue also extends to them. On the other hand, democratic states might fear that unless the burden of admitting them is shared equitably, the democratic quality of certain states could suffer, thereby invoking the second issue. As a result, states have an interest in securing common, democracy-friendly, policies in this area.

Finally, even mature democracies can acknowledge that no democratic process is perfect. So long as the imperfections of any judicial process can also be corrected by a democratic mechanism, then providing a contestatory channel at the international level may allow lessons to be learned from other democracies and certain unfounded parochial biases and prejudices to be challenged.

These three issues can be linked to three criteria for the governance of the international mechanisms that might be established to address them so as to ensure that these in their turn remain consistent with political constitutionalist assumptions.[26]

[23] Ran Hirschl, *Towards Juristocracy: The Origins and Consequences of the New Constitutionalism* (Cambridge, MA: Harvard University Press 2004).

[24] Moravcsik, 'The Origins', 243–6.

[25] Philip Pettit, 'Legitimate International Institutions: A Neo-Republican Perspective' in Samantha Besson and John Tasioulas (eds), *The Philosophy of International Law* (Oxford: Oxford University Press 2010) 139–60, at 152–3.

[26] Pettit, 'Legitimate International Institutions', 153–8; Christiano, 'Democratic Legitimacy', 122–4, 126–9.

First, these courts and the international arrangements of which they form a part must promote and be compatible with the possibility for all individuals to live in legitimate states that possess democratic systems where collective decisions are made in ways that show them equal respect and concern through being under their shared and equal control. Second, these international mechanisms should be under the equal control of such states. If the legitimacy of democratic states stems from them offering reasonably effective mechanisms for the identification and equal advancement of the interests of their citizens, then the legitimacy of international systems stems from them doing likewise through being in their turn under the shared and equal control of the signatory states. Third, membership of such international systems should be voluntary. Not all states will have an equal stake in collective arrangements on a given issue, and many will not have equal bargaining power. Voluntary arrangements allow states to tailor their international commitments to the interests of their populations and ideally to negotiate the terms of their adherence accordingly.

The basic institutional model of the international order stemming from these issues and criteria is that of a voluntary and fair association among democratic states. Such an association offers a 'two-level' political constitution,[27] whereby a political constitution at the international level renders an IHRC and IHRCts subject to the democratic authorization and accountability of the representatives of the contracting democratic states, who are in their turn democratically authorized and accountable to those they represent through a political constitution at the domestic level. A number of recommendations follow from this account as to the competences and scope of judicial review by IHRCts, on the one hand, and the democratic organization of IHRC systems, on the other. I shall take each in order below.

With regard to competences and scope, four remarks are in order. First, as Thomas Christiano has noted,[28] this model grounds certain international *jus cogens* norms concerning the performance of agreements duly made and against slavery, genocide, and aggressive war, since these norms are prerequisites of, or internal to, such an arrangement and the importance it places on the value of consent. Therefore, there can be no problem with IHRCts seeking to uphold such norms unconditionally.

Second, a prime focus of such Conventions should be the interactions between states and those who either lack democratic representation or operate outside adequate democratic control, such as refugees and multinational corporations respectively.

[27] Robert Putnam, 'Diplomacy and Domestic Politics: The Logic of Two-Level Games' (1988) 42 *International Organization* 427–60.

[28] Christiano, 'Democratic Legitimacy', 123.

Third, if IHRCts are to respect the integrity of the democratic process, particularly in their judgments on domestic legislation and policies, they must be restricted to weak review. Moreover, contestation ought to be limited to cases where domestic political and judicial avenues have been exhausted and only involve those rights that might be considered basic to each citizen within a given polity being able to publically advance their interests on equal terms to others, though controversy exists as to whether these involve only core civil and political rights or also certain minimum social and economic rights too.[29] Allowance also has to be made for the variety of ways different legal systems may choose to specify a given right and the numerous circumstances that may lead legislatures to limit the scope of one right in order to secure other rights.

Fourth, given courts may be as mistaken as legislators, the possibility for a democratic override of an IHRCt judgment must also exist, with such decisions resting with a consensus among the representatives of the democratic governments, who should be ultimately charged with monitoring state compliance with the Court's rulings. A number of benefits stem from this arrangement. For a start, from the perspective of the democratic state challenging the judgment, this would be a decision of peers.[30] The governments of other democratic states would appreciate the need to attune rights to domestic situations and the adverse reaction an IHRCt decision perceived as insensitive to such considerations and in error might arouse. Yet, that need not mean they would tolerate almost any objection to a ruling that proved inconvenient for the government concerned—quite the contrary. For they would also be fully alive to the dangers of allowing states to renege on their solidaristic obligations and of undermining the Court's authority through frivolous or self-serving challenges—particularly with regard to democratizing states.

The issue of democratic organization enters here, with three points being pertinent. First, this model is compatible with granting IHRCts a degree of independence from the states that bring them into being so long as the participating states have the right of exit and can determine the competences of these courts. In other words, the functionaries of the IHRC, such as the judges, may act independently but the system itself must be democratically dependent on the contracting states.

Second, the democratic legitimacy of such dependence rests on the agents of the states involved adequately reflecting the views and concerns of the populations they represent. Consequently, signatories to IHRCs should be limited to states that are at least credibly democratizing. The evidence suggests that non-democratic states do not respect the decisions of such bodies in any case—their formal adherence merely serves to give a spurious legitimacy to such regimes.[31] Meanwhile,

[29] Christiano, *The Constitution of Equality*, 273–4.

[30] Fritz Scharpf, 'Legitimacy in the Multilevel European Polity' (2009) 1 *European Political Science Review* (2009) 173–204, at 199–200.

[31] Beth Simmons, *Mobilizing for Human Rights: International Law in Domestic Politics* (Cambridge: Cambridge University Press 2009).

given the discretion executives of even democratic states have been accustomed to enjoy in foreign affairs, it is important to ensure the state officials involved remain accountable for their decisions to the legislature and ultimately the electorate.

Finally, if the system as a whole is to offer equal consideration to the interests of the democratic peoples that it serves, then the signatory states ought to exercise equal control over the IHRC. For example, all states should have an equal vote in decisions regarding changes to the Convention, the selection of judges and instructions as to their working methods, the implementation of the Court's judgments, the budget, and so on.

How do these arrangements fare against the four objections? With regard to the first, exclusive democratic control, objection, that is met at a base line level by insisting that entry into these arrangements are voluntary and include a right of exit. Moreover, their purpose and operation is structured around respect for democratic self-government. As we saw, this goal lies behind both the three issues motivating the establishment of this system and the three criteria guiding its competences and organization. In particular, its governance structure does not involve a simple transfer of authority from a domestic to an international actor. Rather, it places domestic actors, who remain democratically accountable to citizens or their representatives, in control on an equal and democratic basis. This structure overcomes the second, global democratic deficit, objection without assuming either a global *demos* or democracy. Instead, the arrangement is one of a democratic international association of democracies and their *demoi*. This sort of 'two-level' arrangement has been characterized as *demoi*cratic. The fact that the system is an outgrowth of domestic democratic systems reduces the force of the third objection regarding the need for a constitutional transition. There is not so much a transfer of competences as the creation of a jointly controlled mechanism to tackle those common problems that domestic institutions lack the competence to deal with alone. Finally, the fourth objection, of undue judicial discretion, is met through rendering the IHRCt systemically dependent on the collective democratic decisions of the contracting states with regard to their competences and, in the last instance, judgments. Judges may be independent but only with respect to weak review.

Clearly, many problems stand in the way of realizing this system and in practice institutional arrangements may not necessarily always meet the criteria or answer all relevant issues. In particular, there is the problem of asymmetric bargaining between richer and more powerful states and poorer and weaker states, though coalitions among the latter can to some degree counteract the influence of the former.[32] As with all domestic democratic systems, the international *demoi*cratic system is work in progress, with various groups employing the existing processes to further,

[32] Christiano, 'Democratic Legitimacy', 125–6; Pettit, 'Legitimate International Institutions', 158–60.

and occasionally to hinder, its development. This section has aimed simply at formulating its normative and institutional underpinnings.

4. THE POLITICAL CONSTITUTION OF THE ECHR

A measure of the plausibility of this approach can be gauged by the significant degree to which the ECHR can be assimilated to it. All signatories must meet certain minimal democratic standards. The Court and Convention are overseen by the Council of Europe, the governance structure of which consists of the Committee of Ministers, comprising the foreign ministers or their permanent representatives of all forty-seven member states, along with the Parliamentary Assembly of the Council of Europe (PACE). The Committee decides the Council's budget, negotiates the treaties and conventions governing its competences, and monitors the implementation of Court decisions. PACE, which includes between two and eighteen members, depending on population size, from the national parliaments of each of the signatory states, selects the judges—one from each member state—and the Secretary General of the Council from lists supplied by the Committee of Ministers. As a result, there is a degree of legislative oversight of executive action in this area, with PACE also receiving regular reports from and making recommendations to the Committee of Ministers. The danger of overlooking domestic or transnational minorities is also lessened through the involvement of a Congress of Local and Regional Authorities of the Council of Europe, composed of elected members from these bodies within the member states, charged with exploring the enhancement of local democracy and, in an advisory role, the International Non-Governmental Organisations (INGOs) Conference of the Council of Europe.

Meanwhile, the Court applies a margin of appreciation in making its judgments, especially where no common standard exists across the Council of Europe and it may be necessary to balance rights and other interests,[33] thereby taking account of the diverse ways a right may be specified within different legal systems. Moreover, the Court has generally applied a wider margin when the case involves a choice that has been publically debated by a democratic legislature and where opinions reasonably differ, and narrowed it where a legislature has enacted or re-enacted a measure without due consideration.[34] Its judgments also only apply to the given jurisdiction and do not necessarily serve as precedents for rulings in similar cases in another state, thereby minimizing the 'one size fits all' problem. The Brighton

[33] See *Rasmussen v. Denmark* (1984) 7 EHRR 371 [40]–[41] for the lack of a common approach, and *Dickenson v. United Kingdom* (2008) 46 EHRR 41, GC [77]–[79] for the issue of balance.

[34] *Hatton v. United Kingdom* (2003) 37 EHRR 28 GC [97]; *Draon v. France* (2006) 42 EHRR 40, GC [106]–[108], and—for the converse argument—*Hirst v. United Kingdom (No. 2)* (2006) 42 EHRR 41; *Sukhovetsky v. Ukraine* (2007) 44 EHRR 57 [65]–[67]; and the analysis in Andrew Legg, *The Margin of Appreciation in International Human Rights Law* (Oxford: Oxford University Press 2012) esp. ch. 4.

declaration proposed formally incorporating both the margin of appreciation and the principle of subsidiarity into the Preamble of the Convention,[35] thereby underlining that the primary duty for the implementation of Convention rights rests with domestic legal and especially political organs. Indeed, it suggested that all parliaments should adopt the enhanced pre-legislative scrutiny procedures currently found in the UK and Nordic countries. In fact, the record suggests that the ECtHR already operates at the margins so far as mature democracies are concerned. For example, since 1966, 97 per cent of the cases brought against the UK have been deemed inadmissible, while only 271 out of the 443 cases that were heard were held to involve an infraction—61 per cent or an average of 6.15 cases per year, less than 2 per cent of all cases brought. Five countries—Russia, Ukraine, Romania, Turkey, and Italy—currently account for over half the cases brought before the Court, with Russia alone responsible for 27 per cent of them.

These features of the Council of Europe correspond quite closely to the criteria and corresponding recommendations given in the last section for ensuring an international association of democracies itself meets democratic criteria. Not only is it under the equal control of the representatives of democratic states, but these representatives are not simply from the executive branch. The involvement of parliamentary representatives and, to a lesser extent, representatives from local government and non-governmental organizations (NGOs) as well, increases the likelihood that state policies are more democratically representative of domestic interests than is often the case in foreign affairs, including minority interests. As a result, it meets the concerns behind the 'global democratic deficit' objection in ways that address at least some of the worries behind the 'exclusive democratic control' objection. The EHRC can be regarded in some ways as having the qualities of an international legislative charter of rights, with reports from PACE often leading to changes to the Convention or procedures by the Council of Ministers. Last but not least, the ECtHR is politically dependent, in being chosen and overseen by a representative body of the contracting states, and is constrained to respect to a high degree their domestic rights enforcing mechanisms. As a result of these two aspects, the force of the judicial discretion objection is also weakened to a considerable extent.

That said, the ECHR system falls down in two key respects. First, notwithstanding the margin of appreciation, strictly speaking the ECtHR does not adopt weak review. Under article 46 of the Convention its judgments have binding force on the High Contracting Parties and once a final ruling has been given by a Grand Chamber there are no further grounds of appeal. Still, it does not disapply national laws—they remain in force until the relevant domestic legislature changes them and can only offer a remedy in international not domestic law. To that extent, the

[35] High Level Conference on the future of the ECtHR Brighton Declaration 19/20 April 2012 <http://hub.coe.int/en/20120419-brighton-declaration/>.

ECtHR could be described as applying a 'soft' version of strong review. Yet, the system could be adapted to deliver weak review relatively easily. As I noted, the Committee of Ministers is responsible for implementation of these judgments and can sanction a member for failing to comply and even expel them. However, it would be perfectly possible to allow the Committee to become the final court of appeal as proposed above.

Second, hitherto, the focus of the ECtHR has been on the issue of domestic compliance with the ECHR. Although the Council of Europe has explored common issues affecting the relations between states, these have been at the margins. That would change if the proposed accession of the EU to the ECHR went ahead, which will introduce monitoring of inter-state economic agreements for compliance with human rights. Already, an important difference between the ECtHR and the CJEU with regard to labour rights suggests ways in which this move might lead to greater equal respect and concern between the states involved for their internal democratic processes.[36] Yet, how far that happens is likely to depend on the degree to which both the Council of Europe and the EU are regarded as being bound by a political rather than a legal constitution.

5. THE DISADVANTAGES OF LEGAL COSMOPOLITANISM AND THE ADVANTAGES OF THE POLITICAL CONSTITUTIONAL APPROACH

So far I have simply argued that it is possible to provide a political constitutionalist account of IHRCs that meets the four objections. I have said relatively little about the broader advantages that might derive from a political constitutionalist rather than a cosmopolitan legal constitutionalist perspective that rejected the four objections in the first place. Such a cosmopolitan position can take a number of forms. Here, I shall consider a relatively modest version, which avoids controversial ontological and epistemological claims as far as possible. This version might grant that some reasonable disagreement about rights exists, but note that in practice most democracies agree on the broad outlines of at least some basic rights, such as those in the ECHR, and that for pragmatic as much as principled reasons, rights-based judicial review of domestic legislation by independent international courts offers a way of correcting for local prejudices, self-interest, or myopia.[37] These pragmatic arguments can be roughly grouped together under the legal norm of '*nemo iudex in sua causa*'.[38] In this section, I shall argue that many of these concerns prove

[36] Judy Fudge, 'Constitutionalizing Labour Rights in Europe' in Tom Campbell, E. D. Ewing, and Adam Tomkins (eds), *The Legal Protection of Human Rights: Sceptical Essays* (Oxford: Oxford University Press 2011) 244–67.

[37] Buchanan, *Justice*, 297–8.

[38] Buchanan and Powell, 'Constitutional Democracy', 330–6.

misplaced and that weak review within a political constitutionalist structure offers a more effective and coherent approach to rights promotion than strong review by an IHRCt cut off from democratic control.

For a start, it can be questioned how far it is applicable to regard a democratic state as being a 'judge in its own cause'. This position treats a state as a unitary actor, deciding an issue of rights in its own self-interest. However, given that the decisions in question tend not to be about inter-state relations, it seems inappropriate to regard these judgments as challenging the self-interest of states. The exceptions might be policies concerning access to citizenship or entry to and continued residence in a state for asylum seekers or immigrants. These cases are additionally strong given that neither group can influence the relevant domestic legal and political system via the democratic process, while most of the first and many of the second will either be citizens of regimes that are not democratic, or only minimally so, or stateless persons. However, we saw in Section 3 that democratic states have incentives to create collective arrangements to deal with such issues that can balance the rights of their citizens against those of aspirant and non-citizens, and ultimately aim to promote democracy among all states. As a result, such arrangements only require weak review. Given it is mutually advantageous for all the contracting states to a Convention to comply with them, this would not be an issue where governments would be likely to regard an ICtHR as exceeding its competence.

It is also worth noting that what is perhaps the strongest case for strong review is also the least developed in practice. In the standard cases, which concern purely domestic measures that only affect citizens, the notion of the state being 'judge in its own cause' proves harder to sustain.[39] The democratic decision-making process that leads to the disputed law involves a large number of different and often opposed actors. Elected executives will have had to gain the assent of representatives in Parliament and indirectly a majority of citizens, while domestic courts will have also held the measure to be acceptable. Moreover, as we have seen, these domestic processes may well have been scrupulous in their attention to rights considerations. There will have been no single actor 'judging in its own cause' in this situation. Within most democratic systems, an electoral majority is built on a coalition of diverse groups of voters, with the executive and legislative majority often made up of a shifting coalition of different parties. In many systems, measures have to be approved by two chambers and are subject to review by domestic courts.

It will be objected that nonetheless certain 'discrete and insular' or widely dispersed minorities, with little or no bargaining power, might still be consistently ignored by these democratic and legal mechanisms. Those social groups who are likely to form part of the electoral majority and the domestic legal and political

[39] Kristen Hessler, 'Resolving Interpretive Conflicts in International Human Rights Law' (2005) 13 *Journal of Political Philosophy* 29–52, at 41–2.

elite may suppress these minorities' individual rights—be it through self-interest, prejudice, myopia, ignorance, carelessness, or plain error. Indeed, one or more of these factors could lead a majority to pay insufficient attention to their own rights in the face of an overzealous, inept, misguided, or corrupt executive, as some commentators have alleged has been the case with excessively restrictive anti-terrorist legislation. In such instances, an IHRCt offers even a well-run domestic legal and political system the benefit of an 'outsider's' perspective. For example, other legal systems may provide instances of policies that challenge the local prejudices and assumptions of the state in question. Through being more disengaged from the circumstances that give rise to a given policy, such bodies can also help guard against precipitate overreactions to a shocking incident, such as a terrorist bomb or the abduction of a child, and point to the longer-term adverse consequences of overhasty legislation.

Though such reasoning may prove valid in certain circumstances, it is again doubtful that it offers a general case for anything beyond 'weak review'. Indeed, the drawbacks political constitutionalists note with relying on courts for the defence of rights may be amplified in the case of judicial review by IHRCts, in part for the very reasons that their proponents advance in their defence. For a start, the 'outsider's' view may overlook how the specification of a particular right within a given legal system forms part of a more general approach to rights, that balances different rights considerations and which taken overall is reasonable and reflects local circumstances and concerns.[40] Ruling on a single case does not allow for all these various factors to be taken into account and IHRCts are likely to be even less aware of the impact on other rights and moral concerns of citizens than a domestic court. An IHRCt may also be moved to assume 'one size fits all' and seek to apply a minimal standard that overlooks substantive differences between different cases and systems.

Distance also exacerbates the potential for the under protection of rights that can arise when IHRCts are perceived as the key agents of rights protection. Whereas political constitutionalism stresses *ex ante* rights scrutiny, courts operate *ex post*. If a higher court comes to be regarded as the prime instrument of rights protection, there is a danger that the subordinate bodies—particularly executives and legislatures—will be less scrupulous themselves and only take rights into consideration to the extent that they believe they may be legally challenged to do so. An IHRCt may exacerbate this tendency by adding to the already high costs in time and money of mounting a legal challenge. Meanwhile, though IHRCts can help dilute the influence of local factions, weakening the effects of their rent seeking and prejudices, they may also give undue weight in their turn to those groups able to organize transnationally. As we noted, states can unjustifiably

[40] Hessler, 'Resolving', 43–4.

exclude underprivileged groups, such as refugees or poor migrants. However, certain exclusionary state policies—such as those regulating wages or health and safety—may serve to provide social protection for the more vulnerable within their borders. Yet, those seeking to dismantle exclusions of the latter kind, such as corporations, are likely to have more resources and be better able to mount legal challenges at the international level than those seeking to remove exclusions of the former kind, such as the global poor.[41]

There has been a move recently to enshrine some of these social protections in IHRCs. However, many of these issues are matters of reasonable disagreement within most democracies and closely related to the left–right divide that forms the dominant political cleavage within them. As we noted, courts also have limitations when deciding general issues of public policy and often feel they lack the expertise as well as the legitimacy to do so. All rights are costly and how far any state may be able to meet its rights commitments will be a matter of degree, involving various trade-offs that courts invariably feel reluctant to make. Again, distance can add to the timidity of courts in areas that may entail more rather than less state action. Unsurprisingly, the empirical record suggests the constitutionalization of social rights has little impact per se. The key factors are the degree of development of the country concerned and the ability of the underprivileged to organize themselves through unions and parties capable of promoting their interests.[42]

It might be thought that when courts fail to correct an injustice their influence is neutral—they have simply failed to right a wrong. That is not the case. Under strong review they add legitimacy to that wrong and render its righting harder. Courts may also make mistakes and in doing so commit a double wrong. Not only have the rights of those individuals directly affected by the particular decision been infringed, but so has the right of all citizens to have an equal say in defining their rights. Weak review may commit the first wrong but in escaping the second also makes the rectification of the first easier to effect.

Given the legitimacy of democratic processes to decide rights issues depends on their providing an adequate means for giving equal consideration to the views and interests of those concerned, it has been argued that even if courts ought not to offer substantive rulings on the nature of rights, they do have a role in deeming whether democratic procedures meet the appropriate standards for their decisions to have authority.[43] Moreover, the argument for not being judge in one's own cause appears particularly strong in this case. Those in power will always have an

[41] Danny Nicol, 'Business Rights as Human Rights' in Campbell, Ewing, and Tomkins (eds), *The Legal Protection*, 229–43.

[42] Evan Rosevear and Ran Hirschl, 'Constitutional Law Meets Comparative Politics: Socio-economic Rights and Political Realities', in Campbell, Ewing, and Tomkins (eds), *The Legal Protection*, 207–28.

[43] John Hart Ely, *Democracy and Distrust: A Theory of Judicial Review* (Cambridge, MA: Harvard University Press 1980).

incentive to alter the rules of the game in their favour. The difficulty is that process issues can be as subject to reasonable disagreement as substantive questions. Citizens may agree that procedures should show those involved equal respect and concern, yet disagree as to how best to interpret these requirements. These procedural disagreements will most likely reflect their substantive disagreements. Even when agreement exists on a given understanding of political equality, the institutions most likely to bring it about are difficult to specify and likely to depend on the social circumstances in which they are located. Therefore, it can be hard for courts to offer an impartial or satisfactory decision in such cases, with IHRCts once again hampered by distance and a lack of local knowledge.

Although a human right to democracy is controversial,[44] it might be thought central for political constitutionalists—even the 'right of rights'[45]—and so render strong judicial review legitimate.[46] In this area, courts could be said not just to restore the rights of those individuals who have been unjustly excluded from the process but also the rights of all those involved in it, because by ensuring their inclusion a court reinstates the authority of the process as a whole.[47] Yet, the principled and pragmatic objections to strong review remain given that courts may fail to uphold the democratic rights of citizens or even hamper attempts by the legislature to do so. For example, compare *Buckley v. Valeo*, where the US Supreme Court prevented the legislature limiting campaign finance, to the British Parliament's considered preparedness to override potential judicial objections to its regulation of political advertising in the *Communications Act 2003*. Both cases concerned freedom of speech and the appropriate way to secure its promotion.[48] The difference between the Supreme Court's perspective and that of the UK (and US) legislatures was not between a rights-based view and a non-rights-based view, but over which measures best secured this right within a democratic society. Again, the argument points at best to weak review because while it is important to draw attention to potential individual rights infringements, a court may not offer the most suitable forum for ensuring rights protection remains consistent with equal concern and respect for all citizens. In this case, it could be argued it was precisely because the

[44] Joshua Cohen, 'Is There a Human Right to Democracy?' in Christine Sypnowich (ed.), *The Egalitarian Conscience: Essays in Honour of G. A. Cohen* (Oxford: Oxford University Press 2006) 226–50.

[45] Waldron, *Law and Disagreement*, 232.

[46] Robert A. Dahl, *Democracy and its Critics* (New Haven, CT: Yale University Press 1989) 191 and 359 n. 9.

[47] Christiano, *The Constitution of Equality*, 275–7.

[48] The UK Parliament (Communications Act 2003 (U.K.), 2003, *c.* 21 ss 319–21) sought to ensure political equality at election time by regulating political broadcasts—a move that had cross-party support but which it anticipated, in part because of decisions such as *Buckley v. Valeo* 424 US 1 (1976), might be ruled as contrary to art 10 ECHR, leading to a Ministerial declaration to legislate notwithstanding a potential incompatibility with the HRA, as is allowed under section 19 HRA. Influenced by Parliament's reasoning, the British courts subsequently upheld the measure in *R. (Animal Defenders International) v. Secretary for Culture, Media and Sport* [2008] UKHL 15, esp. Lord Bingham at [7]–[21].

politicians had an interest in the decision that they appreciated the need for regulation to ensure a roughly level playing field for fair and equal elections.

Finally, the argument against being judge in one's cause is in some respects deployed selectively and ultimately lacks coherence. For it is inescapable that some person or institution will be so. After all, superior courts generally claim the competence to decide their own competences. Political constitutionalists argue that, to the extent this is true of domestic democratic legislatures, it can at least be justified by the countervailing principle that 'what touches all should be decided by all'. This doctrine embodies the important epistemic principle that decisions are best made by those with sufficient stake in the matter to decide responsibly. IHRCts, by their very nature as outsiders, lack that incentive.

6. CONCLUSION

The upholding of IHRCs by IHRCts has been criticized for lacking democratic legitimacy. Such criticisms have emanated from certain legal constitutionalist regimes, such as the United States and Germany, but have been particularly strong in political constitutionalist regimes, such as the UK. Indeed, senior Conservative politicians and academics, as well as some Labour politicians and supporters, have proposed at various times that Britain withdraw from all such arrangements.[49] As I noted in the Introduction, paradoxically these critiques reflect opposed views of the nature of the decisions of the ECtHR, with the right criticizing its expansive, and the left its restrictive, reading of rights. Both agree, though, albeit the left more convincingly than the right, that this involves judicial discretion illegitimately encroaching on areas that should be left to democratic legislation. This chapter has taken these two objections seriously but has argued they can be met by IHRCts in ways that address the 'global democratic deficit' and 'constitutional transfer' objections by regarding IHRC instruments as forming part of a 'two-level' political constitution resulting from an association of democratic states. In fact, the ECHR, which has borne the brunt of recent attacks on IHRCts within the UK, largely conforms to this model. This arrangement also renders IHRCts consistent with legal constitutionalism at the domestic level by allowing national constitutional courts to legitimize and control their competences in the name of their respective *demoi*. Finally, limiting IHRCts to weak review, as this system requires, proves not only a more democratically legitimate but also a more effective means of protecting rights than the strong review advocated by a legal cosmopolitan approach.

[49] For the right-wing critique, see 'Protecting Human Rights in the UK: The Conservatives' Proposals for Changing Britain's Human Rights Laws', 3 October 2014 and Malcolm, 'Human Rights and Political Wrongs', whose view parallels that of Sumption, *Trials of State*. For the left-wing critique, that more truly aligns with political constitutionalism, see the articles in the Judicial Power Project publication, Ekins and Gee (eds), *Judicial Power and the Left*.

PART 3

THE JUDICIAL CHALLENGE—DEMOCRACY THROUGH COURTS?

6

Must Politics Rest on Law?

1. INTRODUCTION

A common critique of political constitutionalism and its grounding in the need for fair political procedures to resolve 'reasonable disagreements' is that this argument produces an infinite regress.[1] If we prioritize procedures to settle persistent disagreements, these critics ask, then which procedures do we employ to select these procedures? Surely, some procedure will be needed to identify the preferred procedure? Yet how can that procedure avoid being subject to reasonable disagreements in its turn, requiring yet another procedure to settle that dispute, and so on ad infinitum? These critics maintain that the only way around this dilemma must be to determine the minimum rights required for a legitimate procedure and to see these as the legal constitutional basis for—and potential constraints upon—any acceptable form of democracy.

This chapter explores this criticism by way of an examination of Cormac Mac Amhlaigh's stimulating article challenging the coherence of political constitutionalism.[2] Mac Amhlaigh helpfully identifies four linked claims that, taken together, constitute the main elements of this critique. First, he argues that political constitutionalists contend disagreement goes 'all the way down'; second, that given they maintain this disagreement applies to processes as much as outcomes, there is no impartial, Archimedean, point from which to assess the rival claims of different procedures, and hence no way they can argue for the superiority of political over legal constitutionalism; third, that contrary to their assertion that process matters more than outcomes, the normative legitimacy of any process must rest on an outcome assessment of its preserving certain minimal standards, such as upholding basic rights; and fourth, that they can only defend a preference for political over legal constitutionalism where it is already in place and meets these minimal legitimacy requirements.

Needless to say I disagree—not unreasonably I hope—with the validity of all four criticisms, at least in regard to my own characterization of political

[1] e.g. Thomas Christiano, 'Waldron on Law and Disagreement' (2000) 19(4) *Law and Philosophy* 521; Frank I. Michelman, 'How Can the People Ever Make the Laws? A Critique of Deliberative Democracy' (1997) 17(4) *The Modern Schoolman* 311–30; Henry Richardson, *Democratic Autonomy: Public Reasoning about the Ends of Policy* (Oxford: Oxford University Press 2002) 67.

[2] Cormac Mac Amhlaigh, 'Putting Political Constitutionalism in Its Place' (2016) 14 *International Journal of Constitutional Law* 175–97.

Defending the Political Constitution. Richard Bellamy, Oxford University Press. © Richard Bellamy 2026.
DOI: 10.1093/9780191826986.003.0009

constitutionalism (although much of what I say in my own defence may well apply to Jeremy Waldron's views as well, the other main target of Mac Amhlaigh's critique).[3] I believe that Mac Amhlaigh (like other critics) mischaracterizes what I have called 'the circumstances of disagreement', and in doing so adopts a position that is itself self-defeating. At the heart of our disagreement lie two different conceptions of constitutionalism that only partially overlap with the distinction between legal and political constitutionalism. The first conception can be characterized as a form of what Bernard Williams termed political moralism.[4] It conceives a constitution as a moral structure that provides foundations for, and constraints upon, the political and, in some versions, also goals for politics to enact. The second conception aligns itself more with what Williams called political realism.[5] It gives greater autonomy to political concerns related to the need for an authoritative process of decision-making that are distinct from morality. Both conceptions could be institutionalized in ways that involved either judicial or legislative supremacy. For example, democratic institutions could be so designed that they promote a given conception of justice,[6] as a political moralist would advocate, or courts be viewed simply as a necessary political mechanism to provide authoritative decisions,[7] as a political realist would argue.

What gives my account of political constitutionalism its distinctively political cast is its political realist starting point rather than the advocacy of legislative supremacy per se. It is this political realist character that leads to the emphasis on constitutional process rather than the achievement of certain constitutional outcomes, such as political moralists would advocate. As I suggest below, this process-based view does ultimately favour legislative over judicial supremacy. However, even if it provides no clear knock-down argument for the former, it certainly alters how we should conceive of the latter.

In what follows, I draw on Williams to suggest why all four of Mac Amhlaigh's claims misfire through invoking a political moralist as opposed to a political realist conception of constitutionalism. As a result, he is led into making a second order critique of the grounding of any first order constitutional reasoning, the necessity for, and plausibility of which, I largely deny. It is for that reason that he fears an infinite regress in the face of ubiquitous disagreement, whereas I am content

[3] The main targets of his argument are Richard Bellamy, *Political Constitutionalism: A Republican Defence of the Constitutionality of Democracy* (Cambridge: Cambridge University Press 2007) (hereafter *PC*) and Jeremy Waldron, *Law and Disagreement* (Oxford: Oxford University Press 1999).

[4] Bernard Williams, 'Realism and Moralism in Political Theory' in Bernard Williams, *In the Beginning Was the Deed* (Princeton, NJ: Princeton University Press 2005) 1–2.

[5] Williams, 'Realism and Moralism in Political Theory', 3.

[6] e.g. Philippe Van Parijis, *Just Democracy: The Rawls–Machiavelli Programme* (Colchester: ECPR Press 2011).

[7] e.g. Martin Shapiro's characterization of the European Court of Justice (ECJ) in Martin Shapiro, 'The European Court of Justice' in Paul Craig and Gráinne de Búrca (eds), *The Evolution of EU Law* (Oxford: Oxford University Press 1999) 321–7.

to regard it as a permanent and unavoidable feature of the human condition and simply to start from where we are.

2. ALL THE WAY DOWN? THE 'CIRCUMSTANCES OF DISAGREEMENT'

Though Mac Amhlaigh puts the phrase 'disagreement all the way down' in quotation marks, it is not one I ever employed in *Political Constitutionalism*, though it does figure once in Waldron's *Law and Disagreement*.[8] Of course, even without using the phrase, my argument that 'politics goes all the way down' and defence of 'the basic normative case for a thorough-going proceduralism that goes all the way down' might be thought to entail such a position,[9] whether I realized it or not. However, I believe that overstates my argument and is neither necessary to, nor supportive of, my case for political constitutionalism. Indeed, to the extent Mac Amhlaigh appears to embrace this position himself, at least for the purposes of his article, I shall argue it undermines the alternative case he wishes to make.

The belief that disagreement goes 'all the way down' might be taken as a form of what Ronald Dworkin called 'external' scepticism.[10] Such a position would be sceptical about the whole enterprise of legal and political argument. It would maintain that the fact we disagree suggests that no moral and political view could ever be right. Yet that goes too far, as it would negate the very holding of a substantive position in the first place. Such 'external' scepticism can be deemed ontological. By contrast, what Dworkin called 'internal' scepticism reflects the experience of anyone who takes moral and political argument and their own positions within it seriously. It is the acknowledgement that the presence of other views to one's own, including views that involve criticisms of one's views, mean that one may be wrong. Such 'internal' scepticism can be regarded as epistemological—it reflects the limitations of our practical reasoning which make us prone to error.

Hypothetically, an objective and just resolution of people's disagreements may exist—not necessarily *sub specie aeternitatis*, a notion I criticize below, but of a kind that makes sense to people in a given historically contingent situation. That supposition provides us with something to disagree about, rather than disagreeing for disagreement's sake. After all, both political and legal constitutionalists agree that protecting certain rights and guarding against particular ways of exercising power are important. However, they disagree about why, how, when, and by whom—even

[8] Waldron, *Law and Disagreement*, 295, where he states, 'It looks as though it is disagreement all the way down, so far as constitutional choice is concerned'. The subsequent sections of that chapter go on to address similar issues to those raised by Mac Amhlaigh and others.

[9] Bellamy, *Political Constitutionalism*, 152, 174.

[10] Ronald Dworkin, 'Objectivity and Truth: You'd Better Believe It' (1996) 25 *Philosophy and Public Affairs* 87–139.

among themselves. Practically, nobody has access to an objective perspective from which to resolve these disputes. Stupidity, ignorance, or self-interest no doubt all play a part in creating much disagreement. Yet, disagreement also arises among the wise and well-intentioned because our individual perspectives on what ought to be done are inevitably partial in the sense of being both incomplete and reflecting a personal bias.[11] Lacking omniscience, our knowledge of others and of the causes or effects of any action or policy will always be flawed, making our reasoning fallible and opening up the prospect that, with the best will in the world, we are prone to errors that may have profoundly damaging consequences. Similarly, our values and judgements tend to reflect our own experience and knowledge—however hard we try, it proves highly improbable that we could entirely satisfactorily place ourselves fully in the shoes of those whose ways of thinking and social context may be either metaphorically or literally outside our ken. These two forms of partiality together comprise the 'circumstances of disagreement'.

As I have remarked in Chapters 1 and especially 2, these 'circumstances of disagreement' have political and legal importance because of what Rawls, following Hume, termed the 'circumstances of justice'.[12] Scarce resources and limited altruism mean that no one can assume that they will either have enough to satisfy all they need for their projects, or can count on the spontaneous forbearance or support of others when necessary. As a result, conflicts will arise, leading to the need for collective rules assigning who is entitled to or owed what by whom, when, and how. Yet, we must collectively agree on these necessary collective rules in the light of extensive disagreement about their substance, sources, subjects, sphere, and scope. Such disagreements about the nature and application of rights and justice, combined with the need for collective agreements about them, together comprise what Waldron has called 'the circumstances of politics'.[13]

The circumstances of politics make necessary the establishment of some form of political authority capable of determining our rights despite our disagreements. As I remarked in Chapter 2, Bernard Williams regarded this necessity for the authoritative 'securing of order, protection, trust and the conditions of co-operation' as 'the first political question' because 'it is the condition of solving, indeed posing, any others'.[14] In that sense, politics goes 'all the way down', as I noted I did say, because it is fundamental. Yet, how are we to ensure such an authority is also constitutional? Clearly, it will be constitutive of the political community, but how could we agree on its meeting constitutional norms despite our disagreements about those norms? This is the question to which political constitutionalism attempts to provide an answer, with Mac Amhlaigh contending that response to be inadequate.

[11] Thomas Christiano, *The Constitution of Equality: Democratic Authority and Its Limits* (Oxford: Oxford University Press 2008) 88–96.

[12] John Rawls, *A Theory of Justice* (Cambridge, MA: Harvard University Press 1971) 126–30.

[13] Waldron, *Law and Disagreement*, 107–13.

[14] Williams, 'Realism and Moralism in Political Theory', 3.

If the circumstances of disagreement were ontological, then any attempt to take constitutional norms such as rights seriously would be futile. This scenario belongs to what H. L. A. Hart famously termed the Nightmare of certain schools of American jurisprudence.[15] It appears to assume that without unambiguous second order grounds for the truth and objectivity of our first order arguments; any view we express or agreement we reach will be arbitrary. Political constitutionalists have no need to adopt this position. They can sensibly engage in first order arguments about their situation in terms that make sense to us in the here and now without answering or even asking second order questions concerning the cosmic validity of these terms.[16] This is what most people do most of the time about most of the things that matter to them. Yet, what Hart characterized as the Noble Dream of appealing directly to a correct understanding of certain rights and other constitutional norms—even of a basic 'minimal' kind, such as Mac Amhlaigh proposes—will not work either. Disagreement at the epistemological level means that the basis for such an appeal does not exist. Rather, rights and other constitutional norms can only be taken seriously in the manner whereby the necessary decisions about them are argued for and made. These decisions are not only political in purpose, as we saw, but also need to be regarded as being decided politically. Such political decision-making must aim at legitimacy, which I define below in Section 4, without being able to show that the decision reached is the most just or the best—indeed, it must do so because it cannot show that to be the case. Consequently, all that can be shown is that the process of decision-making has treated the norms at issue as important and that people's different views about them have been respected and debated.

Herein lies the normative case for my advocacy of 'a thorough-going proceduralism that goes all the way down'. Namely, that there is no other way to take constitutional norms seriously than through the way our arguments and decisions about them proceed. We cannot avoid starting with procedures. Yet, it can be noted, that is no different to many other areas of human enquiry. For example, acceptance of the findings of natural science turn likewise on the methods employed to validate them, which are similarly subject to continuous refinement. Different types of process are appropriate to different fields of enquiry. The claim made here is that the process for deciding constitutional issues cannot but be political in the broad sense of providing a politically necessary resolution of disputes between political opponents about the values to be realized in their collective life.

The priority of politics and the inescapability of procedures of a broadly political kind provide two key features of a politically realist constitutionalism. Together, they motivate the move away from the focus on a legal document as a statement of

[15] H. L. A. Hart, 'American Jurisprudence through English Eyes: The Nightmare and the Noble Dream' (1977) 11 *Georgia Law Review* 969–89.

[16] Williams, 'Realism and Moralism', 11.

moral principles as the hallmark of constitutionalism and towards a concentration on the manner in which constitutional norms are politically debated, decided, and determined—both in general and in particular cases. Nevertheless, not enough has been said at this stage to definitely tip the scales towards political rather than legal processes of debate. These criteria might be satisfied by a broadly political account of legal constitutionalism—one, say, that characterized the moral reading of the constitution not as the enactment of the Noble Dream, as Hart assumed Dworkin conceived it,[17] but, as was arguably nearer Dworkin's position, as a political debate in legal terms about the moral principles a democratic society should uphold.[18] Yet, if we disagree as much about procedures as we do about outcomes, how can we decide between different kinds of political and legal processes? It might seem we can only escape the frying pan of ontological scepticism by entering the fire of an epistemological scepticism that involves an infinite regress regarding process.

3. NO ARCHIMEDEAN POINT: PROCEDURES AND THE PROBLEM OF INFINITE REGRESS

As Mac Amhlaigh observes, political constitutionalists may embrace a proceduralist view of constitutionalism but they do not thereby adopt the view of someone such as John Hart Ely, who believed that judicial review of the process of democratic decision-making is acceptable in ways that the review of the substantive decisions of democratic bodies is not.[19] Political constitutionalists argue that procedures are as controversial as the decisions made by them—indeed, the two are intrinsically linked given that the validation of any decision comes through the way it is made. Yet, for that self-same reason, they can resist the futile attempt to find a perfect procedure from which we can assess the best procedure for all situations and purposes. On this account, there is simply no Archimedean point and so no need for an infinite regress towards some originating procedure that might

[17] Dworkin denied he held this 'silly' view in *Taking Rights Seriously* (2nd edn, London: Duckworth 1978) 293.

[18] As Jeremy Waldron has noted, Dworkin famously rejected the notion of any Archimedean point, remarking that the notion that there was a 'right answer' 'locked up in some transcendental strongbox' was 'nonsense' (*Taking Rights Seriously*, at 216). On his account, we can only have arguments about right answers, and these must always be open to counter-arguments. His support for legal over political constitutionalism largely stems from the alleged superiority of legal argumentation—a process view in other words—which, as Waldron remarks, depended on a contestable understanding of political processes. See Jeremy Waldron, 'The Rule of Law as a Theatre of Debate' in Justine Burley (ed.), *Dworkin and his Critics* (Oxford: Blackwell 2004) 319–36, at 326–7. Nevertheless, as Williams, 'Realism and Moralism', 12, discerned, Dworkin's account of law trades on the possibility of political moralism. A more truly political realist account of courts as a model of public adversarial deliberation can be found in Stuart Hampshire, *Justice is Conflict* (Princeton, NJ: Princeton University Press 2000) esp. 89–90, where he discusses the US Supreme Court.

[19] John Hart Ely, *Democracy and Distrust: A Theory of Judicial Review* (Cambridge, MA: Harvard University Press 1981). See the critique of his position in *PC*, 107–18.

provide such a point.[20] We can only start from the procedures we have and seek to improve them through voicing our disagreements within them and thereby motivating changes to them. Moreover, we do not need to engage in a second order reflection on the best possible procedure to offer sensible first order reflections on the adequacy of current procedures for our present needs.

This reasoning underlies my scepticism regarding the supposed special merits of constitutional conventions as mechanisms for legitimizing subsequently entrenched constitutions. Such proposals suppose these conventions might offer such an Archimedean point by representing an especially elevated and serious political process that would be superior to all subsequent processes. However, the evidence for a sharp distinction between constitutional and normal politics seems thin and hard to justify if all processes are potentially challengeable. Rather, there is a need for the processes that establish and adjudicate on constitutional questions to be permanently open to criticism and change.[21]

Mac Amhlaigh and others have raised a number of potential problems with this process of continually re-building the constitutional ship at sea. First, he and fellow critics worry that such incessant re-building might undermine the authority of the prevailing process if it, and the decisions it has made, become liable to continuous challenge. The capacity of a political authority to settle issues will be weakened, damaging its capacity to respond to Williams's first political question. However, this worry seems exaggerated given these same objectors generally accept that either constitutional or supreme courts can and do overrule their precedents and revise their competences without a descent into anarchy. After all, many important and wide-ranging reforms to our democratic processes, such as woman's suffrage, have come about without wholesale revolution. Even when these reforms involved and were precipitated by protests outside the established processes, such as acts of civil disobedience, they invariably ended up being formally enacted and legitimated within them. In part, that was because even such radical reforms could be put forward not so much as wholesale rejections of these processes but rather as better understandings of the practical requirements demanded by their inner rationale.

Mac Amhlaigh's second objection, that using a process, such as majority rule, to decide on the suitability of that same process is both illegitimate and illogical, fails for similar reasons. How, he asks, can a system of majority rule, say, be used to determine whether to employ, constrain, or extend majority rule or not? He implies, though he does not spell this out, that it would be illegitimate because it involves being 'judge in one's own cause'.[22] Yet, that seems almost inevitably the case. Even if one handed a decision to a totally external body, such as an international court,

[20] See *PC*, 173–4,

[21] See Richard Bellamy and Justus Schönlau, 'The Normality of Constitutional Politics: An Analysis of the Drafting of the EU Charter of Fundamental Rights' (2004) 11 *Constellations* 412–33.

[22] I examine this objection in *PC*, 118–20 and see too Waldron, *Law and Disagreement*, 296–8.

it would need to express an opinion on its own competences. Moreover, total independence risks removing a key incentive to impartial and equitable decision-making—namely, that one should have to live equally under the laws that one makes on equal terms with others. After all, this forms the core of Locke's argument for replacing rule by 'one good and excellent man' who, experience reveals, sadly cannot be counted on to always act impartially and non-arbitrarily, with rule by a representative legislature, by 'which means every single person became subject, equally with other the meanest men, to those laws, which he himself, as part of the legislative, had established'.[23]

Of course, though those invoking the *nemo iudex in sua causa* tend to ignore or dispute this point's validity, justices on a domestic supreme or constitutional court usually are themselves citizens, and so are subject to their own decisions. Yet, a court judgment does not meet the Lockean reasoning for having those making the law being subject to it, and so may be more exposed to the critics' objection than a legislature. Why is that? The 'judge in one's own cause' argument gains its force in instances where an individual or group in a dispute with another group or individual can make a decision in its own favour without consulting the other party. Yet that is not the case in a situation where the people as a whole is determining what legislation and rights are in the best interests of their political community. Here, following the Lockean rationale for rule by a legislature rather than a monarch that broadly informs the argument of Chapters 2 and 3, ensuring all are equal under the law requires that it be made by all those with an equal interest in it. As Waldron notes, in this case, the appropriate Latin tag would seem to demand that 'what touches all, should be decided by all' (*Quod omnes tangit ab omnibus decidentur*).[24] The danger of a court deciding such matters might be that the religious or political views of particular judges may place them precisely in a situation whereby they make a decision in which they have an interest without having to consult the opposing views and treat them on equal terms.

The logical aspect of this objection takes a slightly different tack. According to this line of reasoning, even if the 'judge in your own cause' objection proves inappropriate, there is still something question-begging about having a majority democratic decision to justify or decide the validity of a majoritarian democratic decision.[25] However, this argument seems once again to depend for its coherence on the belief that some perfect procedure might exist that could determine all other procedures, thereby triggering the very infinite regress that these critics accuse political constitutionalists of being committed to. Yet this dilemma only

[23] John Locke, *Two Treatises of Government* (Peter Laslett ed., Cambridge: Cambridge University Press 1988) Second Treatise, ch. VII, sec. 94: 329.

[24] Waldron, *Law and Disagreement*, 298.

[25] This point is also raised and discussed in Waldron, *Law and Disagreement*, 298–301.

exists for those who believe such an Archimedean point might exist. Without that possibility, the criticism misfires—there simply is no alternative than to grasp the procedural nettle as we find it. Not all decision procedures are inherently biased in their operation to the status quo—a system of making decisions on the toss of a coin, for example, offers an equal chance to any alternative to continuing the practice. Majority rule in and of itself has no inherent bias to majority rule. Rather, for well-known reasons,[26] it is neutral between the options it is used to decide between, gives all involved an equal say, and responds positively to what people choose. Consequently, it is unsurprising that majority systems in Canada, New Zealand, and the UK have introduced both Bills of Rights and, in some instances, proportional representation (PR), admittedly in certain cases by allowing for an alternative to the ordinary legislative process to decide the issue, albeit usually one, such as a referendum, involving a form of majority rule, though a form different to that prevailing in making normal legislation. Still, that decision itself was made and implemented by majority rule within the legislature. Moreover, these critics of majority rule within legislatures have little if anything to say about its similar use by judges in multimember courts to resolve their disputes.[27]

I have still said nothing that need decisively favour legislative over judicial supremacy. True, a defence of judicial supremacy in purely 'output' terms is ruled out by the argument that the credibility and appropriateness of any outcome always turns on the character of the process employed to support it. However, legal constitutionalists can and do make just such a case in noting qualities of the legal process, such as its purported impartiality and even-handedness, which supposedly render it superior in these respects to political processes as a forum of constitutional principle.[28] By the same token, though, nothing here rules out the possibility for political constitutionalists to challenge a prevailing legal constitutionalist system either, as Mac Amhlaigh proposes must be the case. I return to that argument in Section 5. Before doing so, I want to explore Mac Amhlaigh's third claim that the political constitutionalist position implies that there are no criteria of legitimacy that could allow a criticism of any process, even that of a totalitarian regime. According to this objection, constitutionalism in and of itself must assume some criteria that stand outside any process—a role he ascribes to a minimum theory of legal legitimacy.

[26] Kenneth O. May, 'A Set of Independent Necessary and Sufficient Conditions for Simple Majority Decision' (1952) 20 *Econometrica* 680–4.

[27] For a discussion, see Jeremy Waldron, 'Five to Four: Why Do Bare Majorities Rule on Courts?' (2014) 123 *Yale Law Journal* 1692–1730.

[28] Most famously, Ronald Dworkin, 'The Forum of Principle' in Ronald Dworkin, *A Matter of Principle* (Cambridge, MA: Harvard University Press 1985) 33–71, but see too Hampshire, *Justice is Conflict*.

4. POLITICAL NOT METAPHYSICAL: THE BASIC LEGITIMATION DEMAND

In addressing this point, it is helpful to return to Williams's account of the political. As I noted in Chapter 2, he argued that it was not enough for a political system to answer the 'first political question'; it must also meet the 'Basic Legitimation Demand' (BLD).[29] To do so, the response to the first political question must offer 'an "acceptable" solution', one that can provide a justification of the political system's right to rule to each person subject to it. While he distinguished the two analytically, noting that an answer to the first political question provides a necessary but not a sufficient condition for meeting the BLD, he saw the two as interconnected since the first political question could not be answered adequately without meeting the BLD. As he elaborated it, 'acceptable to each' turns out to be a threshold condition—that there should be no group 'so radically disadvantaged' by the prevailing regime that they conceive themselves as enemies of the polity and its rulers.[30]

Mapping Williams's account onto both Mac Amhlaigh's argument and the discussion of the circumstances of politics above, we can see the first political question as responding to the need for an authority capable of providing a stable set of rules of justice capable of coordinating the social activities of the members of a political community. Yet, if disagreement goes all the way down, then the criteria of legitimacy needed to decide if the BLD has also been met will themselves be subject to the disagreements that give rise to the need for such a political authority in the first place. As a result, Williams seems open to a parallel criticism to that levelled by Mac Amhlaigh at those political constitutionalists who appear to argue in similar terms: namely, that he must either concede that there are moral criteria of legitimacy that arise outside politics or accept that either might could define right or that whatever works must be legitimate enough.[31]

Williams conceded that the BLD is a moral principle but not one that is 'prior to politics'. Rather, 'it is a claim that is inherent in there being such a thing as politics: in particular, because it is inherent in there being a first political question'.[32] Developing this point, Williams reasoned that the first political question is unlikely to be answered in a stable way, that acknowledges the disagreements and conflicts that stand behind the very need for politics and raise the question in the first place, unless rulers can avoid their rule so radically disadvantaging a given group that that group could never find it acceptable in the sense of being preferable to open war. A situation in which a group of people hold power by terrorizing another group does not provide an answer to the first political question but rather

[29] Williams, 'Realism and Moralism', 4.
[30] Williams, 'Realism and Moralism', 5.
[31] e.g. Charles Larmore, 'What Is Political Philosophy?' (2013) 10 *Journal of Moral Philosophy* 291.
[32] Williams, 'Realism and Moralism', 5.

represents the very circumstance that the political is supposed to address. Might never implies right in and of itself because 'the power of coercion offered simply as the power of coercion cannot justify its own use'.[33] In other words, might alone does not supply an account of political authority.

Nevertheless, this last argument might appear to imply that the BLD could be satisfied by acceptable 'outputs', as Mac Amhlaigh proposes, without involving any special sort of political 'inputs'. However, that possibility would suggest that the legitimacy of a given regime can result from its promoting a certain moral ideal that lies outside of politics, in the sense of being beyond reasonable disagreement. For example, certain basic human rights and a minimal account of social justice might be defended, as Mac Amhlaigh and many other theorists do, as moral norms that ought to be accepted and acceptable to all because they avoid any group being radically disadvantaged by another. Yet, realists maintain that position cannot be plausible if the whole point of politics arises from disagreement about which moral ends and modes of moral reasoning are to be preferred. Rather, the 'acceptance' required of citizens must be with the way the political system operates and whether its operation is systematically skewed against a given group, so that they are consistently disadvantaged from participating, expressing their views, or influencing decisions. Satisfying these requirements relates to input rather than output features of a political system, to the conduct of the decision-making process rather than the decisions themselves, though the two will be to some degree related. Such generally acceptable input features aim at avoiding any group being so radically disadvantaged in putting its views that it could be regarded as being dominated by some other group or groups within that political society. However, that need not mean that no group should ever be disadvantaged by any decision, merely that such discriminating decisions should be duly made in a non-dominating fashion.

The argument being made here is that the quality of the process carries some normative weight of an independent kind from either its pragmatic virtues or lack of them, on the one side, or its conduciveness to realizing some desirable normative outcome, on the other. That weight consists in the way those subject to political decisions feel they are regarded within the decision-making process itself—the equality of concern and respect they are accorded. As I argued in the last section, this issue cannot be cashed out in terms of a definitive set of procedural rights, given these too are subject to disagreement. Williams has been accused of assuming a prior moral claim that all human beings matter equally or that authority requires universal consent,[34] notions that might ground such a set of pre-political procedural rights. However, like political constitutionalists, his argument

[33] Williams, 'Realism and Moralism', 5–6.

[34] Matt Sleat, 'Bernard Williams and the Possibility of a Realist Political Theory' (2010) 11 *European Journal of Political Theory* 247–72. For a critique, see Edward Hall, 'Bernard Williams and the Basic Legitimation Demand: A Defence' (2015) 63 *Political Studies* 446–80.

is purely political—it is a claim that derives from the nature of political authority itself towards those who are subject to it. How it gets cashed out has varied and been elaborated in different ways over time, but the rationale lies within the nature of political processes themselves rather than some pre-political morality. Nor is it to argue, as Lon Fuller attempted with the idea of the rule of law,[35] that all that is of normative value could be packed into the idea of legitimate procedures so that no bad politician could subvert them nor any bad outcome ever be produced by them. Rather, as I also observed, it merely shows that the legitimacy of outcomes cannot be separated from that of process and that addressing this last has to have priority in our constitutional thinking.

Does doing so favour legislative over judicial supremacy? Yes and no. I do not dispute that legal and political constitutionalists can both claim their respective processes accord dignity to the individuals who employ them. Moreover, both schools believe their respective mechanisms to be complementary in doing so in various respects—that both need the other. However, as I remarked in Section 1, a key component of the 'circumstances of disagreement' lies in the inevitable partiality of any person's judgement about him or herself and others. As I argued in Chapter 3, democratic mechanisms seek to address that structural problem in a public way by allowing all an equal say in their collective deliberations, albeit usually indirectly through their influence over their elected representatives. On this account, the only way to realize justice in our relations with others is through public deliberation about justice in which each has an equal say. What touches all must involve all. Of course, how far democratic procedures succeed in this endeavour can be questioned but the political constitutionalist claim is that not even to attempt to develop such a process involves in and of itself an injustice precisely because the circumstances of disagreements makes processual and outcome issues so intertwined in this regard. It becomes difficult for justice to be done in any other way than by trying to show it has been done through the equal involvement of those concerned. As J. S. Mill noted in his *Considerations on Representative Government* (in part, echoing the reasoning behind the Lockean argument referred to earlier):

> it is a personal injustice to withhold from any one . . . the ordinary privilege of having his voice reckoned in the disposal of affairs in which he has the same interest as other people.[36]

Legal constitutionalists can and have sought to address this issue by noting the 'democratic' qualities of their own procedures—a claim I assess in Chapter 7.

[35] Lon Fuller, 'Positivism and Fidelity to Law: A Reply to Hart' (1957) 71 *Harvard Law Review* 630–72, at 637.

[36] John Stuart Mill, *Considerations on Representative Government* in John Stuart Mill, *On Liberty and Other Essays* (Oxford: Oxford University Press 1998) 329.

Indeed, judicial review has been frequently characterized as a means for rectifying precisely this 'personal injustice' in the case of 'discrete and insular minorities'.[37] But that is to shift the debate in the direction political constitutionalists desired in mounting their challenge. It moves the argument away from seeing constitutionalism as a moral framework for, and supplement to, democracy, to a view of it as somehow intimately connected to how democracy operates, so that even a legal constitutionalism requires certain democratic characteristics in its processes, rather than simply offering an alternative, and corrective, to the supposed inherent shortcomings of such processes—a supposition that political constitutionalists have sought to reveal as unwarranted.

5. 'NOW AND AROUND HERE': A STATUS QUO BIAS?

This point brings me neatly to Mac Amhlaigh's final claim. He argues that so long as a prevailing constitutional system, be it legal or political, satisfies his minimal theory of legitimacy, then, given disagreements about process, a political constitutionalist could defend the continuance of that system where it exists but could not argue for its adoption and a move away from legal constitutionalism. The reason for this dismal conclusion arises from the supposed self-defeating nature of political constitutionalist arguments. In Mac Amhlaigh's view, political constitutionalists are so caught up in an infinite regress that they are doomed to cling on to the turtle on which they find themselves or risk plunging into the abyss.[38]

The political constitutionalist does accept that we must look at what makes sense 'now and around here',[39] sharing the view of legal constitutionalists that legitimate political rule within modern, pluralist societies involves certain normative and institutional elements of both constitutionalism and democracy that are characteristic of liberal and republican political theories and those systems that seek to enshrine their values. Yet the reason for this view being shared by most members of contemporary democracies does not turn on any grand metaphysical consensus. It suffices to draw on the recent historical experience of various forms of illiberal authoritarianism and compare life under them with that in more liberal democratic regimes. As a result, constitutional government, be it of a legal or a political kind, is likely to be accepted as broadly legitimate where it exists because it offers us a largely stable solution to the first political question. However, its capacity to do so in either way remains to a degree historically contingent—the BLD has been met

[37] *United States v. Carolene Products Co.* 304 US 144 at 152 n. 4 (1938); Ely, *Democracy and Distrust*, 75–7, and see *PC*, 110, 249–58.

[38] The reference here is to the phrase 'Turtles all the way down' that alludes to the myth that the earth rests on the back of a great turtle, leading to the question of what the turtle rests on thereby triggering an infinite regress of turtles resting on yet another turtle.

[39] Williams, 'Realism and Moralism', 8.

by non-liberal legal and political systems for most of human history, while established liberal democratic regimes are currently losing popular support and being challenged by extreme right populist movements with authoritarian and illiberal tendencies.

Does this contingency mean, as Mac Amhlaigh suggests, that political constitutionalism can only be defended where it already exists, no doubt within the confines of suitably obscure specialist journals? That would only be the case if the non-arbitrary defence of either form of constitutionalism had to be grounded on some imaginary ultimate turtle. However, unlike his minimal theory of legitimacy, the BLD has no need of such question-begging second order foundations. It can be grounded in the very idea of a legitimate state capable of answering the first political question.[40] Where this question receives a satisfactory response, as it more or less still does 'now and around here', we can (and, certainly these days, most urgently should) still ask sensible first order political questions about the capacity of different systems to continue to be seen as legitimate in the type of societies we live in and the forms of disagreement they generate. That possibility rests open to *both* legal and political constitutionalists, with each prompting the other—as in this exchange—to improve their case. Yet that exercise can best be achieved not through abstract theorizing about the moral foundations of constitutional values, which by and large political and legal constitutionalists share for the historical reasons given above, so much as through engagement with the ways legal and political institutions work and people's capacity to employ and relate to them. The contribution of political constitutionalism lies in showing the normative necessity and worth of such an engagement, noting how it proceeds from the logic of the very arguments legal constitutionalists employ, such as treating people with equal concern and respect. Such an approach—which I seek to apply to the democratic challenges posed by populism and globalization in Chapters 8, 9, and 10—seems all the more necessary in times such as the present, when there is widespread disaffection with the current operation of liberal democracy on the part of many citizens.

In this regard, a certain irony arises from Mac Amhlaigh's proffered 'defence'. A chief motivation behind political constitutionalism has been the critique of the conservative status quo bias of legal constitutionalism, which, by seeking to entrench certain historically given constitutional norms, risks locking in the privileges and biases of those favoured by the prevailing system. Indeed, the desire for hegemonic groups to preserve their dominance has been shown to motivate many moves from political to more legal forms of constitutionalism.[41] Political constitutionalism challenges such hegemonic projects, indicating the dangers they pose to the legitimacy of the constitutional process in the long term. In seeking to foreclose

[40] Williams, 'Realism and Moralism', 8.

[41] Ran Hirschl, *Towards Juristocracy: The Origins and Consequences of the New Constitutionalism* (Cambridge, MA: Harvard University Press 2004).

such challenges, Mac Amhlaigh's argument proves intellectually reactionary, the misguided idealization of a given turtle as the best of all possible turtles. As I argue in Chapter 8, the legal constitutional entrenchment of democracy risks reinforcing criticisms of liberal democratic systems as unresponsive and serving the interests of elites. Moreover, it has been a strategy adopted by populist politicians to give their regimes a spurious legitimacy and protect their hold on power. By contrast, political constitutionalism emphasizes the need to empower citizens in ways that encourage, on the one hand, governments to equally advance their interests, and, on the other hand, they themselves to treat each other as equals and hear and harken to their views and concerns. As I sketched in Chapter 3, the democratic mechanisms involved are likely to be as complex and plural as contemporary societies. And, as these societies evolve, must themselves be open to reform.

6. CONCLUSION: CONSTITUTIVE VS. CONSTITUTED POLITICS

Mac Amhlaigh conceives of legal constitutionalism as constituting politics.[42] Yet to do so, he becomes enmeshed in the very infinite regress he regards as bedevilling political constitutionalism. By contrast, political constitutionalism avoids this dilemma by dropping the legal constitutionalist view of a constitution as establishing a just foundation and framework for politics. Instead, it conceives a constitution as a set of political mechanisms for preserving the civic freedom of citizens to negotiate their different views of rights and justice and reach collective agreements that avoid mutual domination.

This move proves necessary precisely because disagreements about the nature of rights and justice inevitably spill over into debates concerning who is recognized as worthy of respect and how their beliefs are represented. Disagreement enters into the form of politics, therefore, producing an ongoing process whereby a polity is continually reconstituted more appropriately to recognize, respect, and represent the opinions of its members—often producing modifications to majoritarian rule, as in federal and consociational systems, or even calls for secession. Herein lies the constitutive role of politics.

We can analyse this phenomenon via the ways political recognition, respect, and representation get mediated through four intersecting dimensions of any polity: namely, the *sphere*, *subjects*, *scope*, and *styles* of politics. The *sphere* of politics refers to where politics takes place. As I noted in Chapter 3, these borders involve not only the external frontiers of the polity but also its internal administrative

[42] This section draws on Richard Bellamy 'Constitutive Citizenship vs. Constitutional Rights: Republican Reflections on the EU Charter and the Human Rights Act' in T. Campbell, K. D. Ewing, and A. Tomkins (eds), *Sceptical Essays on Human Rights* (Oxford: Oxford University Press 2001) 19–21.

divisions. These tend to be both territorially and functionally defined, with different functions usually mapping onto different territorial units and occasionally cutting across them. They are also frequently subdivided into more localized units that implement and inform central decisions. There are also demarcations between the political and non-political areas of life, as in attempts to distinguish a public from a private sphere.

The *subjects* of politics concern the definitions of rulers and ruled, or who decides for and over whom. Even in a democracy, where the designated demos are potentially both governors and governed, the criteria for voting can be different to those for standing for election. Meanwhile, no polity identifies citizens simply with those physically present within a relevant sphere. Citizenship is standardly associated with certain capacities and commitments that only a subset of residents will possess.

The *scope* of politics has to do with its aims and the claims it makes upon people within its designated spheres. Different areas of political life may warrant a greater or lesser degree of intervention and be more or less demanding than others. A politics aimed at ensuring noninterference and forbearance will have a very different character and impact from a politics demanding positive action to promote equality and support public goods.

Finally, the *styles* of politics relate to the different ways politics is undertaken as a result of the various types of formal and informal consultation and influence that the political system allows. These may range from voting as determined by the electoral system, through membership of political parties, unions, and various lobbying organizations, to consultative meetings, letter-writing campaigns, demonstrations, direct action, and even—in extreme circumstances—terrorism and civil war.

These four dimensions of politics are clearly related, with the character of each influencing that of the others. Thus, the boundaries marking the sphere of politics will partly, though not entirely, determine its subjects, scope, and styles by creating certain constituencies and designating which areas are political or not. Recognizing a region as a legitimate sphere of politics by granting it a degree of political autonomy may be tied implicitly or explicitly to recognition of a national minority as a subject of politics. Giving them a degree of self-government, however, will also lead to acceptance that the claims of language or culture fall within the scope of politics, and that new styles of politics may be necessary to allow certain minority groups to participate according to their particular linguistic and cultural traditions. Similarly, if the scope of politics consists simply of upholding negative rights, then its legitimate sphere, subjects, and styles will differ from a view that includes positive rights. For example, it is more likely that the economy will be treated as a largely private sphere, employees not recognized as political subjects, and certain styles of consultation, such as workplace democracy, deemed inappropriate. And so on. When citizens struggle to be recognized as political subjects, therefore, they are not simply demanding access to a pre-constituted set of political rights. For that recognition will invariably have profound consequences for the other dimensions of politics and hence for the very constitution of the political. Moreover, disagreements between citizens over any of the other dimensions, such as the appropriate scope of politics, will equally have constitutional consequences for how we conceive its sphere, subjects, and styles.

Because political disagreements invariably turn on the definition of one or more of these dimensions, political debates and struggles play a pivotal and continuous constitutive role in the transformation and reformation of political communities across all four of these dimensions. In the nineteenth century, for example, nationalist movements played a significant part in defining the sphere of politics as the nation-state. Frequently tied to revolutionary and democratic movements, these struggles for national self-determination also served to make 'the people' the subject of politics and in the process altered both its scope and forms. Similarly, later struggles to extend the franchise to women and workers have not only expanded the subjects of politics but, as we noted above, inevitably changed its sphere, scope, and styles. Though the US constitution is sometimes treated as the archetypal rights-based document, establishing the republic on 'self-evident' just constitutional principles, its true foundations lie in 'we the people'. As Bruce Ackerman has shown,[43] citizens have transformed it through successive waves of constitutional politics, from the extreme case of civil war, through the Depression years that gave rise to the New Deal, to the civil rights movement of the 1960s. In all these cases, citizens were struggling to construct a framework within which their concerns would be recognized and respected. Yet that has not been simply a matter of getting noticed under the established rules but, as we have seen, has inevitably meant challenging those rules as well.

Three features of these constitutive political struggles need emphasizing. First, some commentators grant that such constitutional moments occasionally arise, but like Ackerman, regard them as exceptional, with 'normal' politics occurring within the framework set by the last constitutional struggle.[44] To some degree that is inevitably true. Revolutions are rare, and even then attempts to start totally anew prove impossible. The constitutional ship is necessarily rebuilt at sea, with modifications in one area being realized through the established practices in another. Nevertheless, this is a more incremental and everyday process than Ackerman and others allow, with momentous transformations usually the cumulative result of a gradual alteration in public opinion produced by numerous small shifts within debates on a variety of particular issues.

Second, past struggles by workers, women, and ethnic minorities (and occasionally majorities) are sometimes contrasted with current struggles over gender

[43] Bruce Ackerman, *We the People: Foundations* (Cambridge, MA: Harvard University Press 1991).
[44] Ackerman, *We the People*, 3–33.

and multiculturalism.[45] The former are typified as struggles for inclusion within the established framework—as demands that the cooperatively produced benefits and burdens of the political community be shared more equitably. In sum, they are struggles for a fuller realization of justice. By contrast, the latter are characterized as struggles to be recognized as different and to enjoy an exclusive status. They seek a more diverse rather than a more equal society. Certain critics go so far as to vilify them for promoting injustice by seeking to entrench the very inequities and hierarchies that past groups struggled to overturn. The foregoing analysis, however, suggests far greater continuity between the two.[46] Like contemporary struggles, those of the past involved demands for recognition as well as distribution. They sought not only admission to, but also a reconstitution of, the political community and the forms of justice and equality it inscribes. Thus, the enfranchisement of women brought with it an enlargement of the sphere of politics to include the domestic arena, a corresponding extension of the scope of politics to include issues such as sexual harassment and marital rape, and demands for new and less confrontational styles of politics. Like past struggles, those of the present are for a more inclusive and equitable society. However, once again these demands involve reconceptualizing how political goods are produced and distributed. As we saw, the struggles of workers and national minorities entail parallel transformations of the sphere, scope, subjects, and styles of politics.

Third, and most importantly, it is impossible to say *a priori* what the 'best' conception of these dimensions and their relations to each other might be. Any criteria we might come up with will not only have to be tailored to varying and highly contingent circumstances in ways that are impossible to specify in advance, but also will be subject to diverse judgements and interpretations by citizens themselves. Indeed, divergent priorities and values may lead groups to propose different criteria. Meanwhile, as one group alters the ways in which it is recognized by others, that has knock-on effects both for the ways these others are recognized and for how they recognize themselves. Thus, new struggles are spawned as identities, ideals, and interests change in response to the new structures, producing in their turn further struggles for new forms of recognition. Consider, for example, how in recent times gains in certain domains by the feminist movement have given rise to 'post-feminist' discourses, on the one hand, and a reappraisal of masculine gender, on the other, fostering a further spate of political dialogue and change.

The need to find agreement in circumstances of ongoing disagreement produces struggles over how different groups and individuals are recognized, respected, and represented which are directly related to the ways the polity is constituted. The answer to the First Political Question cannot be framed in a non-political way in

[45] e.g. Nancy Fraser, *Justice Interruptus* (London: Routledge 1997) ch. 1.

[46] J. Tully, 'Struggles over Recognition and Distribution' (2000) 7 *Constellations* 469–82.

terms of a pre- or supra-political legal constitution because the terms whereby it meets the Basic Legitimation Demand will be a matter of ongoing political negotiation. Precisely because reasonable disagreements go all the way down to the constitutional foundations of politics, the process of politically reconstituting the polity is necessarily a continuous one.

7

Democracy through Courts?

1. INTRODUCTION

Rights-based judicial review of legislation by constitutional courts has long been criticized as undermining democracy, particularly when it involves a strike down power and a claim to judicial supremacy, a position associated—albeit contentiously—with the US Supreme Court in particular.[1] However, recent criticisms—such as those developed in this book—have given a new twist to this objection. These critiques do not turn on an assumed clash between democratic and constitutional norms. Rather, they rest on the comparative legitimacy and effectiveness of democratic and judicial processes as mechanisms to realize these norms. Within this latest phase of the debate, democracy, on the one hand, and constitutionalism and rights, on the other, are conceived as involving the self-same norms associated with treating autonomous individuals with equal concern and respect. The key claim of the advocates of democracy—and of this book—has not been that constitutionalism is at odds with or less justified than democracy but that the democratic process has superior constitutional properties to the judicial process.[2] As we have seen, political constitutionalists hold that democracy, understood as a procedure involving regular elections for competing parties, universal suffrage based on one person one vote, and majority rule provides a mechanism whereby all citizens can see they are treated as equals by virtue of having an equal say in making the collective decisions and rules that shape their common institutions and social interactions, albeit indirectly through their electorally authorized and accountable representatives in the legislature. As such, this system meets the constitutional norms of fairness and impartiality by offering an instrument for ensuring public institutions and arrangements are committed to the equal advancement of the interests of those subject to them. It does so by treating the views individuals have about their own and their society's interests with equal concern and respect and constraining the pursuit of collective policies by the need for governments and the administration to take those views into account. Political constitutionalists

[1] Learned Hand, *The Bill of Rights* (Cambridge, MA: Harvard University Press 1958).

[2] Mark Tushnet, *Taking the Constitution Away from the Courts* (Princeton, NJ: Princeton University Press 1999); Jeremy Waldron, *Law and Disagreement* (Oxford: Clarendon Press 1999); Richard Bellamy, *Political Constitutionalism: A Republican Defence of the Constitutionality of Democracy* (Cambridge: Cambridge University Press 2007).

Defending the Political Constitution. Richard Bellamy, Oxford University Press.
DOI: 10.1093/9780191826986.003.0010

contend that courts cannot achieve this task as legitimately or effectively because the legal process lacks those features of the democratic process that allow citizens to define and protect their rights on an equal basis. Consequently, courts cannot show their judgments about the rights and rules governing our public lives avoid bias and respect the reasonable disagreements we have about them.

This objection challenges head on a hitherto standard defence of the role of courts that has located their legitimacy and efficacy precisely in their *not* operating in a democratic manner.[3] According to this latter line of argument, judicial review is justified as a counter-weight to potentially myopic, prejudiced, careless, and occasionally tyrannous majorities and the democratically elected politicians who feel obliged to respond to their demands. Courts are said to avoid such problems through being isolated from the electoral process and independent from government interference. Their reasoning is guided by legal norms and standards of natural justice inculcated by the professional training judges receive, and the expectations and conventions of legal and judicial practice and modes of argument. As a result of this independence, it is claimed that courts take decisions that are less emotive and precipitate than those of democratically accountable legislators and executives, are more likely to give due weight to the rights and interests of overlooked or unpopular minorities, and accord due weight to long-term advantages and considerations of justice over short-term gains, administrative convenience, and collective utility. However, the democratic critique responds that this model of judicial decision-making involves biases of its own. Given the complexity and plurality of modern societies and the diversity of interests, ideals, and experiences of those that live in them, even with the best will in the world the judgements of all individuals will inevitably be partial and limited by their backgrounds and knowledge.[4] Therefore, insulating the judicial system from democratic pressures runs the risk of rendering courts cognitively biased towards the assumptions and attitudes of those best placed to get their voices heard by entering the legal profession or making use of the courts.[5]

To overcome these worries, courts themselves will need to possess certain democratic qualities that can ensure their commitment to the equal advancement of the interests of all persons subject to their authority by demonstrating that they will be treated impartially and in a publicly equal way. For example, it will be important to show that the constitution provides a people's rather than a lawyer's charter and does not unjustifiably favour certain groups within the community at the expense of others; that access to justice is not biased or inequitable; and that

[3] Alexander Bickel, *The Least Dangerous Branch: The Supreme Court at the Bar of Politics*, (2nd edn, New Haven, CT: Yale University Press 1986) 24–6.

[4] Thomas Christiano, *The Constitution of Equality: Democratic Authority and Its Limits* (Oxford: Oxford University Press 2008) 88–95.

[5] Ran Hirschl, *Towards Juristocracy: The Origins and Consequences of the New Constitutionalism* (Cambridge, MA: Harvard University Press 2004).

the judiciary and lawyers do not form a class apart, out of touch with the circumstances and values of the broader society, and that their recruitment is open and meets equal opportunities criteria.

This chapter explores three arguments that seek respectively to address each of these points by proposing that courts not only uphold democratic values but also embody them, by providing a democratic forum for public deliberation, popular participation, and the representation of insular minorities. According to the first argument, a constitution should be seen as expressing the principles essential to a democratic society, which courts debate in relation to a given case in a deliberative manner. As such, their judgments can be seen as the product of an ideal democratic procedure that expresses the public reasoning of a democratic community. The second argument sees litigation as providing citizens with an additional and more direct avenue for advancing their interests and contesting their neglect or suppression by governments. The third argument conceives judges as representatives who can be expected to act on behalf of citizens because of the quality of the process of authorization and the values they may be presumed to hold. Though analytically distinct, they prove mutually supportive and necessary to each other, with the first the lynch-pin of the other two.[6]

All three arguments treat these alleged democratic qualities as intrinsic properties of well-designed constitutions and an associated legal and judicial process. They are held to operate independently of any electoral process—indeed, they are believed to result largely from that independence. On these accounts, therefore, courts may be counter-majoritarian but they are not anti-democratic.[7] Rather, they offer a superior form of democracy that can legitimately oversee and correct the supposed failings of electoral forms of democracy. This claim will be challenged below. Instead of viewing courts as defining and maintaining the democratic qualities of the political system, it proves more appropriate to reverse this perspective and note how courts possess important and necessary democratic qualities precisely because they are embedded within and framed by a democratic political system.

The three arguments discussed below have long figured in the normative literature. They are especially prominent among those North American legal and political philosophers who regard the Supreme Court as encapsulating the 'American ideal' of ensuring government 'under principle' by giving final authority to judges charged with a 'moral reading' of the constitution. Ronald Dworkin even describes this arrangement as 'the most important contribution our [i.e. the United States's] history has given to political theory'.[8] Yet, as Alex de Tocqueville observed as early

[6] e.g. Ronald Dworkin, 'Introduction' in Ronald Dworkin, *Freedom's Law: The Moral Reading of the American Constitution* (Oxford: Oxford University Press 1996) 6–7.

[7] Dworkin, *Freedom's Law*, 7, 17–19.

[8] Dworkin, *Freedom's Law*, 6.

as the 1830s, there is something aristocratic about this arrangement.[9] He noted (approvingly, it has to be said) how the privileged role of the law in American society assured those who studied it a certain superiority, making them—especially judges—'a rank apart'. Their training and role as the arbiters of people's disagreements and conflicts produced a certain 'disgust at the actions of the multitude' and rendered them 'secretly contemptuous of government by the people'. As such, they performed what he regarded as a necessary counter-democratic function, not least in protecting the property rights of the wealthy.[10] In what follows, I shall argue that the recent 'democratic' defences of judicial review explored below retain the aristocratic 'discomfort' with the processes of electoral democracy Tocqueville identified among the legal class of his time—an unease that Robert Unger has labelled one of the 'dirty little secrets of contemporary jurisprudence'. As Unger noted, this wariness manifests itself in:

> the ceaseless identification of restraints on majority rule . . . as the overriding responsibility of . . . jurists; . . . in the effort to obtain from judges . . . the advances popular politics fail to deliver; in the abandonment of institutional reconstruction to rare and magical moments of national refoundation; in an ideal of deliberative democracy as most acceptable when closest in style to a polite conversation among gentlemen in an eighteenth-century drawing room . . . [and] in the . . . treatment of party government as a subsidiary, last-ditch source of legal evolution, to be tolerated when none of the more refined modes of legal resolution applies.[11]

These prejudices inform all three of the arguments for courts as an alternative democratic avenue—one their proponents typically regard as superior to, and so justifiably constraining of, electoral and legislative politics. As we shall see, this claim proves flawed, both normatively and empirically.

All three arguments tend to be presented as largely logical and conceptual in nature. However, they rest on a number of implicit and occasionally explicit empirical assumptions about the merits of courts and the demerits of electoral democracy of the kind highlighted by Unger. Although empirical work has questioned how far these empirical assumptions meet these theorists' normative expectations

[9] Alex de Tocqueville, *Democracy in America* (Eduardo Nolla ed., James T. Schleifer tr., vol. 1, Indianapolis: Liberty Fund 2012) ch. 8. See too Nikolas Bowie, 'The Contemporary Debate over Supreme Court Reform: Origins and Perspectives', Written Statement to the Presidential Commission on the Supreme Court of the United States, 30 June 2021, 2.

[10] And thereby promoting economic inequality. See Jose Antonio Cheibub, Fernando Limongi, Adam Przeworski, and Ye Wang, 'Anti-majoritarianism and Democracy: Effects of Judicial Review on Rights, Economic Growth, and Inequality' (4 September 2024), available at SSRN <http://dx.doi.org/10.2139/ssrn.5069081> 20.

[11] Roberto Unger, *What Should Legal Analysis Become?* (London: Verso 1996) 72. See too Jeremy Waldron, 'Dirty Little Secret' (1998) 98 *Columbia Law Review* 510–30; Waldron, *Law and Disagreement*, 8–10.

about the legal and political process,[12] much normative work still defends the democratic legitimacy of judicial supremacy and litigation campaigns on the basis of faulty empirics.[13] The main thrust of the following analysis will accordingly be to challenge the conceptual and normative underpinning of these arguments, while drawing attention to their largely questionable historical and empirical grounding.

The argument here is with the strong judicial review of legislation—and, in the United States and other federal polities, more specifically with the strong judicial review of federal legislation. That is not to deny that courts supplement democracy in valuable ways—not least in ensuring the impartial and equitable application of democratically determined legislation, including through the review of executive action and the enforcement of federal law with regard to state law and officials. However, I shall maintain that the necessary democratic qualities courts possess in doing so derive from the legal and judicial system being part of a democratic society characterized by political equality. The reason for this being so is simple: namely, that the only way to ensure all citizens enjoy an equal status is to subject state institutions—including courts—to a process that provides them with an equal say. Given citizens disagree about the principles and interpretations of them that best realize democratic equality, they cannot be defined or applied entirely outside a democratic process without losing democratic legitimacy and failing to treat citizens with equal concern and respect as having an equal stake in the configuration of their political community—a point I developed at length in Chapter 1. As I remarked in Chapter 3, democratic processes and democratic outcomes are linked. However, as I insisted in Chapters 1, 2, 4, and 5, that does not mean that courts cannot play a key role in alerting legislatures to the adverse impact of legislation on individual rights through 'weak review'.

These democratic arguments for the judicial review of legislation can be regarded as reflecting a crisis with this practice. As Learned Hand predicted sixty years ago,[14] the more the Supreme Court comes to be viewed as a 'third legislature', the more the known or expected political convictions of its members have become an important determinant in their appointment. As a result, the judgments of Supreme Court Justices now reliably reflect the political views expressed at their confirmation hearings.[15] Analogous developments have arisen in other countries as courts have been drawn into making decisions in controversial areas where there is deep disagreement. Meanwhile, attempts to depoliticize courts by rendering them independent from political involvement in the appointment process seem to

[12] For useful summaries of this research, see Jeff King, 'The Democratic Case for a Written Constitution' (2019) 72 *Current Legal Problems* 13 and n. 30; Tushnet, *Taking the Constitution Away*, chs 6 and 7.

[13] e.g. Peter H. Irons, *The Courage of Their Convictions* (New York: Free Press).

[14] Hand, *The Bill of Rights*, 71.

[15] Jeffrey A. Segal and Albert D. Cover, 'Ideological Values and the Votes of U.S. Supreme Court Justices' (1989) 83(2) *American Political Science Review* 557–65.

have weakened their social and political legitimacy—not least because these processes can lack transparency and appear to support the self-selection of a judicial elite that in any case offers no guarantee that judges will be free from certain ideological and value biases (indeed how could they not be),[16] thereby providing a justification for reforms that increase political interference.[17] Therefore, even if we could, I doubt we should return to the aristocratic view of a judiciary as somehow above or immune to the partial perspectives of their fellow citizens. Instead, we need to confront their political partiality. I suggest a fourth argument that might improve the democratic legitimacy of courts in doing so—namely, that they be indicatively representative of the range of political opinion. However, I shall argue that this form of politicization should not be seen as a means to improve the democratic quality of judicial deliberations, so that they can be seen as a rival democratic forum to legislatures. Rather, they can serve to incentivize courts to deliberate in impartial and non-partisan ways.

2. COURTS AND IDEAL DEMOCRACY

The first argument holds that constitutional courts are not counter-democratic but upholders of the democratic ideals enshrined in the constitution and that their deliberations can themselves be regarded as exemplary of a true democratic process. This thesis has been given a procedural and a substantive reading: as ensuring that either the processes or the outcomes of democratic decision-making are consistent with democratic values.[18] Advocates of the procedural, input, approach maintain it is less contentious then the substantive, outcome, approach. However, in practice each tends to shade into the other. If theorists from the substantive camp propose those procedures they believe most conducive to producing certain outcomes, those from the procedural camp tend to draw substantive conclusions from procedural arguments, as when they argue that the functioning of a given process assumes certain substantive social and economic preconditions. Space prevents

[16] Nuno Garoupa and Tom Ginsburg, 'Guarding the Guardians: Judicial Councils and Judicial Independence' (2009) 57(1) *American Journal of Comparative Law* 103–34 <https://doi.org/10.5131/ajcl.2008.0004>; Uwe Kischel, 'Party, Pope, and Politics? The Election of German Constitutional Court Justices in Comparative Perspective' (2013) 13(4) *International Journal of Constitutional Law* 972.

[17] See Amal Sethi, 'Politicising Constitutional Court Appointments in Europe'(2025) 21(2) *European Constitutional Law Review* 193–229; M. Urbániková, and S. Šipulová, 'Failed Expectations: Does the Establishment of Judicial Councils Enhance Confidence in Courts?' (2018) 19(7) *German Law Journal* 2105–36; D. Kosař, J. Baroš, and P. Dufek, 'The Twin Challenges to Separation of Powers in Central Europe: Technocratic Governance and Populism' (2019) 15(3) *European Constitutional Law Review* 427–61.

[18] For the substantive reading, see Dworkin, *Freedom's Law*; for the procedural reading, see John Hart Ely, *Democracy and Distrust: A Theory of Judicial Review* (Cambridge, MA: Harvard University Press 1980); Jürgen Habermas, *Between Facts and Norms: Contributions to a Discourse Theory of Law and Democracy* (William Rehg tr., Cambridge: Polity Press 1996).

my surveying all the variations on this argument.[19] Here I restrict my analysis to one prominent example, that of John Rawls.[20] Rawls attempts to cut through the substantive-procedural distinction by conceiving the public reasons that justify both substance and process as matters of political right or justice that are distinct from—but compatible with—any reasonable conception of the good that a democratic politics might be employed to promote.[21] He seeks a consensus around a distinctively democratic mode of argumentation that can be employed by courts to justify their judgments. Whereas some such move offers a necessary underpinning for the view that courts possess democratic legitimacy in and of themselves, I shall argue that it cannot secure the consensual support it requires if it is to provide a source of democratic legitimacy independent of any democratic process.

Rawls claims that the Supreme Court 'is the exemplar of public reason' and that its standing in this regard is triply democratic.[22] First, it upholds the principles that are intrinsic to the democratic public sphere. It may override certain decisions of that democratic process but only to preserve democracy. Second, the Supreme Court deliberates in an ideally democratic way because it is constrained when it comes to deciding issues that raise 'constitutional essentials' to only employ public reasons—reasons that simply reflect the values of a democratic society and process—when reaching its judgment. Thirdly, the Supreme Court has a democratic mandate from the people, as the authorizers of the constitution and the ultimate arbiters of how it should be interpreted. These democratic credentials are mutually sustaining, yet ultimately fail. Given, as we shall see, the first proves suspect and gains little or no support from the third, the basis for the second collapses.

Rawls's theory rests on a view of the constitution as the repository of those public reasons that democratic citizens can reach 'practical agreement' about in relation to two sets of 'constitutional essentials'. These two sets concern, respectively, 'the general structure of government and the political process', on the one hand, and the 'equal basic rights and liberties of citizenship that legislative majorities are to respect', on the other.[23] As such, his account encompasses both the procedural and the substantive reading, given that the second set is not limited to those rights and liberties that are inherent to the democratic process. Nevertheless, his scheme is limited to 'political justice', its aim being to fix 'once and for all' the procedures through which citizens 'can express ... their reasoned democratic will' and the protections necessary for 'guaranteeing the security and independence of citizens'.[24]

Rawls sees disagreement about the nature of the good life as 'reasonable' and inevitable in a liberal society, committed to tolerating a plurality of values and ideas

[19] For such a survey, see Bellamy, *Political Constitutionalism*, ch. 3.
[20] John Rawls, *Political Liberalism* (New York: Columbia University Press 1993).
[21] Rawls, *Political Liberalism*, 213.
[22] Rawls, *Political Liberalism*, 216, 219.
[23] Rawls, *Political Liberalism*, 227.
[24] Rawls, *Political Liberalism*, 232.

and promoting experiments in living. Yet, he considers it a matter of 'the greatest urgency' that citizens agree on the basic rules of the political game which determine how these disagreements are to be conducted and limit the extent to which they can be concluded by closing off the possibility of dissent or the capacity to adopt alternative ways of living.[25] Consequently, he believes the public reasons that derive from political justice must be as far as possible separate from any given conception of the political (or any other) good citizens may hold. They are intended to be reasons that all citizens can acknowledge as guiding the pursuit and promotion of their different and often conflicting and incompatible conceptions of the good within the public sphere, so as to show the views and activities of others equal concern and respect. These reasons do not follow from or seek to determine *what* good citizens should pursue. They merely constrain *how* they can use politics or the law to protect or support whatever good they may value and to regulate their interactions with others.[26]

Public reasons contrast with the 'private' reasons of the various non-public associations and bodies found in civil society or of autocratic or aristocratic regimes that serve the particular interests of a given group of people rather than the public as a whole.[27] A private association such as a Church need only be open to those who share its system of beliefs. It can even be hierarchically ordered, with believers accepting the authority of priests in matters of religious doctrine by virtue of their learning and devoutness. Likewise, firms can require employees for the purposes of their work to share their goals and follow the directions of the management as to how best to achieve them. Nevertheless, these private associations, like the political authorities that may regulate them, must operate in ways that are consistent with a public framework which allows their peaceful co-existence with other associations and that does not impinge on their members' status as citizens. Once they enter the public sphere, they have a moral duty of civility to couch their views in ways consistent with public reasons.

Rawls claims such public reasoning is 'characteristic of a democratic people'[28] but is ambiguous as to whether it is a necessary feature of all democratic politics. Although he starts by asserting that 'many if not most political questions do not concern those fundamental matters' that invoke public reason,[29] he later backtracks to suggest that all public policies may touch on them but in ways that are not always entirely clear.[30] Whereas he thinks agreement on what public reason dictates for how power is acquired and limited is both more urgent and easier to reach

[25] Rawls, *Political Liberalism*, 227.

[26] Rawls, *Political Liberalism*, 216–20.

[27] Rawls, *Political Liberalism*, 220–2. As Rawls notes, there is no purely personal 'private' reason, so even these reasons are 'social'. However, they are not 'public' in his sense of addressing other members of society in their guise as fellow citizens, as opposed to, say, fellow believers.

[28] Rawls, *Political Liberalism*, 213.

[29] Rawls, *Political Liberalism*, 214.

[30] Rawls, *Political Liberalism*, 215.

because what is required is relatively straightforward to specify, he believes social and economic arrangements allow for 'wide differences of reasonable opinion' given 'they rest on complicated inferences and intuitive judgments that require us to assess complex social and economic information about topics poorly understood'.[31] However, given all collective decisions involve state coercion to some degree, not just politicians but also citizens should seek to justify their view of them in terms of public reason, regardless of their personal grounds for voting a certain way on a given matter. Indeed, though Rawls's account appears initially parsimonious in its foundations and limited in application, he concludes by considering that public reason will ultimately involve convergence on the 'most reasonable' view of justice, a position for which he proposes his own theory.[32] This hubristic move proves both unavoidable and fatal to his thesis.

Rawls regards the democratic integrity of a constitutional court's position as depending on a consensus on political justice that can be applied in a reasonably clear-cut manner, at least so far as securing the equal rights and liberties of citizens in the operation of political procedures is concerned. As we saw in Chapter 1, Rawls regards disagreement among 'comprehensive religious, philosophical, and moral doctrines' as inevitable and reasonable, and so dissents from Dworkin's view that a constitutional court can appeal to 'a conception of morality as such' or even 'political morality'.[33] Nevertheless, he sees agreement on political justice as vital if we are to have a stable basis on which to conduct these disagreements about religion, morality, and so on.[34] Yet, it is unclear that disagreement about political justice—including Rawls's own theory of justice—is any less reasonable than disagreement about conceptions of the good.

As we also noted in Chapter 1, Rawls attributes moral disagreement to what he terms 'the burdens of judgment'.[35] We have seen how these burdens refer to the normative and empirical difficulties that attend our practical reasoning. The normative difficulties arise from the problems of assessing which factors are morally relevant to a given issue or how moral factors of different kinds might be combined or prioritized, the overcoming of the vagueness of our concepts, especially when it comes to hard cases, and of reconciling the divergent moral views that people's different life experiences may lead them to adopt. The empirical difficulties reflect the problems within complex and open societies of weighing up evidence, identifying causal processes, and estimating the consequences of different decisions and policies. Yet precisely such normative and empirical difficulties characterize disagreements about issues of political justice such as the limits to freedom of speech, the propriety of particular anti-terrorist measures, the scope of privacy, and so on.

[31] Rawls, *Political Liberalism*, 228–9.
[32] Rawls, *Political Liberalism*, 227.
[33] Rawls, *Political Liberalism*, 236 n. 25.
[34] Rawls, *Political Liberalism*, 228.
[35] Rawls, *Political Liberalism*, 54–8.

Here too, concepts are vague, different life experiences lead to divergent assessments of what is morally important, and the bearing of evidence is hard to assess and causal processes difficult to read.

Proponents of different conceptions of the good can certainly hold similar views of the right, so that there can be Catholic, Protestant, and Humanist Rawlsian liberals, say. However, those who embrace the same conceptions of the good may also differ about the right, so that there can be Catholic, Protestant, and Humanist Burkean conservatives as well. As Rawls concedes, these differences may reflect to some degree their different understandings of their various conceptions of the good. Yet, even if they manage to put these conceptions to one side—which, as we shall see in the next section, may be doubted—their differences over the right will be characterized by the self-same burdensome judgements that characterize their disagreements about the good. Conservatives and liberals will each understand rights and justice in different ways, with their ideological disagreements being mired in identical normative and empirical difficulties to those Rawls associates with their differing comprehensive philosophical conceptions.

The need for democratic politics flows as much from disagreements about the right as about the good.[36] Debates between (and within) Labour and Conservatives in the UK or Democrats and Republicans in the United States are not disagreements about how to apply agreed principles of democratic justice but about which among a number of rival principles to apply, be they libertarian, conservative, social democratic, or a mix of all three. Yet despite these disagreements, some collective policies will need to be decided upon. The 'burdens of judgment' and the resulting partiality and potential fallibility of all human reasoning about the right as well as the good, mean that no individual or group of individuals can claim to be a better judge of another individual's interests than him or herself. Consequently, fairness dictates that collective decisions should be made in such a way that those persons whose common world is shaped by them can advance their interests on an equal basis to everyone else. In this regard, as I argued in Chapter 1, democracy embodies the 'right to have rights' of citizens—it offers the mechanism through which their different views on justice and the good are treated with equal respect and their interests and ideals may be shown equal concern.[37]

It might be argued that this process requires at the very least that we agree on the rights intrinsic to democratic procedures.[38] As we saw, though Rawls contends there is more to political justice than purely procedural matters, he believes these are easier and the most important to reach agreement on.[39] However, turning to process rather than substance provides no solution to the above difficulties. Not

[36] Waldron, *Law and Disagreement*, 105–6.
[37] Waldron, Law and Disagreement, ch. 11.
[38] Ely, *Democracy and Distrust*; Habermas, *Between Facts and Norms*.
[39] Rawls, *Political Liberalism*, 215, 22–30.

only are citizens' substantive positions often implicated in their views of process, so that they judge a process by how far it is likely to achieve substantive results they approve of, but also there can be purely procedural disagreements over issues such as whether deliberation promotes group think or better informed decision-making, the relative merits of different electoral systems, the value of second chambers, and so on. Procedural judgments prove as burdensome as substantive ones. Even basic procedural issues, such as the right to vote, can be controversial. For example, Rawls's dissent from the Supreme Court's judgment in *Buckley v. Valeo* 424 US 424 (1976), that decided the limits on expenditures imposed by the Election Act Amendment of 1974 were unconstitutional, turns not on the Court failing to consider democratic values but, rather, on his view that its reasoning was faulty with regard to the normative and empirical assumptions it made when interpreting those values.[40]

Rawls believes disagreement cannot go all the way down to the very constitution of the democratic process without placing the upholders of democracy in a dilemma. For if there is disagreement about the nature of democracy, a democratic process that many participants within it feel is not truly democratic cannot be a legitimate means to decide questions about the nature of democracy itself. To the degree that is so, though, having a court decide these issues offers no solution to the dilemma.[41] In the absence of an agreed conception of political justice, there is no reason to suppose the composition, competences, and decisions of any court will be any less contentious than those of elected representatives in the legislature. Nor, as is sometimes suggested, can it be supposed the decisions of a court on the democratic process will be less self-interested or more independent than those of an elected legislature.[42] For its members have the same interest in the democratic process as all other citizens, while many of their decisions will implicitly and sometimes explicitly touch on its own role in the legal and political system. However imperfectly, a less than ideal democratic process will at least offer a roughly equal measure of popular participation in deciding these disagreements.

A one-off constitutional referendum also offers no help in legitimizing the democratic standing of a constitutional court. Following Bruce Ackerman,[43] Rawls distinguishes 'normal' from 'constitutional' politics and argues that a constitutional democracy is 'dualist'. Normal legislation is democratically legitimized by an electoral process involving majority rule but is subject to the higher law of the constitution which acquires democratic legitimacy in a more demanding, super-majoritarian, way through garnering the overwhelming support of the people as a whole at an exceptional constitutional moment, when the very character of the

[40] Rawls, *Political Liberalism*, 359–60.
[41] Waldron, *Law and Disagreement*, 298–9.
[42] Waldron, *Law and Disagreement*, 296–8.
[43] Bruce Ackerman, *We the People: Foundations* (Cambridge, MA: Harvard University Press 1991).

political regime as a whole comes into question.[44] Though imperfect and potentially fallible, Rawls considers such real instances of popular constitutionalism as the best available approximation to the ideal democratic contract that grounds his theory. They show the principles of political justice that order a given democratic society are 'plain truths now widely accepted'.[45]

This argument confuses popular sovereignty with democracy.[46] 'We the people' may be sovereign but that does not make whatever institutions or mechanisms they choose *ipso facto* democratic, for they may deploy that sovereign power to establish a non-democratic political system. Yet democratic legitimacy requires the system be democratic in its operation and not merely in its establishment. One reason is that constitutional documents continue to be controversial and in need of interpretation so long as reasonable disagreement about justice persists. If reasonable disagreement about political justice proves ongoing, and so present within almost all debates on public policy in elections and the legislature, then no valid reason exists for assuming that the popular determination at time t should prevail over that at t + 1, when changes in society and in the people and their views that compose it, suggest a new determination of fundamental questions. To make such changes subject either to the evolving views of the judiciary or a super-majority of citizens as a whole in a special referendum denies the very essence of democracy—the equal right of citizens to participate in the framing of their common life. It effectively weights the privileges of the past or of a few judges over those of citizens. As such, it fails the criteria of equal concern and respect.

Rawls accepts that a legislature may be the 'exemplar of public reason' in certain democratic societies.[47] What has been argued above is that it has a superior basis for that role than constitutional courts through being the forum for the ongoing reasoning of the public—a place where citizens may voice their reasonable disagreements about the basis of their collective co-existence, albeit through their duly elected representatives. If these disagreements extend to the very rules of the game then there will be no set of undisputed democratic values and certainly no authoritative way of interpreting them that might justify the exemplary role Rawls accords to the Supreme Court. That need not mean that a role could not exist for courts to be a forum for individuals or groups to contest the fairness and equity of legislation in relation to particular cases. However, it does suggest that, as with the UK Human Rights Act, discussed in Chapter 4, the final word should rest with the legislature. It is only then that courts can offer an alternative and democratically legitimate forum for popular participation in public reasoning—either directly or

44 Rawls, *Political Liberalism*, 232–5.
45 Rawls, *Political Liberalism*, 225.
46 Waldron, *Law and Disagreement*, 258–9.
47 Rawls, *Political Liberalism*, 234–5, esp. n. 21.

through the judiciary as their representatives. Otherwise, they will be forced to rely on flawed arguments similar to those of Rawls criticized above.

3. COURTS AND PARTICIPATORY DEMOCRACY

Few would deny that the electoral process often fails to engage citizens or to adequately reflect or respond to the important concerns of a significant number of them. Indeed, most democracies have experienced falling voter turnout in recent years. By contrast, participation in a range of other kinds of political activism remains comparatively buoyant. Many see support for litigation by public interest groups, such as consumer, environmental, or anti-discrimination campaigners, as among the most important of these alternative forms of civic engagement.[48] Yet, how democratic is it? Following Philip Pettit, we can distinguish three forms of democracy—'authorial', 'editorial', and 'contestatory'.[49] I shall explore each in turn and argue all suffer from the oligarchic and anti-democratic qualities they associate with electoral democracy and seek to correct.

3.1. Authorial Democracy

Authorial democracy involves citizens authoring collective policies. Within electoral systems this arises from their indirect influence over legislation and the policies of elected government officials. As we have seen, the claim to democratic legitimacy stems from the electoral process being a public mechanism that allows citizens to advance their interests on an equal basis to each other. In the case of authorial litigation, the aim is to point to a failure on the part of the authorities to meet their as yet unrecognized legal obligations with regard to some issue that places a new requirement on elected governments and administrations to legislate or act on this matter. Such litigation thereby indirectly authors new legislation and action. An example would be the growing use of climate change litigation to effect increased governmental and legislative action to reduce emissions on the grounds that a failure to do so breaches human rights.[50]

[48] Aileen Kavanagh, 'Participation and Judicial Review' (2003) 22 *Law and Philosophy* 451–86. See also Rachel Cichowski, 'Mobilisation, Litigation and Democratic Governance' (2013) 49 *Representation* 321–33; Daniel Keleman, 'Judicialisation, Democracy and European Integration' (2013) 49 *Representation* 295–308; Lisa Vanhala, 'Civil Society Organisations and the Aarhus Conventions in Court' (2013) 49 *Representation* 309–20; Cristina Lafont, *Democracy Without Shortcuts. A Participatory Conception of Deliberative Democracy* (Oxford: Oxford University Press 2020) ch. 8.

[49] Philip Pettit, 'Democracy: Electoral and Contestatory' in Ian Shapiro and Stephen Macedo (eds), *Designing Democratic Institutions* (New York: New York University Press 2000) 105–44.

[50] J. Setzer and C. Higham, *Global Trends in Climate Change Litigation: 2025 Snapshot* (London: Grantham Research Institute on Climate Change and the Environment, London School of Economics and Political Science 2025) report that in 2024 there were at least 180 such cases globally. Key cases include the Dutch cases *Urgenda Foundation v. State of the Netherlands* (2015; 2019) and *Milieudefensie*

The democratic credentials of such cases are held to rest in part on their being initiated by popular associations of citizens, such as the Senior Women for Climate Protection in Switzerland or the Urgenda Foundation, a Dutch environmental group, in Holland. However, even given a declining electoral turnout, national elections in most democracies typically engage the participation of over 50 per cent of the electorate, often amounting to several million voters.[51] No litigation campaign achieves anything like the same degree of support or involvement. Likewise, campaigning organizations typically have even lower levels of membership than political parties. For example, the Senior Women started as a group of forty and by April 2024 its membership had only risen to around 2,500, while the Urgenda Foundation represents around 900 citizens. Even when such groups do enjoy a significant following, as is the case with Milieudefensie (Friends of the Earth Netherlands), they lack anything equivalent to the electoral incentive, explored in Chapter 3, that leads parties to weigh the views and interests of all citizens on a sufficiently equitable basis to secure a majority, usually by appealing to the median voter—be it alone or as part of a winning coalition.[52]

Of course, it could be argued that within the context of a given case, a court will hear from representatives of all affected parties. In this way, the legal forum comes to reflect the wider political forum. However, the incentives for rival groups mounting or blocking legal challenges are not symmetrical to the electoral incentives of parties. In the legal case, it will be the specific impact of a particular policy that will be at issue. To litigate, there must also be a case in law, with only certain parties have standing. As a result, a whole range of views and interests of potentially affected persons may be excluded. Meanwhile, those with deep pockets can have an even more disproportionate influence in the legal than they do in the political sphere. However wealthy they may be, rich party funders must ultimately win the votes of those poorer than themselves. They cannot straightforwardly buy an advocate to argue their case on an equal basis to a much more poorly resourced advocate supported by very many more people. Imperfect and inequitable though electoral processes frequently are, legal processes risk being even more so. For example, particularly in the United States, but also elsewhere, fossil fuel corporations have begun to engage in litigation designed to roll back the gains made by climate groups through anti-regulatory challenges, lawsuits contesting the legitimacy of environmental and social governance, strategic litigation against public participation aimed at silencing activists and their

et al. v. Shell (2021), the European Court of Human Rights (ECtHR) case *Verein KlimaSeniorinnen Schweiz and Others v. Switzerland* (2024), and the Advisory Opinion on the 'Obligations of States in Respect of Climate Change' of the International Court of Justice (ICJ) of 23 July 2025.

[51] Colin Hay, *Why We Hate Politics* (Cambridge: Polity 2008) 13–14.

[52] Peter C. Ordeshook, *Game Theory and Political Theory* (Cambridge: Cambridge University Press 1986) 245–57.

supporters, and rights-based cases claiming climate change measures fall disproportionately on certain disadvantaged groups—such as workers in these industries or the traditional practices of indigenous groups—raising issues related to just transition norms. Around 27 per cent of climate-related litigation brought in 2024 fell into one or more of these categories,[53] the most prominent case being Shell's successful appeal in the Dutch Supreme Court against *Milieudefensie et al. v. Shell* (2021).

Above all, the final determination of a case lies not with the litigators but the judiciary. It is their vote alone that counts in court—indeed, nobody else has a right to vote. Even if the campaigns and hearings themselves were as free and equal as the electoral process, a crucial element is missing—it is not the parties to this process who determine the outcome. Litigation offers the right to petition for rights but is not itself a right to define and determine the rights of the collectivity. Thus, the credentials of litigation as a mode of 'authorial' democracy are weak. That exposes such litigation to the charge of being itself anti-democratic and prompting a democratic backlash. For example, the *Verein KlimaSeniorinnen Schweiz and Others v. Switzerland* (2024) encountered strong criticism in the Swiss media, provoking the Swiss Parliament to vote to reject the European Court of Human Rights (ECtHR) ruling upholding their cause on 12 June 2024, claiming the government already had an effective climate policy, with the government issuing a statement concurring with this view on 28 August. Likewise, Lord Sumption—a former UK Supreme Court justice—saw the ruling as a typical case of judicial overreach by the ECtHR, writing that it had 'become an avowed enemy not just of democratic decision-making but of good government'.[54]

Certain of the imperfections and inequities of the legal process could be said to be balanced by the constraints of the law itself. Not all arguments will be valid. That may exclude certain injustices getting a legal hearing but it will also rule out certain unjust views being presented and allow many that have been legislated for to be challenged—not least by groups whose views may not have gained an adequate consideration within the electoral process. Moreover, the judges can only decide a case on the basis of legislation or a constitution that has itself been democratically endorsed. These constraints move litigation towards the model of 'editorial' democracy, whereby the aim is not to author new legislation to realize certain supposed rights standards so much as to strike down existing legislation for a lack of conformity with these standards. Here the aim is to litigate against commissions more than omissions by the elected authorities. That might seem a less contentious and more moderate aim than 'authorial' litigation, but turns out to raise parallel problems.

[53] Setzer and Higham, *Global Trends in Climate Change Litigation*, 42.

[54] Jonathan Sumption, 'ECHR's climate change ruling is its boldest intrusion yet', *The Times*, 14 April 2024.

3.2. Editorial Democracy

The democratic legitimacy of 'editorial democracy' rests on the constitution reflecting a democratic consensus on the procedural and substantive norms of a democratic polity that can be applied in an impartial way that reflects this consensus by the relevant courts. However, the strongest case for the democratic legitimacy of this practice depends on something like Rawls's argument about public reason that I criticized in the last section. In other words, it assumes that the editorial rules provided by the constitution reflect a democratic consensus as to the norms of a democratic society and that they can be applied in an impartial way that reflects this consensus by the court. If neither is true, then the danger exists that the court may edit out what needs editing in or vice versa, inventing or interpreting supposedly democratic norms in a largely arbitrary way. For example, think of the Lochner period when the state and federal courts in the United States struck down some 150 pieces of labour legislation, including measures to outlaw child labour, on the grounds that they violated freedom of contract.[55] Or consider the Canadian Court's declaration that restrictions on tobacco advertising undermined freedom of speech.[56]

Editorial democracy presumes to offer public criteria that can distinguish between groups that are heard within the democratic process but fail to convince, on the one hand, from those who either fail to get a hearing at all or whose very right to be treated as worthy of a hearing is being denied, on the other. As a result, those who litigate in this spirit argue that either the process was deficient or that the decision itself denies them their democratic rights. Yet, we saw how these matters prove impossible to determine without the judiciary taking a position on the very disagreements about political justice that may have been at issue in the legislative process. Thus, an intense minority, who feel very strongly in favour of a policy that the rest of the population feel moderately opposed to, may argue the electoral process has let them down by not appropriately weighting the intensity of their views. However, even if this case is treated as a 'mere' procedural issue it raises contentious and burdensome judgements over process rights. For example, who deserves more of a say: residents of an area where an airport is to be built or the general population? That could be treated as a matter of the appropriate competences or a balance between local and national decision-making, but unless there was a very clear and settled view in law on the issue it is doubtful the judiciary could invoke a consensus on this topic. They may be simply reconsidering a question that legislators had themselves thought long and hard about when deciding to build the airport where they did. It is also more than likely that most views of the

[55] Waldron, *Law and Disagreement*, 288.

[56] Ran Hirschl, *Towards Juristocracy: The Origins and Consequences of the New Constitutionalism* (Cambridge, MA: Harvard University Press 2004).

procedural question will involve a stance on what an acceptable outcome would be and hence of the relative importance of the interests involved. Once again, though, these points may have been raised and deliberated on already, with the legislature's decision itself seeking to balance the impact on residents, environmental concerns, and the needs of the economy on as equitable and fair basis as possible.

As a result, in deciding the question on either procedural or substantive grounds, the court will be deliberating like a legislature, even if it deploys the rhetoric of constitutionalism when doing so. It need not be that the legislature or administration ignored democratic rights, they just offered a different interpretation of them to that favoured by the litigators or—if convinced by the litigants' reasoning—the court. But why then should this second view prevail? The danger arises that litigation simply offers a venue for those who lose fair and square in politics to gain a second hearing by concentrating all their resources on winning on a particular issue in law. It may distort rather than support the democratic process by diverting political resources to fighting a battle that the majority felt had already been legitimately settled in a way that offered a more rounded and comprehensive appreciation of all the rights and views of rights at issue.[57]

What about examples that most people would regard as legitimate? Rawls sees the civil rights movement in the United States as a prime instance of editorial democracy.[58] He argues the democratic legitimacy of the campaign rested on its leaders being able to appeal to the public reason of the constitution, thereby validating the rights of a minority group. However, this example proves problematic in a number of respects. First, as Rawls acknowledges, the rhetoric of the campaign was typically couched in terms of a more comprehensive conception of the good, often religious in character, to reinforce their contention that, in this area, equal could not mean differential or separate treatment. Rawls argues such religious arguments were acceptable in this case because they met what he calls 'the proviso' of supporting the public reasons of constitutional values, and their case was capable of being defended in these terms.[59] However, the Supreme Court had had a history of interpreting these very values in ways that upheld racial inequality even after the Civil War and the broad public condemnation of its ruling in *Dred Scott* of 1857. In particular, the Court had interpreted the 13th, 14th, and 15th post-Civil War constitutional amendments in the 1883 *Civil Rights Cases* in ways that largely gutted the anti-discrimination legislation proposed by Congress to give these amendments practical effect, claiming they unfairly privileged black people as 'the special favourite of the laws'.[60] Indeed, in 1896, the Court explicitly upheld segregation as 'equal but separate' in *Plessy v. Ferguson*.[61] Given this context, it is perhaps

[57] Tushnet, *Taking the Constitution Away*, 138–40.

[58] Rawls, *Political Liberalism*, 249–51.

[59] John Rawls, 'The Idea of Public Reason Revisited' (1997) 64(3) *The University of Chicago Law Review* 776, 784–6.

[60] Civil Rights Act of 1866, ch. 31: 14 Stat. 27; *Civil Rights Cases* 109 U.S. 3, 25 (1883).

[61] *Plessy v. Ferguson* 163 U.S. 537 (1896).

unsurprising that later civil rights campaigners should feel a need to justify a particular reading of the constitution in terms of a wider set of considerations than the narrow public reasons deployed in the legal argumentation of the Court. In other words, their aim was not to appeal to a constitutional consensus on democratic values that had been ignored by either the legislature or a federal democratic majority but to contest and change the dominant *judicial* understanding of those values.

Second, Rawls's account largely overlooks this history of Court decisions that undermined democratic attempts at the federal level to secure minority rights. This dire judicial legacy has tended to be eclipsed by the Court's judgment in *Brown v. Board of Education*,[62] that reversed *Plessy*. This case has been seen as legitimizing judicial review as a mechanism for ensuring discrete and insular minorities have their constitutional rights to be regarded as equal citizens upheld. However, not only had these rights been expressly denied by the courts up to that point, but also this case was not an instance of the Court overruling Congress and disapplying a federal law. Rather, as Nikolas Bowie has pointed out,[63] it involved the enforcement of a federal law, the Ku Klux Klan Act of 1871, which earlier Court rulings had largely invalidated but a section of which prohibited state officials from violating federal law or the constitution.[64] Moreover, segregation was only effectively ended with the passing by Congress of the Civil Rights and Voting Rights Acts in 1964 and 1965:[65] federal legislation that had to overcome earlier Supreme Court precedents and that subsequent judgments, notably *Shelby*, have eroded.[66] The success of the civil rights movement depended—and still depends—on the democratic rather than the judicial arena.

None of the above denies that there can be excluded and unpopular groups who, through prejudice or oversight, fail to have their interests adequately considered within the electoral process. Measures that appear generally beneficial may also have unintended and unanticipated harmful consequences for particular individuals or in certain unforeseen circumstances. There is a risk of injustice and rights violations whichever institution is ultimately favoured. As I argued in Chapter 3, democracy can minimize such risks through incorporating checks and balances into the operation of the democratic process and its institutionalization. I also noted in Chapters 1 and 4 how 'weak' review by the courts can be seen as a further check and balance that may provide a valuable fire alarm in such cases by allowing groups or individuals to raise such concerns.[67] However, given there is

[62] *Brown v. Board of Education* 347 U.S. 483 (1954).

[63] Bowie, 'The Contemporary Debate over Supreme Court Reform', 7–8, 23–4.

[64] The section now known as 42 U.S.C. § 1983.

[65] Gerald Rosenberg, *The Hollow Hope: Can Court Bring About Social Change* (Chicago: University of Chicago Press 1991).

[66] *Shelby County v. Holder* 570 U.S. 529 (2013).

[67] On 'weak' versus 'strong' judicial review, see Jeremy Waldron, 'The Core of the Case Against Judicial Review' (2006) 115 *Yale Law Journal* 1346–1406, at 1354–6. This term is also used by Mark Tushnet, 'Alternative Forms of Judicial Review' (2003) 101 *Michigan Law Review* 2781–2802. Whereas

no uncontentious way a court could decide these questions on the basis of democratic reasons alone, the only true democratic forum for the final decision must surely be one that is itself subject to an inclusive democratic process—namely, the legislature.[68]

3.3. Contestatory Democracy

These criticisms of judicial review as a form of editorial democracy also apply to Cristina Lafont's recent participatory interpretation of the democratic case for judicial review as a form of contestatory democracy—the most sustained normative argument yet for this position.[69] This third form of litigation involves certain aspects of the previous two. Like editorial democracy, it appeals to democratic constitutional norms, but it moves towards authorial democracy in stimulating a popular debate as to how they should be understood and appropriately enacted with regard to a given policy. On this account, even losing cases can be seen as a series of steps in a campaign to change judicial opinion that will ultimately produce a change in how the law is interpreted or even in the law itself.[70]

Lafont maintains that though judicial review may be 'counter-majoritarian' that need not make it anti-democratic. She contends that critics adopt an excessively 'juricentric' perspective, that ignores, or minimizes, the role played by citizens in initiating litigation before the courts, and their reasons for doing so. She contests the view,[71] alluded to above, that litigants are 'poor losers', who having lost fair and square in the political sphere seek to win in a legal sphere 'undisciplined by the principles of political equality',[72] in which all citizens have an equal voice. Rather, she portrays litigants as exercising an equal right to legal contestation with the aim of getting a 'fair hearing'. Such litigation provides members of minority groups in particular with an equal right to be treated with equal concern in the protection of their rights. Moreover, she remarks that litigants do not themselves make decisions—so they are not exercising an additional, and so unequal, 'authorial' vote.[73] Indeed, she maintains that judges do not 'author' law or policy either, given

'strong' form judicial review, as found in the United States, allows a court to strike down and disapply a law it deems to be incompatible with the constitution, 'weak' review, as in the UK under the Human Rights Act, leaves the offending law in place and merely requests the government and legislature to consider revising it.

[68] Bellamy, *Political Constitutionalism*, ch. 6.
[69] Lafont, *Democracy Without Shortcuts*, 222 ff.
[70] For an empirical account of such strategies, see Lisa Vanhala, 'Legal Opportunity Structures and the Paradox of Legal Mobilization by the Environmental Movement in the UK' (2012) 46(3) *Law and Society Review* 523–56.
[71] Lafont, *Democracy Without Shortcuts*, 226–8.
[72] Jeremy Waldron, 'The Core of the Case Against Judicial Review' (2006) 115 *Yale Law Journal* 1395.
[73] Lafont, *Democracy Without Shortcuts*, 230.

they are constrained in their judgment by the terms of a constitution that often has a democratic provenance and that can be changed through democratic pressures.[74] Rather, echoing Dworkin, she argues that courts and legal reasoning can elevate political debates to a principled level, where decisions are grounded in rights, justice, and integrity, rather than just power or compromise. Litigation becomes a way to translate political disagreements into constitutional questions, forcing governments to justify their actions in terms of fundamental values, thereby stimulating a more deliberative and principled debate of issues among the citizenry.[75]

Lafont concedes that her argument turns on the court being a 'forum of principle' in Dworkin's (and Rawls's) sense in a way that she believes a legislature cannot (and should not) be. She argues there is a division of labour between legislatures and courts. The former rightly reflect majority opinion to determine those policies that are in most people's interest. But these decisions may be either self-interested, and so indifferent or even antagonistic to certain minority rights, or (quoting Dworkin) involve 'compromises that may subordinate important issues of principle'.[76] By contrast, the latter are designed to take rights seriously and to focus on the constitutionality of the measure. However, Section 2 above questioned the idea of an overlapping consensus on fundamental democratic rights that could place judicial views on issues of principle beyond the different comprehensive or other views individual judges may hold with regard to policies. Rights are subject to the 'burdens of judgment' and hence give rise to reasonable disagreements that reflect the inevitably partial views of those involved when the bearing of different evidential and moral factors on a given case or issue is at stake. Consequently, the reasoning of judges regarding rights is likely to parallel that of citizens and their representatives. True, judges may feel constrained by precedent and conformity with the terms of the higher law of a codified constitution, but these are weak constraints—especially if judges conceive their role as making Herculean efforts to offer judgments that reflect their reading of the moral integrity of the entire body of law.[77] Not only can diametrically opposed positions be rendered compatible with such criteria—as we saw, though Rawls might view *Buckley v. Valeo* as wrongly decided, formally speaking it could be seen as simply an alternative reading to his of a US tradition of prioritizing freedom of speech, as could *Citizens United v. Federal Election Commission*, 558 U.S. 310 (2010). But also, courts have the power to ignore such constraints—as occurred in *Dobbs v. Jackson Women's Health Organization* 549 U.S. 215 (2022), which overturned both *Roe v. Wade* 410 U.S. 113 (1973) and

[74] Lafont, *Democracy Without Shortcuts*, 220.

[75] Lafont, *Democracy Without Shortcuts*, 238 (quoting, in n. 52, Ronald Dworkin, *A Matter of Principle* (Cambridge, MA: Harvard University Press 1985) 70 and in n. 53, Dworkin, *Freedom's Law*, 345).

[76] Lafont, *Democracy Without Shortcuts*, 234 (quoting Dworkin, *Freedom's Law*, 30).

[77] Think of the way Adrian Vermeule in *Common Good Constitutionalism* (Cambridge: Polity 2022) adopts Ronald Dworkin's approach in *Law's Empire* (London: Fontana 1986) to justify a Conservative Catholic reading of the constitution.

Planned Parenthood v. Casey 505 U.S. 833 (1992). Indeed, in certain instances it may even be justified to override precedents if earlier decisions involved a grave injustice, as was the case with *Dred Scott v. Sandford* 60 U.S. (19 How.) 393 (1857).

Lafont suggests that even 'bad' or 'wrong' decisions may have a positive effect by constitutionalizing political debate. However, she ignores the negative effect they have in politicizing the court and its reading of the constitution. If the decision on whether a law has been authored in a constitutionally consistent way rests with a court, then political effort is likely to get directed at obtaining a majority on the court—as indeed has been the case in the United States. The judicialization of politics will lead to the politicization of the judiciary.[78] The resulting switches in both membership of the Court and its interpretation of the constitution need not be the product of an epoch-changing 'constitutional moment', reflecting a deep moral change among the public, as Ackerman contends.[79] They may be better characterized as an aggressive form of normal politics by a party willing to play constitutional hardball.[80] Consequently, there is a danger that a court's role in upholding the rule of law by consistently applying duly made democratic legislation in an impartial manner will be undermined if it becomes an adjudicator on the justifiability of the law. *Pace* Lafont, that may be a role best left to legislatures—in part for the very reasons she objects to them.

To the extent we can have reasonable disagreements about rights, the complex majorities of legislative politics and the compromises they entail may be fairer than the simple majorities of courts. After all, as we saw in Chapter 3, legislative majorities need to be built—often across two representative chambers, and the millions of voters they represent. In the case of the United States, that means getting a majority of the 435 representatives and 100 senators. As a result, far from being oppressed by tyrannous majorities, minorities can often have considerable bargaining power. Such coalition-building may require compromise, yet that need not be unprincipled—it can reflect mutual recognition of the various sides to a reasonable disagreement.[81] By contrast, Supreme Court decisions require a simple majority of five out of a mere nine justices. Moreover, as Jeremy Waldron has argued, such a simple judicial majority lacks the epistemic and fairness justifications associated with democratic majorities—at best it offers an efficient means for overcoming deadlock—but then, why not toss a coin if majority rule in such circumstances lacks further justification?[82] Of course, courts in some jurisdictions both

[78] Tom Ginsburg, 'Democratic Backsliding and the Rule of Law' (2018) 44 *Ohio Northern University Law Review* 363–4.

[79] Ackerman, *We the People*.

[80] Mark Tushnet, *Taking Back the Constitution: Activist Judges and the Next Age of American Law* (New Haven, CT: Yale University Press 2020).

[81] Richard Bellamy, *Liberalism and Pluralism: Towards a Politics of Compromise* (London: Routledge 1999) ch. 4.

[82] Jeremy Waldron, 'Five to Four: Why Do Bare Majorities Rule on Courts?' (2014) 123 *Yale Law Journal* 1693–1730.

have a larger membership and decide by either consensus or a super-majority, so that a number of swing voters will need to be won over. However, as Cass Sunstein has noted, courts in such situations may well be apt to avoid overly principled decision-making and seek instead 'incompletely theorised agreements' grounded in case by case analogical reasoning.[83] Such deliberations may be little different to those of a legislature—especially if, as is the case in many Commonwealth countries—legislators have a statutory duty to take fundamental rights seriously in their decisions.[84]

Like Rawls, Lafont ignores the history of the Supreme Court and 'its antidemocratic influence on American law, one that has undermined federal attempts to eliminate hierarchies of race, wealth, and status'.[85] As Bowie observes, the only minority rights it has consistently upheld are those of the wealthy—not least because they have the resources to litigate until they do so.[86] True, she illustrates her argument with an apparent exception to the rule—*Obergefell*,[87] that overturned the Defence of Marriage Act (DOMA) of 1996 and affirmed the right of same-sex couples to marry on the basis of the due process and equal protection clauses of the 14th amendment.[88] She argues that religious prejudice on this issue, whereby marriage could only be heterosexual—was overcome by couching it in terms of the public reasons of constitutional rights. However, this case cannot be viewed as a knock-down argument for her position. The Court divided 5–4 and in his concurring opinion for *Dobbs*, one of the dissenters, Justice Clarence Thomas, suggested that the Court should also review *Obergefell*, prompting Congress to pass the Respect for Marriage Act repealing DOMA in December 2022. Of course, Lafont could argue Congress's reaction reflects the change in public opinion brought about by the litigation that led to *Obergefell* and the framing of the issue in terms of rights—but the fact remains that litigation can also allow a well-organized minority to constrain majority democratic opinion in regressive ways. Meanwhile, elsewhere, democratic legislatures have legalized same-sex marriage, as the Marriage (Same Sex Couples) Act 2013 did for England and Wales—something that the High Court had not recognized as a matter of fundamental rights under the European Convention of Human Rights (ECHR) or the UK Human Rights Act in its ruling on *Wilkinson v. Kitzinger* in 2006, where the judge more or less took the view of the US legislature in DOMA.[89] As others have pointed out, we should avoid

[83] Cass Sunstein, *Legal Reasoning and Political Conflict* (Oxford: Oxford University Press 1996) chs 2 and 3.

[84] Stephen Gardbaum, 'The New Commonwealth Model of Constitutionalism' (2001) 49 *American Journal of Comparative Law* 707–60.

[85] Bowie, 'The Contemporary Debate over Supreme Court Reform', 1.

[86] Bowie, 'The Contemporary Debate over Supreme Court Reform', 10.

[87] *Obergefell v. Hodges* 576 U.S. 644 (2015).

[88] Curiously she does not mention *Obergefell* by name, but Lafont, *Democracy Without Shortcuts*, ch. 7 nn. 46–50, and the related text at 214–16, make plain this is the issue and case to which her argument refers.

[89] *Wilkinson v. Kitzinger and Others* [2006] EWHC 2022 (Fam) (31 July 2006) [122].

associating same-sex marriage with 'bold judicial pronouncements on constitutional rights [since] much of the worldwide progress for same-sex relationship recognition has occurred at the legislative level, often without overt prompting from courts'.[90]

Of course, like courts, legislatures may get it wrong—as she notes, they cannot necessarily anticipate all possible cases and the potential negative impact a given measure may have for certain individuals. Again, that's why I advocate 'weak review'—it promotes a dialogue between the courts and legislature that can be mutually beneficial. It also, when combined for a pre-legislative process of rights compatibility, as in the UK, obliges the legislature to reason in a principled way. But this is not a pragmatic choice, based on empirical circumstances, as Lafont suggests.[91] It's a normative choice, based—as was argued in Chapters 1 and 2 in particular—on considerations of democratic legitimacy. Those advocating this position are not denying her normative claim that citizens should have a right to legal contestation. As was argued in Chapter 2, such a right forms a basic requirement of a democratic account of the rule of law.[92] Rather, the argument is that handing a constitutional court the final say on such matters exceeds what can be legitimately claimed given reasonable disagreement about constitutional essentials. The empirics largely confirm this point in showing how arbitrary judicial decisions can be—being largely dependent on the composition of the court, and offering inconsistent support at best to minority rights.[93]

4. COURTS AND REPRESENTATIVE DEMOCRACY

Perhaps, though, a court could claim democratic legitimacy if it could be regarded as representative of the people. Proponents of this argument have tended to adopt either a negative and/or a positive thesis—the one to dispute the aforementioned democratic qualities of the legislature, the other to buttress those of the courts.[94] According to the negative thesis, the democratic critique of courts fails because in representative democracies legislation cannot be regarded as reflecting the popular will. Rather, it results from the deliberations of representatives in the legislature.

[90] Kenji Yoshino and Michael Kavey, 'Immodest Claims and Modest Contributions: Sexual Orientation in Comparative Constitutional Law' in Michel Rosenfeld and András Sajó (eds), *The Oxford Handbook of Comparative Constitutional Law* (Oxford: Oxford University Press 2012) 1091, cited in Psygkas Athanasios, 'The Hydraulics of Constitutional Claims: Multiplicity of Actors in Constitutional Interpretation' (2018) 69(2) *University of Toronto Law Journal* 240—whose analysis yields similar conclusions.

[91] Lafont, *Democracy Without Shortcuts*, 224 and n. 19, 230 n. 39. It is not entirely clear what empirical factors she regards as decisive here.

[92] As does Waldron, Lafont's main antagonist.

[93] See Cheibub, Limongi, Przeworski, and Wang, 'Anti-majoritarianism and Democracy', 8–12.

[94] Dimitrios Kyritsis, 'Representation and Waldron's Objection to Judicial Review' (2006) 26 *Oxford Journal of Legal Studies* 733–51.

However, representatives are neither delegates nor proxies of their constituents. Instead, they are more like trustees.[95] As such, a democratic case against judicial review based on the equal right of citizens to participate in legislation proves as telling against the legislature as it does against constitutional courts. For legislators likewise possess a superior voting weight to ordinary citizens and exercise their independent moral judgement when making decisions concerning the whole of the political community, often going against the express wishes of the citizens that voted for them. The positive thesis notes that judges may likewise be considered as trustees, acting in this sense as representatives in an analogous way to most members of the legislature. However, once again, their chief democratic quality rests on their engaging in conscientious and impartial deliberation on the public good.[96]

Robert Alexy offers a good example of the positive thesis.[97] At one level, he concedes the democratic argument, arguing that 'the only way to reconcile constitutional review with democracy is to conceive of it, too, as representation of the people'.[98] Yet, he also admits that such representation cannot be based on elections and will need to make a case to be superior to that which is. To make this case, he ends up—like Lafont—adopting a version of the Rawlsian view of constitutional courts as exemplars of public reason. Judges, he claims, represent constitutional arguments. He considers these as being akin to what Rawls's calls public reasons. As such, they reflect a potential consensus among rational and reasonable persons. To the extent a constitutional court's decisions involve such reasoning, therefore, it can be regarded as providing a source of 'argumentative representation'.[99] As with trustees, the judge represents through enacting the public reasoning of 'constitutional persons'. Given that 'sound and correct' arguments are superior to those that are flawed and wrong, the priority of 'purely argumentative representation' over 'representation based on election and re-election is no longer difficult'.[100] However, the difficulty, as we have seen, lies in the fact that the 'burdens of judgment' and the possibility of reasonable disagreement render such claims to represent how the public would argue (or at least should, were they reasonable and rational) hard to sustain.

The chief weight of the representation argument, therefore, rests on the negative thesis. Yet, the delegate–trustee distinction on which it relies proves too sharply drawn and fails to consider the full range of representative roles politicians play. Not only do delegation and trusteeship form the end-points of a continuum rather than being opposed and incompatible concepts,[101] but also these and other

[95] Kyritsis, 'Representation', 743–4.
[96] Kyritsis, 'Representation', 748–50.
[97] Robert Alexy, 'Balancing, Constitutional Review, and Representation' (2005) 3(4) *International Journal of Constitutional Law* 572–81.
[98] Alexy, 'Balancing, Constitutional Review, and Representation', 578.
[99] Alexy, 'Balancing, Constitutional Review, and Representation', 579–80.
[100] Alexy, 'Balancing, Constitutional Review, and Representation', 580.
[101] Hanna Fenichel Pitkin, *The Concept of Representation* (Berkeley, CA: University of California Press 1967) 121.

roles can be combined. The key is how the processes of authorization and accountability influence the behaviour of representatives by respectively screening for certain qualities and sanctioning their subsequent failure to meet expectations. For example, Jane Mansbridge has distinguished promissory, anticipatory, and gyroscopic representation.[102] The first category corresponds most to the delegatory model, with representatives assessed by their fidelity to their electoral promises. Indeed, most representatives belong to parties and are subject to party discipline, and the findings of the manifesto research group suggest that, once elected, parties do keep faith to their electoral promises to a remarkable degree.[103] Of course, manifesto promises are often vague policy goals, so representatives may still act as trustees and deliberate over the appropriate means to meet these promised ends. Yet, they are also sensitive to changing attitudes among the electorate in response to new circumstances or the success or failure of different policies. As such, representatives also operate as per the second category and anticipate what they think voters will approve at the next election. Finally, representatives will always have to face unanticipated decisions. However, in doing so, voters may be able to expect they will decide in ways consistent with their previously expressed views without external incentives because they have been selected on the basis of their prior beliefs and opinions. Here, representatives fit into the third category and act as gyroscopes, rotating around a set of relatively stable convictions. Even so, although their authority derives for the most part from the process of authorization, they are liable to be held accountable should they act other than expected.

In all these cases, representatives are sensitive to voter preferences and in dialogue with them in a way that the judiciary largely are not. To the degree that is the case, it is because judges operate in a democratic environment. Thus, they can sometimes be categorized under gyroscopic and anticipatory representation. The gyroscopic model operates where the selection of judges is subject to direct political control, as in the United States, with ideological attitudes as well as professional merit being among the qualities that decide the selection of Supreme Court Justices. By and large, the attitudes expressed in Senate hearings correlate remarkably well with their subsequent decisions.[104] Yet, even where there is greater independence from direct political interference, courts will wish their decisions to gain acceptance by governments and citizens alike. Otherwise, they risk both a loss of legitimacy and an implementation deficit, given there are many ways a judgment can be blocked or undermined through half-hearted, underfunded, or delayed compliance. As a result, they practice a weak form of anticipatory representation,

[102] Jane Mansbridge, 'Rethinking Representation' (2003) 97 *American Political Science Review* 515–28.

[103] Hans-Dieter Klingermann, Richard I. Hofferbert, and Ian Budge, *Parties, Policies and Democracy* (Boulder, CO: Westview Press 1994).

[104] Jeffrey Segal and Harold Spaeth, *The Supreme Court and the Attitudinal Model* (Cambridge: Cambridge University Press 1993).

so that 'courts follow the polls' to the extent of reflecting sustained, national popular opinion.[105]

5. COURTS AND INDICATIVE DEMOCRACY

Anticipatory representation of the kind referred to above only works to the extent a court takes its broad democratic legitimacy among all citizens seriously enough to be responsive to long-term and widely shared trends in popular opinion. Court responsiveness of this kind aspires to be non-partisan and seeks merely to avoid seeming out of touch with what the vast majority of people think: be it by failing to track how people's views have evolved, or by moving in a direction that departs too far from what people are prepared to accept. Such responsiveness to long-term and widely shared trends in popular opinion seems desirable, without which people will cease to recognize the law as theirs but rather as an aristocratic imposition by the judges.

However, such responsiveness becomes much harder when public opinion is polarized. In these circumstances, it becomes difficult for court judgments relating to key social and political issues not to seem partisan. As a result, there will be an increased focus on the politics of the judiciary, with pressure groups and politicians placing ever more effort into ensuring like-minded candidates are appointed. Such appointees obtain their position not as representatives who are in some way responsive to those they represent but as representatives whose views resemble those who appointed them. Whereas with responsive representation the representee will seek to track the reasoning of those they represent, in the case of representation as resemblance things work the other way around.[106] With so-called indicative representation, we can expect the represented to hold similar views to their representee.

There can be good reasons why we might wish the responsiveness of judges to be muted. As I remarked in Chapter 2, political constitutionalists agree with the formal account of the rule of law and its stress on the need for consistency and equity in the framing and application of the law. If we are to be able to count on law as offering a stable framework for social interactions and planning, we need the judicial process to possess features apt to ensure a fair hearing and equality before the law. If the judiciary is subject to intermittent interference by elected governments or rendered responsive to short-term fluctuations in public opinion, then these features may be impaired. Hence, a certain independence from democratic responsiveness seems justified to preserve the rule of law and to maintain the

[105] Robert A. Dahl, 'Decision-making in a Democracy: The Supreme Court as National Policymaker' (1957) 6 *Journal of Public Law* 279–95. See too Robert McKeever, *Raw Judicial Power? The Supreme Court and American Society* (2nd edn, Manchester: Manchester University Press 1995).

[106] Philip Pettit, 'Representation, Responsive and Indicative' (2010) 17(3) *Constellations* 426–34.

popular legitimacy of the court as making 'legal' rather than simply 'political' judgments (even if the two cannot be as neatly distinguished as legal constitutionalists maintain).

However, these risks to the rule of law and legitimacy can be even greater in the case of indicative representation, based on the resemblance of judicial appointees to those who appoint them. If the appointment process gets captured by a single party and lobbyists tied to particular interests and ideological convictions, who choose indicative representatives as their appointees, then precedent and deliberation as well as broad popular responsiveness are likely to carry little weight with them. Instead, such appointees will seek to simply follow and promote their partisan beliefs. As a result, the court's view of the law will depend solely on the particular views of its individual members, and will change as its membership changes. In such a situation, the rule of law becomes little more than the arbitrary rule of those persons empowered to interpret it as they will. Insulated from even informal accountability by the separation of powers and secure salaries and tenure, and unwilling, and (when in a majority) absolved from, engaging with contrary opinions, such judges can ignore not only the precedents set by earlier judges but also long-term and widely shared trends in popular opinion. Instead, they are free to pursue an agenda that resembles only the narrow views of the powerful groups that promoted them.

The decision in *Dobbs* offers a vivid illustration of how this scenario currently obtains so far as the US Supreme Court is concerned. Moreover, it has been replicated in other countries, such as Hungary and Poland, where governments have sought to weaponize the legal constitution in their favour—a phenomenon discussed further in Chapter 8. As a number of commentators have noted, this development has provoked a crisis in the practice of judicial review.[107] In the United States, trust in the Supreme Court has reached a historic low, with 58 per cent of respondents in a recent Gallup poll disapproving of 'how it did its job'.[108]

What is to be done? The Report of the Presidential Commission of the United States canvasses a range of options in regard to the Supreme Court, from removing life tenure to increasing the Court's membership and packing it with Democrat nominees. However, I agree with those who consider a more thoroughgoing democratic reform is required.[109] In part, that involves rendering its role more compatible with democracy by limiting its remit to some form of weak review. But that in itself would be insufficient. It is also necessary to instil within the Court similar incentives to 'hear the other side' to those associated with the democratic process

[107] Jeremy Waldron, 'The Crisis of Judicial Review', H.L.A. Hart Memorial Lecture, 25 May 2023. See too *Final Report by the Presidential Commission on the Supreme Court of the United States*, December 2021 <whitehouse.gov/pcscotus/final-report/>.

[108] <https://news.gallup.com/poll/4732/supreme-court.aspx>.

[109] Ryan D. Doerfler and Samuel Moyn, 'Democratizing the Supreme Court' (2021) 109(5) *California Law Review* 1703–70; Bowie, 'The Contemporary Debate over Supreme Court Reform'.

in Chapter 3. As I noted there, that involves institutionalizing elements of the balance of power.

How might that be achieved in ways that avoid the pitfalls of the judiciary being overly responsive, on the one side, and only partially indicative, on the other? One way may be to enhance the indicative character of judges so that courts contain representatives of all the main currents of political and legal opinion. After all, this plays an important role in legal processes involving juries. In common law systems, those accused of a felony are entitled to be subject to the judgment of their peers as to whether they are legally liable or not. This requirement seeks to avoid arbitrariness and domination by taking this determination out of the hands of an individual or administrative agency, such as a prosecutor, a judge, or the police, and handing it to a jury that is indicatively representative of the people as a whole. A single individual or agency, however scrupulous, will be partial in numerous ways—some potentially badly motivated, many others not. By contrast, juries are generally chosen at random from the local citizenry. Like everyone else, jurors will have their own individual partialities. However, in deliberating together to reach agreement—usually a consensus or super-majority—they will need to hear and harken to the diverse perspectives of the different jurors. In so doing, they will be motivated to reason on the basis of commonly avowable and accessible arguments that reflect the reasoning of the community as a whole. Most importantly, they will reason in ways that the accused can be assumed to share—or could be expected to share. As such, their judgment will not be dominating—the arbitrary imposition of a partial individual will.

As with the judiciary, responsive representation would be inappropriate for a jury. After all, we would not want them to be responsive to the Mafia, for example, or indeed to any other particular group. Yet, like a jury, we might wish the judiciary to be indicative of the community—particularly in those cases, such as most constitutional decisions, where there is no jury. If the bench consists largely of white, privately educated, privileged men then, despite their best efforts, they risk being partial to their own experiences and appearing as such. As we have noted, that risk becomes a certainty if they are deliberately chosen on the basis of their holding certain partisan political and moral views. In both cases, it may be hard for many people to recognize their own reasoning in that of the court. Instead, we need to have a broadly indicative judiciary, the composition of which is not controlled or controllable by any partial group of selectors, and that is large enough to be representative of the range of political opinions and experiences and sufficiently balanced to motivate engagement and the search for commonly avowable resolutions.

Daniel Epps and Ganesh Sitaraman have made a proposal that points in this direction for the US Supreme Court.[110] What they call the 'Supreme Court Lottery'

[110] Daniel Epps and Ganesh Sitaraman, 'How to Save the Supreme Court' (2019) 129 *Yale Law Journal* 148–206.

involves treating all judges on the federal courts of appeal as associate judges of the Supreme Court.[111] Randomly selected panels of nine judges would hear cases, with no more than five justices nominated by a President of a single political party and with decisions needing to be made 6–3. Clearly, this proposal reflects the constitutional and institutional features of the United States. However, the German system of electing judges for the Federal Constitutional Court, whereby a two-thirds majority of the Bundesrat and the Bundestag each chooses four of the eight members of each Senate, who are appointed for a maximum and non-renewable term of twelve years, with compulsory retirement at sixty-eight regardless of whether they have completed their term or not, can be seen as being similarly motivated. Like Epps and Sitaraman's proposal, the German system is aimed at ensuring a mix of political affiliations within the judiciary that is broadly proportional to party representation in each chamber and that, due to changes in the composition of those chambers as a result of regular elections, will at any time include both government and opposition appointees. Moreover, to get the requisite super-majorities, candidates generally need to be able to win cross-party support—so could not be too partisan.[112]

Both Epps and Sitaraman's proposal and the German system seek to render the respective constitutional court more broadly representative and ideologically balanced in ways that are less manipulable and politicized but can claim a certain democratic justification, not least in encouraging decision-making that treats those affected with equal concern and respect by taking into account the varied interests and ideals of society as a whole.[113] Neither rests on an aristocratic myth of impartiality or superior reasoning among the judicial class to achieve these goals. Rather, they seek to democratize the representativeness and reasoning of the judiciary in ways that oblige judges to recognize the reasonable disagreements that characterize any pluralist democratic society. As a result, the court is more likely to enjoy both political and social legitimacy. For one thing, politicians will find it harder to demonize the court as an undemocratic elite out of touch with the political values of the people. For another, citizens will be more likely to consider the court to be theirs.

A politically diverse membership, containing both government and opposition appointees, means that majority decisions will require coalitions to be built across multiple ideological divides. That requirement should incentivize judges to avoid excessive partisanship in their judgments and rather to seek mutually acceptable

[111] Epps and Sitaraman, 'How to Save the Supreme Court', 181–2. They also make a second proposal, 'the Balanced Bench' that, as the name suggests, has similar aims but adopts a different mechanism to achieve them.

[112] For a discussion of the German system of appointments see Kischel, 'Party, Pope, and Politics?', 962–80.

[113] For general guidelines (what he calls a 'template') that follow a similar route drawing on the European experience, see Sethi, 'Politicising Constitutional Court Appointments in Europe', 15–21.

rulings likely to remain stable over time. As I remarked above, that situation may well encourage them to abstract from their personal moral reasoning and rely instead on 'incompletely theorised agreements' grounded in case by case analogical reasoning.[114] Such reasoning proves more likely to possess the desirable qualities of consistency and stability associated with the formal account of the rule of law and so provide a legal framework that can survive changes in government.

6. CONCLUSION

Constitutional courts have increasingly sought to justify their role on democratic grounds. They claim to uphold democratic values, provide a venue for democratic participation and contestation, and to act as representatives of the people. These three functions prove interdependent even if analytically distinct. A court only allows for democratic participation and represents the people's democratic interests insofar as it accurately upholds commonly avowable democratic values. In their turn, these democratic values can only be regarded as reflecting public reason to the extent they find support in the actual reasons of the public and judges accurately represent their views.

However, none of these conditions is likely to be met outwith an actual democratic process. The view of constitutional democrats that courts and constitutions offer an ideal democratic framework for the real democratic process proves the opposite of the reality. The legitimacy of democratic processes derives from their own inherent constitutional properties as mechanisms for citizens to engage with each on other on equal terms. To the extent courts possess similar qualities, they do so because of the indirect influence of that process. Political equality promotes equality before and in the law, not vice versa.[115] It is because—or to the extent that—citizens have acquired a roughly equal share of political power that legal institutions likewise place them on an equal footing. In part, that is because the political, civil, and social norms embodied in law can only be taken advantage of insofar as the citizens to whom they apply are sufficiently organized to be able to exploit them. In other words, courts may offer a forum for participation and contestatory democracy but their ability to do so depends on the democratic opportunity structure within the social and political systems as a whole. In part, that is because democratic justice cannot be separated from the good of the democratic society as defined by its citizens. As a result, judges cannot be viewed simply as trustees of a fixed democratic good, but need to be responsive to, and represent, widespread and sustained popular opinion.

[114] Sunstein, *Legal Reasoning and Political Conflict*, chs 2 and 3.

[115] Stephen Holmes, 'Lineages of the Rule of Law' in José María Maravall and Adam Przeworski (eds), *Democracy and the Rule of Law* (Cambridge: Cambridge University Press 2003) 19–61.

These are not arguments for electing judges and holding regular referenda on the constitution in order to democratize them directly. To do so would unnecessarily and confusingly duplicate the task of the legislature and neglect that of the judiciary to provide the consistent and impartial application of duly enacted law to particular cases. However, it remains important that courts undertake their proper tasks in an appropriately democratic spirit—not least by treating all citizens equitably and acting as representatives of the public interest. The argument has been that they cannot do so because of any inherently democratic qualities of the constitution or the judicial process. Democratic norms can only be legitimately and justifiably defined and applied through a democratic electoral and legislative process. Courts supplement this democratic process in a number of ways—by applying democratic legislation consistently and equitably and by signalling how a given case may reveal that legislation has overlooked, or unduly minimized, certain adverse consequences for particular individuals in given circumstances. To do so, judges need to act independently while being responsive to long-term and widely held public opinion. Moreover, they need to be incentivized to take a democratic stance in their adjudication process, that gives all sides an equal hearing. I have suggested this can be best achieved through courts being broadly indicatively representative of the political community. Yet, however designed, no court can ever substitute for a truly responsive democratic system in which the people and their elected representatives prove exemplars of constitutional reasoning. As Learned Hand observed, absent that condition, no court can save democracy, where it prevails no court need save it, while the attempt to entrust that responsibility to the courts can only erode its presence among voters and politicians alike.[116]

[116] Hand, *The Bill of Rights*, 155–65.

PART 4

THE POPULIST CHALLENGE: DEMOCRACY AS THE WILL OF THE PEOPLE?

8

Populism and the Democratic Challenge

Does Political Constitutionalism Facilitate or Counter Democratic Backsliding?

1. INTRODUCTION

The effectiveness of political constitutionalism in upholding both democracy and constitutional values has been disputed since at least Tom Paine's critique of Edmund Burke's defence of the British constitution in *The Rights of Man* (1791).[1] The contemporary debate goes back to the late 1970s, when Conservative critics of the then Labour administrations of Harold Wilson and James Callaghan contended it offered little more than a recipe for 'elective dictatorship'.[2] Liberal and some Labour opponents of the subsequent Thatcher administration repeated this charge once these erstwhile critics assumed power and left the political constitution largely unreformed and arguably even more centralized, with the executive more dominant than ever.[3] The referendum on Britain's membership of the European Union (EU) and the decision to leave (Brexit), explored in the next chapter, has reignited these debates. A number of commentators have seen the referendum and its result as symptomatic of the rise of populism within established democracies—a development they regard political constitutionalism as ill-suited to preventing and possibly even as fomenting.[4] That view was reinforced by

[1] Thomas Paine, *Rights of Man, Common Sense, and Other Political Writings* (Mark Philp ed., Oxford: Oxford University Press 1995) 122–4, 248–54.

[2] Lord Hailsham, *The Dilemma of Democracy: Diagnosis and Prescription* (Glasgow: Collins 1978) 127.

[3] Pivotal in the left–liberal constitutional critique of Thatcherism was Charter 88. For an example of their arguments, see David Beetham, 'Civil Liberties, Thatcherism and Charter "88"' (1989) 60(3) *The Political Quarterly* 273–9 <https://doi.org/10.1111/j.1467-923X.1989.tb00772.x>.For a critical overview of the British debate from Hailsham to the passing of the Human Rights Act, see Richard Bellamy, *Liberalism and Pluralism: Towards a Politics of Compromise* (London: Routledge 1999) 180–9. As Chapter 4 indicates, I have become less critical since.

[4] Vernon Bogdanor, *Beyond Brexit: Towards a British Constitution* (London: I.B. Tauris 2019). Bogdanor asserts, contentiously in my view (see Chapter 10 and Richard Bellamy, *A Republican Europe of States: Cosmopolitanism, Intergovernmentalism and Democracy in the* EU (Cambridge: Cambridge University Press 2019) ch. 6), that membership of the EU had subjected the UK to a written and codified constitution, which post-Brexit the UK must re-establish—not least because, as he just as contentiously maintains (see Chapter 9), the referendum itself had undermined the UK political constitutional order by replacing parliamentary sovereignty with the more populist-friendly sovereignty of the people.

Defending the Political Constitution. Richard Bellamy, Oxford University Press. © Richard Bellamy 2026.
DOI: 10.1093/9780191826986.003.0012

the premiership of Boris Johnson in particular, whose actions during the Brexit negotiations and in subsequent legislation, notably the Dissolution and Calling of Parliament Act 2022, had a decidedly anti-constitutional tendency in undermining the right of Parliament as well as the courts to question or hinder the executive.[5] As such, his term of office has been characterized as a salutary lesson in how the political constitution can be weaponized against itself, and of the need for a legal constitution to protect against that possibility.[6] Yet, one could arguably characterize the Trump presidency in a parallel way as providing a similar warning of how a legal constitution can be likewise abused to undermine legal constitutional constraints.[7] Indeed, a number of commentators contend that Trump could only have been stopped through strengthening the political constitution and hence democracy.[8] The relative roles of legal and political constitutionalism in enabling and/or constraining the rise and establishment of populism is a contested issue, therefore.

Matters are further muddied by criticisms of political constitutionalism's relationship to populism pointing in two apparently contradictory ways. On the one hand, as I have already indicated, it is charged with legitimating—or at least as being unable to curb—populist politics. As I mentioned, these critics point to the appeal to 'the will of the people' via a referendum with regard to Brexit, and attempts by the executive to by-pass Parliament and avoid scrutiny of its proposals for exiting the EU. They contend the executive was only hampered by appeal to the courts and the UK's common law legal constitution,[9] and often claim that had the referendum been regulated by what they assume (not necessarily correctly) would be the norms inscribed in any legal constitution, most notably a super-majority threshold, it would not have been successful.[10] Such critics also note how political constitutionalism has been appealed to by supporters of democratic backsliding regimes in Hungary and Poland.[11] On the other hand, though, other critics censure political constitutionalism for being insufficiently open to popular participation.

[5] David Sanders, 'One Man's Damage: The Consequences of Boris Johnson's Assault on the British Political System' (2023) 94(2) *The Political Quarterly* 166–74.

[6] See too Jeff King, *From Constitutional Crisis to Poisoned Chalice: A Letter from London, VerfBlog*, 28 June 2024 <https://verfassungsblog.de/from-constitutional-crisis-to-poisoned-chalice/> DOI: 10.59704/8163652a51cb5c78.

[7] Sam Moyn, 'Resisting the Juristocracy', *Boston Review*, 5 October 2018 <https://www.bostonreview.net/articles/samuel-moyn-resisting-juristocracy/>.

[8] Ryan D. Doerfler and Sam Moyn, 'Don't count on the courts to save democracy: Giving courts the last word is part of what got us into this mess. It won't get us out', *Washington Post*, 20 March 2025 <https://www.washingtonpost.com/opinions/2025/03/20/supremecourt-trump-democracy-crisis/>.

[9] See T. Konstadinides, N. O'Meara, and R. Sallustio, 'The UK Supreme Court's Judgment in *Miller/ Cherry*: Reflections on Its Context and Implications', UK Const. L. Blog (2 October 2019) <https://ukconstitutionallaw.org/>; yet note also Michael Gordon, 'The Prorogation Case and the Political Constitution', UK Const. L. Blog (30 September 2019) <https://ukconstitutionallaw.org/>.

[10] e.g. A. C. Grayling, *Democracy and its Crisis* (London: Oneworld 2017) 189–97. I return to this argument in Chapter 9.

[11] Tímea Drinóczi and Agnieszka Bień-Kacala, 'Illiberal Constitutionalism: The Case of Hungary and Poland' (2019) 20 *German Law Journal* 1140–66, at 1161–2.

A doctrine focused on the constitutional qualities of representative democracy and the role of Parliament, these critics see political constitutionalism as involving an essentially elite model of politics. Notwithstanding its political character, they contend it lacks adequate popular responsiveness and thereby encourages an anti-system politics of a populist character.[12]

Underlying these contrasting assessments are differing conceptions of the nature of populism and its relationship to both democracy and constitutionalism, and hence to political constitutionalism. Accordingly, this chapter begins by exploring these terms. Section 1 starts by defining populism as a form of anti-system politics. However, political scientists divide as to whether populism should be seen as the product of a socio-cultural or an economic backlash. Right-wing populism tends to align with the former, and opposes those aspects of constitutionalism designed to protect the minority rights of cultural and ethnic groups and allow for pluralism. By contrast, despite involving some similar tropes, left-wing populism is largely associated with the latter. Moreover, it generally favours pluralism on socio-cultural issues and instead opposes forms of constitutionalism linked to limited government as a socio-economic doctrine. Therefore, how far—and how justifiably—populism clashes with constitutionalism depends to some degree on which populism and what aspect of constitutionalism one has in mind. Consequently, Section 2 turns to exploring two varieties of constitutionalism, each informed by a different regulative ideal: namely, that of limited government and of non-arbitrary rule, respectively. Whereas both ideals and the related forms of constitutionalism provide resources for resisting the socio-cultural backlash of right-wing populism, the latter is more open to the economic demands of left-wing populists than the former. To the extent populism results from a lack of political responsiveness to legitimate democratic demands for greater socio-economic equality for which those constitutional arrangements favouring limited government can be blamed, it may be more appropriate to criticize the related form of constitutionalism rather than populism. Section 3 turns to political constitutionalism and recaps salient aspects of the argument as to its institutional form described in Chapter 3. Political constitutionalists of a republican hue claim that in resting on the ideal of non-arbitrary rule, it favours, and to a degree draws upon, socio-cultural pluralism, while allowing the democratic critique of forms of economic liberalism associated with the ideal of limited government. Moreover, it does so more reliably than any form of legal constitutionalism is likely to achieve. An assessment of political constitutionalism's relationship to populism must turn on how far these claims can be sustained. Section 4 argues that—at the level of normative theory—political constitutionalism proves incompatible with right-wing populism while capable of addressing the demands of left-wing

[12] Stephen Tierney, 'Whose Political Constitution? Citizens and Referendums' (2013) 14 *German Law Journal* 2185–96.

populism. Yet, what may be true in theory need not prove the case in practice. The reality of political constitutionalism as currently practised in the UK often falls short of the theoretical ideal. To some degree, it falls foul of the first criticism noted above, that of legitimating populism, with regard to right-wing populism, and to the second criticism, that of being insufficiently popular, with regard to left-wing populism. Section 5 turns to legal constitutionalism, and asks whether it might do better, or act as an important supplement to political constitutionalism when it fails. This section offers reasons for doubting it will do so, especially when the legal constitution—as tends to be the case—is informed by the ideal of limited government. Indeed, as the recent experience of the United States suggests, there are reasons for considering political constitutionalism as more apt to combat populism than legal constitutionalism. However, to do so may require democratic reforms to further strengthen the constitutional credentials of the political system, leading to questions as to how apt the political constitution may be to reform itself.

2. VARIETIES OF POPULISM

As Mark Tushnet and Bojan Bugaric have recently remarked, populism is typically defined so as to be 'by definition antithetical to constitutionalism'.[13] However, as they also note, both populism and constitutionalism cover respectively a wide range of very different types of political movement and legal and political system. Drawing on the work of both political scientists and theorists, they contend that populism cannot be simply characterized as a particular style of politics. It also needs to be linked to a specific ideology and local circumstances that together determine the character of its various forms. Broadly speaking, they distinguish a predominantly right-wing authoritarian populism that deploys populist rhetoric, often of a nationalist, anti-libertarian, and xenophobic nature, to legitimize democratic backsliding and entrench the rule of the movement's leadership from a more left-wing, democratic populism that challenges the lack of responsiveness of mainstream parties to the needs of ordinary citizens on egalitarian grounds and calls for greater redistribution and a more participatory form of political engagement.[14] Both types of populism come in a number of variants. Indeed, to some extent there is a gamut of populisms extending between these two types and in certain cases combining elements of each.

[13] Mark Tushnet and Bojan Bugarič, *Power to the People: Constitutionalism in the Age of Populism* (Oxford: Oxford University Press 2021).

[14] For right-wing populism, see Pippa Norris and Ronald Inglehart, *Cultural Backlash: Trump, Brexit, and Authoritarian Populism* (Cambridge: Cambridge University Press 2019); for left-wing populism, see Jonathan Hopkin, *Anti-System Politics: The Crisis of Market Liberalism in Rich Democracies* (New York: Oxford University Press 2020) 64–7.

Despite these differences, there are certain common features that tend to be found in all these varieties of populism. Typically, they are anti-system and anti-elite.[15] That is, they criticize the main centre parties of established liberal democratic systems as forming a cartel, offering a restricted range of policy options consistent with a free market economy. Consequently, their aim is to break this cartel and offer an alternative that appeals to the collective interests of the 'people', characterized as the 'many', not the elite 'few'.[16]

The appeal to a 'popular will' has been seen by many commentators as anti-pluralist and inherently illiberal, justifying the tyranny of the majority over minority rights.[17] This depiction of populism informs the argument that populism is inherently anti-democratic and anti-constitutional.[18] These features certainly characterize aspects of the more authoritarian uses of populist tropes by politicians such as Donald Trump and Viktor Orbán.[19] Such figures do tend to invoke an exclusionary conception of the people as not only members of an ethnic and culturally homogenous 'nation' but also as possessing a commitment to certain narrowly defined traditional values. Moreover, these leaders contend that they and their parties are the sole authentic voice of this homogenous people and their collective interests. This contention allows them to demonize all political opposition as reflecting the concerns of an elite group, whose interests or values diverge from those of the nation or people and their traditions. The rights of ethnic, religious, and other minorities and of immigrant groups are likewise treated as 'foreign' and sinister, as are often those of the LGBTQ + community. As we shall see, these arguments do provide a spurious justification for undermining certain core features of constitutionalism.

However, placed in a different ideological framework, appeals to the people can be regarded as reflecting an egalitarian concern with the public interest consistent with minority rights. As Jonathan Hopkin and Jane Mansbridge and Stephen Macedo, among other analysts, note, there are also populist movements that combine a condemnation of the corruption and self-interest of the ruling elite and their ties to global financial markets and multinational corporations, with socially liberal attitudes and a demand for redistributive polices and investment in public services and infrastructure that will serve the interests of the people.[20] To various degrees, Podemos, Syriza, Bernie Sanders, and Jeremy Corbyn are examples of this type of socially inclusive populism.[21] Like the US Populist party of the nineteenth

[15] Cass Mudde and Cristóbal Rovira Kaltwasser, *Populism: A Very Short Introduction* (New York: Oxford University Press 2017).

[16] Hopkin, *Anti-System Politics*, ch. 2.

[17] Jan-Werner Müller, *What is Populism?* (London: Penguin 2016).

[18] Jan-Werner Müller, 'Populism and Constitutionalism' in Cristóbal Rovira Kaltwasser et al. (eds) *The Oxford Handbook of Populism* (Oxford: Oxford University Press 2017) 590–606.

[19] Norris and Inglehart, *Cultural Backlash*.

[20] Hopkin, *Anti-System Politics*; Jane Mansbridge and Stephen Macedo, 'Populism and Democratic Theory' (2019) 15 *Annual Review of Law & Social Science* 59–77.

[21] Hopkin, *Anti-System Politics*, 65–6.

century, such movements are not anti-pluralist in the same way as the nationalist-populists are, with their appeal to traditional values. Indeed, their view of the 'people' tends to consist of an alliance of groups and classes, albeit united in having interests ignored by—and in certain respects opposed to—those of certain economic and social elites.[22]

Local circumstances are likely to determine which of these types of populism are liable to predominate. As I noted above, scholars divide as to whether they attribute the rise of populism to a cultural or an economic backlash. However, these are clearly not exclusive categories. As Hopkin has noted, both forms can be broadly related to a convergence of the main centre parties of left and right on a larger role for competitive markets, including with regard to what had hitherto been regarded as non-market public institutions and services, and a consequent narrowing of electoral choice.[23] These policies also brought with them a disinclination to increase progressive taxation to fund welfare measures, and growing income inequality. For example, in the UK, the Gini co-efficient for inequality shifted in little more than a decade in the Thatcher years from being comparable to Germany to converging with the United States. Even under New Labour, the share of pre-tax income of the top 10 per cent—and especially the top 1 per cent—increased dramatically from 28.4 to 42.6 per cent. While median income also grew consistently in this period, that all changed with the financial crisis of 2008. As average real wages fell, the alleged trade-off between income growth and greater inequality and insecurity no longer looked remotely plausible.[24]

Against the background of this general political and economic context, a distinction can be drawn between the responses of different social groups and—most importantly here—the way differences in social, economic, and political institutions determined the extent and nature of populist support and impact. By and large, right-wing xenophobic rhetoric has appealed most to older, less educated, white male voters in declining industrial areas, whereas left-wing populism has proved more attractive to younger voters in more economically dynamic urban areas.[25] Meanwhile, as Hopkin shows, a key conditioning factor has been the way institutions managed the crisis in terms of the distribution of economic risks, costs, and benefits.[26] Those political systems where even left-wing parties were inclined to act 'responsibly' in the wake of the crisis, and supported bailing out the banks and financial institutions, and disinclined to act 'responsively' to the resulting economic hardship of many voters, offering instead austerity policies that cut social benefits, have proven to be the most likely to witness increased support for anti-system, populist parties. Indeed, Hopkin describes how the UK—that next to the

[22] Mansbridge and Macedo, 'Populism', 67, 70–3.
[23] Hopkin, *Anti-System Politics*, 58–60.
[24] Hopkin, *Anti-System Politics*, 119–21.
[25] Hopkin, *Anti-System Politics*, 11–12.
[26] Hopkin, *Anti-System Politics*, 67–76.

United States has been the biggest supporter of global and domestic marketization, is likewise prone to trade deficits, and has similarly weakened welfare support—has been among the most open in Europe to populism of both right and left among different social groups, with Brexit a predictable result of this disaffection.[27]

There is a tendency in much writing on populism and constitutionalism to describe populism in purely conceptual terms, as a defective form of democracy,[28] without reference either to the particular social, economic, and institutional drivers that might promote it or to variations in its ideological colouring. It is thereby portrayed as an ever-present potential risk of mass politics that the constitutional constraints placed on popular democracy exist to curtail. Yet, once populism gets related to certain social and economic demands that the prevailing system has failed to respond to, that presentation becomes more problematic. If these demands can be justified in terms of democratic norms, then the legitimacy of certain constitutional mechanisms can themselves be called into question. This possibility suggests we need not only a more complex view of populism but also of constitutionalism, to which we now turn.

3. VARIETIES OF CONSTITUTIONALISM

Within the literature on populism and constitutionalism it has become standard to employ a 'minimal' account of constitutional democracy.[29] This strategy attempts to avoid assessing the constitutionality of populism by potentially controversial standards, that might fail to accommodate a reasonable range of variations in the constitutional systems of different states. In a bid to further reduce controversy, these accounts are presented as descriptive rather than normative, reflecting the core constitutional mechanisms rather than the main elements of constitutionalism as a regulative ideal. Yet, this approach risks reifying certain mechanisms that may themselves be at least partly responsible for populist forms of politics as a result of reducing the responsiveness of the system to reasonable popular demands. To avoid this risk, this section adopts the reverse approach and starts by considering a range of regulative ideals that constitutional systems might adopt. That leads to a variety of types of constitutionalism to match the varieties of populism, and allows a discussion in later sections as to which types of constitutionalism might be likely to encourage or discourage what kind of populism.

Constitutionalism in the most abstract and generic sense simply refers to any political system with rules or conventions establishing who exercises power,

[27] Hopkin, *Anti-System Politics*, 74, 118.

[28] Müller, *What is Populism?*; Nadia Urbinati, *Me the People: How Populism Transforms Democracy* (Cambridge, MA: Harvard University Press 2019).

[29] Tom Ginsburg and Aziz Huq, *How to Save a Constitutional Democracy* (Chicago: Chicago University Press 2018) 10; Tushnet and Bugarič, *Power*, 9–12.

through what processes, and in which circumstances.[30] All political systems of any complexity will have constitutions in this sense, including absolute monarchies and authoritarian dictatorships.[31] That fact merits bearing in mind given that one feature of right-wing populist regimes in Hungary, Poland, and Turkey, as well as Donald Trump's neo-populist presidency in the United States, has been to seek to buttress their hold on power by reinterpreting constitutional conventions, packing the judiciary, and even altering the constitution itself so as to favour their party.[32] While the entrenchment of certain written legal constitutional rules as a higher law to be upheld by a similarly entrenched judiciary has often been regarded as a bulwark against populism, recent right-wing populists have shown how these same mechanisms can be deployed to entrench populist regimes in power. Indeed, such entrenchment may even have supported their rise to office to the extent that they rendered the political system unresponsive to the concerns of significant groups of citizens.

To distinguish authoritarian populist constitutionalism from more genuinely democratic forms, it is necessary to look less at the existence or absence of certain supposedly core features and institutions—such as a written, entrenched, and judicially protected constitution that operates as a higher law—and more at the regulative ideals motivating their design and deployment, and their prospects of success within given social and political conditions. Here I shall consider two regulative ideals—that of limited government and that of non-arbitrary government. While the liberal ideal of freedom from interference informs the first, the republican ideal of freedom from domination animates the second. The first is predominantly a negative, or government-constraining, conception of constitutionalism, whereas the second incorporates a more circumscribed set of government-restraining, negative, features into a more positive, or citizen empowering, conception. My claim—elaborated in later sections—shall be that whereas right-wing populism proves incompatible at a theoretical level with either ideal, and is best characterized as seeking to constitutionalize arbitrary rule through those self-same mechanisms of legal constitutionalism many consider as the best way of limiting their capacity to do so; certain instances of left-wing populism might involve legitimate criticisms of the liberal ideal, while being compatible with the republican.

Constitutionalism is most commonly characterized as a negative regulative ideal of limited government. As Wil Waluchow and Dimitrios Kyritsis (2022) define the term in their entry for the authoritative *Stanford Encyclopaedia of Philosophy*, 'Constitutionalism is the idea, often associated with the political theories of John

[30] John Gardner, 'Can There be a Written Constitution?' in John Gardner, *Law as a Leap of Faith* (Oxford: Oxford University Press 2012) 89–124.

[31] Richard Bellamy and Jeff King, 'Introduction: On Constitutions and Constitutional Theory' in Richard Bellamy and Jeff King (eds), *The Cambridge Companion to Constitutional Theory* (Cambridge: Cambridge University Press 2025) 7.

[32] Ginsburg and Huq, *How to Save*, ch. 4.

Locke and the founders of the American republic, that government can and should be legally limited in its powers, and that its authority or legitimacy depends on its observing these limitations'.[33] Jeremy Waldron has noted how a number of analytically distinct concepts have been associated with the idea of limitations, some more restrictive of the scope and exercise of governmental authority than others.[34] At the most restrictive end of the scale, constitutional limits are associated with a minimal view of the state and hence less government, with constitutional protection given to property rights, freedom of contract, and the laxly regulated laissez faire workings of an allegedly free market. These are economic liberal constraints designed to reduce state interference with an individual's negative liberty, especially the economic liberty to produce and trade goods and services. They potentially constrain many democratic demands for state intervention to improve working conditions, including the right to strike to secure such improvements; to provide better public services—such as more extensive welfare, health, and education systems; to enhance environmental protections; or to upgrade and expand public infrastructure. These demands become liable to challenge not only as misguided from a given neo-liberal economic standpoint, but also—and more far reaching—as legally and politically illegitimate. Less restrictive is the idea of restraint, as in prohibitions on torture, detention without trial, or interference with religious belief. These might be regarded as ethical liberal constraints, concerned to ensure relations of equal respect among citizens and individuals more generally. Finally, at the least restrictive end of the scale, limitation can mean control. As Waldron notes, this need not be a purely negative notion. A driver controls a car not only in the sense that she can prevent it leaving the road and crashing, but also in being able to direct it towards certain destinations by a given route and at a given speed. Government regulation to implement the democratic demands mentioned earlier could be consistent with control in this sense, with citizens being placed in the driving seat through the electoral process.

This last notion of limitation connects to the second, more positive, regulative ideal—that of avoiding arbitrary rule through citizen empowerment to prevent domination. Unlike the liberal notion of freedom as non-interference, freedom as non-domination does not require less government but rather controlled government.[35] On this account, rulers dominate to the extent they can wilfully alter the available choice set for autonomous agents subject to their rule without being obliged to consult their reasons or interests. The possibility for domination arises

[33] Wil Waluchow and Dimitrios Kyritsis, 'Constitutionalism' in *The Stanford Encyclopedia of Philosophy* (E. Zalta ed., 2022) <https://plato.stanford.edu/archives/sum2022/entries/constitutionalism/>.

[34] Jeremy Waldron, 'Constitutionalism: A Skeptical View' in Thomas Christiano and John Christman (eds), *Contemporary Debates in Political Philosophy* (Malden: Wiley-Blackwell 2009) 265–82, at 271–2.

[35] Philip Pettit, *Republicanism: A Theory of Freedom and Government* (Oxford: Oxford University Press 1997) 22–3.

when there is a power imbalance between rulers and ruled, a dependency of the ruled on the ruler, and rulers can exercise personal rule.[36] These circumstances can be overcome within a democratic system that gives the governed equal power and authority in the authorization and holding to account of the government, so that politicians and administrators are incentivized to address the commonly avowable interests of those in whose name they govern. A government controlled in this way need not be limited in its social and economic policies in order to be non-dominating. On the contrary, it may need to extensively and effectively regulate the basic economic and social structures precisely to ensure they operate in an equitable and non-dominating way.

This ideal places citizens in control of the government. Constitutions so conceived are concerned with due process. In Waldron's words, they 'lay down procedures . . . limiting not so much what can be done but *how* it is done'.[37] In so doing, federalism and electoral systems, on the one hand, and bicameral arrangements and checks and balances, on the other, need not be seen simply as ways of dispersing and diluting power, that constrain potentially oppressive legislation or acts. Rather, and more importantly, they can be designed as ways of empowering citizens by bringing a variety of voices into play, enabling them to act in concert and to inform as well as to hold accountable their political representatives, and ensuring public policies are adequately deliberated and scrutinized.[38] As we shall see, political constitutionalism aspires to operate in just such a way, not least by seeing the core of constitutionalism as the equal democratic empowerment of all citizens.

As I noted in Chapter 3, the fault line between the limiting and the empowering regulative ideals of constitutionalism is often located in their views of majority rule.[39] The limiting ideal is more inclined towards a legal constitutionalism that is designed, at least in its minimal state version, in large part to curb democratic demands for more active and redistributive government on the grounds that they reflect the 'tyranny of the majority'. As such, it is usually happy to deploy non-majoritarian institutions (NMIs), such as central banks, international organizations, and constitutional courts—to lock in liberal values and policies. However, as Michael Zürn has recently argued, the increasing deployment of such institutions, combined with the cartelization of parties noted above, offers a political explanation of the rise of populism that can combine aspects of the cultural and economic explanations.[40] As he observes, both these developments have over time decreased

[36] Frank Lovett, *A General Theory of Domination and Justice* (Oxford: Oxford University Press 2010) 119–20.

[37] Waldron, 'Constitutionalism', 273.

[38] Jeremy Waldron, *Political Political Theory: An Essay on Institutions* (Cambridge, MA: Harvard University Press 2016) chs 3–5.

[39] Waldron, 'Constitutionalism', 275.

[40] Michael Zürn, 'How Non-Majoritarian Institutions Make Silent Majorities Vocal: A Popular Explanation of Authoritarian Populism' (2022) 20(2) *Perspectives on Politics* <https://doi.org/10.1017/S1537592721001043> 788–807.

the responsiveness of the political system and pushed the narrative of a permanent, discrete, and isolated silent majority that has been increasingly marginalized by unrepresentative elites. Zürn associates the rise of catch-all parties, on the one side, and NMIs, on the other, to the bargain between capital and labour whereby the institutionalization of international free trade post-Second World War went hand in hand with the establishment of national welfare states capable of absorbing economic shocks and uncertainties. He charts how, as that bargain came under increased strain from the 1980s onwards, trust shifted away from the majoritarian processes of electoral democracy. As parties lost their mass base and even electoral support, power (and blame) was shifted to supposedly trustworthy independent institutions. Consequently, NMIs grew in number and prominence and became more politicized, while parties themselves became more professionalized parts of the state, as per the cartelization thesis. He contends that a new political cleavage developed between the liberal cosmopolitan elite represented within both NMIs and the cartel running the established centrist parties, on the one hand, and the 'silent' majority who became increasingly attracted to populism, on the other.[41]

By contrast, the empowering ideal is more inclined towards a political constitutionalism that is designed to prevent arbitrary rule by controlling, and to some degree restraining, government by making it responsive to democratic majorities.[42] On this account, as I argued in Chapter 3, majority rule is seen as a fair process for citizens to reconcile their disagreements on the moral norms governing their society—one that motivates politicians to appeal to those norms most people can share as in their common interest. Within a pluralist society, in which majorities need to be constructed from various fluctuating minorities, majority rule encourages the attempt to settle on both processes and policies likely to treat all with equal concern and respect. As a result, it not only reflects the egalitarian norms of the democratic process but also supports those of a democratic society more generally.

However, the political constitution can itself be deformed by the same trends traced by Hopkin, Zürn, and others. It relies on parties being genuinely competitive and representing and responding to the plurality of society. It is sometimes argued that a democratic system and society presupposes certain norms and practices related to ensuring political equality but cannot be assumed to create or sustain them.[43] As such, they are pre-political and need to be enshrined in a legal constitution and judicially protected from challenge—including by the democratic process itself. At best, they can gain direct democratic legitimacy through being enacted in exceptional moments of political solidarity, such as after a war

[41] Zürn, 'How Non-Majoritarian', 789–91.

[42] Bellamy, *Political Constitutionalism*, ch. 6.

[43] Ronald Dworkin, 'Introduction: The Moral Reading and the Majoritarian Premise' in Ronald Dworkin, *Freedom's Law: The Moral Reading of the American Constitution* (Cambridge, MA: Harvard University Press 1996) 1–38; John Hart Ely, *Democracy and Distrust: A Theory of Judicial Review* (Cambridge, MA: Harvard University Press 1980).

or some other crisis, in a singular constitutive act of the people as a whole.[44] Yet, these accounts leave the power of the judiciary itself unchecked and assume that these norms reflect either objective moral principles or, in the absence of a popular constitutional amendment, views that the current 'people' can be regarded as acquiescing in—even if the constitutive act was several generations ago. Both the 'objective' and the 'popular' view of constitutional norms underestimate the significance of moral disagreement and the moral capacities of citizens.[45] Meanwhile, each gives rise to a paradox. On the one hand, the 'objective' view seems to justify the establishment of the very NMIs that on some accounts have led to the development of populism. On the other hand, using 'popular' methods, such as a referendum, for changing the constitution risk being themselves populist. By contrast, as was argued in Chapters 1–3, the reasonableness of moral disagreement among citizens forms the starting point of political constitutionalism, which seeks to provide a mechanism for their fair and equitable resolution in ways that recognize the ontological status of the competing values and judgements while being popular without being populist.

4. POLITICAL CONSTITUTIONALISM, DISAGREEMENT, AND REPRESENTATIVE DEMOCRACY

As earlier chapters (especially 1–3) have detailed, political constitutionalism proceeds from the argument that the laws determining the terms of social and political co-existence, including the basis and interpretation of fundamental rights, are matters of reasonable disagreement among those who are subject to them.[46] Political constitutionalists claim that the most appropriate way of recognizing the contested nature of these terms and rights is to subject them to a collective decision-process as to their content and implementation that treats all involved impartially and promotes reciprocity among them, so all are regarded with equal respect and concern.[47] Representative democracy linked to parliamentarism is held to satisfy these desiderata in a manner that embodies certain qualities standardly associated with constitutionalism.[48]

As I noted above, these constitutional qualities are achieved not through legal mechanisms that hold politicians and the administration to the norms of a codified and entrenched constitution that acts as a higher law, but through the electoral and

[44] Bruce Ackerman, *We the People: Foundations* (Cambridge, MA: Harvard University Press 1991).

[45] Waldron, 'Constitutionalism', 275–6.

[46] Bellamy, *Political Constitutionalism*, 4–5; Jeremy Waldron, *Law and Disagreement* (Oxford: Clarendon Press 1999) 107–18.

[47] Bellamy, *Political Constitutionalism*, ch. 4; Waldron, *Law and Disagreement*, ch. 11.

[48] Griffith, 'The Political Constitution'; Tomkins, *Our Republican Constitution*, 1–10; Bellamy, *Political Constitutionalism*, 12, 259, 260; Gordon, 'Parliamentary Sovereignty', 131–3.

legislative operations of a democratic political system.[49] As I argued in Chapter 3, such systems incorporate two key constitutional devices—those of checks and of balances, reflecting respectively the negative, or constraining, and the positive, or empowering, aspects of constitutionalism outlined in the previous section.[50] On the one hand, governments are checked through requiring authorization by, and being held regularly accountable to, citizens through the electoral process. These mechanisms provide checks on arbitrary rule and the protection of individual rights. As I observed in Chapters 1 and 4 in particular, they can also be supplemented by weak form judicial review, that highlights the adverse impact of general legislation on the rights of particular individuals. On the other hand, governments, and indirectly those citizens supporting them, are balanced by having to compete against opposition parties—both in elections and in the legislature, and hence must 'hear the other side'. These balances promote the participation in decision-making by citizens so as to support the need for politicians to appeal to their commonly avowable reasoning and interests and enhance identification with the public good. As I noted in Chapter 3, bicameralism, federalism, and a proportional electoral system can all, where appropriate, provide further sources of balance that foster deliberation and the need to address all sections of the community.[51]

As I indicated in the Introduction, all these mechanisms can be seen as sharing a lineage with the ancient notion of the mixed constitution, which aimed at achieving a degree of mutual checks and balances between the different classes of a society.[52] Although in their modern incarnation they involve democracy, their virtues lie not as means for collective self-rule or popular will formation, as in certain theories of deliberative and direct democracy. Rather, as per the neo-Roman republican tradition, their core concern is with the promotion of freedom as non-domination and relatedly of equality.[53] From this perspective, what matters is that public authorities cannot act arbitrarily: that is, simply as they will, without consulting on an equal basis the views and interests of those subject to their rule.

By advocating an institutional framework for a non-dominating system of democratic government, political constitutionalism seeks to achieve a form of rule that treats all with equal respect and concern. The securing of equal respect can be regarded as both an intrinsic and an instrumental feature of political constitutionalism. Regular free and fair elections based on one person one vote and majority rule have the intrinsic quality of treating all citizens as possessing equal status, and provide a mechanism that gives equal weight to their views and interests and that

[49] Bellamy, *Political Constitutionalism*, ch. 6.

[50] Bellamy, *Political Constitutionalism*, ch. 5; N. W. Barber, *The Principles of Constitutionalism* (Oxford: Oxford University Press 2018) 2–9.

[51] See too Waldron, *Political Political Theory*, chs 3–5.

[52] See too Richard Bellamy, 'The Political Form of the Constitution: The Separation of Powers, Rights and Representative Democracy' (1996) 14 *Political Studies* 436–56.

[53] Tomkins, *Our Republican Constitution*, ch. 2; Bellamy, *Political Constitutionalism*, ch. 4.

is neutral and impartial with regard to their worth for any collective decision.[54] However, this intrinsic aspect of the democratic process also proves instrumental to securing equal concern and the negative and positive constitutional purposes of protecting rights and fostering participation and the public interest respectively.[55] The balancing features of the political constitution encourage reciprocity among citizens and a willingness to compromise to create viable party programmes with broad popular appeal. For example, competition between different parties incentivizes politicians to fish for votes and construct programmes that build coalitions between different groups of citizens that appeal to the median voter—usually that set of preferences that represent the Condorcet winner across the electorate.[56] As Robert A. Dahl famously observed, within pluralist societies majority rule tends to be the rule of an alliance of various minorities.[57] Given many minorities could swap allegiance, this motivates both a regard for minority rights and the need to frame policies in terms of their benefit to the public interest rather than particular sectional interests.

Meanwhile, the prospect of future elections constrains arbitrariness by governments, which will be held accountable for their failings when they next seek authorization to rule.[58] That parties may alternate in power also creates a reason to wish the rules of the game to remain fair and for the judiciary to be independent and ensure all are equal under the law. The prospect of a change of government is also basic to ensuring 'loser's consent' when elections fail to go their way. It gives those who voted for the defeated party an equal chance of securing their preferred policies in a future election. That fact also means that no government can afford entirely to ignore the views and interests of those who may have voted against them: come the next election, they may need their support. As noted above, bicameralism—especially where the second chamber is selected by different electoral rules to the first—may likewise provide a spur to inclusive deliberation and a regard for the public interest. As I noted in Chapter 3, the precise nature of these institutional arrangements will tend to reflect the social characteristics of the polity concerned.[59]

As will be argued in the next section, a well-functioning political constitution ought in principle to be capable of meeting the respective challenges posed by right- and left-wing populism. On the one hand, minority rights should be

[54] Thomas Christiano, *The Constitution of Equality: Democratic Authority and Its Limits* (Oxford: Oxford University Press 2008).

[55] A. J. McGann, 'The Tyranny of the Supermajority: How Majority Rule Protects Minorities' (2004) 16 *Journal of Theoretical Politics* 53–77, at 56, 71.

[56] Peter C. Ordeshook, *Game Theory and Political Theory* (Cambridge: Cambridge University Press 1986) 245–57.

[57] Robert A. Dahl, *Democracy and Its Critics* (New Haven, CT: Yale University Press 1989) 218.

[58] Adam Przeworski, 'Minimalist Democracy: A Defense' in Ian Shapiro and Casiano Hacker-Cordon (eds), *Democracy's Value* (Cambridge: Cambridge University Press 1999) 23–55.

[59] Dahl, *Democracy and Its Critics*, 251 ff.

protected through their pivotal role in the formation of majority coalitions. On the other hand, governments should be responsive to policies promotive of economic equality. After all, as I remarked in the last section, political constitutionalism is informed by the regulative ideal of non-arbitrary rather than limited government, while its openness to majority rule favours policies likely to be promotive of the interests of the many rather than the few. Yet, what happens in circumstances when the political constitution is not well-functioning? Is the political constitution capable of defending and reforming itself, or must it rely on the protection offered by a legal constitution? We shall turn to these questions in the section after next.

5. POLITICAL CONSTITUTIONALISM AND POPULISM

As a form of government, populism—even in its right-wing variant—differs from authoritarianism in claiming, and to some degree possessing, democratic support and credentials. Although populists seek to reform certain democratic structures and constitutional checks, they do so on the basis of an alleged democratic mandate to enhance more direct popular influence and control, replacing rule by and for a minority/ies with rule by and for the majority, defined as the people as a whole, and thereby supposedly rendering policy-making more responsive and less elitist.[60] This appeal to democracy produces a certain superficial similarity with political constitutionalism. That resemblance proves potentially justified in the case of left-wing populism. By contrast, right-wing populism proves opposed to the very features of democracy that provide it with the constitutional features political constitutionalists admire and advocate.

5.1. Right-wing Populism and Political Constitutionalism

There are five interrelated core features of right-wing populism that render its advocacy of democracy unconstitutional in a manner inimical to political constitutionalism. First, it is anti-pluralist.[61] Its advocates appeal to a unitary conception of 'the people'—based on nationality, ethnicity, or class—with those not sharing the preferred markers being not part of the people. Second, and as a consequence, majority rule is not a construct of a certain form of political system that equally weighs the different preferences of all individuals. Rather, it is the pre-existing will of an already existing collective agent.[62] Third, as a result, complex electoral systems

[60] Ginsburg and Huq, *How to Save*, 77–8.
[61] Müller, *What is Populism?*, 13, 32, 69.
[62] Albert Weale, *The Will of the People. A Modern Myth* (Cambridge: Polity 2018).

are denigrated by comparison with exercises of direct democracy, such as referendums, that can be portrayed as allowing the collective expression of a supposed popular will.[63] Fourth, for parallel reasons, intermediaries between the people and the executive, such as parties and representatives, are deemed elitist. Populist political leaders claim a direct, intuitive, connection to the people.[64] Fifth, since there is only one 'true' people, who speak with one voice, there is no requirement to 'hear the other side'. Political competition, scrutiny, and critical debate are delegitimized. There is no notion of 'loyal' opposition. Rather, alternative proposals and criticism are by definition 'against' the people.[65]

These five features serve to legitimize the centralization of power under the executive within right-wing populist regimes, and the transformation of the legislature into a rubber stamp of executive decrees. They also pave the way for the politicization of the bureaucracy and judiciary. Most relevantly here, they challenge the validity of the checks and balances of the political constitution, particularly those designed to prevent arbitrary rule by the executive, on the one hand, and to secure a voice for minority groups and the opposition, on the other. Both become unjustified constraints on the will of the people.[66] These arguments also go hand in hand with the advocacy of national self-interest and the related opposition to liberal cosmopolitan elites. Yet, the appeal to national popular solidarity tends to be turned outwards—against immigration, foreign imports, and international agreements and institutions—rather than inwards—in favour of redistribution and social equality among national citizens. Domestically, right-wing populists have tended to remain advocates of market economies.[67] By contrast, these latter demands inform left-wing populism.

5.2. Left-wing Populism and Political Constitutionalism

As was noted earlier, left-wing populism can be regarded as involving a critique of neo-liberal economic policies and the constitutional doctrine of limited government that has often been employed to legitimize and uphold them.[68] In the international sphere, such limitations have been defended and imposed by bodies such as the International Monetary Fund (IMF), World Trade Organization (WTO), and the Court of Justice of the European Union (CJEU) through their emphasis on free trade and the consequent pressures to remove tariff barriers, to privatize public utilities and services and open them up to competition, including by foreign

[63] Ginsburg and Huq, *How to Save*, 81.
[64] Ginsburg and Huq, *How to Save*, 79–80.
[65] Ginsburg and Huq, *How to Save*, 81–2.
[66] Ginsburg and Huq, *How to Save*, 80–1.
[67] Hopkin, *Anti-System Politics*, 11, 61–2.
[68] Hopkin, *Anti-System Politics*, 65–7.

providers, and the need for low inflation and balanced budgets.[69] Domestically, these limits have been endorsed, implemented, and extended by central banks, regulatory agencies, and constitutional courts—particularly with regard to the limits placed on trade unions and wage bargaining on the grounds of upholding freedom of contract, and the adoption of strict public spending targets, with a consequent reduction of welfare programmes, sometimes accompanied by tax cuts.[70] However, as important has been the parallel critique of the lack of responsiveness of actually existing democratic systems.[71] Here, the complaint has been that the main parties of left and right have converged in ways that have effectively depoliticized and removed or blocked the established democratic channels whereby such policies might be challenged. Instead, these parties have prioritized economic responsibility over political responsiveness, leading—in the wake of the Euro crisis—to their providing massive bank bailouts while implementing austerity policies to tackle the associated sovereign debt.[72]

This latter complaint can be seen as a criticism of the political constitution for failing to perform its constitutional task of preventing arbitrary rule. Following Zürn and Hopkin, I remarked above how the development of catch-all parties of the centre right and left—the result of the post-war consensus on a model of embedded liberalism—led to a more professionalized and technocratic, non-ideological form of politics, that produced a growing sense of disaffection between parliamentary representatives and party members and voters.[73] This development has produced a steady decline in electoral turnout across almost all established democracies. The resulting cartelization of the party system undermines the political constitution, exacerbating certain generic criticisms levelled at representative democracy.[74] Critics focus on the elite character of representative systems, the lack of responsiveness of parties, and the ways collusion between them can keep key issues off the electoral agenda, and the resulting disempowered nature of citizen participation, limited as it is to a periodic vote on the, often overlapping, programmes offered by politicians.[75] These failings are held to largely depoliticize democracy and limit both its checking and balancing capacity, thereby weakening its negative and positive constitutional qualities. If parties fail to adequately contest each other and offer clear alternatives, then it becomes harder to check governments

[69] For a discussion and critique of such measures within the context of the EU, see Richard Bellamy and Albert Weale, 'Political Legitimacy and European Monetary Union: Contracts, Constitutionalism and the Normative Logic of Two-Level Games' (2015) 22(2) *Journal of European Public Policy* 257–74.

[70] See Sandra Fredman, 'The New Rights: Labour Law and Ideology in the Thatcher Years' (1992) 12 *Oxford Journal of Legal Studies* 24–44.

[71] Zürn, 'How Non-Majoritarian', 792, 794; Hopkin, *Anti-System Politics*, 72.

[72] Peter Mair, *Ruling the Void: The Hollowing Out of Western Democracy* (London: Verso 2013).

[73] Zürn, 'How Non-Majoritarian', 792–4; Hopkin, *Anti-System Politics*, 37–9.

[74] Richard Katz and Peter Mair, 'Changing Models of Party Organisation and Party Democracy: The Emergence of the Cartel Party' (1995) 1 *Party Politics* 5–28.

[75] Tierney, 'Whose Political Constitution?', 2187–8; Stephen Tierney, *Constitutional Referendums. The Theory and Practice of Republican Deliberation* (Oxford: Oxford University Press 2012) 3–4.

and hold them to account or to incentivize them to pursue policies that address the commonly avowable interests of the public as a whole. Likewise, if the main parties ignore the preferences of certain groups of citizens and take them off the electoral agenda, then these preferences will carry no weight in the balance of political priorities within any of the party programmes. All these potential failings have been held to increasingly characterize democratic systems.[76] The resulting danger is less that of the tyranny of the majority as of a tyranny of a minority—a feature exacerbated in plurality electoral systems such as those of the United States and UK, which reduce the number of viable parties in play, and result in parliamentary majorities that rarely represent a majority of voters. Small wonder that recent studies have documented a pronounced oligarchic tendency within contemporary representative democracies,[77] that leads them to reflect the preferences of the wealthiest sections of society and ignore those of the vast majority of citizens. While that trend has been particularly evident in the United States given the lack of adequate checks on the influence of money in politics,[78] similar trends have been noted in Europe and elsewhere.[79] Moreover, the same features that have allowed for the capture of government by the wealthy have facilitated—often in collusion with them—that of right-wing populists, notwithstanding their anti-elitist rhetoric. Indeed, again contrary to their professed desire to increase the influence of the people, they have standardly sought to further reduce the responsiveness of the political system through electoral gerrymandering. In these circumstances, a natural question has been whether the political constitution is capable of renewing itself, or if legal constitutionalism must come to the rescue—an issue to which we now turn.

6. CAN LEGAL CONSTITUTIONALISM DO BETTER?

Recent instances of democratic backsliding by populist politicians in not only comparatively recent democracies, such as Hungary and Poland, but also established democracies, such as in the UK under the Johnson administration, in Italy under Georgia Meloni, and, most dramatically, in the United States under President Trump, as well as the growing danger of something similar happening in France and Germany with the dramatic growth of far right parties in these countries, has

[76] Mair, *Ruling the Void*.

[77] Larry M. Bartels, *Unequal Democracy: The Political Economy of the New Gilded Age* (Princeton, NJ: Princeton University Press 2008) ch. 9.

[78] Jeffrey A. Winters, and Benjamin I. Page 'Oligarchy in the United States?' (2009) 7(4) *Perspectives on Politics* 731–51; Martin Gilens and Benjamin I. Page, 'Testing Theories of American Politics: Elites, Interest Groups, and Average Citizens' (2014) 12(3) *Perspectives on Politics* 564–81.

[79] Noam Lupu and Zach Warner, 'Affluence and Congruence: Unequal Representation around the World' (2022) 84(1) *Journal of Politics* 276–90; Ruben Mathisen, 'Affluence and Influence in a Social Democracy' (2023) 117(2) *American Political Science Review* 751–8.

led to a revived interest in militant democracy and the use of legal constitutional measures to defend democracy.[80] The rationale behind this revival derives from the fact, remarked on earlier, that populist politicians have come to power through winning elections and then deployed formally legal means to entrench their power. The alleged advantages of legal constitutionalism in this regard are held to derive from two features of this arrangement: the entrenchment of constitutional rights and processes, including the rules of the democratic game, and the supposed independence of the judiciary. Its proponents claim that these two features make it harder for populists to subvert the democratic process and abrogate core rights. They contend that even if certain substantive issues should arguably be left to the democratic process, that process itself requires protection to ensure it operates in a free, equitable, and open way.[81]

However, it can be doubted whether these mechanisms are likely to address either the democratic backsliding by right-wing populists or the democratic disappointments of left-wing populists. With regard to the former, they have typically used the following six techniques to subvert the legal constitution.[82] First, they exploit the fact that even written constitutions often function on the basis of good will and conventions, which they either ignore or interpret in tendentious and partisan ways. For example, Republicans in the United States exploited filibuster conventions in the Senate to block some confirmations of Barak Obama's nominations to the federal judiciary and, most importantly, refused to consider any nominee to replace Antonin Scalia in 2016 on the spurious grounds that it would be illegitimate to allow an appointment given the upcoming presidential election—a position they reversed when it came to Donald Trump's nomination of Amy Coney Barrett in 2020 only days before the election. Second, they pack the judiciary with supporters or seek to make them more susceptible to political pressure. Third, they attempt to change the constitution to increase or even abolish term lengths for the executive and enact changes to fundamental values that favour their programme. Fourth, they seek to alter electoral rules and constituencies to gain advantages over opposition parties. Fifth, they use libel and funding regulations to limit freedom of speech and association, and criminalize opposition. Finally, they regulate the media in ways that shrink the public sphere.

Theoretically, an independent judiciary upholding a constitution enshrining fair democratic standards could block such moves. Lars Vinx has even suggested

[80] Jan Werner Müller, 'Militant Democracy' in Michel Rosenfeld and András Sajó (eds), *The Oxford Handbook of Comparative Constitutional Law* (Oxford: Oxford University Press 2012) 1254–69; T. Ginsburg, A. Z. Huq, and T. Khaitan, *The Entrenchment of Democracy* (Cambridge: Cambridge University Press 2024) 13–21.

[81] e.g. Rosalind Dixon, *Responsive Judicial Review: Democracy and Dysfunction in the Modern Age* (Oxford: Oxford University Press 2022); and the essays in Ginsburg, Huq, and Khaitan, *The Entrenchment of Democracy*.

[82] Ginsburg and Huq, *How to Save*, 90–119; Mark Tushnet, *Taking Back the Constitution: Activist Judges and the Next Age of American Law* (New Haven, CT: Yale University Press 2020) Parts 1 and 2.

that a militant democratic approach that seeks simply to entrench those democratic processes needed to secure an equal chance for voters supporting opposition parties in the future is a requirement of political constitutionalism.[83] I agree with the logical claim that leads him to this conclusion: that, *pace* Kelsen, there is no necessary contradiction in a committed democrat seeking to uphold democracy by defending processes that are sufficiently free and fair to be termed democratic—a standard Vinx associates with securing an equal chance for voters that their preferred party could win not only in the past but also in the future.[84] I can regard President Trump as having democratic legitimacy as a result of winning an election that met a minimal threshold of fairness to count as democratic; but that does not mean that I need regard acts by his administration that would lead the next election to fall below that threshold as democratically legitimate. However, he suggests that defending that claim as the core task for a legal constitution, allowing non-procedural issues to be decided by the democratic process, renders his argument essentially political constitutionalist.[85] Yet, as I noted in Chapter 2, a procedural legal constitutionalism cannot avoid straying into substantive issues and raises similar problems.

For a start, as he concedes,[86] the judiciary may prove unwilling if not unable to uphold militant democratic constitutional clauses.[87] First, a lack of democratic legitimacy may make the judiciary reluctant to intervene unless an explicit constitutional provision applies to the case at hand. That often is not the case. Second, greater activism by the courts risks politicizing the constitution and judiciary, prompting attempts to change the former and capture the latter. As a result, such measures may only provide a temporary buffer. Indeed, third, if these attempts prove successful they can work to entrench the position of the right-wing populist regime. Fourth, even if the constitution is unchanged, constitutional norms tend to be sufficiently abstract to allow for a variety of different interpretations with quite divergent policy consequences. Consider majority minority districts in the United States, for example. At one level, these can be seen as a progressive measure, akin to special representation rights for certain groups in a number of countries, that promotes the representation of minorities in Congress. Yet, they can also indirectly support gerrymandering that favours white majority districts. Or consider how in *Citizens United v. Federal Election Commission* (FEC), the Supreme Court ruled that political spending was a form of free speech and hence protected by the first amendment, thereby deeming campaign finance reform unconstitutional.[88]

[83] Lars Vinx, 'Democratic Equality and Militant Democracy' (2020) 27 *Constellations* 685–701.
[84] Vinx, 'Democratic Equality', 686, 689, 690.
[85] Vinx, 'Democratic Equality', 695.
[86] Vinx, 'Democratic Equality', 696–7.
[87] Ryan D. Doerfler and Samuel Moyn, 'Democratizing the Supreme Court' (2021) 109 *California Law Review* 1703–72; Ryan D. Doerfler and Samuel Moyn, 'The Ghost of John Hart Ely' (2022) 75 *Vanderbilt Law Review* 769–821.
[88] *Citizens United v. Federal Election Commission* 558 U.S. 310 (2010).

Finally, these different interpretations often reflect reasonable disagreements as to how certain principles should be understood. Taking such controversies out of politics risks at best promoting disillusionment with democracy and at worst rendering political debate ever more unprincipled and anti-constitutional, given they will no longer be the responsibility of citizens or politicians.

As we saw, it is precisely such limitations on democracy that drive the rise of left-wing populism. Much of the liberal constitutionalist case rests on the assumption that the key danger to individual rights stems from the tyranny of the majority, and that strong form review by an independent constitutional court on the basis of an entrenched Bill of Rights performs better. However, no such empirical correlation exists. If one looks at standard indices for the protection of civil and political liberties, such as the Freedom House Reports, then a majority of the highest performing countries, many ranked far higher than the United States, do not have strong form judicial review: these include the four Scandinavian countries, which have a very weak form of review; the Netherlands and Australia, that do not permit judicial review of statutes in rights cases; the UK and New Zealand, that have declaratory powers but leave the law in force; and the Canadian constitution that permits Parliament a legislative override.[89] By contrast, majoritarian democracy has more than a contingent link to human rights protection because in sharing power equally, at least in formal terms, it favours the promotion of public policies that support the equal rights of voters.[90] By contrast, as the traditional utilitarian criticism of natural rights contended, there is a danger that appeals to rights that are unrelated to, and even deployed against, the public welfare, serve merely to protect the unwarranted entitlements of privileged minorities. That danger risks being exacerbated by the narrower and less accessible forum of a court—not least if that court has been captured by the privileged minority, as seems to be the case in *Citizens United*. Indeed, a *Washington Post*–ABC News poll at the time showed a majority of both Republicans and Democrats opposed the Supreme Court's judgment, while 72 per cent thought Congress should act to restore some limits to political spending.

Counter-majoritarian mechanisms, including entrenched constitutions and judicial review aimed at upholding democracy, form part of the problem rather than a solution. As I remarked in Chapter 3, a key role in this regard is played by the nature of the electoral system itself. Plurality systems tend to promote anti-system politics more than proportional systems. True, the latter make it easier for populist parties of the right and left to gain representation, yet that can act as a safety valve against total disillusionment with the democratic system. By contrast,

[89] Jeff King, 'The Democratic Case for a Written Constitution' (2019) 72 *Current Legal Problems* 1–36, at 13 and n. 30.

[90] Thomas Christiano, 'An Instrumental Argument for a Human Right to Democracy' (2011) 39 *Philosophy & Public Affairs* 142–76.

plurality systems can magnify and lead to a build-up of voter discontent, eventually leading to more dramatic breakthroughs, as in the UK and United States.[91] More importantly, proportional representation (PR) tends to favour greater social equality because it leads to a broader range of social interests being involved in the policy-making process.[92] In other words, we need to strengthen rather than weaken political constitutionalism, by enhancing those democratic features on which its constitutional qualities depend.

That raises the issue of whether the political constitution can renew itself. A standard critique of even attempting to do so is that this would involve politicians and those they represent being 'judge in their own cause'. Yet, those raising this objection tend not to complain of court's ruling on their own competence to adjudicate on a given issue. To a degree, this will be an unavoidable feature of whatever body has the final say on constitutional questions in a given system. Even so there are democratic mechanisms that can be deployed to reduce the likelihood of self-interested, rushed, or poorly conceived proposals being adopted. For example, proposals could be drafted by a body of experts nominated and approved by all parties and involving the input of randomly selected citizens juries; while the resulting legislation might require endorsement by parliaments either side of an election or need approval in a referendum.[93] These seem more legitimate ways of making and approving changes to the rules of the democratic game than a decision by a court as to what it believes are mandated by certain constitutional norms. Moreover, that need not mean these democratic deliberations are unconstitutional. On the contrary, broad agreement is likelier the more proposals can be shown to align with commonly avowable principles of a constitutional nature, such as political equality.

Of course, nothing is guaranteed. People need to be convinced change is needed—that the system of governance needs fixing and not just individual politicians.[94] And that perceived need has to be sufficiently broad as to be to some degree cross-party, so that the public rather than just sectional interests will prevail. To a certain extent, the same can be said with regard to constitutional innovations by judges. Courts tend to reflect sustained trends of national public opinion, with judges often feeling most confident to act when they feel their judgments will meet with broad popular support.[95] But the potential for the tyranny of the minority is much greater, especially if courts involve a small membership with lengthy terms of office, as is the case in the United States. In these cases, entrenchment and

[91] Hopkin, *Anti-System Politics*, 74.

[92] Torben Iversen and David Soskice, 'Electoral Institutions and the Politics of Coalitions: Why Some Democracies Redistribute More than Others' (2006) 100 *American Political Science Review* 165–81.

[93] King, 'The Democratic Case'.

[94] Alan Renwick, *The Politics of Electoral Reform: Changing the Rules of Democracy* (Cambridge: Cambridge University Press 2011).

[95] Robert A. Dahl, 'Decision-Making in A Democracy: The Supreme Court as a National Policy Maker' (1957) 6 *Journal of Public Law* 279–95.

independence become disadvantages rather than advantages precisely because there is a lack of popular responsiveness.[96]

7. CONCLUSION

Populism tends to be regarded as a latent potential within democracy that a legal constitution provides protection against. Political constitutionalism thereby becomes suspect as enabling the emergence of populism. This chapter has disputed this view. It distinguished right- from left-wing populism, arguing that only the former seeks a deformation of democracy that is at odds with its constitutional qualities. It also distinguished a form of constitutionalism linked to the ideal of limited government from one linked to non-arbitrary government. Legal constitutionalism typically embraces the first ideal. However, that can be seen as a driver both of right- and even more of left-wing populism, that may produce certain kinds of arbitrary rule that can be exploited by democratic backsliding and illiberal regimes. By contrast, political constitutionalism involves the second ideal and is inherently at odds with right-wing populism. Nevertheless, left-wing populism can be seen as related to failings in contemporary democratic systems to secure political responsiveness and equality, and thereby perform their constitutional role to prevent arbitrary rule. Yet, strengthening legal constitutionalism is unlikely to remedy these shortcomings. Instead, the solution lies in exploring how democratic politics might be deployed to enable the political constitution to renew itself. It is to the pros and cons of one way of doing so—namely, through a referendum—that I now turn.

[96] Mark Tushnet, *Taking the Constitution Away from the Courts* (Princeton, NJ: Princeton University Press 1999); Doerfler and Moyn, 'Democratizing the Supreme Court'.

9

Referendums and the Case of Brexit

Towards a Populist Constitutionalism?

1. INTRODUCTION

Referendums have increased in frequency and number in democratic states across the globe over the past fifty years.[1] Between 1975 and 2000, the fifty-eight functioning democracies with populations above three million held some thirty-nine referendums,[2] and since then they have become four times more common.[3] These referendums have been categorized into four main types relating to the sort of issue they address.[4] The first type deals with the very existence or shape of the polity, be it to approve secession from an existing state and the founding of a new state, as occurred in South Sudan in 2011, or the remodelling of the polity by the granting of greater sub-state autonomy, as in the failed Bolivian referendum of 2006. The second focuses on the approval of reforms to the polity's regime, be it to endorse the creation and proposal for a new constitutional order, as in Venezuela in 1998 and 1999 or Chile in 2020 and the failed referendum of 2022; or to ratify constitutional amendments, as occurred with regard to the rights to abortion, divorce, and blasphemy in Ireland in 2018. The third is a hybrid type and involves international treaties raising both polity and regime issues as a result of membership of an international organization, such as NATO or the European Union (EU), whereby accession or reforms involve the transfer of certain state competences to supranational or intergovernmental bodies and/or changes to how those competences are exercised. Notable examples include both the failed French and Dutch referendums on the Treaty establishing a Constitution for Europe, and the UK's 'Brexit' referendum on whether to leave or remain in the EU of June 2016—a focus of this chapter. A final type—potentially of a non-constitutional nature, at least in the strict sense, relates to particular policies, as is often the case with various local Swiss referendums.

[1] Lawrence LeDuc, *The Politics of Direct Democracy: Referendums in Global Perspective* (New York: Broadview Press 2003) 29.

[2] Stephen Tierney, *Constitutional Referendums. The Theory and Practice of Republican Deliberation* (Oxford: Oxford University Press 2012) 1.

[3] Dennis F. Thompson, 'Why Representative Democracy Requires Referendums' in J. A. Gardener (ed.), *Comparative Electoral Law* (Cheltenham: Elgar 2022) 195.

[4] Stephen Tierney, 'Constitutional Referendums: A Theoretical Enquiry' (2009) 72(3) *Modern Law Review* 360.

Defending the Political Constitution. Richard Bellamy, Oxford University Press. © Richard Bellamy 2026.
DOI: 10.1093/9780191826986.003.0013

Referendums of the first three kinds are often praised or criticized as instances of popular sovereignty, through which the people possess the constituent power to determine both the locus of legal and political authority, and as such who, where, and what will be subject to it, and the terms and conditions of its exercise, and consequently how and with what limitations such authority can be deployed. Supporters of such referendums see them as valuable instances of popular self-determination, that can provide legal and political systems with democratic legitimacy. They contend they offer a mechanism through which citizens can participate in shaping a polity and its regime and identify with them as 'theirs'.[5] Meanwhile, the fourth type provides an additional channel for citizens to enhance the responsiveness of politicians, either by challenging unpopular policies or proposing new ones that parties have kept off the electoral agenda. By contrast, opponents caution against the potentially populist and plebiscitary character of referendums.[6] They believe referendums can diminish democracy and remove important liberal constraints on majority tyranny.[7] Contrary to populist claims, these critics consider referendums more susceptible to elite manipulation and less deliberative than electoral, representative democracy, not least through reducing complex issues to a simple binary choice. Meanwhile, as alleged expressions of a putative singular popular will that lie outside the constitution, they may fail to attend to minority voices and rights—not least when 'the people' gets framed by rightist populists in native, ethnic terms. On this account, referendums only prove legitimate when they supplement rather than supplant representative democracy, and operate within rather than outside the extant constitutional framework.[8]

These critics see the Brexit referendum as 'a textbook example of how *not* to conduct a referendum',[9] offering 'a clear and unambiguous lesson on what democracies ought *not* to do'.[10] Indeed, it has become common to assess quite different referendums—from the Columbian peace agreement referendum of October 2016 and the Chilean referendum on a new constitution of September 2022, to the above mentioned Irish referendums of 2018—on the basis of how far they supposedly repeated or avoided the alleged mistakes of the Brexit referendum.[11] That

[5] Tierney, *Constitutional Referendums*.

[6] Claus Offe, 'Referendum vs. Institutionalized Deliberation: What Democratic Theorists Can Learn from the 2016 Brexit Decision' (2017) 146(3) *Daedalus* 14–27.

[7] R. Van Crombrugge, 'Are Referendums Necessarily Populist? Countering the Populist Interpretation of Referendums Through Institutional Design' (2021) 57(1) *Representation* 111–13.

[8] Van Crombrugge, 'Are Referendums Necessarily Populist?'; Leah Trueblood, 'Are Referendums Directly Democratic?' (2020) 40(3) *Oxford Journal of Legal Studies* 425–48.

[9] Leah Trueblood, 'Brexit and Two Roles for Referendums in the United Kingdom' in Richard Albert and Richard Stacey (eds), *The Limits and Legitimacy of Referendums* (Oxford: Oxford University Press 2022) 183.

[10] Offe, 'Referendum vs. Institutionalized Deliberation' 22.

[11] Roberto Gargarella, 'Rejection of the New Chilean Constitution: Some Reflections', *Oxford Human Rights Hub* (14 September 2022) <https://ohrh.law.ox.ac.uk/rejection-of-the-new-chilean-constitution-some-reflections/>.

said, commentators often disagree as to how far and in what ways these different referendums paralleled or differed from Brexit, these disagreements reflecting differing views of the coherence and legitimacy of appeals to constituent power and popular sovereignty, notions that play a key role in many constitutional traditions.[12] Determining how far, and in what ways, the Brexit referendum can be regarded as flawed or not potentially has a wider significance, therefore.

Critics of that referendum see it as being both at odds with, and indicative of the weaknesses of, the UK's political constitution. On the one hand, they regard what they see as the referendum's appeal to popular sovereignty to decide a complex issue as being at odds with the doctrine of parliamentary sovereignty,[13] which forms the keystone of the political constitution.[14] As we have seen, according to this political conception it is the representative and parliamentary processes that give the democratic system its constitutional qualities. These allow citizens to hold governments and the administration accountable either indirectly through elections or directly via elected parliaments and the need for the government to govern and legislate with the support of a plurality of the population and a majority of MPs.[15] By contrast, referendums produce a populist disfigurement of democracy,[16] that denies the pluralism and tolerance of representative democratic decision-making through emphasizing the existence of a mythical and singular people's will.[17]

On the other hand, though, these critics believe the referendum highlights the weaknesses of the political constitution as a curb on populism and a potential tyranny of a democratic majority.[18] They claim that not only can any government possessing a stable parliamentary majority act as an 'elective dictatorship' and make and interpret the law as it wishes,[19] but also the executive can further overrule Parliament by appealing directly to a popular majority in a plebiscite, as Prime Ministers Theresa May and Boris Johnson both attempted to do in order to avoid parliamentary scrutiny of their respective proposals for leaving the EU.

[12] S. Verdugo, 'On the Democratic (but Limited) Virtues of the Chilean Exit Referendum', IACL-AIDC Blog (4 October 2022) <https://blog-iacl-aidc.org/new-blog-3/2022/10/4/on-the-democratic-but-limited-virtues-of-the-chilean-exit-referendum>.

[13] Offe, 'Referendum vs. Institutionalized Deliberation', 18, 21–2.

[14] Keith David Ewing, 'The Resilience of the Political Constitution' (2013) 14 *German Law Journal* 2111–36, at 2118; Michael Gordon, 'Parliamentary Sovereignty and the Political Constitution(s): From Griffith to Brexit' (2019) 30 *King's Law Journal* 125–47, at 133–7.

[15] J. A. G. Griffith, 'The Political Constitution' (1979) 42 *Modern Law Review* 1–21; Adam Tomkins, *Our Republican Constitution* (Oxford: Hart Publishing 2005) 1–10.

[16] Nadia Urbinati, *Me the People: How Populism Transforms Democracy* (Cambridge, MA: Harvard University Press 2019).

[17] Albert Weale, *The Will of the People. A Modern Myth* (Cambridge: Polity 2018); Van Crombrugge, 'Are Referendums Necessarily Populist?', 115–16.

[18] Trueblood, 'Brexit and Two Roles for Referendums in the United Kingdom'.

[19] Lord Hailsham, *The Dilemma of Democracy: Diagnosis and Prescription* (Glasgow: Collins 1978) 127; Philip Pettit, 'Republican Freedom and Contestatory Democratization' in Ian Shapiro and Casiano Hacker-Cordón (eds), *Democracy's Value* (Cambridge: Cambridge University Press 1999) 163–90, at 176.

These critics claim that a codified constitution that acts as a higher law that frames the operation of politics would have ensured that both the referendum and the parliamentary process operated in an inclusive way, that protected minority voices.[20]

Needless to say, defenders of the referendum tend to dispute both these points. They argue that representative democracy can be prone to elitism and a lack of responsiveness to popular concerns, and provide insufficient space for citizen participation through more truly democratic avenues. They consider referendums as a truer form of political constitutionalism, offering an opportunity for the direct expression of popular political sovereignty on which the legitimacy of Parliament's legislative sovereignty ultimately rests.[21] Meanwhile, they note that many legal constitutions explicitly recognize popular sovereignty as the constituent power, with some constitutions explicitly authorizing this power to operate outside constitutional limits, given that it may initiate and approve a thorough reform of the extant constitution.[22] To that extent, legal constitutionalism per se cannot be viewed as offering a necessary constraint on popular sovereignty.

This chapter challenges the views of both opponents and proponents of the Brexit referendum. Putting to one side the strictly legal issue of the compatibility of the referendum with prevailing UK public law, it explores the broader normative issue of the compatibility of referendums in general, and this one in particular, with the very notion of a political constitution based on parliamentary rather than popular sovereignty. Referendums are not foreign to the UK, which has held eleven of them since 1973. Indeed, A. V. Dicey, whose *Introduction to the Study of the Law of the Constitution* offers the *locus classicus* of the doctrine of parliamentary sovereignty,[23] was the first to advocate the referendum in Britain.[24] Although Dicey's position has been viewed as 'paradoxical',[25] I shall argue that referendums can play a valid political constitutional role as part of a system of checks and balances on executive authority so long as they are appropriately embedded within a system of representative democracy.

On this account, referendums need not displace parliamentary sovereignty with an unmediated popular sovereignty. They can allow an important role for the people while nevertheless relying upon Parliament to structure the debate and

[20] Vernon Bogdanor, *Beyond Brexit: Towards a British Constitution* (London: I.B. Tauris 2019) ch. 3; Vernon Bogdanor, 'Brexit Means Britain Needs a Constitution', *Foreign Policy* (8 October 2019) <https://foreignpolicy.com/2019/10/08/brexit-means-britain-needs-a-constitution//>.

[21] Stephen Tierney, 'Whose Political Constitution? Citizens and Referendums' (2013) 14 *German Law Journal* 2185–96.

[22] J. Colón-Riós, *Constituent Power and the Law* (Oxford: Oxford University Press 2020).

[23] A. V. Dicey, *Introduction to the Study of the Law of the Constitution* (8th edn, London: MacMillan 1915 [1885]) Part II, chs 13, 402, 405.

[24] A. V. Dicey, 'Ought the Referendum to be Introduced into England?' (1890) 57 *Contemporary Review* 489–511.

[25] Vernon Bogdanor, 'Western Europe' in David Butler and Austin Ranney (eds), *Referendums Around the World: The Growing Use of Direct Democracy* (Basingstoke: Palgrave 1994) 34.

oversee the decisions' implementation. As a result, they can encourage popular participation without producing populism. So conceived, referendums supplement representative democracy on those constitutional issues where allowing the elected government to decide would make it 'judge in its own cause'—notably, changes to the electoral system or to the demos.[26] I shall argue that the Brexit referendum was such a case, given it involved changes to the demos and hence to the scope of parliamentary sovereignty. However, while it can be regarded as meeting certain minimal standards of democratic legitimacy, the process could certainly have been improved—even if the result might well have remained the same.

The argument proceeds as follows. First, I explore how far referendums can be said to be compatible with the constitutional qualities political constitutionalists associate with a parliamentary representative democracy while potentially addressing some of the limitations that critics attribute to it. I shall argue this can be possible to the extent referendums can be nested within, and made a component of, the standard picture of the political constitution so as to form part of a system of political checks and balances with constitutional qualities. Second, I turn to the Brexit referendum and consider whether, while far from perfect, it was so nested and can be regarded as democratically and constitutionally legitimate in terms of the political constitution, performing an important supplementary function appropriate to such constitutive issues. Though flawed, the failings of the referendum rested more with those putting the argument for remain rather than the process per se. Finally, I conclude by noting that there are positive as well as negative lessons that can be drawn from the Brexit referendum concerning the ways referendums can enhance both representative democracy and constitutionalism as part of a political constitution.

2. THE CONSTITUTIONAL QUALITIES OF REFERENDUMS

As was noted above, referendums typically fall into four rough issue types. This categorization by issue relates to whether they deal with constitutive, constitutional, international, or policy matters.[27] Thus, the first type involves decisions that redefine either the polity, as in referendums on secession—such as the recent Scottish referendum on independence, or the fundamental form of its regime, as in referendums on an entirely new constitution. The second relates to more limited amendments to an already existing written constitution or constitutional statute, which operate within the prevailing constitutional structures with regard to both the polity and the regime, such as the recent Irish referendum on abortion or the

[26] Thompson, 'Why Representative Democracy Requires Referendums', 196.
[27] Tierney, *Constitutional Referendums* 11–15.

UK referendum on changing the electoral system. The third relates to the ratification of international treaties that raise constitutive, constitutional, and possibly policy issues. Finally, the fourth concerns policies ranging from changes in local planning regulations, as is common in Swiss communal and some English Parish referendums, to major policy decisions, such as the California Proposition 218 that—while technically a constitutional amendment—was designed to give voters a direct say over levels of local government taxes. As this last example indicates, there can be some overlap between the issue types– a policy issue can have constitutional implications, as in this case, while most constitutive referendums will raise both constitutional and policy issues, as was the case with Scottish independence and is likely to be true of referendums on international treaties, such as Brexit. It will also be a matter of degree as to how far a constitutional amendment can be regarded as altering the nature of the regime or polity, as might have been the case with electoral reform, or in referendums on establishing elected mayors.

These four issue types can take two broad forms with two distinctive modalities. With regard to forms, referendums can be regarded as either top down, where the government calls and frames the referendum, or bottom up, where a process exists for citizens to request a referendum—for example, by gathering a prescribed number of signatures. There are also hybrid forms that combine elements of both, such as the Irish use of citizen juries to identify issues on which referendums might be called. With regard to modalities, referendums may be negative, called to abrogate an existing law or arrangement; or positive, aimed at approving a proposal for a new measure or arrangement. Once again, this distinction may not be clear cut. In some cases, a successful negative referendum may entail the need for new positive measures or arrangements, though the precise nature of these may not be clearly specified. Likewise, if a positive proposal has failed to get approval it has by implication been abrogated.

The degree to which referendums can be regarded as either possessing themselves constitutional qualities or complementing those of representative and parliamentary forms of democracy will depend on the particular ways the issue, forms, and modalities interact with each other and, where relevant, with the system of representative democracy.[28] Broadly speaking, the intrinsic securing of equal respect appears strongest in referendums that are bottom up and allow citizens to propose new policies, and weakest in those that are top down and merely seek approval of a government measure.[29] Referendums of the former type, that belong to the policy issue category, take a bottom up form and involve a positive modality, approximate most closely to exercises of direct democracy that can be characterized as embodying popular sovereignty. As such, *prima facie* at least, they appear

[28] Lord, 'Referendums and Democratic Theory'.

[29] Francis Cheneval and Alice el-Wakil, 'The Institutional Design of Referendums: Bottom-Up and Binding' (2018) 24 *Swiss Political Science Review* 294–304.

best placed to counter the criticism of representative democracy for its lack of participation and elitism. However, these types of referendum are also those where critics have most doubted their instrumental constitutional qualities. These worries involve the limitations of referendums with regard to collective policy-making, citizen competence, and elite manipulation; majority tyranny; and the lack of accountability or undermining of the role of representatives.[30] I shall consider each of these worries in turn, although—as we shall see—they relate in various ways to each other.

The key problem for referendums with regard to collective policy-making relates to the weighting of citizens' preferences across the whole domain of policy options.[31] A referendum necessarily focuses on a single issue, whereas elections focus on party programmes that bundle together a range of policies and seek to weigh them against each other, including giving consideration for the knock-on effects of decisions in one policy area for decisions in others.[32] A decision on a policy taken in isolation from others risks producing policy incoherence—as when voters vote for tax cuts that would undermine the government's ability to fund public services and infrastructure that they wish to see expanded.[33] True, the Ostrogorski paradox suggests the possibility that bundling may involve putting together a number of policies, many of which taken on their own are not supported by a majority.[34] In this scenario, a bottom up, positive, policy referendum might be justified to challenge parties having taken off the agenda or ignored a majority view in a given area. However, that would depend on the policy being discrete, which in most cases is unlikely.

The policy implications of a popular vote may also be imprecise. This is especially true of negative, abrogative, referendums, where what is to be put in place of the rescinded measure—if anything—may be unclear. Yet, positive referendums may also be imprecise unless the policy proposal is clearly specified. A related issue stems from the binary nature of many referendums, whereby the two options on offer may be arbitrary and suppress alternatives that would have been the most preferred (i.e. the Condorcet winner[35]), particularly if voters could rank their preferences among multiple possibilities.[36] Of course, voters could be given multiple

[30] Tierney, *Constitutional Referendums*, 22–4; Trueblood, 'Are Referendums Directly Democratic?', 435–41; Lord, 'Referendums and Democratic Theory', 35.

[31] Richard Bellamy, 'Majority Rule, Compromise and the Democratic Legitimacy of Referendums' (2018) 24 *Swiss Political Science Review* 312–19, at 314–16.

[32] Tierney, *Constitutional Referendums* 37.

[33] John Haskell, *Direct Democracy or Representative Government? Dispelling the Populist Myth* (Boulder, CO: Westview 2001) 16.

[34] Maija Setälä, 'On the Problems of Responsibility and Accountability in Referendums' (2006) 45 *European Journal of Political Research* 699–721; Lord, 'Referendums and Democratic Theory', 34.

[35] The Condorcet winner is that option (be it a candidate, party, policy, or programme) that would defeat all the other options in a one on one (or pairwise) contest.

[36] Weale, *The Will of the People*, 62–6; Bellamy, 'Majority Rule', 317–18.

options to choose from and allowed to rank them, as occurs in some Swiss referendums.[37] Yet, these are likely to still be options relating to a single policy.

Worries about citizen competence enter here. Some advocates of policy referendums claim they benefit from the 'wisdom of crowds'.[38] However, that depends on citizens possessing sufficient knowledge about the relevant policy area to be able to make a reasonable guess as to which of the available options might be best. Meanwhile, the aforementioned problems regarding policy connectedness and the representativeness of the options on offer still apply. Even referendums that emerge from a popular initiative can be subject to elite manipulation,[39] as they will generally arise as a result of a campaign led by a small group of activists, who will then seek to shape the referendum question so as to favour their preferred result. In the absence of personal expertise, most voters will also follow elite cues from media and other campaigns.[40] In these respects, referendums may at best allow for a similar degree of misrepresentation and manipulation as elections, and at worst an even greater degree given party ideology tends to act as a relatively stable indicator of the overall direction of the policies advocated taken as a whole, whereas such guides may be lacking when it comes to a single issue. Of course, as advocates of these initiatives note, the issue concerned may be one that divides parties, with support and opposition cutting across standard party lines.[41] A referendum in such circumstances may help overcome such divisions. Yet, it could also be seen as an abnegation of responsibility by politicians to take a difficult decision. After all, free votes in legislatures can often be among the most deliberative precisely because politicians do not simply follow the party lead. By the same token, though, the fact that politicians have no clear mandate for how they would vote could be seen as legitimizing a popular debate and decision.

Nevertheless, so far as policy issues are concerned, the disadvantages of referendums may outweigh the advantages. As was noted in Chapter 3, the need to fish for votes from a diverse electorate and build a coalition for a party programme helps support minority interests. But when it comes to a vote on a single issue, the need for coalition-building is likely to be less. That increases the danger of majority tyranny, since the need for compromise and accommodation is greatly reduced, as is the capacity, within the procedure, to develop a compromise.[42] Meanwhile, policies that are so decided tend to become entrenched—politicians will be wary of

[37] Lord, 'Referendums and Democratic Theory', 36.

[38] e.g. Hélène Landemore, *Democratic Reason: Politics, Collective Intelligence, and the Rule of the Many* (Princeton, NJ: Princeton University Press 2013).

[39] Iseult Honohan, *Civic Republicanism* (London: Routledge 2002) 220–30.

[40] Honohan, *Civic Republicanism*, 218.

[41] A. Glencross, 'History' in J. Smith (ed.), *The Palgrave Handbook of European Referendums* (Basingstoke: Palgrave Macmillan 2021) 49–66, 57–8.

[42] Bellamy, 'Majority Rule'; Donald Haider-Markel, Alana Querze, and Kara Lindaman, 'Lose, Win, or Draw? A Reexamination of Direct Democracy and Minority Rights' (2007) 60 *Political Research Quarterly* 304–14.

reversing a measure possessing a popular mandate, even if they regard the policy as deleterious. Moreover, they will bear no personal responsibility for it and so cannot be held to account for its failings. Once again, the worry is that referendums may not only lack adequate instrumental constitutional qualities themselves but also undermine those associated with representative democracy.

These concerns arise when referendums are seen as exercises of direct democracy, involving the exercise of popular sovereignty. Some theorists have argued that while referendums with this quality may be inappropriate on policy issues, they are suitable for constitutive and constitutional issues.[43] As I noted above, referendums on these two issues concern respectively the definition of the polity and its demos; and the character of the regime—particularly the rules of the democratic game. Both these issues have been regarded as being suitably conceived as expressions of 'we the people'.[44] In the first case, a referendum could be seen as providing a way for those concerned to contract to form a people who then subject themselves to a common authority under their mutual control. In the second case, a referendum allows the secondary rules that define the legal and political system to be authorized directly by the people to whom they will apply, encouraging them to identify with these rules as theirs.

Two additional claims are often made in regard to both issues: first, that these are matters of collective and common interest, that transcend the particular interests individuals may have with regard to specific policies; and second, that referendums spark a more participatory and deliberative debate of a kind that promotes public reasoning on a topic that defines both the public or demos and their public interactions.[45] On this account, constitutive and constitutional referendums form part of a dual democracy:[46] they provide a democratic mechanism for bringing into being a democratic system that can address policy issues. Yet, it is disputable whether they can escape the problems identified above with regard to policy referendums. To do so, it must be assumed that the referendum does indeed take the form of a contract whereby all citizens agree on fair terms of cooperation and consent to them, with constitutional and constitutive politics differing in deliberative and epistemological quality to normal politics, such that citizens are moved by the better argument and avoid the conflicts of interest and ontological disagreements typical of policy debates.[47] However, there is no compelling reason to believe this will be the case.[48]

43 Tierney, *Constitutional Referendums*; Tierney, 'Whose Political Constitutions?'.

44 See Ackerman, *We the People.*

45 Tierney, *Constitutional Referendums*, 12–15; Tierney, 'Whose Political Constitutions?'.

46 Ackerman, *We the People.*

47 Jürgen Habermas, *Between Facts and Norms: Contributions to a Discourse Theory of Law and Democracy* (William Rehg tr., Cambridge: Polity Press 1996) 278–9.

48 Richard Bellamy and Justus Schönlau, 'The Normality of Constitutional Politics: An Analysis of the Drafting of the EU Charter of Fundamental Rights' (2004) 11 *Constellations* 412–33.

If, as political constitutionalists argue, rights and procedural rules can be matters of reasonable disagreement, then no consensus is likely to be reached on them through a public wide discussion and referendum any more than in a legislative debate. Nor are such discussions necessarily any more bottom up and lacking in elite manipulation, given that as with policy proposals they are likely to be prompted by political entrepreneurs and the debate heavily influenced by the media. Meanwhile, such a discussion may lack the incentives of checks and balances that lead to legislators 'hearing the other side'. Indeed, as the 2009 Swiss referendum on minarets, recurrent Swiss referendums on immigration and residence of foreign criminals, and California Proposition 8 illustrate,[49] such exercises of popular democracy may allow minority rights to be abrogated by tyrannous majorities. Some such checks might be incorporated into the referendum process—for example, it might be necessary to have a threshold for the turnout of over 50 per cent and/or to achieve a super-majority if the measure is to carry. However, while these requirements may prevent certain unjust proposals carrying they can also inhibit reforms that remove injustices from the prevailing status quo.[50] They can only be justified if it is reasonable to assume that most changes would be likely to be worse than the prevailing system—hardly an endorsement of popular sovereignty. Arguably, a comprehensive constitutional reform might allow for more compromise to arise of a balancing kind between the representatives of different groups, and—as with the Icelandic constitutive assembly—there could be a direct crowd sourcing of ideas by the public, with the whole package then put to a referendum. However, this proposal seems to suggest that constitutive and constitutional referendums become more acceptable the more they develop the characteristics of representative, competitive party politics.

Although there is some evidence that Dicey may have come to regard referendums in this light,[51] the development of his argument seems to have been driven by the desire to stop Irish Home Rule at any price.[52] However, that need not mean that referendums could not be incorporated into a Diceyan version of political constitutionalism where political sovereignty lies with the people but legal sovereignty rests with Parliament, which retains both constitutional and legislative authority.[53] Dicey's point—at least until 1911—seems to have been that an executive required a significant level of popular political authorization for major constitutional change.

[49] Daniel Moeckli, 'Of Minarets and Foreign Criminals: Swiss Direct Democracy and Human Rights' (2011) 11 *Human Rights Law Review* 774–94; J. Hainmueller and D. Hangartner, 'Does Direct Democracy Hurt Immigrant Minorities? Evidence from Naturalization Decisions in Switzerland' (2019) 63 *American Journal of Political Science* 530–47; Bruno Frey and Lorenz Goette, 'Does the Popular Vote Destroy Civil Rights?' (1988) 42 *American Journal of Political Science* 1343–8.

[50] Melissa Schwartzberg, *Counting the Many: The Origins and Limits of Supermajority Rule* (Cambridge: Cambridge University Press 2013).

[51] Rivka Weill, 'Dicey was not Diceyan' (2003) 62 *Cambridge Law Journal* 474–94.

[52] Richard Cosgrove, *The Rule of Law: Albert Venn Dicey, Victorian Jurist* (Chapel Hill, NC: University of North Carolina Press 1980) 105–10, 247.

[53] Weill, 'Dicey', 474–5.

However, as with the Great Reform Act of 1832, he considered—at least initially—an election victory in which the change figured prominently in the campaign as sufficient.[54] He only turned to advocating a referendum as Home Rule appeared unlikely to be opposed. The logic of his argument was not to consider the people as possessing legislative sovereignty, though, as some have argued. Rather, he saw referendums as a means for exercising a popular political constraint on the legislature in the case of significant constitutive or constitutional laws that paralleled—and could even be exercised by—the withdrawal of their authorization of a government at an election.[55]

In a similar manner, Eoin Daly has argued that referendums may be considered as forming a part of the mixed constitution, adding another political channel for checks and balances in areas that legislatures may be ill-suited to provide for themselves.[56] Rather than being bottom up and positive exercises of popular legislative sovereignty, and as such rivals to parliamentary sovereignty, he contends that referendums are better seen as negative and top down, serving a contestatory function aimed at guarding against arbitrary rule and promoting public justification.[57] As such, they can contribute to the negative and positive instrumental constitutional functions identified above, usefully supplementing representative democracy in the process.

Daly considers referendums of this kind as particularly relevant for constitutive and constitutional issues. Both these issues could be regarded as relating to areas where politicians might have an interest at variance with those they represent. For example, a government might wish to introduce electoral reforms or constitutional amendments that make it more likely they remain in power or the policies they favour are entrenched. He contends that forcing governments to put proposals on these two sorts of issues to a referendum can promote a wider public discussion and promote civic participation. As he notes, in Europe, Ireland, Switzerland, and Denmark all have mandatory constitutional amendment referendums for issues of this kind,[58] as does Australia.[59] Even in Germany, which had been thought averse to referendums given their use by the Nazis, the Basic Law has been amended to allow for a referendum on changes to the Basic Law itself (A146).[60] Their aim is to reinforce the likelihood such measures treat all with equal respect and concern by giving all citizens an equal vote on them while having the proposal itself and its implementation the product of coalition-building and compromise by parties in the legislature, whose actions remain electorally authorized and accountable.

[54] Weill, 'Dicey', 478–9.

[55] Weill, 'Dicey', 480–8.

[56] Eoin Daly, 'A Republican Defence of the Constitutional Referendum' (2015) 35 *Legal Studies* 30–54, at 32.

[57] Daly, 'A Republican Defence', 37.

[58] Daly, 'A Republican Defence', 38.

[59] Daly, 'A Republican Defence', 41.

[60] Lord, 'Referendums and Democratic Theory', 31.

Daly distinguishes referendums that still retain parliamentary legislative sovereignty from those, such as De Gaulle's 1962 referendum amending the rules on presidential elections, that involve a direct populist appeal by a political leader to the 'people's will' in order to by-pass parliamentary amendment procedures.[61] He likens referendums of the former type to the role of a second chamber that adopts a different form of representation to the first and primary legislative chamber. As a form of multicameralism,[62] referendums both support the representation of all relevant interests on such important questions, and promote their balancing through enhancing the scrutiny to which they are subjected.

Daly's argument presents an account of referendums that can be reconciled with political constitutionalism insofar as it distinguishes political and legal sovereignty, leaving the latter with Parliament. So conceived, referendums introduce a check and balance that possesses the intrinsic and instrumental constitutional qualities of democracy that political constitutionalists seek to deploy, at least when they are embedded within a system of representative democracy and act as a supplement to it. However, his account gives referendums a largely negative, contestatory, role. They operate not to propose change so much as to approve or reject changes proposed by the legislature. As such, they only partly address the alleged failings of representative democracy. They operate against elites when they are acting against the public interest, but not when they are failing to act in the public interest. Yet, though any given individual act of omission may pose less of a danger than any single act of commission, taken cumulatively over time they may do as much, if not more, to undermine popular support for democracy.

Even in plurality systems such as that of the UK, though, electoral competition may work against parties successfully colluding to take certain constitutional issues completely off the agenda. For example, although the two main parties have generally opposed any move towards proportional representation (PR) for national elections, the hung Parliament of 2010 gave the Liberal Democrats the opportunity to push for electoral reform. Given the type of issue and the fact that no parliamentary majority probably existed for this measure, putting a proposal to a referendum could be regarded as a legitimate alternative to canvass the support of the broader public for such a fundamental reform. Likewise, the referendums on Northern Ireland remaining part of the UK (1973); the Good Friday Agreement (1998); and the Scottish (1979, 1997) and Welsh (1979, 1997, 2011) referendums on devolution, and in the case of Scotland independence (2014), all deal with constitutional issues where it is conceivable no majority would exist at Westminster for the change, and those voters with a strong interest in the issue lacked sufficient representation. Even though not all of these detailed the precise form the proposal would take, they can be seen as a means for checking against potential inaction by

[61] Daly, 'A Republican Defence', 36–7.
[62] Daly, 'A Republican Defence', 43.

politicians on a core constitutive or constitutional issue through canvassing the wider and more diverse chamber of the relevant public as a whole. It would be misleading to regard them as operating as expressions of popular sovereignty or consent.

As I have noted, international treaties can raise both constitutive and constitutional issues, and as such seem apt as an issue for referendums. However, article 75 of the Italian constitution, that allows abrogative referendums, explicitly excludes referendums on 'laws authorising the ratification of international treaties' along with those on 'tax, budget, amnesty or pardon laws'. This first exclusion has been justified as necessary to ensure credible commitments to international agreements regardless of changes in the popular mood. However, many treaties contain provisions allowing one or more of the parties to it to 'denounce' it in specific circumstances and to terminate or suspend participation in it. Indeed, 216 of the 561 international organizations created between 1815 and 2006 have ceased to exist.[63] If domestic constitutive and constitutional questions are valid subjects for referendums, then international agreements that raise similar questions should be too. After all, international agreements no less than domestic arrangements may either be negotiated by politicians who fail to adequately represent the concerns of citizens or cease to match changing circumstances that politicians with a vested interest in their continuance collude in keeping off the electoral agenda. In that respect, these agreements differ from the other exclusions of article 75, involving policy issues where the citizens themselves might be regarded as acting as 'judge in their own cause' and which are far more likely to be subject to electoral competition and change. The exception might be when these issues, most notably tax and budget matters, are themselves entrenched within international agreements. But then it is precisely the inappropriate constitutionalizing of a policy issue that renders it justified to allow its challenge in a referendum.[64] It remains to be seen whether the Brexit referendum can be justified on similar grounds to those discussed in this section.

3. THE BREXIT REFERENDUM AND POLITICAL CONSTITUTIONALISM

The Brexit referendum has been subjected to a high degree of criticism, especially, but not solely, by those favouring remaining in the EU. These criticisms have ranged from concerns about the misleading character of the Leave campaign,

[63] Mette Eilstrup-Sangiovanni, 'Death of International Organizations' (2020) 15 *Review of International Organizations* 339–70.

[64] Richard Bellamy and Albert Weale, 'Political Legitimacy and European Monetary Union: Contracts, Constitutionalism, and the Normative Logic of Two-Level Games' (2015) 22(2) *Journal of European Public Policy* 257–74.

including financial irregularities, misinformation, and the use of algorithms for media advertising that derived from dubiously obtained personal information,[65] to dissatisfaction with the franchise, especially for its failure to include resident EU nationals or to reduce the voting age to sixteen.[66] The evaluation developed here focuses on the second set of criticisms relating to the referendum's institutional design and constitutional credentials rather than the first set relating to its conduct. However, neither the referendum's conduct nor design need to be perfect for it to be legitimate. Though both were flawed in various ways, it was arguably no worse in these respects than current general elections in the UK or, indeed, in most other established democracies, such as the United States. These too rightly attract criticism for their many shortcomings. For example, similar campaign techniques to those of the Brexit referendum feature in normal elections in these countries, while a case exists in both the UK and United States for allowing permanent residents to vote, lowering the age of the franchise, and changing the electoral system to some form of PR. Yet, though undoubtedly improvable, both systems are regarded as possessing sufficient democratic qualities to be legitimate processes. The Brexit referendum arguably met a similar threshold of legitimacy, despite its manifold faults.[67] Granting this to be the case, my concern is whether it could be regarded as compatible with political constitutionalism along the lines given in the last section.

Note, if it can, that would offer a different ground for the referendum's legitimacy than was given by not only many Leave supporters but also others, such as the former Prime Minister Theresa May, who supported Remain but felt obliged to honour the referendum's result: namely, that it was an expression of the people's will, with popular sovereignty trumping parliamentary sovereignty.[68] It also provides a response to those who considered the referendum as unconstitutional—either in principle, or due to the absence of its procedures forming part of a legal constitution.[69] Instead, it could be seen not as a form of direct democracy requiring constitutional regulation but rather as a constitutional form of democratic politics as part of a mixed political constitutional system.

To fit this role, a referendum needs to be both embedded within and regulated via the system of representative democracy, and as such subject to the legal authority of parliamentary sovereignty, while offering a justified check and balance

[65] Sten Hansson and Sandra Kröger, 'How a Lack of Truthfulness can Undermine Democratic Representation: The Case of Post-Referendum Brexit Discourses' (2021) 23 *The British Journal of Politics and International Relations* 609–26.

[66] A. C. Grayling *Democracy and its Crisis* (London: Oneworld 2017) 189–97; Offe, 'Referendum vs. Institutionalized Deliberation', 18–21.

[67] Electoral Commission. (2016). The EU referendum: Report on the 23 June 2016 referendum on the UK's Membership of the European Union <https://www.electoralcommission.org.uk/data/assets/pdf_file/0008/215279/2016-EU-referendum-report.pdf>; Richard Bellamy, 'Was the Brexit Referendum Legitimate, and Would a Second One Be So?' (2019) 18 *European Political Science* 126–33.

[68] Weale, *The Will of the People*, ix–x.

[69] Grayling, *Democracy*, 189–97.

upon it issuing from the political authority of the people taken as a whole. The argument of the previous section suggested this is most likely to be the case in referendums on constitutive and constitutional issues, or those on international agreements that combine one or other or both, which are top down and related to affirming or contesting a proposal from the executive, and that can only take place when legislated for by a duly elected legislature, which retains the responsibility for acting on the result as its members think fit. How far was this true of the Brexit referendum?

The decision to call the referendum resulted from a manifesto pledge of the Conservative Party in the 2015 election. That origin has been viewed as somehow tainted—a hypocritical move to blunt the electoral threat posed by the UK Independence Party (UKIP) to the Conservatives. Yet, it could equally be seen as a mechanism for giving voice to an issue that the major parties had largely kept off the electoral agenda. True, the Conservatives had tried to make the EU an electoral issue in the 2001 and 2005 elections without success, a point to which I return below. However, to the extent that EU membership forms a constitutive issue as to the very nature of the polity, then it can be regarded as rightly a matter on which the people as a whole should be consulted. Indeed, across the EU that has steadily become the norm, including in Germany where the Constitutional Court has recently argued that the development of a 'federal state' at the European level could reach a point that would require 'a decision of the German people beyond the present application of the Basic Law'.[70] If a referendum is increasingly seen as necessary for not only joining the EU but also for any significant deepening of European integration, then the same should hold for a decision to leave the EU altogether. Making that possibility a manifesto pledge within an election can be regarded as providing a democratic test of its significance for the electorate. Meanwhile, doing so to fend off a challenge from a small party with significant but diffuse support (UKIP has only won one parliamentary seat in an election, which was held by a popular MP who had defected from the Conservative Party), can be regarded as providing a form of balance within a plurality system for views that might otherwise go unheard.

I also noted how referendums are likely to most fit with political constitutionalism to the extent they are regulated by parliamentary legislation. Here too that was the case. Legislation governing referendums in general had been passed under the Political Parties, Elections and Referendums Act 2000, and this was specifically applied to the Brexit referendum in the European Referendum Act 2015. This Act was passed with an overwhelming majority in the Commons of 544 to 53 in favour, with only the Scottish National Party (SNP) voting against.

[70] German Federal Constitutional Court (GFCC), Judgement of the Second Senate of 30 June 2009, 2 BE 2/08 (Lisbon Treaty) https://www.bundesverfassungsgericht.de/SharedDocs/Entscheidungen/EN/2009/06/es20090630_2bve000208en.html paras 179, 263.

As I remarked above, the main complaints with this legislation related to the franchise, the lack of super-majority rules, the length and rules for the conduct of the campaign and the alleged vagueness of the question posed. The relevant question to ask here is whether the proposed changes could be justified as necessary for the referendum to perform its checking and balancing role. My claim will be that at best they were unnecessary for the constitutional legitimacy of the referendum and at worst they would have been illegitimate.

With regard to the franchise, the referendum adopted that used for national elections under the provisions of the Representation of the People Acts 1983 and 2000. Although those provisions are contestable, they are largely consistent with those found in other established democracies. A related but distinct issue is whether a reasonable case can be made for keeping to those provisions, or whether not to depart from them in this case involved an unequivocal injustice. Here it is useful to distinguish between who can be legitimately included in making a decision and the side constraints that might arise with regard to those affected by a decision. In the case of a constitutive referendum, which concerns the very shape of the demos, a reasonable case can be made for restricting the decision to citizens. On the stakeholder account of political rights and obligations,[71] the claim to being a citizen of a given sovereign political community belongs to those whose freedom and rights are inherently linked to the collective self-government and flourishing of this polity over time. This argument links citizenship rights to the performance of civic and social duties and a commitment to the political community and its members, including to future generations. On this view, rightful inclusion in the demos depends on assuming the obligations entailed by long-term membership of a community, not least by naturalizing as a citizen of the host country—something that was relatively easy for long-term resident EU citizens to do. This view also seems the most consistent with political constitutionalism, which concerns the ability for citizens to decide the rules governing their social co-existence on an equitable basis. It would be inapposite to include in such a process those who are not committed to living under those rules over time. That said, EU citizens are certainly affected by the decision, and for any Brexit deal to be legitimate it should also be constrained in ways that acknowledge their legitimate expectations regarding their rights to remain—as the EU negotiators justifiably insisted.

What about the argument that the franchise ought to have included sixteen-year-olds? Critics of this decision argue that it excluded those most directly affected by the proposal. They note that while those aged over sixty-five, many of whom may never have had to live with the consequences of their vote, divided 66–34 pro-Leave, the excluded younger generation, whose future will be

[71] Rainer Bauböck, 'Morphing the Demos into the Right Shape. Normative Principles for Enfranchising Resident Aliens and Expatriate Citizens' (2015) 22 *Democratization* 820–39.

profoundly shaped by Brexit, were 73–27 pro-Remain.[72] Again, these are important objections. Cohort injustices are possible, and some have even suggested disenfranchising the elderly from voting on certain issues.[73] Still, the elderly tend to have children and grandchildren, so are not entirely without any concern for securing the interests of future generations, while any economic downturn as a result of Brexit would also have short-term and direct effects on their pensions and access to health care.

Super-majority thresholds are often required for constitutional and constitutive referendums. For example, the 1979 referendums on devolution in Scotland and Wales required the approval of at least 40 per cent of the eligible electorate rather than just a majority of those who voted, a threshold they failed to meet. Neither did the Brexit referendum, where the majority of 51.89 per cent on a participation rate of 72.21 per cent represented just 37.4 per cent of the electorate—although it was achieved by the 1975 referendum, which had a lower turn out (64.62%) but a higher majority in favour (67.23%). The argument favouring such criteria is that the (constitutional or quasi-constitutional) infrastructure of a polity should be relatively stable, particularly in those respects where it matters greatly for some members (perhaps a minority) in the society: for example, they have built their lives around the assumption that it will remain in place. Putting part of that infrastructure up for a 50–50 vote is like playing dice. This may be because there will always be some who vote against the status quo on the basis of frustration with the government on any front or because those affected will not realize, until it is too late, how badly they will be affected. For any such reason there will always be noise in the system, so to speak. This is an important consideration. However, a super-majority is an illegitimate way to address this point. For a super-majority violates a basic democratic and liberal norm that decision-making processes should be impartial and neutral between views in order to be fair.[74] Super-majorities entrench the status quo and may consequently lock in inefficient or unequal measures that generate injustices.[75] Instead, the issue was addressed in part by the referendum being advisory to Parliament, which subsequently had to debate and implement relevant legislation. In that sense, there was an opportunity for Parliament to deliberate the implications of the decision, and for it to be reconsidered by the electorate—a point I return to below.

A slightly different version of the super-majority argument is whether the vote should have obtained a majority among—or even in all of—the different

[72] H. D. Clarke, M. Goodwin, and P. Whitely, *Brexit: Why Britain Voted to Leave the European Union* (Cambridge: Cambridge University Press 2017) 155.

[73] Philippe Van Parijs, 'The Disenfranchisement of the Elderly, and Other Attempts to Secure Intergenerational Justice' (1998) 27 *Philosophy & Public Affairs* 292–333.

[74] Kenneth O. May, 'A Set of Independent, Necessary and Sufficient Conditions for Simple Majority Decision' (1952) 20(4) *Econometrica* 680–4.

[75] Schwartzberg, *Counting the Many*.

'nations' of the UK. The devolved regions argued that the UK included at least four demoi: those of Scotland, Wales, and Northern Ireland, as well as England. Indeed, a case could even be made for suggesting that London, with a population almost as large as that of Scotland and Wales combined and devolved powers of its own, represented a fifth demos. Of these five, only two: Wales and England (minus London), voted to leave the EU. This requirement could be conceived as an additional political check and balance necessary in multinational political systems. However, it is not at present one that exists within the UK for non-devolved matters. Rather, power is devolved downwards from Westminster to these authorities for the purpose of managing domestic issues. The UK at present is not formally a federation and even if it has federal-like features, federative powers with regard to the sovereignty of the UK state, such as the ability to contract obligations under international law, remain at Westminster, for which purpose the UK operates as a single nation—much as the EU represents all the member states in those areas where competences have been conferred upon it, notably the negotiation of trade issues within the World Trade Organization (WTO). Nor is this an unusual arrangement—it is true of federations such as the United States and Germany, for example. It reflects the fact that the federal parts ultimately form a unitary state, which in the area of external affairs has to be able to act as a single unit, for example on issues such as defence. The two parts of the UK most likely to leave—Scotland and Northern Ireland—had had respectively referendums on independence (2014) and joining the Republic of Ireland (1973), with the referendum on the Good Friday Agreement (1998) also, in part, a referendum on the conditions under which Northern Ireland might leave the UK and join the Republic—and although Brexit may prompt them to be repeated sooner rather than later, at the time of the EU referendum a reasonable case existed for saying that for these purposes the UK formed a single demos.

With regard to the question posed, unlike the referendum on electoral reform of 2011, the electorate were not asked to accept or reject a specific constitutional proposal, which would then automatically become legislation. Formally speaking, as with the other UK referendums hitherto, it was a consultative referendum and the EU Referendum Act did not include any requirement that the government implement the decision. As such, it was consistent with parliamentary legislative sovereignty. Instead, the question was 'Should the United Kingdom remain a member of the European Union or leave the European Union?' However, this could be seen as a referendum on whether to accept or reject David Cameron's, the then Prime Minister's, renegotiation of the terms of Britain's EU membership. In other words, it offered a check on the prevailing view of the government and in the legislature more generally—and, indeed, was the first—and so far the only time—that view has been rejected in a referendum. The issue then turned to what terms of leaving the EU should follow from that decision, and should the electorate have been consulted via a second referendum on them?

The argument against a repeat referendum tended to take the form that these should be a once in a generation exercise. Adapting a parallel argument to Thomas Jefferson's for a periodical ratification of the terms of the US constitution to ensure they still reflected 'we the people',[76] the argument goes that repeat referendums should only occur once the generation that decided the original referendum no longer form a majority. The reasoning is that with constitutive and constitutional referendums, which concern the basic political and legal framework, there is a need for continuity of a kind associated with the rule of law, whereby individuals can plan ahead. That criterion was met in 2016 with regard to the first EU referendum of 1975, but would require at least a decade for a repeat of the 2016 referendum to be legitimate. However, that objection does not really address two different arguments for a second referendum: one addressing the case for a super-majority in a way more consistent with democratic norms, and that fits with the checks and balances rationale given for them here, the other raised by the need for a ratification of the terms of the withdrawal from the EU.

With regard to the first argument, the case for a second referendum might proceed as follows. In his novel, *The Life and Opinions of Tristram Shandy Gentleman*, Laurence Sterne has Shandy, the novel's narrator, report, misremembering Herodotus on Persian customs, that the ancient Goths of Germany took major decisions twice: first drunk and second sober, with only those drunken resolutions that met with sober approval being acted on.[77] Shandy remarks that his father was much taken with this argument but being teetotal adapted it to involve discussing important domestic matters with his wife on the first Saturday night of the month and then on the following Sunday morning, referring to these two deliberative occasions as his 'beds of justice'.[78] Adapting this argument, it can be maintained that, for the reasons given earlier, decisions involving changing the very rules of the political game deserve to be considered especially carefully. At the same time, such consideration ought to respect democratic norms and allow all views to be fairly weighed and expressed. Balancing passionate frustration with the possible inadequacies of the status quo against reflective consideration of the consequences of changing it, potentially for an even worse arrangement, reflects a well-established deliberative norm of 'hearing the other side' that informs adversarial debate in Parliament and the courts as well as normal elections. Indeed, Sterne's 'two bed' argument has been employed to justify bicameralism, in which the second chamber acts as a scrutiny chamber, and could be equally employed to allow for judicial review.[79]

[76] Thomas Jefferson, Letter to Madison of September 6, 1789, in Thomas Jefferson, *Writings* (M. Petterson ed., New York: Library of America 1984).

[77] Laurence Sterne, *The Life and Opinions of Tristram Shandy Gentleman* (vol. 6, London: T. Becket and P. A. Dehondt 1762) ch. 17.

[78] Jeremy Waldron, *Political Political Theory: Essays on Institutions* (Cambridge, MA: Harvard University Press 2016) 76, 327, n. 29.

[79] Waldron, *Political Political Theory*, 77.

This argument responds to the common criticisms of the first referendum while reflecting general considerations that derive from the reasoning underlying political constitutionalism rather than being ad hoc arguments that reflect one's view of the issue the referendum sought to decide. Unfortunately, the early triggering of article 50 rendered it impossible to hold a second referendum before time ran out. However, arguably doing so for this reason would have been appropriate from a political constitutionalist perspective, and not to do so was a missed opportunity.

The second argument, that a vote should have been held on the specific terms of withdrawal, rather than the general issue of whether to withdraw at all, is more problematic. This moves the decision from a strictly constitutive and constitutional issue to something more like a policy issue, where as we saw referendums prove more problematic. Parliament—arguably like the public as a whole—was divided between (1) remaining in the EU; (2) leaving and staying in the single market (roughly the position of Norway and countries within the European Economic Area (EEA)) or customs union; (3) leaving and not staying in the single market and customs union (a version of which would have been Theresa May's amended Chequers deal or the withdrawal agreement ultimately negotiated by Boris Johnson); and (4) leaving without a deal (and trading according to WTO rules). One solution, proposed by Justine Greening, would have been to offer voters these choices and accept either the plurality winner or, using a Borda or Condorcet count, the most preferred of these options. However, that would still not have necessarily weighed the impact of these options against the full range of other policies of importance to voters. For this purpose, a General Election in which voters have an opportunity to see how these options fit into a programme of government offers a better solution. As it happens, voters were given such a choice, with elections in both 2017 and 2019. The latter election, which the government fought on the slogan 'Get Brexit Done', gave Boris Johnson's Conservative Party a landslide victory, with the party winning 43.6 per cent of the vote—the highest percentage obtained by a party since 1979, and a parliamentary majority of eighty seats. Arguably, therefore, the second argument was met and there can be no doubting that 'getting Brexit done' was the settled preference of the British electorate.

Of course, criticisms continue about the conduct of both the election and referendum campaigns and especially the misinformation and failure to discuss certain key issues, notably Northern Ireland. Yet, these failings are arguably down as much to the failure of the opposition parties as the process itself. After all, the referendum and election were overseen by an independent regulator, the Electoral Commission, which in its report argued that no procedural failures were serious enough to invalidate the result. In other words, while flawed and improvable, the process cannot be regarded as so defective as to justify being annulled. Indeed, recent opinion polls suggest that even with the many problems attendant on leaving the EU already having become apparent, most voters have not changed their minds. Though a re-run of the referendum might now produce a different result, that is largely down to demographic changes whereby older voters have died and been replaced by younger voters unable to vote in the original referendum.

4. CONCLUSION

Disillusionment with the result of the Brexit referendum has led many critics to dispute the democratic or constitutional validity of referendums in general. They are seen as populist instances of popular sovereignty that are at odds with a properly constituted form of democracy.[80] Indeed, though the failings of the referendum have often been attributed to the UK's lacking a legal constitution, the direct appeal to the people has been regarded by many as incompatible with political constitutionalism as well, given that it arguably undermined parliamentary sovereignty. By contrast, this chapter has challenged both the constitutional criticisms of referendums in general and of the Brexit referendum in particular, defending the compatibility of both with the norms of democratic legitimacy at the heart of political constitutionalism.

This book has portrayed political constitutionalism as providing a system of checks and balances for resolving disagreements in a fair manner, which forces citizens and politicians to 'hear the other side'. I have argued that referendums can form a justifiable part of such a system, especially with regard to constitutive and constitutional issues where representatives may act as 'judges in their own cause' and international agreements that raise similar concerns. However, such referendums should remain subject to the sovereignty of Parliament in being regulated by parliamentary legislation and subject to approval by Parliament—a check that also operates against their being used as executive-led plebiscites. Some constitutional theorists have contended that such referendums ought to be restricted to providing a potential negative check on government proposals on such questions.[81] However, a failure to consider reforms may be as legitimate to address as a proposal for reform. Consider how the two main British parties have kept electoral reform off the agenda. An open referendum can be a way of forcing Parliament to deliberate on proposals for constitutional or constitutive reform, and then to put either a consensual proposal or a range of proposals to a second referendum. In this regard, I have suggested that a key failing of the Brexit referendum was not that of raising the constitutive question of leaving the EU, but rather the attempts of both the May and Johnson administrations to avoid adequate parliamentary debate of the withdrawal agreement or to submit it for popular approval. In this respect, they did end up challenging the UK's political constitution.

[80] Weale, *The Will of the People*.

[81] Daly, 'A Republican Defence of the Constitutional Referendum'; Trueblood, 'Brexit and Two Roles for Referendums in the United Kingdom'.

Notwithstanding those failings, I have nevertheless claimed that the 2016 Brexit referendum itself can be viewed as consistent with political constitutionalism and met a reasonable threshold of democratic legitimacy. *Contra* May and Johnson, that did not mean Parliament and the electorate were obliged to accept a 'hard' Brexit as reflecting 'the will' of the British people. Rather, they had an obligation to accept that the plurality of citizens who voted for this result made their case in a fair way that was suitably checked and balanced, and that Parliament was therefore obliged to deliberate how best to effect this change. Meanwhile, those of us who supported Remain should acknowledge the failures of our campaign, which relied less on the positive case for staying in the EU and emphasized instead the negatives of leaving—justified as these concerns may well have been. That weakness was compounded by a failure of those opposed to the 'hard' Brexit proposed by May and particularly Johnson to cooperate to defeat it either in Parliament or the subsequent election. One reason for embedding referendums within representative democracy is to allow representatives to negotiate electorally attractive policy packages capable of obtaining the approval of the electorate. The Remain camp failed to do that—although, unlike the 2022 Chilean referendum, where a similar failure resulted from the large number of independents within the constitutional convention,[82] this failure was less a matter of institutional design than of the politicians themselves.

All of which is to recognize that institutional design cannot—and arguably should not—guarantee those outcomes one thinks best.[83] Indeed, liberals consider that individuals have the right to make mistakes, hoping they—or at least the rest of us—may learn from them. Those of us who consider leaving the EU to be such a mistake, as I do,[84] can continue to try and convince others of their view, campaign for better terms with the EU,[85] and ultimately—in ten years or more, as per the Jeffersonian principle discussed earlier—seek a further referendum on rejoining. This suggestion, however, might be thought to be at odds with what turned out to be a key theme of the referendum: namely, that membership of the EU was itself at odds with the UK's political constitution and that leaving was necessary to 'take back control' and re-establish parliamentary sovereignty. It is to this argument that we now turn.

[82] S. Verdugo, 'The Paradox of Constitution-Making in Democratic Settings. A Tradeoff between Party Renewal and Political Representation?', *International Journal of Constitutional Law Blog* (24 September 2022) <http://www.iconnectblog.com/2022/09/the-paradox-of-constitution-making-in-democratic-settings-a-tradeoff-between-party-renewal-and-political-representation/>; J. Couso, 'Making Sense of Chile's Failed Constituent Process', *International Journal of Constitutional Law Blog* (4 October 2022) <http://www.iconnectblog.com/2022/10/making-sense-of-chiles-failed-constituent-process/>.

[83] Crombrugge, 'Are Referendums Necessarily Populist?', 122–3.

[84] See Richard Bellamy, *A Republican Europe of States: Cosmopolitanism, Intergovernmentalism and Democracy in the EU* (Cambridge: Cambridge University Press 2019) xiii–xv.

[85] Albert Weale, 'The Democratic Duty to Oppose Brexit' (2017) 88 *Political Quarterly* 170–81.

10

Taking Back Control?

The Political Constitution of the European Union

1. INTRODUCTION

The Brexit referendum was won on the slogan 'taking back control'. The resonance of this slogan with British voters could be seen as confirming the longstanding complaint regarding the European Union's (EU) democratic deficit. Yet, shifting democratic authority away from national parliaments to the European Parliament might likewise be seen as a loss of control so far as the various peoples or *demoi* of the member states are concerned. After all, similar reasoning has led national minorities within many of these states to voice demands for a greater devolution of democratic authority and even secession. At the same time, though, in an interconnected world how far democracy can be realized in one country has become increasingly doubtful.

The EU and its member states confront a dilemma, therefore—one that paradoxically the very formation of the EU was in part designed to resolve. On the one hand, interconnectedness renders it necessary for states to form multiple agreements with each other. Only then can their citizens, albeit through their elected governments, have any prospect of exercising some control over their inevitable interactions. The EU simply takes this unavoidable process a step further by forming a more comprehensive set of agreements among its member states. On the other hand, this situation poses multiple questions relating to the most appropriate locus of democracy. For example, can it remain possible for the citizens of these states to remain as in control as before once these agreements are in place? Is the only solution to place the citizens of the various states in direct control of the system of agreements? Yet, if so, how can that occur without these citizens losing control as a self-governing people of a particular state?

This democratic dilemma entails a parallel dilemma for political constitutionalism to that posed by the European Convention of Human Rights (ECHR) and deference to the judgments of the European Court of Human Rights (ECtHR) explored in Chapter 5. As we have seen, political constitutionalism turns on the legal system being subject to the sovereignty of a democratically elected Parliament.

Defending the Political Constitution. Richard Bellamy, Oxford University Press. © Richard Bellamy 2026.
DOI: 10.1093/9780191826986.003.0014

However, both EU-phile[1] and EU-sceptical[2] scholars (and citizens)—the one favourably and the other critically—have considered membership of the EU as involving subjection to the EU Treaties, on the one hand, and EU-level institutions and decision-making processes, on the other. The first are held to form a legal constitution over which the Court of Justice of the European Union (CJEU) has the competence to determine and enforce its applicability with regard to domestic legislation. Meanwhile, the second formulate policy in those areas that have been conferred on the EU by its member states, with national parliaments being required simply to transpose EU legislation into domestic law. Both these developments are held to undermine the constitutional and parliamentary sovereignty of the member states, and as such are incompatible with political constitutionalism. As I remarked in the Introduction, the *Factortame* case has been seen as a key exemplar of this circumstance.[3] In this judgment, the House of Lords held itself bound to disapply an Act of the UK Parliament that the then European Court of Justice (ECJ) had found to be in conflict with the European Community (EC) treaties. They reasoned that when Parliament enacted the European Communities Act, enabling the UK to accede to the Treaty of Admission admitting it to the then EC, it necessarily derogated from its own future sovereignty—at least for as long as it did not repeal that Act, which it retained the competence to do—as was subsequently explicitly acknowledged in article 50 of the Treaty on European Union (TEU).

In what follows, I shall develop the argument made in Chapter 5 and contend that this dilemma can be resolved by seeing the EU as an association of democratic states, in which their agreements reflect the normative requirements of a two-level game.[4] To do so, these agreements must meet the dual conditions of being both mutually negotiated and consented to by their duly elected governments in line with their domestic constitutional arrangements and endorsed by their respective citizens.

This account conforms to the arrangement that Kalypso Nicolaïdis has termed *demoi*-cratic.[5] In other words, it conceives of the EU not as a *demos*-cracy in the making but as a form of co-governance by the different national *demoi* of the member states through which they exercise mutual control. As such, it reflects a more confederal rather than a federal conception of the EU.[6] A federal perspective

[1] e.g. Vernon Bogdanor, 'Brexit Means Britain Needs a Constitution', *Foreign Policy* (8 October 2019) <https://foreignpolicy.com/2019/10/08/brexit-means-britain-needs-a-constitution//>.

[2] e.g. Martin Loughlin, *Against Constitutionalism* (Cambridge, MA: Harvard University Press 2022) 20, 187.

[3] *R. v. Secretary of State for Transport exp. Factortame* [1991] AC 603; [1991] 3 All ER 769; C221/89.

[4] Robert Putnam, 'Diplomacy and Domestic Politics: The Logic of Two-Level Games' (1988) 42 *International Organization* 427–60; Deborah Savage and Albert Weale, 'Political Representation and the Normative Logic of Two-Level Games' (2009) 1 *European Political Science Review* 63–81.

[5] Kalypso Nicolaïdis, 'European *Demoi*cracy and its Crisis' (2013) 51 *Journal of Common Market Studies* 351–69.

[6] As Nick Barber has noted (Nick W. Barber, 'The Two Europes' in Nick W. Barber, M. Cahill, and R. Ekins (eds), *The Rise and Fall of the European Constitution*. (Oxford: Hart Publishing 2019) 89–104), confederal and federal are terms of art, involving descriptive and normative elements. As such,

on the EU characterizes its institutional framework as one in which authority is divided between different levels, in the EU case between the supranational and the member state level, with each level having the final decision on different issues, and with a federal court—the CJEU—adjudicating disputes concerning federalism.[7] By contrast, the confederal perspective questions the first two elements, noting that the supranational level has strong intergovernmental aspects, and is a form of shared authority between the constituent parts.[8] For parallel reasons, explored below, it also disputes the third element of the federal perspective, contending that national constitutional courts and the CJEU likewise share authority as to which competences have been conferred on the EU and on what terms.

Within such a confederal arrangement, the main problem is not that of a democratic deficit at the EU level but of what could be called a *demoi*cratic disconnect[9] between EU decision-making and the various national groupings of citizens at the member state level. Reconnecting the national *demoi* to EU decision-making involves enhancing the role of national parliaments (NPs) rather than that of the European Parliament (EP). This move may lead to a more differentiated process of integration, yet that may be both more equitable and effective than promoting uniformity at the expense of diversity.[10] At the same time, it might be argued that such a model of Europe would be incompatible with, and hence constrained and undercut by, the operation of EU law, and in particular by the Court's claims to primacy and direct effect. This chapter contends this objection can be met by proposing a *demoi*-cratic constitution for the EU. Drawing on constitutional pluralist accounts of the EU, I shall argue that not just accession to (as well as withdrawal from) the EU have to be in conformity with domestic constitutional requirements, but also—as is implied by the principle of the conferral of competences as per articles 4 and 5 TEU—so must the ongoing operations of the EU. As a result, the EU's constitutional arrangements are likewise subject to an ongoing two-level game, which renders the EU consistent with political constitutionalism.[11]

they can be used in a number of confusingly diverse and even conflicting ways by different analysts of the EU. I have defined the two terms in the sentences that follow in ways that are consistent with the distinction between a *demoi*-cratic and a *demos*-cratic vision of the EU.

[7] D. Kelemen, 'The Structure and Dynamics of EU Federalism' (2003) 36(1–2) *Comparative Political Studies* 185.

[8] Nicolaïdis, 'European *Demoi*cracy and its Crisis', 351.

[9] See Peter Lindseth, *Power and Legitimacy: Reconciling Europe and the Nations State* (Oxford: Oxford University Press 2010).

[10] Richard Bellamy and Sandra Kröger, 'Differentiated Integration as a Fair Scheme of Cooperation' (2023) 81(1) *Review of Social Economy* 61–83.

[11] This reasoning reflects that of the German Federal Constitutional Court (GFCC) on Mr Manfred Brunner and others' challenge to the validity of Germany's accession to the Maastricht Treaty (2BvR 2134/92 and 2159/92 JZ 1993. 1100; cf. [1994] I CMLR 57), in which the Court held that—contrary to the reasoning of the ECJ, it retained the competence to decide whether further EU integration remained consistent with the German constitutional order and the continuing sovereignty of the German people. I follow here the argument of Neil MacCormick in 'The Maastricht-Urteil: Sovereignty Now' (1995) 1 *European Law Journal* 259–66.

2. FROM *DEMOS*-CRACY TO *DEMOI*-CRACY

The basic problem outlined above can be formulated in terms of what Dani Rodrik has called 'the fundamental political trilemma of the world economy':[12] namely, the impossibility of simultaneously achieving democracy, national self-determination, and economic globalization—one of these has to give.[13] As he explains, 'If we want to maintain and deepen democracy, we have to choose between the nation state and international economic integration. And if we want to keep the nation state and self-determination, we have to choose between deepening democracy and deepening globalization.'[14]

Given most (if not all) people regard national autarky as a non-starter, and unregulated free global markets unjust as well as likely to be inefficient and prone to failures, many have concluded that the only answer is to give up national self-determination and subsume national democracy and citizenship within some broader scheme for global democracy. Most federally minded Europeans adopt this line of thinking, regarding the development of supranational democracy at the EU level as the first stage in such a process.[15] However, the concern with the EU's democratic deficit enters at this point, with Europhiles joining in an unholy alliance with Eurosceptics to argue that in many core areas decisional authority has passed upwards to Brussels without adequate democratic oversight. By and large, proposals for addressing this alleged deficit have turned on the practicality and justifiability of enhancing the powers of the EP and electing the Commission, be it directly or indirectly, and invariably get linked to arguments for further political integration. Unsurprisingly, the main counter-arguments have mirrored this reasoning. They come from those opposing the justifiability of the integration process on democratic grounds. These critics regard the shift of political authority from national to European political structures as at best diluting the democratic influence of each individual voter, and at worst indefensibly undermining the self-determination of sovereign peoples. This argument suggests that the EU could never be democratically legitimate—indeed, that further empowering the EP or electing the Commission might deepen rather than lessen the democratic deficit.

These latter concerns are further buttressed by the fact that the EU has the promotion of economic globalization broadly hardwired into its constitutional structure.[16] Initially, at least, the integration process was deliberately pursued in non-democratic ways, in part to avoid potential resistance from the different

[12] Dani Rodrik, *The Globalization Paradox: Why Global Markets, States, and Democracy Can't Coexist* (Oxford: Oxford University Press 2011) xviii.

[13] Rodrik, *The Globalization*, xix, 200–5.

[14] Rodrik, *The Globalization*, xix, 200.

[15] Jürgen Habermas, 'Democracy in Europe: Why the Development of EU into a Transnational Democracy Is Necessary and How It Is Possible' (2015) 21 *European Law Journal* 546–57.

[16] Turkuler Isiksel, *Europe's Functional Constitution: A Theory of Constitutionalism Beyond the State* (Oxford: Oxford University Press 2016).

demoi of the member states.[17] Meanwhile, the rights that came to be associated with Union citizenship were largely tied to mobility and the economic opportunities provided by the single market. As a result, they were exercised by less than 5 per cent of the EU population. Of course, the exception is the right to vote for the EP, but the exercise of this right had hitherto steadily fallen since its inception in 1979 and been below 50 per cent since 1999, reaching the low of 42.61 per cent in the 2014 election. In the 2019 election, possibly as a result of Brexit, turnout did go up to 50.66 per cent, with dramatic increases in a number of West European countries, such as Germany. However, Portugal and many Central and Eastern European countries continue to register figures around and often below 30 per cent, while—as has been the case domestically across the EU—the share of the vote of centre left and right parties (the European People's Party and the Party of European Socialists) went down, so that they lost their majority within the EP for the first time (it fell further in the 2024 EP elections). As I note below, the fracturing of the EU grand coalition may offer an opportunity for the positive politicization of EU decision-making. Nevertheless, that is unlikely to be achieved unless mainstream domestic parties are prepared to engage with EU affairs in a more proactive way, rather than simply seeking to counter growing Euro scepticism from left and right. Meanwhile, it remains true that the EP has been a far weaker venue for the exercise of citizen preferences than that offered by EU law to economic enterprises and social groups seeking to challenge directives and regulations that have been negotiated at the national level.[18]

Part of the problem confronting the democratic legitimacy of the EP has been that the transfer of allegiance to the EU has been fairly shallow. Attachment to nationality remains considerably stronger in all member states than attachment to the EU.[19] So long as the EU was associated with the post-war period of peace and prosperity, it has enjoyed 'output' legitimacy and sustained a broad degree of 'banal' identification for the security and economic benefits with which it has been credited.[20] But the euro crisis and the more recent association of the EU in many countries with widespread austerity policies and the reduction of public spending, especially on social welfare, have sorely tested the 'permissive consensus' of European citizens with the integration process. As Brexit indicated, those sceptical of the EU, who account for as much as a third of the electorate in many countries

[17] Jan-Werner Müller, *Contesting Democracy: Political Ideas in Twentieth-Century Europe* (New Haven, CT: Yale University Press 2011) 128, 142.

[18] Isiksel, *Europe's Functional Constitution*, 143.

[19] Special Eurobarometer 508 Values and Identities of EU Citizens, October–November 2020 (2021), 29 and 30. In the Eurobarometer Survey 91.5 of the European Parliament—2019 Post-Electoral Survey: Have European Elections Entered a New Dimension, at 46, only 25% said they voted because they were in favour of the EU and just 12% because they felt they were European or a citizen of the EU.

[20] Kathleen McNamara, *The Politics of Everyday Europe: Constructing Authority in the European Union* (Oxford: Oxford University Press 2015).

across the EU, garnering roughly a sixth of the seats in the EP in 2024, are typically far more vocal and passionate than its supporters tend to be.

Again, many pro-Europeans have seen the obvious response as being the adoption by the EU of more socially integrative policies—such as an EU-wide basic income[21]—that might support a transfer of democratic political authority to the EU level. Yet, such a move begs the question of whether EU citizens desire greater social integration in the first place. To many, such a move would be yet another top down imposition, with a very real risk of further undermining the incomplete, but nevertheless far superior, social welfare systems existing at the national level, along with the democratic systems that facilitated their emergence.[22]

How might we avoid this impasse? As Rodrik notes, an alternative response to the global 'trilemma' involves collaboration between democratic states to collectively regulate globalization in 'smart' ways, as he believed Keynes's design of the Bretton Woods system achieved for the post-war period.[23] From this perspective, the democratic legitimacy of the EU lies in its strengthening and legitimizing the democratic systems of the member states rather than by offering an alternative to them. However, that cannot be achieved by treating the national self-determination of one state in isolation from that of other states—either morally or practically. The democratic decisions of almost all states affect, and are themselves affected by, the democratic decisions of other states, whether they are formally associated within a structure such as the EU or not. To the extent that democratically made decisions of one state undercut those of other states, or reduce the options available to them, while being in their turn partially determined by these other states, all states risk losing democratic legitimacy. Meanwhile, as I noted above, domestic democracy is further diminished by its inability to tackle problems that require cooperation between states, either because these problems are by their nature global in character—such as global warming—or involve transnational activities and processes among multinational organizations, be it financial movements, migration flows, or terrorism. Therefore, a domestic democratic deficit exists from the very fact of democratic states being part of an interconnected world in which autarky no longer offers a plausible or desirable option.[24]

Meeting this challenge requires some regulation of the interactions between states and a mechanism for fostering cooperation among them. To achieve that purpose while still retaining meaningful forms of self-determination for the peoples of these states, we need to reconceive the purpose of supranational bodies.

[21] Philippe Van Parijs and Yannick Vanderborght, *Basic Income: A Radical Proposal for a Free Society and A Sane Economy* (Cambridge, MA: Harvard University Press 2017) 235–41.

[22] Wolfgang Streeck, *Buying Time: The Delayed Crisis of Democratic Capitalism* (London: Verso 2014).

[23] Rodrik, *The Globalization.*

[24] Richard Bellamy, '"An Ever Closer Union Among the People of Europe": Republican Intergovernmentalism and Demoicratic Representation within the EU' (2013) 35 *Journal of European Integration* 499–516.

Instead of being superior and independent sources of democratic authority to their constituent states, we should see them as mechanisms that allow democratic communities to co-exist on mutually agreed and equitable terms. As such, these bodies have to remain subordinate to their constituent members as a delegated authority under their joint and equal control.

As I noted above, this proposal constitutes a '*demoi*-cratic' solution to the democratic legitimacy issue, whereby, in Kalypso Nicolaïdis's felicitous phrase, the peoples of the EU 'govern together but not as one'.[25] On my account, they achieve this result through a form of 'republican intergovernmentalism'.[26] For decision-making to be legitimate in the republican sense it must be non-dominating—that is, the decision cannot be the product of the arbitrary will of the decision-maker, with no need on that agent or agency's part to track the reasons and interests of those subject to the decision.[27] To ensure that is the case and domination avoided, legal and political authority must be subject to the equal influence and control of those subject to it. Republican intergovernmentalism achieves this condition by institutionalizing a practice of reaching agreements among democratic states, in which governments must both act credibly as the democratic representatives of their respective peoples and respect each other as the democratically authorized and accountable representatives of their respective peoples.[28] To do so, governments need both to agree amongst each other on an equal basis at the international level, while at the same time securing the long-term democratic agreement of their citizens. The aim is for international decision making to achieve the dual goal of avoiding governments dominating either the citizens of the state they represent, on the one side, or the citizens of other states with which they interact, on the other side. In so doing, they can simultaneously meet republican criteria for non-domination both internally and externally when making collective agreements to regulate their interactions, including the possibility for citizens to move freely among the states of the association, and to secure justice and common goods at the regional or global level.

3. FROM THE DEMOCRATIC DEFICIT TO THE *DEMOI*-CRATIC DISCONNECT

The problem of democratic legitimacy thereby changes from being one of a democratic deficit at the supranational level to that of a *demoi*cratic disconnect between

[25] Nicolaïdis, 'European *Demoi*cracy', 351.

[26] Bellamy, 'An Ever Closer Union'; Richard Bellamy, *A Republican Europe of States: Cosmopolitanism, Intergovernmentalism and Democracy in the EU* (Cambridge: Cambridge University Press 2019).

[27] Philip Pettit, *Republicanism: A Theory of Freedom and Government* (Oxford: Oxford University Press 1997); Bellamy, *A Republican Europe*, ch. 2.

[28] Philip Pettit, 'A Republican Law of Peoples' (2010) 9 *European Journal of Political Theory* 70–94.

the peoples of the constituent states and the inter- and multi-national decisions their domestic representatives make in their name, including the creation and control of supranational regulatory bodies.[29]

If empowering the EP has provided the standard response to the EU's supposed democratic deficit, then empowering NPs provides the obvious route to overcoming the *demoi*cratic disconnect. As Sandra Kröger and I have argued, the aim of such empowerment is to promote a *demoi*cratic reconnection of the EU through the 'domestication' of EU politics, by relating it to the everyday concerns of citizens, and 'bringing it back home', by placing EU decision-making in a context that is closer to citizens and that they understand.[30] At the same time, EU decision-making needs to be 'normalized'. The current politicization of the EU is mainly along the axis of 'pro-' or 'anti-', 'in' or 'out'. Instead, it needs to be polarized along the 'left' or 'right' and other cleavages—'green', 'feminist', 'multicultural', etc.—which inform domestic politics. Political debate about the EU can thereby be shifted from 'should the EU exist at all?' to a more nuanced 'what is the best way for it to do the useful things it does?' and 'what should those things be?'

Steps in this direction have already been made.[31] The Lisbon Treaty mentioned the NPs as participants in the EU's decision-making for the first time. Since then, the role of NPs in EU affairs has been greatly strengthened. All NPs established European committees to scrutinize EU proposals and the actions of their own representatives in the various European Councils of heads of government or ministers where EU policy is largely made. NPs can also send 'reasoned opinions' highlighting issues to the Commission. Additionally, NPs obtained certain negative powers that allow them to challenge whether an EU measure is truly necessary or not, or might be better undertaken by the member states—the so-called Early Warning Mechanism. This is not an individual veto as at least one third of NPs must raise an objection for the measure to be reconsidered (a 'yellow' card) or 55 per cent for it to be withdrawn (an 'orange' card). Collaboration between NPs is facilitated through COSAC—the French acronym of the Conference of Parliamentary Committees for Union Affairs. There are also two inter-parliamentary committees comprising representatives of all NPs and the EP: one to foster oversight and cooperation in Common Foreign, Defence and Security Policy, and the other to oversee policy relating to the European Fiscal Compact under the article 13 of the Treaty on Stability, Coordination and Governance (TSCG).

[29] Richard Bellamy and Albert Weale, 'Political Legitimacy and European Monetary Union: Contracts, Constitutionalism, and the Normative Logic of Two-Level Games' (2015) 22 *Journal of European Public Policy* 257–74.

[30] Richard Bellamy and Sandra Kröger, 'A Demoicratic Justification of Differentiated Integration in a Heterogenous EU' (2017) 39 *Journal of European Integration* 625–39.

[31] Katrin Auel and Thomas Christiansen, 'After Lisbon: National Parliaments in the European Union' (2015) 38 *West European Politics* 261–81.

These measures have provided an incentive for some national politicians to become more informed about EU affairs and has prompted the EP and Commission to interact more with NPs so as to be alert and responsive to potential opposition. They have also encouraged cooperation and the sharing of information among NPs—not least in Brussels itself, where almost all NPs now have an office and a representative. However, two major problems stand in the way of their further and more positive involvement as mechanisms for the 'normalization' and 'domestication' of European politics.

First, the main centre-left and centre-right parties have felt inhibited about politicizing EU affairs. Part of the reason lies in their belonging to the grand coalition of governmental parties within the EP. As a result, they feel they cannot criticize policies that they have played an indirect role in bringing about. Worse, they fear that to politicize the EU opens up a Pandora's box from which the more EU-sceptical left- and right-wing parties have more to gain than them. As a result, the main EU political debates tend to be between those in favour of the European project and those opposing it, rather than about different policy options that the EU might adopt.

Second, the establishment of the single market and the austerity measures associated with the euro crisis have led citizens to feel that the EU undercuts political debate and constrains policy-making at the national level, creating a domestic democratic deficit. Governments cannot act responsively with regard to their voters. Rather, they must act responsibly and simply implement the public spending cuts demanded by the guardians of the eurozone. Indeed, thanks to the TSCG and the Treaty Establishing the European Stability Mechanism (ESM Treaty), the governance of the euro area operates through a variety of institutions that have evolved outside the European treaties and so involve comparatively little democratic scrutiny by either NPs or the EP.[32] This is particularly true of the central institution of this system of governance, the Eurogroup, a collective term commonly employed for the monthly informal meetings of the finance ministers of the eurozone in combination with the Commissioner for economic and financial affairs, taxation and customs and the President of the European Central Bank (ECB).[33] Moreover, schemes for financial assistance have been conditional on the relevant member states undertaking far-reaching austerity and public spending measures. There have even been moves under the European Semester's Macroeconomic Imbalance Procedure (MIP) for eurozone members more generally to be encouraged to constitutionalize such conditionality practices and be subject to fines for failing to make the requisite structural measures, thereby constraining considerably domestic democratic choice on macroeconomic policy. As a

[32] Stéphanie Hennette, Thomas Piketty, Guillaume Sacriste, and Antoine Vauchez, *How to Democratize Europe* (Cambridge, MA: Harvard University Press 2019) 2–3, 63.

[33] Hennette et al., *How to Democratize*, 1.

result, EU-level decision-making has steadily moved into core social and political areas of the member states, such as social policies, pensions, labour law, and public spending and taxation more generally.[34]

Two proposals have recently emerged that potentially address each of these problems respectively. While I am sympathetic to both, I offer here some variations on each of them geared towards reinforcing their *demoi*cratic credentials. The first proposal is for a 'Green' Card whereby NPs could play a broader role in amending and proposing legislative proposals. Various forms of this proposal were put forward from 2013–15 by the Dutch and Danish NPs and the UK House of Lords, with a 2015 COSAC working group finding support from around half of the EU's parliamentary bodies for some form of legislative input.[35] My own version (developed with Sandra Kröger) puts forward what we call a Parliamentary Legislative Initiative, whereby a third of MPs in a quarter of NPs may make a legislative proposal for the Commission to put forward.[36] This proposal seeks to address the first problem by providing incentives for political debate among all national parties to be about which policies the EU should pursue rather than simply whether it ought to exist at all. It aims to support national parties to develop different positive policies on the EU by facilitating their ability to argue and campaign for them, rather than being reduced to simply accepting or rejecting whatever is put to them. The comparatively low threshold allows opposition party groups the possibility of putting forward proposals, perhaps with the support of certain rebels from the governing party(ies). Otherwise, the danger might be that the Green card would never be used, as governments could be assumed to have already agreed with current EU policy.

The second proposal is that of Hennette, Piketty, Sacriste, and Vauchez for democratizing the eurozone by developing the Interparliamentary Conference on Stability, Economic Coordination and Governance into a Parliamentary Assembly to oversee the European Stability Mechanism (ESM).[37] A number of commentators have argued that the only adequate way to manage the euro and avoid a further crisis is to move towards both a fiscal and a deeper political Union, that effectively turns the EP into a European legislature and the Commission into an elected EU government with tax and spend powers. Hennette et al. raise a number of pragmatic problems with this argument.[38] First, it would involve a major treaty change, which would likely meet with considerable domestic opposition. Second, not all member

[34] Hennette et al., *How to Democratize*, 180.

[35] Cristina Fasone and Diane Fromage, 'From Veto Players to Agenda-Setters? National Parliaments their "Green Card" to the European Commission' (2016) 23 *Maastricht Journal of European and Comparative Law* 294–316, at 303.

[36] For details see Sandra Kröger and Richard Bellamy, 'Beyond a Constraining Dissensus: The Role of National Parliaments in Domesticating and Normalising the Politicization of European Integration' (2016) 14 *Comparative European Politics* 131–53.

[37] See Hennette et al., *How to Democratize*.

[38] Hennette et al., *How to Democratize*, 178–82.

states are in the euro or wish to be so. If the EP was responsible for monitoring the Euro group, that would involve the twenty-eight member states currently belonging to the EU defining the policies for the nineteen states of the euro area. Third, handing such responsibilities to the EP would deprive NPs of their core power to control the supply of funds and spending priorities of elected governments, thereby creating a domestic democratic deficit and rendering the *demoi*cratic disconnect between the national and the EU levels even more problematic.

Their proposal seeks to overcome all three of these difficulties. Rather than revisiting the EU Treaties, they suggest replicating the *modus operandi* of the TSCG and ESM Treaty with a Treaty on the Democratisation of the Governance of the Euro Area (or T-Dem).[39] The new Assembly to oversee the ESM would consist of 400 members, 320 from NPs based on the population of the member state and 80 from the EP. As such, they believe that it empowers NPs in the euro arena without necessarily disempowering the EP. Indeed, they contend that as the new Assembly would operate outside the EU Treaties, the position of the EP within the EU structures remains untouched.

In many respects, the T-Dem proposal adopts the *demoi*cratic logic proposed here.[40] As they note, any positive policies for additional funding and investment need the support of national taxpayers. The reason the EU has turned to austerity policies rests on limited solidarity between states, itself the product of a perceived lack of control. Empowering NPs in this area enables them to take back control. That said, the common policies they hope might be legitimized through such an Assembly could risk imposing inappropriate 'one size fits all' regulations on the highly diverse economies of the EU, in ways likely to benefit the richer more developed states at the expense of the poorer and less developed.[41] The different *demoi* of the member states might also continue to block redistributive policies from one state to another.

Therefore, to avoid these problems, my version of this second proposal seeks to limit its scope by restricting the eurozone to a banking union rather than a fiscal union. It gives such an Assembly of NPs a key role in overseeing an EU banking union but leaves fiscal policy a member state competence. Completing the banking union would allow fiscal policy to be returned to national governments by reducing the danger that fiscal mismanagement in one country could spread to others and potentially upset the banking system. If governments make bad decisions, and over-spend, they would need to restructure their debts rather than receiving a bailout from other states. A genuine European Monetary Fund would replace the ECB and European Commission as lender of last resort, able to ensure

[39] Hennette et al., *How to Democratize*, 65.

[40] See the commentary of Kalypso Nicolaïdis, 'For a Demoicratization of Eurozone Governance', in Hennette et al., *How to Democratize*, 100–8.

[41] Christian Joerges, 'The Economy Is a Polity: Implications for the New Modes of Economic Governance in the EU', in Hennette et al., *How to Democratize*, 122–30, at 127–8.

liquidity, and providing for a European debt-restructuring programme. The fund could be overseen by a Parliamentary Assembly based on the Interparliamentary Conference on Economic and Financial Governance of the European Union that was set up under article 13 of the TSCG. As a result, the process of granting an emergency loan could be given '*demoi*cratic' legitimacy.

4. FROM UNITY TO DIFFERENTIATION

The *demoi*cratic view of the EU naturally allows for differentiated integration within the EU, in much the same way that liberal egalitarian commitments to multinationalism and multiculturalism allow for differentiation within most democratic states,[42] including many of the member states of the EU. Procedurally, that means ministers in the Council should be responsive to their respective NPs. Likewise, parties in the EP should be linked more strongly to their national parties, with NPs gaining a more direct and collaborative role in EU policy-making. Substantively, it allows for a more differentiated system of integration—one in which, on democratic grounds, states may collaborate more or less than other states, depending either on the greater or lesser stake they have in pursuing collective policies at the EU level, or when collective policies infringe domestic constitutional and cultural norms.[43] In the former case, so-called 'capacity' differentiated integration permits a member state to be excluded or exempted from a policy because they could not meet their obligations under it (as has been the case with membership of the eurozone). In the latter case, so-called 'sovereignty' differentiated integration allows a member state to opt out from transferring certain state powers to the EU level, as when Ireland negotiated a protocol to the Maastricht Treaty to avoid being forced to accept abortion and Denmark's protocol to the Maastricht and subsequent Treaties allowing it to decide if and when it would join the euro.[44]

Of course, all states have a moral obligation to participate in those collective policies necessary to secure such basic rights as are to be found in conventions such as the ECHR.[45] Similarly, they have to guard against such clear collective harms as

[42] Will Kymlicka, *Multicultural Citizenship: A Liberal Theory of Minority Rights* (Oxford: Oxford University Press 1995); Will Kymlicka, *Politics in the Vernacular: Nationalism, Multiculturalism and Citizenship* (Oxford: Oxford University Press 2001).

[43] Bellamy and Kröger, 'A Demoicratic Justification'. For a full account of this vision of the EU, see Richard Bellamy, Sandra Kröger, and Marta Lorimer, *Flexible Europe: Fairness, Democracy, and Differentiated Integration* (Bristol: Bristol University Press/Policy Press 2022).

[44] I take the terms 'capacity' and 'sovereignty' differentiated integration from Thomas Winzen, 'From Capacity to Sovereignty: Legislative Politics and Differentiated Integration in the European Union' (2016) 55(1) *European Journal of Political Research* 100–19.

[45] Thomas Christiano, 'Replies to David Álvarez, David Lefkowitz, and Michael Blake' (2017) 4 *Law, Ethics, and Philosophy* 221–36.

global environmental catastrophe and to assist what John Rawls called 'burdened societies'[46]—that is, societies so burdened by extreme poverty, a lack of natural resources, and low human capital that basic rights cannot be secured and they lack the means to order themselves effectively in a democratic manner. Yet, the vast majority of the EU's competences operate beyond the morally obligatory. Here, it is appropriate to seek to protect the variety of capitalisms and related welfare systems of the member states,[47] while allowing cooperation to ensure greater efficiency and equity in their interrelations. As Christian Joerges notes, the chief failing of the response to the eurozone crisis—a product of the EU's *demoi*cratic disconnect—has been to try and impose structural convergence between the southern and northern economies, ignoring that market economies do not operate uniformly not only because of their different institutional configurations but also because of their diverse ideational commitments.[48]

Nevertheless, the EU has the option of moving in a different and less unitary direction.[49] The intergovernmental and developing interparliamentary processes of the EU and the forms of differentiated integration they produce can and should be regarded not as pragmatic compromises but as matters of principle, whereby the EU seeks to achieve equality of concern and respect among the peoples of Europe.[50] After all, the EU prides itself as seeking unity in diversity. If, as liberal intergovernmental scholars have noted, the role of member state governments has been a key factor in moderating the EU's democratic deficit,[51] the role of NPs can mitigate its *demoi*cratic disconnect. Nor need stressing that the EU is a union of national *demoi* rather than a European *demos* in the making undercut the value of EU citizenship. The core right of this status is not voting for the EP but the possibility of free movement between the member states by citizens of these different peoples. This possibility ensures no individual is disadvantaged through having been born in one state rather than another.[52] It gives all citizens an equal opportunity to choose where to live and work without discrimination on the basis of nationality. Yet, at the same time, freedom of movement preserves, and to some degree facilitates, the ability of the different states of Europe to pursue and experiment with different social and economic arrangements.

[46] John Rawls, *The Law of Peoples* (Cambridge, MA: Harvard University Press 1999) 90, 106.

[47] Peter Hall and David Soskice (eds), *Varieties of Capitalism: The Institutional Foundations of Comparative Advantage* (Oxford: Oxford University Press 2001).

[48] Joerges, 'The Economy is a Polity', 127.

[49] Bellamy, 'An Ever Closer Union'.

[50] Bellamy, Kröger, and Lorimer, 'Introduction', in *Flexible Europe*; Bellamy and Kröger, 'Differentiated Integration as a Fair Scheme of Cooperation'.

[51] Andrew Moravcsik, 'The Myth of Europe's "Democratic Deficit"' (2008) *Intereconomics* 331–40.

[52] Richard Bellamy, 'A Duty-Free Europe? What's Wrong with Kochenov's Account of EU Citizenship Rights' (2015) 21 *European Law Journal* 558–65; Bellamy, *A Republican Europe*, ch. 5.

5. THE *DEMOI*CRATIC POLITICAL CONSTITUTION OF THE EU

It will be objected that I have so far ignored the main obstacle to a *demoi*cratic and more differentiated EU: namely, the uniformity of EU law and its primacy and direct effect as interpreted by the most powerful EU institution, the CJEU. The process of integration by law and its close links to the construction of the single market has led to the judicial creation of what has been termed an economic constitution for the EU. Here I explore the extent to which these legal constraints can be rendered compatible with the *demoi*cratic account of the EU given above—and, as a result, with political constitutionalism.

As a number of commentators have noted, the EU's legal structures as often as not exemplify a remarkable degree of constitutional pluralism.[53] Indeed, some claim 'constitutional toleration', whereby the European legal order involves member states and the EU mutually recognizing and accommodating their legal systems in a non-hierarchical manner to each other—to offer the distinctive EU legal model.[54] That claim may be under increasing strain,[55] as its chief advocate acknowledged from the start,[56] but it suggests the possibility of a *demoi*cratic constitutional alternative.[57] In what follows, I shall first defend constitutional pluralism as a plausible and attractive account of a *demoi*cratic EU legal order, and then suggest how it might be rendered compatible with political constitutionalism.

5.1. Constitutional Pluralism and *Demoi*cracy

Constitutional pluralists contend that the conferral of competences upon the EU not only takes place in conformity with the different constitutional processes of the various member states but also remains constrained by them. EU law, therefore, has a plurality of different national sources. Meanwhile, the validity of EU law's claims to primacy 'results from [each] state's amendment of constitutional and sub-constitutional law to the extent required to give direct effect and applicability

[53] Neil MacCormick, 'Beyond the Sovereign State' (1993) 56 *Modern Law Review* 1-18; MacCormick, 'The Maastricht-Urteil: Sovereignty Now'; Klemen Jaklic, *Constitutional Pluralism in the EU* (Oxford: Oxford University Press 2014).

[54] J. H. H. Weiler, 'In Defence of the Status Quo: Europe's Constitutional Sonderweg' in J. H. H. Weiler and M. Wind (eds), *European Constitutionalism Beyond the State* (Cambridge: Cambridge University Press 2003) 7–25, at 20–1.

[55] J. H. H. Weiler, 'In the Face of Crisis: Input Legitimacy, Output Legitimacy and the Political Messianism of European Integration' (2012) 34 *Journal of European Integration* 825–41; Daniel Kelemen, 'On the Unsustainability of Constitutional Pluralism' (2016) 23 *Maastricht Journal of European and Comparative Law* 136–50.

[56] J. H. H. Weiler, *The Constitution of Europe: 'Do the New Clothes Have an Emperor?' and Other Essays on European Integration* (Cambridge: Cambridge University Press 1999) 90–101.

[57] Weiler, *The Constitution of Europe*, 346–7.

to Community law'.[58] EU law may itself constitute a distinct legal system and the CJEU be the highest authority with regard to the interpretation of its norms, as the CJEU insists, but the same holds for the highest courts in each of the member states with regard to their national legal systems, which thereby retain the competence to interpret the validity of EU law in its interaction with domestic law.[59] Consequently, the potential exists for a stand-off, such as has arisen with certain judgments of the German Federal Constitutional Court (GFCC),[60] whereby the CJEU asserts some right or obligation is binding under EU law for a person within a given national jurisdiction, which a national court argues to be either *ultra vires*, going beyond what has been conferred, or invalid, going beyond what is conferrable in terms of the identity of the national constitution. As a result, 'the same human beings and corporations are said to have or not have a certain right'.[61] Indeed, national and EU law are now so intertwined that domestic courts may find themselves having to decide whether to accept the supremacy claims of the CJEU or of the national constitutional court.[62] However, although constitutional pluralism allows for the possibility of such a stand-off, it may never happen in practice. As has occurred so far, the conflicting authorities may reach a compromise or find a way to agree to disagree.

From a *demoi*cratic perspective, constitutional pluralism follows from a reading of article 4 TEU as requiring that respect for the equality of member states before the treaties entails showing equal concern and respect for their 'national identities, inherent in their fundamental structures, political and constitutional, inclusive of regional and local self-government'.[63] As such, it is hardwired into the very structure of the EU and necessitated by the heterogeneity of its member states and their citizens.[64] So conceived, constitutional pluralism adopts the pluralist rationale for constitutionalism within states and applies it to relations between them. Just as pluralism among the persons constituting a *demos* within a state mandates democratic mechanisms that allow for critical opposition by citizens that protect their rights and limit the capacity of governments to act arbitrarily, so pluralism between *demoi* justifies mechanisms fostering opposition by the member states to protect their rights and avoid arbitrary rule by federal agencies, such as the CJEU. Such

[58] Neil MacCormick, *Questioning Sovereignty* (Oxford: Oxford University Press 1999) 117.

[59] MacCormick, *Questioning Sovereignty*, 118.

[60] e.g. BVerfGE 37, 271 [1974] CMLR 540 (Solange I); *Brunner v. The European Treaty* [1994] CMLR 57 (Maastricht Judgment); 2 BvR 2/08, 30 June 2009 (Lisbon Judgment); 2 BvR 1390/12, 12 September 2012 (ESM Treaty).

[61] MacCormick, *Questioning Sovereignty*, 119.

[62] Nick W. Barber, *The Constitutional State* (Oxford: Oxford University Press 2010) 166–7.

[63] It might be objected that this article could be read as not requiring treating equally the national identities and domestic political and legal structures of the member state, but merely respecting them. However, I contend the reading given here is more plausible and reflected in both article 5, on conferral, and article 50, on withdrawal, and consistent with the view of the GFCC, e.g. in its 2009 Lisbon Judgment BVerfG, 2 be 2/08.

[64] Bellamy, *A Republican Europe of States*, 6–7.

an arrangement produces what Miguel Maduro has termed a 'counter-punctual' system of political and judicial decision-making,[65] analogous to domestic mechanisms such as the checks and balances provided by scrutiny by a second chamber, competition from opposition parties, and some form of judicial review. Such a system obliges member states and the EU to hear and harken to each of the others in ways that reflect equal concern and mutual respect.

Arguably, the very introduction of fundamental rights protection into Community law is owed to this process,[66] whereby identity review by the German and Italian constitutional courts in particular led the then ECJ to acknowledge that 'measures which are incompatible with the fundamental rights recognized by the constitutions of [the member states] are unacceptable in the Community'.[67] As Dieter Grimm has noted,[68] integration through law via the competence-stretching judicial decisions of the CJEU has proved a mixed blessing. While it may have filled a political void at times, it has also often tied the EU into policies that are not only inefficient and unfit for purpose, but also lack democratic legitimacy and become a focus for Euroscepticism. In forcing the EU to confront both the efficacy and legitimacy of EU policies, the possibility of a 'counter-punctual' check by a national court can be regarded as both desirable and necessary in a plural and *demoi*cratic constitutional system.

Notwithstanding these potential advantages, the constitutional pluralist understanding of the EU's legal order has given rise to two main criticisms. The first criticism is that this reasoning could be abused to give a spurious legitimacy to attempts by democratic backsliding member states either to request opt-outs from the democratic values enumerated in article 2 TEU, on the grounds that they conflict with the national political and constitutional traditions defended in article 4 TEU, or to challenge EU action against backsliding as *ultra vires*.[69] For example, this worry seemed to be confirmed by the way the then Polish government in 2020 appealed to such arguments in the wake of the *Weiss* judgment of the GFCC. The *Weiss* judgment had deemed the CJEU's ruling on Decision 2015/774 of the ECB as 'arbitrary' and hence lacking the 'minimum of democratic legitimation' necessary under article 23(1) of the German Basic Law (2 BvR 859/15, [2]).[70] This decision

[65] Miguel Maduro, 'Europe and the Constitution: What if this is as Good as it Gets?' in J. H. H. Weiler and M. Wind (eds), *European Constitutionalism beyond the State* (Cambridge: Cambridge University Press 2003) 98–100.

[66] Maduro, 'Europe and the Constitution', 99.

[67] *Hauer* Recital 15, discussed in Weiler, *The Constitution of Europe*, 108–16.

[68] Dieter Grimm, *Constitutionalism: Past, Present, Future* (Oxford: Oxford University Press 2016) ch. 14.

[69] e.g. Daniel Kelemen, 'On the Unsustainability of Constitutional Pluralism: European Supremacy and the Survival of the Eurozone' (2016) 23(1) *Maastricht Journal of European and Comparative Law* 136–50; and his 'Is Differentiation Possible in Rule of Law?' (2019) 17(2) *Comparative European Politics* 246–60.

[70] This case concerned the ECB's Public Sector Purchase Programme (PSPP) programme. The GFCC questioned the compatibility of the PSPP Decisions with the Treaty's prohibition on monetary finance and the principle of conferred powers, and judged the CJEU's ruling on its legality to be

was immediately seized upon by the then Polish government in its legal battle with the Commission and the CJEU over its judicial reforms, with the Ministry of Justice arguing that it vindicated a recent argument of the Polish Constitutional Court disputing claims regarding the superiority of EU over national law in such a domestic matter.[71] This statement prompted thirty-two leading scholars of law and politics to sign a statement asserting that 'national courts cannot override CJEU judgments'.[72] However, to invoke constitutional pluralist arguments is one thing, to be justified in doing so in the matter at hand quite another.[73] Arguments that are sound in themselves ought not to be excluded out of fear that they might be abused. Rather, the issue is whether their use in a given case is consistent with the reasons that underlie and validate constitutional pluralism, and hence legitimate. Its undiplomatic language notwithstanding, the German Court's *Weiss* judgment could be regarded as a justified 'counter-punctual' check that forced the EU to confront both the efficacy and legitimacy of the ECB's mandate and the rules of the economic and monetary union (EMU).[74] By contrast, the Polish government's extrapolation from that ruling to defend its court packing can be viewed as antithetical to the underlying rationale of constitutional pluralism.

Why is that? Constitutional pluralism not only guards against over-reach by EU institutions, but also serves to tame the exclusive and self-interested nationalism of the member states.[75] For, the counter-punctual process described above forces national courts to engage with each other and the CJEU in the development of a system of EU law that entails mutual recognition of their plural orders.[76] However, to operate in this way all the member states must themselves be constitutional democracies and recognize pluralism. The intrinsic and instrumental qualities of democracy required for the equitable and effective functioning of an association of

arbitrary due to a lack of reasoning in its proportionality assessment and the poor standard of review employed. As a result, the CJEU's judgment (C-493/17, *Weiss and Others*), and Decisions of the ECB were deemed *ultra vires* and not applicable in Germany (BVerfG, Judgment of the Second Senate of 5 May 2020 – 2 BvR 859/15).

71 See the Polish Ministry of Justice's statement that *The Judgement of the German Constitutional Court Confirms Poland's Position in the Dispute with the European Commission*. Press Release (12 May 2020) <https://www.gov.pl/web/justice/the-judgement-of-the-german-constitutional-court-confirms-polands-position-in-the-dispute-with-the-european-commission>.

72 Daniel Kelemen, Piet Eeckhout, Federico Fabbrini, Laurent Pech, and Renáta Uitz, 'National Courts Cannot Override CJEU Judgments: A Joint Statement in Defense of the EU Legal Order', VerfBlog (26 May 2020) <https://verfassungsblog.de/national-courts-cannot-override-cjeu-judgments/> DOI: 10.17176/20200527-013240-0.

73 Marcin Baranski, F. B. Bastos, and M. van den Brink, 'Unquestioned Supremacy Still Begs the Question', VerfBlog (29 May 2020) <https://verfassungsblog.de/unquestioned-supremacy-stillbegs-the-question/>.

74 See Ana Bobić and Mark Dawson, 'What Did the German Constitutional Court Get Right in Weiss II?', Op Ed *EU Law Live* (12 May 2020) <https://eulawlive.com/op-ed-what-did-the-german-constitutional-court-get-right-in-weiss-ii-by-ana-bobic-and-mark-dawson/>.

75 Weiler, *The Constitution of Europe*, 341.

76 Weiler, 'In Defence of the Status Quo', 18–22.

states, such as the EU, depends on its member states possessing democratic qualities. Only democratic states can credibly represent their citizens and be counted on to honour their contracts, and so engage in what article 4.3 TEU terms 'sincere cooperation' with other member states on the basis of 'mutual respect'.[77] Therefore, no basis exists for identity or *ultra vires* objections to EU actions in order to defend democratic backsliding, such as those invoked by the Polish Ministry of Justice, since these arguments involve a rejection of pluralism and mutual recognition both internally and externally. Internally, they are designed to protect measures that curtail pluralism and democratic debate and opposition. Externally, far from being part of a 'counter-punctual' move aimed at improving the democratic quality and efficacy of EU decision-making, they are likewise purely self-serving measures on the part of the governments and their judicial appointees proposing them.[78]

The second criticism enters here. Critics contend constitutional pluralism potentially subverts the uniformity and coherence of EU law, which they regard as necessary qualities for its equitable and effective implementation in a manner that treats all EU citizens fairly.[79] They contend these desirable qualities require that the CJEU act as a final and supreme legal authority. They also worry about what happens in the event of either a stand-off, where no party gives way, or, as with democratic backsliding, when the pluralist rules of the game are abused. It should be noted that constitutional pluralism only leads to a stand-off and incompatibility if neither side blinks. Meanwhile, inconsistent laws need not produce inconsistent action.[80] Each side can exercise restraint and either leave the constitutional dilemma unresolved or seek an 'incompletely theorised' compromise,[81] of a kind that often informs majority judgments within multimember apex constitutional courts.[82] As I remarked above, such tacit agreements to disagree form the norm, with derogation the exception, and the feared Mutually Assured Destruction (MAD) so far avoided.[83] Therefore, constitutional pluralism need not give rise to a lack of uniformity in the application of equal rules. Rather, it has been hitherto a way whereby those rules are reciprocally negotiated so as to be implemented in a mutually acceptable way.

Note that such negotiations may be required to allow for differentiated integration because uniform rules would not be equitable. Again, the legitimate driver of

[77] John Rawls, *The Law of Peoples* (Cambridge, MA: Harvard University Press 1999) 16 fn 8, 18–19.

[78] For a description of how democratic backsliding is anti-pluralist and undermines the basic elements of a democratic system, see Richard Bellamy and Sandra Kröger, 'Countering Democratic Backsliding by EU Member States: Constitutional Pluralism and "Value" Differentiated Integration' (2021) 27(3) *Swiss Political Science Review* 622–4.

[79] Kelemen, 'On the Unsustainability of Constitutional Pluralism'.

[80] Barber, *The Constitutional State*, 169–70.

[81] C. Richmond, 'Preserving the Identity Crisis: Autonomy, System and Sovereignty in European Law' (1997) 16(4) *Law and Philosophy* 417; Maduro, 'Europe and the Constitution', 98–9.

[82] Cass Sunstein, *Legal Reasoning and Political Conflict* (Oxford: Oxford University Press 1996) 39–44.

[83] Weiler, *The Constitution of Europe*, 320–1.

such demands stems from pluralism: economic heterogeneity in the case of 'capacity' differentiated integration, and political or cultural heterogeneity in the case 'sovereignty' differentiated integration.[84] From a *demoi*cratic perspective, such arguments for differentiated integration relate respectively to the lack of an equal stake in a given common policy, on the one hand, or claims of cultural difference, on the other.[85] Both these arguments are grounded in equality, whereby like cases are treated alike but relevantly unalike cases are treated differently.[86] As in the case of developing countries seeking 'special and differential treatment' in World Trade Organization (WTO) negotiations[87] or minority groups claiming rights to special treatment within states,[88] to be treated with equal concern and respect may require being treated in distinct and different ways.

The first criticism reappears here, for the fear might persist that such claims to differential treatment may be made in bad faith by a court or state that does not act reciprocally or breaches the very rules and values of the constitutional pluralist process. Does that make constitutional pluralism a 'fair weather' argument?[89] Would it not be necessary in such circumstances for an apex court or political body, such as the European Council in the case of article 7, to be granted the competence to decide the issue? And would that not go against the very idea of constitutional pluralism, revealing a logical incoherence at the heart of the *demoi*cratic account? These critics argue that only the CJEU can have the competence to judge not just compliance with EU law, but also where and when it applies, and hence must have competence over its own competence. Yet, as constitutional pluralists remark, such disputes cannot be resolved by appealing to a higher authority because the dispute turns on the question of supremacy and the fact that *all* the courts involved claim competence over their own competence.[90] Having the CJEU rule on *ultra vires* decisions empowers one of the parties to the dispute. Moreover, the one attempt so far to legitimize such a claim to competence-competence, the attempted constitutional Treaty, failed.[91] The federal solution, therefore, would lack legitimacy, and as such would be liable to exacerbate the problem rather than providing a solution.[92]

Does that make a stand-off between the CJEU and a national court irresolvable, other than by a potentially MAD act risking mutual disintegration? Even with regard to democratic backsliding, the grounds for CJEU competence are potentially

[84] Bellamy and Kröger, 'A Demoicratic Justification', 628–30.
[85] Bellamy and Kröger, 'A Demoicratic Justification', 630–3.
[86] Ronald Dworkin, *Taking Rights Seriously* (2nd edn, London: Duckworth 1978) 227.
[87] See James Christensen, 'Fair Trade, Formal Equality, and Preferential Treatment' (2015) 41 *Social Theory and Practice* 505–26.
[88] See Will Kymlicka, *Multicultural Citizenship: A Liberal Theory of Minority Rights* (Oxford: Oxford University Press 1995).
[89] Kelemen, 'Is Differentiation Possible in Rule of Law?', 254.
[90] Barber, *The Constitutional State*, 167–9.
[91] Weiler, 'In Defence of the Status Quo', 8; Neil Walker, 'Constitutional Pluralism Revisited' (2016) 22(3) *European Law Journal* 333–55.
[92] Grimm, *Constitutionalism*, 300–3.

contentious. Identity and *ultra vires* defences of democratic backsliding may be spurious, but the CJEU's competence-competence to adjudicate on such challenges remains questionable—the concern continues that it will be judge in its own cause. Meanwhile, even if this issue could be resolved, the Treaties are vague or silent on both the institutional mechanisms required to secure the rather broadly defined values in article 2 TEU and the Charter of Fundamental Rights of the European Union, and the basis on which their absence might be litigated. Indeed, to act, the CJEU has had to 'read in' the implication that all member states have an independent judiciary into their legal obligation 'to provide remedies sufficient to ensure effective legal protection in the fields covered by Union law' in article 19(1) TEU and for the proper working of the preliminary ruling mechanism under article 267, or find grounds under the infringement proceedings (arts 258–260 of the Treaty on the Functioning of the European Union (TFEU)).[93] Yet, an extensive use of such weakly based judicial rulings, such as some advocate,[94] risk being treated as lacking either legitimate authority or an adequate basis in EU law, and might even help boost support for the elected governments against which they are used,[95] a point conceded even by some federalists advocating legal sanctions.[96]

These potential legitimacy problems suggest a different approach may be warranted. As I have argued elsewhere,[97] to be legitimate EU action against a backsliding member state must fulfil four criteria that align with the account of a *demoi*cratic constitutional pluralism developed above. First, action must avoid inviting the charge of being an *arbitrary* imposition, which fails to consult the views and interests of the member states and their citizens, or to be accountable to them. Consequently, the European Commission and the CJEU should not be the organs that advise on whether EU action is in order. Rather, the process should gain authority from a body that can credibly represent the pluralism of the member states and be ultimately accountable to the Council. It should also involve actors from civil society and the opposition within the targeted member states. Second, the identification of any democratic failings needs to be undertaken in an *impartial* manner, which applies equally and consistently to all member states.[98] To meet this

[93] For details see European Commission, *Further Strengthening the Rule of Law within the Union*. COM(2019) 163 final, 4.

[94] Armin Von Bogdandy and L. D. Spieker, 'Countering the Judicial Silencing of Critics: Article 2 TEU Values, Reverse Solange, and the Responsibilities of National Judges' (2019) 15(3) *European Constitutional Law Review* 393–405.

[95] B. Schlipphak and O. Treib, 'Playing the Blame Game on Brussels: The Domestic Political Effects of EU Interventions Against Democratic Backsliding' (2017) 24(3) *Journal of European Public Policy* 362.

[96] M. Blauberger and R. D. Kelemen, 'Can Courts Rescue National Democracy? Judicial Safeguards against Democratic Backsliding in the EU' (2017) 24(3) *Journal of European Public Policy* 321–36.

[97] Bellamy and Kröger, 'Countering Democratic Backsliding by EU Member States', 629–32.

[98] Tom Theuns, 'Containing Populism at the Cost of Democracy? Political vs. Economic Responses to Democratic Backsliding in the EU' (2020) 12(2) *Global Justice: Theory Practice Rhetoric*, 151–2 <https://doi.org/10.21248/gjn.12.02.220>.

condition, the monitoring should come from an independent body.[99] Third, sanctions must be *proportionate* to the degree of backsliding and operate according to a pre-determined scale. Fourth, sanctions should *target the government* rather than the entire population.[100]

These criteria provide a political constitutional rather than a strictly legal constitutional response to democratic backsliding. They allow EU action to avoid appearing to be self-authorized—an exercise of 'competence-competence', whereby supranational institutions define on their own account the content of EU democratic norms, when they are contravened, and what penalties should follow. Instead, these institutions can act in ways that appeal to the joint authority of the *demoi* of both the other member states and, to a degree, even the backsliding state. Meanwhile, the *demoi*cratic and confederal arrangements advocated here have the more general benefit of not putting all of our democratic eggs into one basket. If we had a federal EU, what if the EU went populist? In the constitutional pluralist model proposed here, democratic sicknesses at the core need not contaminate the member states, which will retain sufficient legal and political sovereignty to resist them.[101]

5.2. Towards a *Demoi*cratic Political Constitution

As I have noted, the Lisbon Treaty incorporates two important elements for the *demoi*cratic constitution of the EU. First, article 4(2) TEU commits the EU to showing equal respect to the national constitutional identities of the member states, albeit subject to upholding the democratic values outlined in articles 2 and 6 TEU, with the possibility of suspending certain rights of membership under article 7 TEU of those states that fail to do so. Second, articles 10 and 12 TEU gave a role to NPs as part of the EU decision-making process.

The GFCC's *Lisbon*, *OMT*, and *Weiss* judgments testify to a continued willingness by national constitutional courts to push back against incursions by EU law on national understandings of constitutional essentials. So have similar references by the Spanish and Italian courts in *Melloni* and *Taricco*, concerning the European Arrest Warrant and the right to a fair trial under the Spanish constitution and EU VAT law and the nature of legality in Italian constitutional law respectively. Such

99 Schlipphak and Treib, 'Playing the Blame Game on Brussels', 361–2; M. Blauberger and V. van Hüllen, 'Conditionality of EU Funds: An Instrument to Enforce EU Fundamental Values?' (2020) 43(1) *Journal of European Integration* 9–10, 11–12.

100 Blauberger and van Hüllen, 'Conditionality of EU Funds', 6–7.

101 As R. Kaufman, D. Kelemen, and B. Kolcak, 'Federalism and Democratic Backsliding in Comparative Perspective' (2025) 23(1) *Perspectives on Politics* 15–34 note, such resistance is only likely to the extent federal units retain sufficient control over core governmental functions.

moves suggest that the picture of a steady erosion of national constitutional provisions can be exaggerated.

The German Court's *OMT* ruling had turned on its interpretation of article 38(1) of the German Basic Law as requiring that state authority could not be transferred to an extent which it makes democratic control nugatory, and that Germany's obligations under outright monetary transactions could not be such as to undermine the Bundestag's budgetary oversight.[102] That judgment has served to reinforce the role of NPs in other member states. Although the preparedness and capacity of NPs to take on their new functions varies between member states, I suggested above that the possibility for them being the agents of a *demoi*cratic reconnection to EU policy-making existed.

However, these steps of themselves are insufficient. On the one side, they may not suffice to challenge the incremental constitutionalization of the Treaties by the CJEU and the resulting process of ever more negative integration through law. On the other side, there remains the problem of the cumbersome and often dysfunctional character of the Community method as a mode of EU policy-making. Fritz Scharpf has offered two related sets of suggestions that might address each of these issues to some degree.

The first set of suggestions explores the possibility of a political override of CJEU decisions by the European Council.[103] Although constitutional pluralists regard the validity of EU law as ultimately resting on domestic sources of law as interpreted by national constitutional courts, I have noted how that raises the worry of a potential clash between national courts and the CJEU, should the former consider the latter to have overreached its competence—a challenge the CJEU has viewed as per se illegitimate given its own claim to Kompetenz-Kompetenz. In fact, as I remarked above, both sides have carefully steered clear of such a clash, fearing it represents a nuclear option.[104] Yet, in the long term, such avoidance strategies ultimately play into the hands of the CJEU as it increases the sway of European law by a kind of ratchet effect.

Scharpf suggests that a super-majority decision in the Council offers an appropriate mechanism for addressing such situations—and indeed, it would make them possible by offering a *demoi*cratically legitimate mechanism for resolving them.[105] In essence, this mechanism would reduce the role of the CJEU to that of 'weak review'. It would remove judicial supremacy by making clear that elected governments are the Masters of the Treaties. In line with the norms of 'republican intergovernmentalism', a democratic government disputing a CJEU ruling would

[102] Bellamy and Weale, 'Political Legitimacy', 246–65; Dieter Grimm, *The Constitution of European Democracy* (Oxford: Oxford University Press 2017) 170–1.

[103] Fritz Scharpf, 'Legitimacy in the Multilevel European Polity' (2009) 1 *European Political Science Review* 173–204, at 199–200.

[104] Weiler, *The Constitution of Europe*, 320–1.

[105] Scharpf, 'Legitimacy', 199–200.

be submitting to the judgment of its peers among other member states and asking to be treated with equal concern and respect. On the one hand, other democratic governments can be expected to be appreciative of the need to attune decisions to different domestic contexts and in particular the economic and cultural forms of heterogeneity that motivate differential integration. They will also understand the adverse reaction a CJEU decision perceived as insensitive to such considerations and in error might arouse. On the other hand, that need not mean they would tolerate almost any objection to a ruling that proved inconvenient for the government concerned—quite the contrary. For they would also be fully alive to the dangers of allowing states to renege on their solidaristic obligations and of undermining the Court's authority through frivolous or self-serving challenges. A parallel move for undoing the constitutionalization of the Treaties by the Court would involve (1) only permitting litigation and infringement proceedings based on regulations and directives adopted under articles 289–291 TFEU,[106] and (2) allowing the proposed legislative proposals from NPs and the Council to involve partial or total abandonment of parts of the *acquis* for some or all states, subject to the approval of a qualified majority in the Council and a majority in the EP.[107] This last measure would enable the removal of aspects of the *acquis* that no longer command political support, not least because they have outlived their usefulness.

This last proposal links up with the second set of suggestions.[108] If differentiated integration became normalized rather than exceptional as part of a *demoi*cratic EU, not least by allowing challenges to the CJEU and opt-outs from the *acquis*, then majority rule also becomes more legitimate. Indeed, there is a certain symmetry between the two. In areas where majority or qualified majority rule prevails, there should be the possibility for member states to opt out of ordinary legislation. To guard against that occurring in areas where either free-riding or negative externalities might arise, it should be possible to block such requests by qualified majority in the Council and an absolute majority in the EP. Meanwhile, the Community Method and consensus would prevail with regard to treaty-making.

These suggestions aim to facilitate effective and equitable decision-making that remains consistent with the norms and practices of democratic legitimacy. Given the heterogeneity of the EU, that cannot be achieved by simply scaling up democracy to the EU level. However, it can be achieved if the EU adopts a *demoi*cratic constitution that allows for mutually agreed variable geometry among its constituent members. Moreover, it would be wrong to regard such a Union as a pragmatic rag bag, consisting of 'ins' and 'outs'. Rather, it reflects a principled conception of an international community of democratic states based on equal concern and respect.

[106] Fritz Scharpf, 'De-constitutionalisation and Majority Rule: A Democratic Vision for Europe' (2017) 23 *European Law Journal* 315–34.

[107] Fritz Scharpf, 'After the Crash: A Perspective on Multilevel European Democracy' (2015) 21 *European Law Journal* 384–405, at 403.

[108] Scharpf, 'Legitimacy', 400–4; Scharpf, 'De-constitutionalisation', 330–2.

In particular, it allows a shift from free trade to fair trade, not least in distinguishing anti-protectionism at the borders from de-regulation within borders. The first has been broadly beneficial in improving efficiency by allowing countries to play to their comparative advantage. However, the second has led to disembedding markets from the social and political structures that have been democratically negotiated at the state level to maintain production and labour standards and offer social support and training to the potential losers of freer trade.[109] It has been pushed for and exploited by those multinational corporate interests able to benefit from such changes, but has served to enhance the gap between the winners and losers by eroding social protection in the name of market liberalization.[110] Allowing differentiated integration restores a degree of national regulatory autonomy that provides incentives for the EU itself to adopt countervailing measures, such as protection of labour standards and the coordination of corporate tax levels, that can increase domestic political buy-in to a scheme of free trade by balancing its benefits against its inegalitarian redistributive effects and the capacity of states to mitigate them.

6. CONCLUSION

Against the Eurosceptic proponents of Brexit, I have argued we can only exercise control through bodies such as the EU; against some Europhile proponents of political union, I have suggested we achieve control through collaboration among European democracies, not by creating a EU-level democracy. Both the Eurosceptic and the federal Europhile alternatives involve losing control. By leaving the EU, the British government and those who voted for this proposal have committed a moral and political as well as an economic wrong against themselves and others. They have placed themselves in a situation where they will inevitably be controlled and dominated by other states and organizations and can only respond by seeking, largely vainly, to control and dominate them in turn. In terms of Rodrik's trilemma, they have delivered a formal façade of national sovereignty, symbolized by certain immigration controls against the poor and powerless that disregard their moral obligations to assist those in dire need, combined with a total openness to global economic processes over which they will have little or no democratic control. By contrast, attempts to turn the EU into a *demos*-cracy imperil the cultural and socio-economic heterogeneity of the member states. Yet such

[109] J. G. Ruggie, 'International Regimes, Transactions and Change: Embedded Liberalism in the Postwar Economic Order (1982) 36 *International Organisation* 379–415, at 382–3; R. Gilpin, *The Political Economy of International Relations* (Princeton, NJ: Princeton University Press 1987) 355.

[110] Isiksel, *Europe's Functional Constitution*, 173–9; Fritz Scharpf, 'The Asymmetry of European Integration or Why the EU Cannot Be a Social Market Economy' (2010) 8 *Socio-Economic Review* 211–50.

pluralism deserves protection not for purely pragmatic reasons but for normative reasons—it allows for what J. S. Mill called 'experiments in living' and a variety of valuable modes of social life.[111] The *demoi*cratic view conceives the EU as providing a mechanism for enabling the different political and socio-economic cultures of the member states to co-exist on terms of mutual recognition and respect. It achieves that result by regarding the EU as the product of an ongoing form of republican intergovernmental political constitutionalism both within and between states. The EU becomes in this way a means for them retaining rather than losing control.

[111] John Stuart Mill, *On Liberty* (J. M. Robson ed., Toronto: University of Toronto Press 1977) 261.

Conclusion

Whither the Political Constitution?

This book has offered a defence of the normative justification and attractiveness of a democratic political constitution, on the one hand, and of its practical plausibility and advantages, on the other. In both cases, the comparison has been with a liberal form of legal constitutionalism allowing for 'strong form' judicial review, which can strike down both duly made democratic legislation and the executive acts of elected politicians; with this review being undertaken by a constitutional or supreme court with reference to a codified and entrenched constitution that operates as higher law. The book's central claim has been that a democratic political constitutionalism proves more legitimate and more effective than a liberal legal constitution in achieving two core constitutional tasks: first, that of curbing the arbitrary rule of those empowered to govern; and second, that of providing a process of governing that treats the governed with equal concern and respect. These tasks are best achieved via democratic processes that promote the equal advancement of the interests of all citizens by treating them as having equal status and worth in the making of collective decisions. I associate these attributes with a democratic system that institutionalizes a condition of non-domination among citizens, on the one hand, and between them and their elected representatives, on the other. So conceived, democracy can be regarded as possessing constitutional qualities in and of itself, without needing to be defined in, or circumscribed by, a liberal legal constitution. Rather, it gives rise to a detailed if flexible legal constitution that promotes the equality of citizens.[1] From this perspective, a constitutional democracy is a tautology, since a well-functioning democracy will be intrinsically constitutional and constitutive.[2]

[1] I take the distinction between 'entrenched and spare' or more abstract constitutions, on the one hand, and 'flexible and specific' or more detailed constitutions, on the other, from Mila Versteeg and Emily Zackin, 'Constitutions Unentrenched: Toward an Alternative Theory of Constitutional Design' (2016) 110(4) *American Political Science Review* 657–74. As they note (at 659), what Stephen Gardbaum calls *The New Commonwealth Model of Constitutionalism: Theory and Practice* (Cambridge: Cambridge University Press 2013), a model that includes the UK and resembles the form of political constitutionalism defended here, is an example of such a 'flexible and specific' legal constitution. Their analysis is empirical rather than normative. However, they observe that such flexible constitutions tend to predominate over entrenched constitutions, and derive their legitimacy from democratic demands to reduce the discretion of executives and especially the judiciary in the application of the law—not least through the inclusion of explicit commitments to certain redistributive measures.

[2] Richard Bellamy and Dario Castiglione, 'Constitutionalism and Democracy: Political Theory and the American Constitution' (1997) 27 *British Journal of Political Science* 595–618; Richard

An important subordinate claim of the book is that a legal constitution, as well as the legal system more generally, will only prove as normatively appealing and practically effective as the associated political constitution. After all, as I noted in Chapter 2, even authoritarian systems can have practically workable—if normatively despicable—legal constitutions. Though the role of ensuring individuals are treated with equal concern and respect and their basic rights upheld is often attributed to an entrenched legal constitution of a liberal character, in practice that function habitually falls to a political constitution of a democratic kind within which such a legal system is invariably embedded. Indeed, entrenched liberal legal constitutions may often not even mention key features of the political constitution that have developed after its enactment and that prove crucial to performing the two core constitutional tasks mentioned above. For example, the US constitution, like those of many other democracies, contains no mention of political parties or the electoral system.[3] However, such features are typically spelt out in detail in legislation such as the UK's Political Parties, Elections and Referendums Act 2000 issuing from the processes of a political constitution, and that form part of a derivative, and more democratically legitimate, legal constitution.

Part 1, consisting of the first three chapters, provided a defence of the normative aspect of political constitutionalism. A codified, entrenched, and judicially protected legal constitution of a liberal hue is typically viewed as providing a list of fundamental rights that governments and legislatures can be held to respect; the basis for the rule of law by serving itself as a higher law to which all the organs of government are subordinate; and a counter-majoritarian brake on the potentially tyrannous decisions of a popularly elected executive or legislature that deploys its majority support to ignore or suppress the interests of minorities.[4] Chapters 1, 2, and 3 disputed respectively the way liberal legal constitutionalists conceive of each of these points, and offered a political constitutionalist alternative that considers rights, the rule of law, and the avoidance of majority tyranny in democratic terms.

Chapter 1 defended democratic participation as the right of rights. I contended that there are reasonable disagreements about constitutional essentials, including the various dimensions of rights. We disagree about the sources of rights, that is, their philosophical foundations; the subjects of rights, or who possesses them, where, and when; their status with regard to other values, such as utility; their

Bellamy, *Political Constitutionalism: A Republican Defence of the Constitutionality of Democracy* (Cambridge: Cambridge University Press 2007) ch. 3.

[3] Anthony King, *The British Constitution* (Oxford: Oxford University Press 2009) 7; Richard Bellamy and Jeff King, 'Introduction: Of Constitutions and Constitutional Theory' in Richard Bellamy and Jeff King (eds) *The Cambridge Handbook of Constitutional Theory* (Cambridge: Cambridge University Press 2025) 7, 14.

[4] e.g. Ronald Dworkin, 'Constitutionalism and Democracy' (1995) 3 *European Journal of Philosophy* 2–11.

scope, namely, how far given rights might extend and create obligations on others; the ways they might be best secured; how they might be balanced against each other; and so on.[5] As a result, there can be no higher, rights-based constitutional law that sits above or beyond politics. We necessarily frame and apply rights-based judgments within what Jeremy Waldron has termed the 'circumstances of politics'—that is, those circumstances where we may need a collective decision, but still disagree about its basis, content, scope, and the best mechanisms and policies to realize it.[6] We may need rights to coordinate our collective behaviour and offer forms of protection to individuals and groups from the uncertainties and injustices that arise within social life, yet we differ considerably over what the most appropriate system of rights might be. Moreover, any system of rights creates a correlative system of duties, so that a collective agreement on rights must also be an agreement on how and when we should uphold them and the distribution of the burdens of doing so—including the restrictions that upholding one set of rights may place on the exercise of another set of rights. If we consider rights as possessed and claimable by all, and inherent to our equal status as autonomous individuals, then we need a collective process for deliberating on our rights and related obligations, and resolving our disagreements about them, that is consistent with the very basis of these rights themselves.[7] I argued that democracy offers such a process—though it can be consistent with 'weak form' rights-based review on the basis of a legislative Bill of Rights, that can call out but not strike down parliamentary legislation—a point to which I returned in Chapter 4.

Chapter 2 developed this thesis to show how the rule of law is linked intrinsically and instrumentally to the democratic rule of persons. Political constitutionalists can be located broadly within the fold of legal positivism. Obviously, it is possible to be a legal positivist and still advocate a form of legal constitutionalism. However, political constitutionalists, as Jeremy Waldron has noted,[8] give the legal positivist's focus on the institutional sources of law an important twist. For reasons I explored in the first part of the chapter, political constitutionalists consider the democratic provenance of a law to form an essential feature of its legitimacy. Unlike Hobbes, for whom the kind of authority he associated with sovereignty defines law regardless of who that sovereign might be, the political constitutionalist believes that law-making, sovereign power must reside in democratic institutions that embody a plausible conception of political equality. Only then will laws possess the

[5] See e.g. J. A. G. Griffith, 'The Political Constitution' (1979) 42 *Modern Law* 17–18, 20; Bellamy, *Political Constitutionalism*, 20–3; Jeremy Waldron, 'The Core of the Case Against Judicial Review' (2006) 115 *Yale Law Journal* 1366–9, and Jeremy Waldron, *Law and Disagreement* (Oxford: Clarendon Press 1999) 11–12.

[6] Waldron, *Law and Disagreement*, 107–13.

[7] Griffith, 'The Political Constitution', 16–18; Waldron, *Law and Disagreement*, 159–60; Bellamy, *Political Constitutionalism*, 20–6.

[8] See Jeremy Waldron, 'Can There Be a Democratic Jurisprudence?' (2008–09) 58 *Emory Law Journal* 675–712.

formal qualities that even minimalist accounts of the rule of law, such as Joseph Raz's, accept are needed to distinguish laws from arbitrary commands.[9] Moreover, as Waldron also notes,[10] the political constitutionalist thinks it important that not just the source of law be democratic but also the business of recognizing laws by courts and lawyers be reasonably clear and open to lay people, not simply an arcane endeavour of the legal profession. For a democrat, the criteria of legal validity need to be understandable by the citizens whose property the law is. This concern applies particularly to the notion of judge-made law, given the potential mystifications that can arise when the law seems to be a creature of judicial discretion. Consequently, law should be defined through settled parliamentary processes rather than by court judgments expressing a judge's private assessment of the merits of particular cases.

Accordingly, the second part of Chapter 2 deployed this argument to defend A. V. Dicey's democratic account of the rule of law as grounded in the legislative processes of a sovereign Parliament. That account was then compared to various theories that promote the superiority of judicial review as a mechanism for upholding the rule of law on either procedural or substantive grounds. I argued that on both counts democratic legislatures prove superior to courts. Two features explain this superiority: the broader deliberative qualities of legislatures as compared with courts, and the accountability of legislators to citizens. By contrast, I challenged the counter claims of legal constitutionalists that the constraints of legal reasoning and the independence of courts respectively support fair and impartial reasoning about the nature of law—arguing that in many respects these supposed advantages of courts over legislatures can be disadvantages.[11] On the one hand, the need for courts to accommodate both extant law and to consider only those parties with legal standing in a particular case can make them less apt than legislatures to take into consideration all the moral and practical considerations relevant for collective decisions. On the other hand, the electoral accountability of legislators gives citizens equal status as autonomous reasoners and sources of information about the law, strengthening their sense of ownership of legal decisions and enabling them to ensure that the full range of concerns get considered and appropriately weighed. Meanwhile, independence need not guarantee impartiality. Rather, it may simply allow judges to arbitrarily follow their own moral views in their judgments on the basis of spurious legal precedents.

Compared to legislatures, therefore, courts may fail to offer to all citizens as equal a chance for each and every one of their views and apprehensions regarding the collective provision of certain public goods and the protection of their basic

[9] Joseph Raz, 'The Rule of Law and its Virtue' in Joseph Raz, *The Authority of Law: Essays on Law and Morality* (Oxford: Clarendon Press 1979) 214–18.

[10] Waldron, 'Can There Be a Democratic Jurisprudence?', 691–7.

[11] See Griffith, 'The Political Constitution', 16, 20; Waldron, 'The Core'; Tomkins, *Our Republican Constitution*, 27–30, 64–5; and Bellamy, *Political Constitutionalism*, especially part 2.

interests to be counted, challenged, and weighed. Indeed, because courts offer a more restricted forum than legislatures, strong form judicial review tends to favour the privileged over the unprivileged.[12] As the few large n studies that have been carried out in this area indicate, within established democracies strong form judicial review by constitutional courts has tended to be a means for blocking rather than promoting progressive social reform. For it allows hegemonic groups to argue that such measures impose coercive restrictions on the individual rights of the well-off and propertied.[13] By contrast, courts have fared no better—and often considerably worse—than legislatures in promoting the rights of the disadvantaged and those suffering unjust discrimination.[14]

As a result of all the above, I have defended the political constitutionalist's contention that the rights determined by legislators within legislation should be superior to the decisions of courts. Judicial decisions should be guided by legislation and courts should not have the power to strike down legislation but only to raise potential unanticipated worries via weak form review. The supreme court on constitutional issues, including rights, should be Parliament. Chapter 3, therefore, turned to a defence of political equality and majority rule in the context of a system of representative parliamentary government. I argued that the dangers of both legislative and executive tyranny can be best mitigated not by counter-majoritarian measures but rather through what, adapting a phrase of Steffen Ganghof's,[15] I called 'complex majoritarianism'. A complex majoritarian system of representative government ensures that collective decisions are made at the level at which all voters have an equal interest in the overall package of policies, on the one hand, and that those making these decisions are proportionally representative of the relevant electorate, on the other. In the context of regular and fair elections involving competing parties, these criteria ensure that majorities must be constructed from coalitions of minorities and accommodate the concerns of central and local government. The result is a democratic system of checks and balances capable of possessing the constitutional qualities I associated in Chapters 1 and 2 with a well-functioning political constitution.

Parts 2, 3, and 4 of the book explored practical challenges to the arguments of Chapters 1, 2, and 3 respectively. In Part 2, Chapter 4 focused on whether even a statutory Bill of Rights, such as the Human Rights Act, could be compatible with parliamentary sovereignty; while Chapter 5 took this further to ask if an international convention and court, such as the European Convention on Human

[12] Waldron, *Law and Disagreement*, 12; Bellamy, *Political Constitutionalism*, 27–8.

[13] See Ran Hirschl, *Towards Juristocracy: The Origins and Consequences of the New Constitutionalism* (Cambridge, MA: Harvard University Press 2004).

[14] Gerald Rosenberg, *The Hollow Hope: Can Courts Bring About Social Change?* (Chicago: Chicago University Press 1991); Tushnet, *Taking the Constitution Away*, ch. 6.

[15] Steffen Ganghof, *Beyond Presidentialism and Parliamentarism: Democratic Design and the Separation of Powers* (Oxford: Oxford University Press 2021) 6–7, 69–70.

Rights (ECHR) and the associated court might be. In both cases, I suggested a form of weak review, such as that proposed in Chapter 1, was possible.

Certain proponents, as well as opponents, of political constitutionalism conceive of it in terms that suggest it would be incompatible with any form of independent judicial review of either domestic or especially international law.[16] Yet, as I insisted in Chapter 2, I agree with those who contend such a position would be incompatible with even a formal account of the rule of law, in which laws will need to be consistently and predictably applied by those authorized to do so—a task typically entrusted to or upheld by courts. Of course, it can be argued that bills and conventions of rights create more scope for judicial discretion than the rights specified in ordinary legislation. Yet, as I remarked in Chapters 1 and 4, political constitutionalists are not rights-sceptics. Democratic equality requires the protection of certain fundamental interests of all persons of the kind implied by such bills and conventions. Establishing a system of weak review serves as a mechanism through which a well-functioning democracy seeks to remind itself of the importance of taking such rights into consideration in all the acts and legislation of governments. However, it remains possible for Parliament to retain the final say on how such rights are to be balanced and interpreted, and even give a steer to courts on this matter through a process of pre-legislative review by a parliamentary rights committee—itself perhaps the most important democratic mechanism for taking rights seriously.

Part 3 developed this argument further by defending the account of the rule of law developed in Chapter 2. Here I considered two potential objections to that account. In Chapter 6 I responded to the argument that since politics assumes laws that regulate its functioning, political constitutionalism involves either vicious circularity or an infinite regress—as summed up in the apocryphal claim of a believer that the earth rested on a giant turtle and that this turtle in its turn rested on another turtle and so on ad infinitum, so that it was 'turtles all the way down'. I claimed that would be the case only if political constitutionalists embraced some form of ontological scepticism about the very nature of truth. But their scepticism is epistemological—it does not deny truth exists, only that we have imperfect instruments for defining and discovering it. As a result, we are necessarily involved in developing our views against those of others through procedures allowing for ongoing argumentation on the basis of the available facts and reasons. We rebuild the constitutional ship at sea. And this rebuilding is necessarily a political process, since it involves answering what Bernard Williams termed 'the first political question'[17]: namely, who has the authority to bring our disputes over the terms of our social cooperation to at least a temporary close.

[16] At times, Martin Loughlin, *Against Constitutionalism* (Cambridge, MA: Harvard University Press 2022) adopts arguments that could be read in this way.

[17] Bernard Williams, 'Realism and Moralism in Political Theory' in Bernard Williams, *In the Beginning Was the Deed* (Princeton, NJ: Princeton University Press 2005) 3.

Chapter 7 turned to a rather different objection—that of whether courts may not themselves be seen as democratic forums, allowing for deliberation, representation, and participation of a democratic kind. I agreed that it is desirable that courts possess certain democratic qualities—such as treating all as equal under the law, and giving all equal access to the law. As with similar desiderata regarding the electoral process, these qualities may prove to be deficient in practice. Yet that does not make them any the less preferable—and, indeed, core to the legitimacy of both law and the courts. However, courts tend to possess them to the extent the political system in which they are located itself operates democratically, and will reflect the strengths and weaknesses of the prevailing democratic system. That said, courts tend to lack certain features essential to the operations of a democratic political system—notably electoral authorization and accountability, defended in Chapter 3, and indeed it proves inappropriate for them to possess them. To do so, interferes with their role in the impartial application of the law to specific cases. The key, then, is to ensure courts possess the desirable but not the undesirable (for them) features of democracy—both of which relate to their place within a well-functioning political constitution.

Finally, Part 4 looked at what has emerged as the greatest contemporary challenge to both legal and political constitutionalism—the rise of populism and the subversion of constitutional norms and mechanisms by democratically elected far right politicians. That such politicians claim an electoral mandate for their actions may appear to point the blame to democracy and political constitutionalism. However, Chapters 8 and 9 distinguished populism from democracy and popular from political constitutionalism respectively. The populist denial of pluralism and insistence on the possibility of a coherent 'will of the people' deprives the political process of its constitutional qualities. By contrast to popular sovereignty, parliamentary sovereignty involves the equal representation of a plurality of parties and perspectives and encourages policy-making that incorporates different interests and perspectives. Populist decision-making seeks to overturn such democratic checks and balances. Some legal constitutionalists consider 'militant democratic' measures,[18] that involve entrenching democratic norms and banning anti-democratic parties, to be the most effective ways of meeting the populist threat.[19] However, such tactics risk backfiring by either appearing to confirm the populist critique of establishment elites, or providing a spurious legitimacy to the weaponization of the law and constitutions by populists themselves to entrench

[18] The term originates with Karl Loewenstein's two classic articles: 'Militant Democracy and Fundamental Rights I' (1937) 31(3) *American Political Science Review* 417–32 and 'Militant Democracy and Fundamental Rights II' (1937) 31(4) *American Political Science Review* 638–58.

[19] Loewenstein's ideas were adopted in art 21 of the Basic Law of the Federal Republic of Germany, and roughly 30% of extant constitutions contain such clauses that allow for the banning of anti-democratic political parties. See Tom Ginsburg, Aziz Huq, and T. Khaitan, *The Entrenchment of Democracy* (Cambridge: Cambridge University Press 2024) 12–13 and ch. 5.

their position once gained.[20] By contrast, I advocated the further strengthening of the democratic constitutional checks and balances of the political constitution. In particular, I suggested that these measures have the potential of addressing the social and economic injustices that to some degree drive populism.

Meanwhile, Chapter 9 argued that referendums need not be seen as an instance of popular constitutionalism. While the Brexit referendum has been seen as an object lesson in how *not* to conduct a referendum—or even why one should never hold referendums at all, I argued that the main weakness rested with the failings of the campaign to remain in the European Union (EU), and the fragmented opposition in Parliament. Despite claims that it expressed the 'popular will' on leaving the EU, the referendum actually gave no guidance on the terms by which that was to be achieved—with the narrow majority for leaving including a range of very different views. The decisions of how, when, and on what terms (or even—technically—of if at all) to leave lay with Parliament. In that regard, the referendum can be viewed as being consistent with parliamentary sovereignty in that both the terms of the referendum and the response to the vote rested in Parliament's hands. Indeed, so conceived, referendums can be seen positively, as providing a democratic check on changes to the constitutional rules where the executive or Parliament could be seen as acting as 'judges in their own cause' when it came to determining the rules of the democratic game—including, in this case, the very constitution of the state itself as either a member or not of the EU. That does not mean that the process could not have been improved in various respects—such as by having a second referendum to confirm the decision and deliberate the options for leaving. But one should avoid an instance of a poorly conducted referendum serving as a reason for rejecting them altogether. After all, many—such as myself—who regret the vote on Brexit might nevertheless desire a referendum that might, for example, produce a constitutional change they favour, such as an elected and/or federal replacement of the House of Lords.

Last, but not least, I turned to the issue that prompted Brexit—namely, whether it is possible for state-based parliaments to retain democratic control in an increasingly interconnected world, faced with problems requiring global solutions—most notably climate change. Developing the argument of Chapter 5 and that of my 2019 book *A Republican Europe of States*,[21] I contended that states have both functional and moral reasons to become part of global (such as the World Trade Organization (WTO)) and regional (such as the EU) governance arrangements that regulate their interactions in mutually respectful ways. However, these institutional mechanisms can be seen as *demoi*-cratic in character and as involving a two-level game, in which the elected representatives of state governments reach

[20] Ginsburg, Huq, and Khaitan, *The Entrenchment of Democracy*, 13–14; Rune Møller Stopp and Benjamin Ask Popp-Madsen, 'Defending Democracy: Militant and Popular Models of Democratic Self-Defense' (2022) 29 *Constellations* 310–28.

[21] Richard Bellamy, *A Republican Europe of States: Cosmopolitanism, Intergovernmentalism and Democracy in the EU* (Cambridge: Cambridge University Press 2019).

agreements that command the support of their respective nationally elected parliaments and populations. These parliaments can also interact with each other, either complementing or replacing a supranational Parliament. Indeed, given that each state's domestic policies have effects on those of other states, national parliaments can only retain control through such arrangements. Seen from this 'republican intergovernmental' perspective, as I have termed it, the EU can be conceived as a form of international political constitutionalism—a point confirmed by the constitutional pluralist character of the relations between domestic constitutional courts and the Court of Justice of the European Union (CJEU).

Even a long book inevitably has its lacunas—some of which I am all too aware of, while many others almost certainly elude me. The core of the argument lies with Part 1 and Chapters 1–3, which outlined the normative argument and indicated the form a political constitution needs to take if it was to realize those norms. Parts 2–4 can then be seen as indicative of how political constitutionalism might be adapted and improved relative to certain challenges. While these chapters tend to focus on the UK with occasional comparisons with the United States and even more occasionally Germany, the normative model itself is intended as having a general relevance. As I note in the Chapter 8 in particular, what one might call militant political constitutionalism—that is, the coordinated and cooperative action of opposition parties, often accompanied by pushback within urban areas and other centres of local government, such as occurred in Poland, provide perhaps the most effective as well as the most democratic modes of opposition to populist-led democratic backsliding.

Political constitutionalism is an institutional arrangement for inculcating and preserving the constitutional values associated with democratic equality. Yet, one cannot place virtue solely in institutions. All institutions empower as well as constrain. As the populist undermining of even established democracies has shown all too well, autocratically minded politicians willing to make unscrupulous use of their power can, once elected, undermine both entrenched legal constitutions and settled political conventions and procedures. Moreover, they will only be inhibited from doing so to the extent public officials—be they judges, administrators, or the police—and above all citizens regard such behaviour as unacceptable and possess the civic virtue required to resist it. No working democracy can operate well unless not only politicians but also the rest of us view our fellow citizens as equal powerholders, and as such deserving of our equal respect and concern. In other words, a working political constitution requires not just democratic institutions but also a democratic ethos. It is to the stipulation of the virtues animating such an ethos that I hope to turn next.[22]

[22] I provide a taster of what that might involve in Richard Bellamy and Sandra Kröger, 'Truthfulness, Pluralism and the Ethics of Democratic Representation' (2024) 27(3) *British Journal of Politics and International Relations* 1023–43.

Amalgamated Bibliography

Arash Abizadeh, 'Counter-Majoritarian Democracy: Persistent Minorities, Federalism, and the Power of Numbers' (2021) 115(3) *American Political Science Review* 742–56

Arash Abizadeh, 'Representation, Bicameralism, Political Equality, and Sortition: Reconstituting the Second Chamber as a Randomly Selected Assembly' (2021) 19(3) *Perspectives on Politics* 791–806

C. Achen and L. Bartels, *Democracy for Realists: Why Elections Do Not Produce Responsive Government* (Princeton, NJ: Princeton University Press 2017)

Bruce Ackerman, *We the People: Foundations* (Cambridge, MA: Harvard University Press 1991)

Bruce Ackerman, *Revolutionary Constitutions* (Cambridge, MA: Harvard University Press 2019)

Robert Alexy, 'Balancing, Constitutional Review, and Representation' (2005) 3(4) *International Journal of Constitutional Law* 572–81

T. R. S. Allan, *Law, Liberty, and Justice: The Foundations of British Constitutionalism* (Oxford: Clarendon Press 1993)

T. R. S. Allan, 'Book Review: Richard Bellamy, *Political Constitutionalism*' (2008) 67 *Cambridge Law Journal* 423–6

Elizabeth Anderson, 'What is the Point of Equality?' (1999) 109(2) *Ethics* 287–337

Elizabeth Anderson, 'Critical Notice of Amartya Sen, "Rationality and Freedom"' (2005) 114(2) *The Philosophical Review* 253–71

Elizabeth Anderson, *Private Government: How Employers Rule Our Lives (and Why We Don't Talk about It)* (Princeton, NJ: Princeton University Press 2019)

Hannah Arendt, *The Origins of Totalitarianism* (rev. edn, New York: Harcourt 1973)

Aristotle, *The Politics* (T. A. Sinclair tr., rev. edn, Harmondsworth: Penguin 1981)

K. J. Arrow, *Social Choice and Individual Values* (2nd edn, New Haven, CT: Yale University Press 1963)

Psygkas Athanasios, 'The Hydraulics of Constitutional Claims: Multiplicity of Actors in Constitutional Interpretation' (2018) 69(2) *University of Toronto Law Journal* 211–47

Katrin Auel and Thomas Christiansen, 'After Lisbon: National Parliaments in the European Union' (2015) 38 *West European Politics* 261–81

Nicholas Bamforth, *Understanding the Impact and Status of the Human Rights Act 1998 within English Law*, Global Law Working Paper 10/04 <http://www.law.nyu.edu/global/workingpapers/2004/ECM_DLV_015806>

N. W. Barber, *The Constitutional State* (Oxford: Oxford University Press 2010)

N. W. Barber, *The Principles of Constitutionalism* (Oxford: Oxford University Press 2018)

N. W. Barber, 'The Two Europes' in N. W. Barber, M. Cahill, and R. Ekins (eds), *The Rise and Fall of the European Constitution* (Oxford: Hart Publishing 2019) 89–104

Larry M. Bartels, *Unequal Democracy: The Political Economy of the New Gilded Age* (Princeton, NJ: Princeton University Press 2008)

Omar S. Bashir, 'Testing Inferences about American Politics: A Review of the "Oligarchy" Result' (2015) 2(4) *Research & Politics* 1–7

Rainer Bauböck, 'Morphing the Demos into the Right Shape. Normative Principles for Enfranchising Resident Aliens and Expatriate Citizens' (2015) 22 *Democratization* 820–39

Cesare Beccaria, *On Crimes and Punishments* ([1764], Richard Bellamy ed., Cambridge: Cambridge University Press 1995)

Eric Beerbohm, 'The Ethics of Electioneering' (2016) 24(4) *Journal of Political Philosophy* 381–405

David Beetham, 'Civil Liberties, Thatcherism and Charter "88"' (1989) 60(3) *The Political Quarterly* 273–9 <https://doi.org/10.1111/j.1467-923X.1989.tb00772.x>

Richard Bellamy, 'The Political Form of the Constitution: The Separation of Powers, Rights and Representative Democracy' (1996) 44 *Political Studies* 436–56

Richard Bellamy, *Liberalism and Pluralism: Towards a Politics of Compromise* (London: Routledge 1999)

Richard Bellamy, 'Constitutive Citizenship vs. Constitutional Rights: Republican Reflections on the EU Charter and the Human Rights Act' in Tom Campbell, Keith David Ewing, and Adam Tomkins (eds), *Sceptical Essays on Human Rights* (Oxford: Oxford University Press 2001) 15–39

Richard Bellamy, 'The Advent of the Masses and the Making of the Modern Theory of Democracy' in T. Ball and R. Bellamy (eds), *The Cambridge History of Twentieth Century Political Thought* (Cambridge: Cambridge University Press 2003) 70–103

Richard Bellamy, *Political Constitutionalism: A Republican Defence of the Constitutionality of Democracy* (Cambridge: Cambridge University Press 2007)

Richard Bellamy, 'The Republic of Reasons: Public Reasoning, Depoliticisation and Non-Domination' in Samantha Besson and José Luis Martí (eds), *Legal Republicanism: National and International Perspectives* (Oxford: Oxford University Press 2009) 102–20

Richard Bellamy, 'Dirty Hands and White Gloves: Liberal Ideals and Real Politics' (2010) 9 *European Journal of Political Theory* 412–30

Richard Bellamy, 'Political Constitutionalism and the Human Rights Act' (2011) 9 *International Journal of Constitutional Law (I-Con)* 86–111

Richard Bellamy, 'The Democratic Legitimacy of International Human Rights Conventions: Political Constitutionalism and the ECHR' (2014) 25 *European Journal of International Law* 1019–42

Richard Bellamy, 'Rights as Democracy' (2012) 15 *Critical Review of International Social and Political Philosophy* 449–71

Richard Bellamy, 'Democracy, Compromise and the Representation Paradox: On Coalition Government and Political Integrity' (2012) 47(3) *Government and Opposition* 441–65

Richard Bellamy, '"An Ever-Closer Union Among the People of Europe": Republican Intergovernmentalism and Demoicratic Representation within the EU' (2013) 35 *Journal of European Integration* 499–516

Richard Bellamy, 'A Duty-Free Europe? What's Wrong with Kochenov's Account of EU Citizenship Rights' (2015) 21 *European Law Journal* 558–65

Richard Bellamy, 'The Limits of Lord Sumption: Limited Legal Constitutionalism and the Political Form of the ECHR' in N. W. Barber, Richard Ekins, and Paul Yowell (eds), *Lord Sumption and the Limits of the Law* (Oxford: Hart Publishing 2016) 193–212

Richard Bellamy, 'Turtles All The Way Down? Is the Political Constitutionalist Appeal to Disagreement Self-Defeating? A Reply to Cormac Mac Amhlaigh' (2016) 14(1) *International Journal of Constitutional Law (I-Con)* 204–16

Richard Bellamy, 'Majority Rule, Compromise and the Democratic Legitimacy of Referendums' (2018) 24 *Swiss Political Science Review* 312–19

Richard Bellamy, *A Republican Europe of States: Cosmopolitanism, Intergovernmentalism and Democracy in the EU* (Cambridge: Cambridge University Press 2019)

Richard Bellamy, 'I limiti di Lord Sumption: Costituzionalismo giuridico limitato, Costituzionalismo politico e Convenzione Europea dei Diritti dell'Uomo' (2019) 3(3) *Rivista di Diritti Comparati* 3–40

Richard Bellamy, 'Was the Brexit Referendum Legitimate, and Would a Second One be So?' (2019) 18 *European Political Science* 126–33

Richard Bellamy, 'Between Utopianism and Realism: The Limits of Partisanship as an Academic Methodology' (2021) 69(3) *Political Studies* 481–91

Richard Bellamy and Dario Castiglione, 'Constitutionalism and Democracy: Political Theory and the American Constitution' (1997) 27 *British Journal of Political Science* 595–618

Richard Bellamy and Martin Hollis, 'Liberal Justice: Political and Metaphysical' (1995) 45(178) *The Philosophical Quarterly* 1–20

Richard Bellamy and Martin Hollis, 'Compromise, Consensus and Neutrality' (1998) 1 *Critical Review of Social and Political Philosophy* 57–78

Richard Bellamy and Jeff King, 'Introduction: Of Constitutions and Constitutional Theory' in Richard Bellamy and Jeff King (eds) *The Cambridge Handbook of Constitutional Theory* (Cambridge: Cambridge University Press 2025) 1–20

Richard Bellamy and Sandra Kröger, 'A Demoicratic Justification of Differentiated Integration in a Heterogenous EU' (2017) 39 *Journal of European Integration* 625–39

Richard Bellamy and Sandra Kröger, 'Differentiated Integration as a Fair Scheme of Cooperation' (2023) 81(1) *Review of Social Economy* 61–83

Richard Bellamy and Sandra Kröger, 'Countering Democratic Backsliding by EU Member States: Constitutional Pluralism and "Value" Differentiated Integration' (2021) 27(3) *Swiss Political Science Review* 619–36

Richard Bellamy and Sandra Kröger, 'Truthfulness, Pluralism and the Ethics of Democratic Representation' (2024) 27(3) *British Journal of Politics and International Relations* 1023–43.

Richard Bellamy, Sandra Kröger, and Marta Lorimer, *Flexible Europe: Fairness, Democracy, and Differentiated Integration* (Bristol: Bristol University Press/Policy Press 2022)

Richard Bellamy and Justus Schönlau, 'The Normality of Constitutional Politics: An Analysis of the Drafting of the EU Charter of Fundamental Rights' (2004) 11 *Constellations* 412–33

Richard Bellamy and Albert Weale, 'Political Legitimacy and European Monetary Union: Contracts, Constitutionalism, and the Normative Logic of Two-Level Games' (2015) 22(2) *Journal of European Public Policy* 257–74

Meghan Benton and Meg Russell, 'Assessing the Impact of Parliamentary Oversight Committees: The Select Committees in the British House of Commons' (2013) 66(4) *Parliamentary Affairs* 772–97

Isaiah Berlin, 'Two Concepts of Liberty' in Isaiah Berlin, *Four Essays on Liberty* (Oxford: Oxford University Press 1969)

Alexander Bickel, *The Least Dangerous Branch: The Supreme Court at the Bar of Politics* (2nd edn, New Haven, CT: Yale University Press 1986)

Tom Bingham, *The Rule of Law* (London: Penguin 2010)

M. Blauberger and R. D. Kelemen, 'Can Courts Rescue National Democracy? Judicial Safeguards against Democratic Backsliding in the EU' (2017) 24(3) *Journal of European Public Policy* 321–36

M. Blauberger and V. van Hüllen, 'Conditionality of EU Funds: An Instrument to Enforce EU Fundamental Values?' (2020) 43(1) *Journal of European Integration* 1–16

Norberto Bobbio, *The Future of Democracy: A Defence of the Rules of the Game* (Richard Bellamy ed., Cambridge: Polity Press 1987)

Armin Von Bogdandy and L. D. Spieker, 'Countering the Judicial Silencing of Critics: Article 2 TEU Values, Reverse Solange, and the Responsibilities of National Judges' (2019) 15(3) *European Constitutional Law Review* 391–426

Vernon Bogdanor, 'Western Europe' in David Butler and Austin Ranney (eds), *Referendums Around the World: The Growing Use of Direct Democracy* (Basingstoke: Palgrave 1994) 24–97

Vernon Bogdanor, 'The Sovereignty of Parliament or the Rule of Law?', Magna Carta Lecture (15 June 2006) 20 <http://royalholloway.org.uk/About/magna-carta/2006-lecture.pdf>

Vernon Bogdanor, *The New British Constitution* (Oxford: Hart Publishing 2009)

Vernon Bogdanor, *Beyond Brexit: Towards a British Constitution* (London: I.B. Tauris 2019)

Vernon Bogdanor, 'Brexit Means Britain Needs a Constitution', *Foreign Policy* (8 October 2019) <https://foreignpolicy.com/2019/10/08/brexit-means-britain-needs-a-constitution//>

Nikolas Bowie, 'The Contemporary Debate over Supreme Court Reform: Origins and Perspectives', Written Statement to the Presidential Commission on the Supreme Court of the United States, 30 June 2021

Curtis Bradley and Jack Goldsmith, 'The Current Illegitimacy of International Human Rights' (1997) 66 *Fordham Law Review* 319–69

G. Brennan and A. Hamlin, 'A Revisionist View of the Separation of Powers' (1994) 6(3) *Journal of Theoretical Politics* 345–68

Harry Brighouse and Marc Fleurbaey, 'Democracy and Proportionality' (2010) 18(2) *Journal of Political Philosophy* 137–75

D. M. Brinks and A. Blass, 'Rethinking Judicial Empowerment: The New Foundations of Constitutional Justice (2017) 15(2) *International Journal of Constitutional Law* 296–331

Allen Buchanan, 'Political Legitimacy and Democracy' (2002) 112(4) *Ethics* 689–719

Allen Buchanan, *Justice, Legitimacy and Self-Determination: Moral Foundations for International Law* (Oxford: Oxford University Press 2003)

Allen Buchanan and Russell Powell, 'Survey Article: Constitutional Democracy and the Rule of International Law: Are they Compatible?' (2008) 16 *Journal of Political Philosophy* 326–49

James Buchanan, 'Social Choice, Democracy and Free Markets' (1954) 62 *Journal of Political Economy* 114–23

J. M. Buchanan and G. Tullock, *The Calculus of Consent* (Ann Arbor: University of Michigan Press 1962)

Glenn Burgess, *The Politics of the Ancient Constitution: An Introduction to English Political Thought 1603–1642* (London: Macmillan 1992)

Edmund Burke, 'Speech to the Electors of Bristol' in I. Hampshire-Monk (ed.), *The Political Philosophy of Edmund Burke* (Harlow: Longman 1987), 108–11

J. C. Calhoun, *A Disquisition on Government* (1851) in J. C. Calhoun, *Union and Liberty: The Political Philosophy of John C. Calhoun* (Ross M. Lence ed., Indianapolis: Liberty Fund 1992) 3–78

Tom Campbell, *The Legal Theory of Ethical Positivism* (Aldershot: Dartmouth 1996)

Tom Campbell, Keith David Ewing, and Adam Tomkins (eds), *Sceptical Essays on Human Rights* (Oxford: Oxford University Press 2001)

Tom Campbell, Keith David Ewing, and Adam Tomkins (eds), *The Legal Protection of Human Rights: Sceptical Essays* (Oxford: Oxford University Press 2011)

J. Couso, *Making Sense of Chile's Failed Constituent Process*, International Journal of Constitutional Law Blog (4 October 2022) <http://www.iconnectblog.com/2022/10/making-sense-of-chiles-failed-constituent-process/>

Jose Antonio Cheibub, Fernando Limongi, Adam Przeworski, and Ye Wang, 'Anti-majoritarianism and Democracy: Effects of Judicial Review on Rights, Economic Growth, and Inequality' (4 September 2024) <http://dx.doi.org/10.2139/ssrn.5069081>

Francis Cheneval and Alice el-Wakil, 'The Institutional Design of Referendums: Bottom-Up and Binding' (2018) 24 *Swiss Political Science Review* 294–304

Thomas Christiano, 'Political Equality' in J. Chapman and A. Wertheimer (eds), *Majorities and Minorities NOMOS XXXIII* (New York: New York University Press 1990) 151–81

Thomas Christiano, *The Rule of the Many: Fundamental Issues in Democratic Theory* (Boulder, CO: Westview Press 1996)

Thomas Christiano, 'Waldron on Law and Disagreement' (2000) 19(4) *Law and Philosophy* 513–43

Thomas Christiano, *The Constitution of Equality: Democratic Authority and its Limits* (Oxford: Oxford University Press 2008)

Thomas Christiano, 'Democratic Legitimacy and International Institutions' in Samantha Besson and John Tasioulas (eds), *The Philosophy of International Law* (Oxford: Oxford University Press 2010) 119–37

Thomas Christiano, 'An Instrumental Argument for a Human Right to Democracy' (2011) 39 *Philosophy and Public Affairs* 142–76

Thomas Christiano, 'Replies to David Álvarez, David Lefkowitz, and Michael Blake' (2017) 4 *Law, Ethics, and Philosophy* 221–36

Thomas Christiano, 'The Basis of Political Equality' in Elizabeth Edenberg and Michael Hannon (eds), *Political Epistemology* (Oxford: Oxford University Press 2021) 114–34

James Christensen, 'Fair Trade, Formal Equality, and Preferential Treatment' (2015) 41 *Social Theory and Practice* 505–26

Rachel Cichowski, 'Mobilisation, Litigation and Democratic Governance' (2013) 49 *Representation* 321–33

H. D. Clarke, M. Goodwin, and P. Whitely, *Brexit: Why Britain Voted to Leave the European Union* (Cambridge: Cambridge University Press 2017)

J. Colón-Riós, *Constituent Power and the Law* (Oxford: Oxford University Press 2020)

Chiara Cordelli, *The Privatized State* (Princeton, NJ: Princeton University Press 2020)

Chiara Cordelli, 'Kantian Democracy and Administrative Legitimacy: A Reply to My Critics' (2023) 26(2) *Critical Review of International Social and Political Philosophy* 267–76

Paul Craig, 'Formal and Substantive Conceptions of the Rule of Law: An Analytical Framework' (1997) *Autumn Public Law* 467–87

R. H. S. Crossman, 'Introduction' to Walter Bagehot, *The English Constitution* (Glasgow: Collins 1963)

Joshua Cohen, 'Is There a Human Right to Democracy?' in Christine Sypnowich (ed.), *The Egalitarian Conscience: Essays in Honour of G. A. Cohen* (Oxford: Oxford University Press 2006) 226–50

Richard Cosgrove, *The Rule of Law: Albert Venn Dicey, Victorian Jurist* (Chapel Hill, NC: University of North Carolina Press 1980)

Richard Dagger, *Civic Virtues: Rights, Citizenship and Republican Liberalism* (Oxford: Oxford University Press 1997)

Robert A. Dahl, 'Decision-making in a Democracy: The Supreme Court as National Policymaker' (1957) 6 *Journal of Public Law* 279–95

Robert A. Dahl, *A Preface to Economic Democracy* (Berkeley and Los Angeles, CA: University of California Press 1985)

Robert A. Dahl, *Democracy and its Critics* (New Haven, CT: Yale University Press 1989)

Robert A. Dahl, *Democracy* (New Haven, CT: Yale University Press 1998)

R. Dalton, *Political Realignment: Economics, Culture, and Electoral Change* (Oxford: Oxford University Press 2018)

Eoin Daly, 'A Republican Defence of the Constitutional Referendum' (2015) 35 *Legal Studies* 30–54

Gil Delannoi, Oliver Dowlen, and Peter Stone, *The Lottery as a Democratic Institution* (Dublin: Policy Institute 2013)

A. V. Dicey, *Introduction to the Study of the Law of the Constitution* (8th edn, London: MacMillan 1915 [1885])

A. V. Dicey, 'Ought the Referendum to Be Introduced into England?' (1890) 57 *Contemporary Review* 489–511

Charles Dickens, *Our Mutual Friend* (Harmondsworth: Penguin 1971 [1864–65])

Rosalind Dixon, *Responsive Judicial Review: Democracy and Dysfunction in the Modern Age* (Oxford: Oxford University Press 2023)

Ryan D. Doerfler and Samuel Moyn, 'Democratizing the Supreme Court' (2021) 109 *California Law Review* 1703–72

Ryan D. Doerfler and Samuel Moyn, 'The Ghost of John Hart Ely' (2022) 75 *Vanderbilt Law Review* 769–821

Ryan D. Doerfler and Sam Moyn, 'Don't count on the courts to save democracy: Giving courts the last word is part of what got us into this mess. It won't get us out' *Washington Post*, 20 March 2025

Tímea Drinóczi and Agnieszka Bień-Kacala, 'Illiberal Constitutionalism: The Case of Hungary and Poland' (2019) 20 *German Law Journal* 1140–66

John Dunn, *Setting the People Free. The Story of Democracy* (London: Atlantic Books 2005)

Ronald Dworkin, *Taking Rights Seriously* (2nd edn, London: Duckworth 1978)

Ronald Dworkin, *A Matter of Principle* (Cambridge, MA: Harvard University Press 1985)

Ronald Dworkin, 'The Forum of Principle' in Ronald Dworkin, *A Matter of Principle* (Cambridge, MA: Harvard University Press 1985) 33–71

Ronald Dworkin, *Law's Empire* (Cambridge, MA: Harvard University Press 1986)

Ronald Dworkin, *A Bill of Rights for Britain* (London: Chatto 1990)

Ronald Dworkin, 'Constitutionalism and Democracy' (1995) 3 *European Journal of Philosophy* 2–11

Ronald Dworkin, 'Objectivity and Truth: You'd Better Believe It' (1996) 25 *Philosophy and Public Affairs* 87–139

Ronald Dworkin, *Freedom's Law: The Moral Reading of the American Constitution* (Cambridge, MA: Harvard University Press 1996)

Ronald Dworkin, *The Supreme Court Phalanx: The Court's New Right-Wing Bloc* (New York: New York Review of Books 2008)

Ronald Dworkin, *Justice for Hedgehogs* (Cambridge, MA: Harvard University Press 2013)

Ronald Dworkin, 'A New Philosophy for International Law' (2013) 41 *Philosophy and Public Affairs* 2–30

David Dyzenhaus, *Hard Cases in Wicked Legal Systems: South African Law in the Perspective of Legal Philosophy* (Oxford: Clarendon Press 1991)

David Dyzenhaus, *The Constitution of Law: Legality in a Time of Emergency* (Cambridge: Cambridge University Press 2006)

David Dyzenhaus, 'The Incoherence of Constitutional Positivism' in Grant Huscroft (ed.), *Expounding the Constitution: Essays in Constitutional Theory* (Cambridge: Cambridge University Press 2008) 138–60

David Dyzenhaus, 'Are Legislatures Good at Morality? Or Better at it than the Courts?' (2009) 7 *International Journal of Constitutional Law* 46–52

David Dyzenhaus, 'How Hobbes Met the "Hobbes Challenge"' (2009) 72 *Modern Law Review* 488–506

Mette Eilstrup-Sangiovanni, 'Death of International Organizations' (2020) 15 *Review of International Organizations* 339–70

Richard Ekins, *Human Rights and the Rule of Law* (London: Policy Exchange 2024)

Richard Ekins and Graham Gee (eds), *Judicial Power and the Left* (London: Policy Exchange 2018)

Zachary Elkins, Tom Ginsburg, and James Melton, *The Endurance of National Constitutions* (Cambridge: Cambridge University Press 2009)

Mark Elliott, 'Parliamentary Sovereignty and the New Constitutional Order: Legislative Freedom, Political Reality and Convention' (2002) 22 *Legal Studies* 340–75

John Hart Ely, *Democracy and Distrust: A Theory of Judicial Review* (Cambridge, MA: Harvard University Press 1980)

Daniel Epps and Ganesh Sitaraman, 'How to Save the Supreme Court' (2019) 129 *Yale Law Journal* 148–206

Thomas Erskine May, *The Constitutional History of England Since the Accession of George III*, 2 vols (Boston: Crosby and Nicols 1863)

David Estlund, 'Political Quality' (2000) 17 *Social Philosophy and Policy* 127–60

European Commission, *Further Strengthening the Rule of Law within the Union*. COM(2019) 163 final.

Keith David Ewing, 'The Human Rights Act and Parliamentary Democracy' (1999) 62 *Modern Law Review* 79–99

Keith David Ewing, 'The Futility of the Human Rights Act' (2004) June *Public Law* 829–52

Keith David Ewing, *Bonfire of the Liberties: New Labour, Human Rights, and the Rule of Law* (Oxford: Oxford University Press 2010)

Keith David Ewing, 'The Resilience of the Political Constitution' (2013) 14 *German Law Journal* 2111–36

Cristina Fasone and Diane Fromage, 'From Veto Players to Agenda-Setters? National Parliaments their 'Green Card' to the European Commission' (2016) 23 *Maastricht Journal of European and Comparative Law* 294–316

David Feldman, 'The Human Rights Act 1998 and Constitutional Principles' (1999) 19 *Legal Studies* 165–206

Luigi Ferrajoli, 'Beyond Sovereignty and Citizenship: A Global Constitutionalism' in Richard Bellamy (ed.), *Constitutionalism, Democracy and Sovereignty: American and European Perspectives* (Ashgate: Avebury Press 1996) 151–60

Luigi Ferrajoli, *La democrazia attraverso i diritti. Il costituzionalismo garantista come modello teorico e come progetto politico* (Roma-Bari: Laterza 2013)

Robert Filmer, 'The Anarchy of a Limited or Mixed Monarchy' in Robert Filmer, *Patriarcha and Other Political Writings* (J. Somerville ed., Cambridge: Cambridge University Press 1991) 131–71

John Finnis, *Natural Law and Natural Rights* (Oxford: Clarendon Press 1980)

Katrin Flikschuh, 'Reason, Right, and Revolution: Kant and Locke' (2008) 36(4) *Philosophy and Public Affairs* 275–404

Andreas Follesdal and Marlene Wind, 'Nordic Reluctance towards Judicial Review under Siege' (2009) 27 *Nordic Journal of Human Rights* 131–41

Andreas Follesdal, 'Federalism' in Edward N. Zalta and Uri Nodelman (eds), *The Stanford Encyclopedia of Philosophy* (Winter 2022 edn) <https://plato.stanford.edu/archives/win2022/entries/federalism/>

Nancy Fraser, *Justice Interruptus* (London: Routledge 1997)

Sandra Fredman, 'The New Rights: Labour Law and Ideology in the Thatcher Years' (1992) 12 *Oxford Journal of Legal Studies* 24–44

Sandra Fredman, 'Scepticism under Scrutiny: Labour Law and Human Rights' in Tom Campbell, Keith David Ewing, and Adam Tomkins (eds), *Sceptical Essays on Human Rights* (Oxford: Oxford University Press 2001) 197–214

Bruno Frey and Lorenz Goette, 'Does the Popular Vote Destroy Civil Rights?' (1988) 42 *American Journal of Political Science* 1343–48

Judy Fudge, 'Constitutionalizing Labour Rights in Europe' in Tom Campbell, Keith David Ewing, and Adam Tomkins (eds), *The Legal Protection of Human Rights: Sceptical Essays* (Oxford: Oxford University Press 2011) 244–67

Lon Fuller, *The Morality of Law* (New Haven, CT: Yale University Press 1969)

Lon Fuller, 'Positivism and Fidelity to Law: A Reply to Hart' (1957) 71 *Harvard Law Review* 630–72

Steffen Ganghof, *Beyond Presidentialism and Parliamentarism: Democratic Design and the Separation of Powers* (Oxford: Oxford University Press 2021)

Stephen Gardbaum, 'The New Commonwealth Model of Constitutionalism' (2001) 49 *American Journal of Comparative Law* 707–60

Stephen Gardbaum, 'Reassessing the New Commonwealth Model of Constitutionalism' (2010) 8 *International Journal of Constitutional Law* 167–206

Stephen Gardbaum, *The New Commonwealth Model of Constitutionalism: Theory and Practice* (Cambridge: Cambridge University Press 2013)

John Gardner, 'Can There Be a Written Constitution?' in John Gardner, *Law as a Leap of Faith* (Oxford: Oxford University Press 2012) 89–124

Roberto Gargarella, *Latin American Constitutionalism, 1810–2010: The Engine Room of the Constitution* (Oxford: Oxford University Press 2013)

Roberto Gargarella, 'Rejection of the New Chilean Constitution: Some Reflections', *Oxford Human Rights Hub* (14 September 2022) <https://ohrh.law.ox.ac.uk/rejection-of-the-new-chilean-constitution-some-reflections/>

Nuno Garoupa and Tom Ginsburg, 'Guarding the Guardians: Judicial Councils and Judicial Independence' (2009) 57(1) *The American Journal of Comparative Law* 103–34

Conor Gearty, 'Revisiting Section 3 (1) of the Human Rights Act' (2003) 119 *Law Quarterly Review* 551–3

Graham Gee and Grégoire C. N. Webber, 'What Is a Political Constitution?' (2010) 30 *Oxford Journal of Legal Studies* 273–99

Graham Gee and Grégoire Webber, *Political Constitutions* (Cambridge: Cambridge University Press 2026)

Adom Getachew, *Worldmaking after Empire: The Rise and Fall of National Self-determination* (Princeton, NJ: Princeton University Press 2019)

Martin Gilens and Benjamin I. Page, 'Testing Theories of American Politics: Elites, Interest Groups, and Average Citizens' (2014) 12(03) *Perspectives on Politics* 564–81

R. Gilpin, *The Political Economy of International Relations* (Princeton, NJ: Princeton University Press 1987)

Tom Ginsburg, 'Democratic Backsliding and the Rule of Law' (2018) 44 *Ohio Northern University Law Review* 352–69

Tom Ginsburg and Aziz Huq, *How to Save a Constitutional Democracy* (Chicago: Chicago University Press 2018)

Tom Ginsburg, Aziz Huq, and T. Khaitan, *The Entrenchment of Democracy* (Cambridge: Cambridge University Press 2024)

A. Glencross, 'History' in J. Smith (ed.), *The Palgrave Handbook of European Referendums* (Basingstoke: Palgrave Macmillan 2021) 49–66

Marco Goldoni and Christopher McCorkindale (eds), Special Issue on 'Political Constitutions' (2013) 14(12) *German Law Journal* 2103–2292

Marco Goldoni and Christopher McCorkindale, 'Why We (Still) Need a Revolution' (2013) 14(12) *German Law Journal* 2197–2228

Marco Goldoni and Christopher McCorkindale, 'Three Waves of Political Constitutionalism' (2019) 30 *King's Law Journal* 74–96

Jeffrey Goldsworthy, 'Judicial Review, Legislative Override, and Democracy' (2003) 38 *Wake Forest Law Review* 451–72

Jeffrey Goldsworthy, 'Parliamentary Sovereignty and Statutory Interpretation' in Rick Bigwood (ed.), *The Statute: Making and Meaning* (Wellington, NZ: LexisNexis 2004) 187–210

Jeffrey Goldsworthy, *Parliamentary Sovereignty: Contemporary Debates* (Cambridge: Cambridge University Press 2010)

Robert Goodin, 'The Place of Parties', *Innovating Democracies:Democratic Theory and Practice After the Deliberative Turn* (Oxford: Oxford University Press 2008) ch. 10, 204–223

Michael Gordon, 'Parliamentary Sovereignty and the Political Constitution(s): From Griffith to Brexit' (2019) 30 *King's Law Journal* 125–47

Michael Gordon, 'The Prorogation Case and the Political Constitution', UK Constitutional Law Blog (30 September 2019) <https://ukconstitutionallaw.org/>

A. C. Grayling *Democracy and its Crisis* (London: Oneworld 2017)

J. A. G. Griffith, 'The Political Constitution' (1979) 42 *Modern Law Review* 1–21

Dieter Grimm, *Constitutionalism: Past, Present, Future* (Oxford: Oxford University Press 2016)

Dieter Grimm, *The Constitution of European Democracy* (Oxford: Oxford University Press 2017)

J. A. W. Gunn, 'Influence, Parties and the Constitution: Changing Attitudes, 1783–1832' (1974) 17 *Historical Journal* 301–28

W. B. Gwyn, *The Meaning of the Separation of Powers: An Analysis of the Doctrine from its Origin to the Adoption of the United States Constitution* (The Hague: Martinus Nijhoff 1965)

Jürgen Habermas, *Between Facts and Norms: Contributions to a Discourse Theory of Law and Democracy* (William Rehg tr., Cambridge: Polity Press 1996)

Jürgen Habermas, *The Inclusion of the Other: Studies in Political Theory* (Ciaran Cronin and Pablo De Greiff tr. and eds., Cambridge: Polity Press 1998)

Jürgen Habermas, *The Divided West* (Ciaran Cronin tr. and ed., Cambridge: Polity Press 2006)

Jürgen Habermas, 'The Constitutionalization of International Law and the Legitimation Problems of a Constitution for World Society' (2008) 15 *Constellations* 444–55

Jürgen Habermas, 'Democracy in Europe: Why the Development of EU into a Transnational Democracy is Necessary and How It Is Possible' (2015) 21 *European Law Journal* 546–57

Donald Haider-Markel, Alana Querze, and Kara Lindaman, 'Lose, Win, or Draw? A Reexamination of Direct Democracy and Minority Rights' (2007) 60 *Political Research Quarterly* 304–14

Lord Hailsham, *The Dilemma of Democracy: Diagnosis and Prescription* (Glasgow: Collins 1978)

J. Hainmueller and D. Hangartner, 'Does Direct Democracy Hurt Immigrant Minorities? Evidence from Naturalization Decisions in Switzerland' (2019) 63 *American Journal of Political Science* 530–47

Edward Hall, 'Bernard Williams and the Basic Legitimation Demand: A Defence' (2015) 63 *Political Studies* 446–80

Peter Hall and David Soskice (eds), *Varieties of Capitalism: The Institutional Foundations of Comparative Advantage* (Oxford: Oxford University Press 2001)

Alexander Hamilton, James Madison, and John Jay, *The Federalist* (Terence Ball ed., Cambridge: Cambridge University Press 2003)

Ronald Hamowy, 'Law and the Liberal Society' (1978) 2 *Journal of Libertarian Studies* 87–97

Stuart Hampshire, *Justice is Conflict* (Princeton, NJ: Princeton University Press 2000)

Jean Hampton, 'Democracy and the Rule of Law' in Ian Shapiro (ed.), *Nomos* XXVI (New York: New York University Press 1994) 13–44

Learned Hand, *The Bill of Rights* (Cambridge, MA: Harvard University Press 1958)

Sten Hansson and Sandra Kröger, 'How a Lack of Truthfulness can Undermine Democratic Representation: The Case of Post-referendum Brexit Discourses' (2021) 23 *The British Journal of Politics and International Relations* 609–26

Alon Harel, 'The Kantian Case against Democracy' (2023) 26 *Critical Review of International Social and Political Philosophy* 243–50

Alon Harel and Adam Shinar (2023) 12(1) 'Two Concepts of Constitutional Legitimacy' *Global Constitutionalism* 81–2

James Harrington, *Political Works* (J. G. A. Pocock ed., Cambridge: Cambridge University Press 1977)
James Harrington, *The Commonwealth of Oceana and A System of Politics* (J. G. A. Pocock ed., Cambridge: Cambridge University Press 1992) 20–1
H. L. A. Hart, 'Positivism and the Separation of Law and Morals' (1958) 71(4) *Harvard Law Review* 593–629
H. L. A. Hart, 'American Jurisprudence through English Eyes: The Nightmare and the Noble Dream' (1977) 11 *Georgia Law Review* 969–89
H. L. A. Hart, *The Concept of Law* (2nd edn, Oxford: Clarendon Press 1994)
John Haskell, *Direct Democracy or Representative Government? Dispelling the Populist Myth* (Boulder, CO: Westview 2001)
Angus Hawkins, '"Parliamentary Government" and Victorian Political Parties c 1830–1880' (1989) 104 *English Historical Review* 638–69
Angus Hawkins, *Victorian Political Culture: 'Habits of Heart and Mind'* (Oxford: Oxford University Press 2015)
Colin Hay, *Why We Hate Politics* (Cambridge: Polity 2008)
F. A. Hayek, *The Constitution of Liberty* (London: Routledge 1960)
F. A. Hayek, *Law, Legislation and Liberty*, 3 vols (London: Routledge 1973–79)
Stéphanie Hennette, Thomas Piketty, Guillaume Sacriste, and Antoine Vauchez, *How to Democratize Europe* (Cambridge, MA: Harvard University Press 2019)
Kristen Hessler, 'Resolving Interpretive Conflicts in International Human Rights Law' (2005) 13 *Journal of Political Philosophy* 29–52
Janet Hiebert, 'Interpreting a Bill of Rights: The Importance of Legislative Rights Review' (2005) 35 *British Journal of Political Science* 235–55
Janet Hiebert, 'Parliamentary Bills of Rights: An Alternative Model' (2006) 69 *Modern Law Review* 7–28
Ran Hirschl, *Towards Juristocracy: The Origins and Consequences of the New Constitutionalism* (Cambridge, MA: Harvard University Press 2004)
Thomas Hobbes, *Leviathan* (Richard Tuck ed., Cambridge: Cambridge University Press 1991)
Lord Hoffmann, 'The Universality of Human Rights', Judicial Studies Board Annual Lecture (19 March 2009)
Martin Hollis, *The Philosophy of Social Science* (Cambridge: Cambridge University Press 1994)
Martin Hollis, *Trust Within Reason* (Cambridge: Cambridge University Press 1998)
Stephen Holmes, 'Lineages of the Rule of Law' in José María Maravall and Adam Przeworski (eds), *Democracy and the Rule of Law* (Cambridge: Cambridge University Press 2003) 19–61
Iseult Honohan, *Civic Republicanism* (London: Routledge 2002)
Jonathan Hopkin, *Anti-System Politics: The Crisis of Market Liberalism in Rich Democracies* (New York: Oxford University Press 2020)
David Hume, *Essays Moral, Political and Literary* (E. F. Miller ed., Indianapolis: Liberty Fund 1987)
Ronald Inglehart, *Cultural Evolution: People's Motivations Are Changing, and Reshaping the World* (Cambridge: Cambridge University Press 2018)
Peter H. Irons, *The Courage of their Convictions* (New York: Free Press 1988)
Turkuler Isiksel, *Europe's Functional Constitution: A Theory of Constitutionalism Beyond the State* (Oxford: Oxford University Press 2016)
Torben Iversen and David Soskice, 'Electoral Institutions and the Politics of Coalitions: Why Some Democracies Redistribute More than Others' (2006) 100 *American Political Science Review* 165–81
F. Jacobs, *The Sovereignty of Law: The European Way, The Hamlyn Lectures 2006* (Cambridge: Cambridge University Press 2007)
Klemen Jaklic, *Constitutional Pluralism in the EU* (Oxford: Oxford University Press 2014)
Christian Joerges, 'The Economy is a Polity: Implications for the New Modes of Economic Governance in the EU' in Stéphanie Hennette, Thomas Piketty, Guillaume Sacriste, and Antoine Vauchez (eds), *How to Democratize Europe* (Cambridge, MA: Harvard University Press 2019) 122–30

Peter Jones, *Rights* (Houndmills: Macmillan 1994)
Thomas Jefferson, Letter to Madison of September 6, 1789. In Thomas Jefferson, *Writings* (M. Petterson ed., New York: Library of America 1984)
Immanuel Kant, *Practical Philosophy* (Mary Gregor ed., Cambridge: Cambridge University Press 1999)
Richard Katz and Peter Mair, 'Changing Models of Party Organisation and Party Democracy: The Emergence of the Cartel Party' (1995) 1 *Party Politics* 5–28
Robert Kaufman, D. Kelemen, and B Kolcak, 'Federalism and Democratic Backsliding in Comparative Perspective' (2025) 23(1) *Perspectives on Politics* 15–34
Aileen Kavanagh, 'Participation and Judicial Review: A Reply to Jeremy Waldron' (2003) 22 *Law and Philosophy* 451–86
Aileen Kavanagh, *Constitutional Review Under the U.K. Human Rights Act* (Cambridge: Cambridge University Press 2009)
Aileen Kavanagh, *The Collaborative Constitution* (Cambridge: Cambridge University Press 2024)
Daniel Kelemen, 'The Structure and Dynamics of EU Federalism' (2003) 36(1–2) *Comparative Political Studies* 184–208
Daniel Keleman, 'Judicialisation, Democracy and European Integration' (2013) 49 *Representation* 295–308
Daniel Kelemen, 'On the Unsustainability of Constitutional Pluralism' (2016) 23 *Maastricht Journal of European and Comparative Law* 136–50
Daniel Kelemen, 'Is Differentiation Possible in Rule of Law?' (2019) 17(2) *Comparative European Politics* 246–60
Hans Kelsen, *Introduction to the Problems of Legal Theory* (Oxford: Clarendon Press 1992)
Anthony King, *The British Constitution* (Oxford: Oxford University Press 2009)
Jeff King, 'The Democratic Case for a Written Constitution' (2019) 72 *Current Legal Problems* 1–36
Jeff King, 'From Constitutional Crisis to Poisoned Chalice: A letter from London', VerfBlog (28 June 2024) <https://verfassungsblog.de/from-constitutional-crisis-to-poisoned-chalice/> DOI: 10.59704/8163652a51cb5c78
Uwe Kischel, 'Party, Pope, and Politics? The Election of German Constitutional Court Justices in Comparative Perspective' (2013) 13(4) *International Journal of Constitutional Law* 962–80
Hand-Dieter Klingermann, Richard I. Hofferbert, and Ian Budge, *Parties, Policies and Democracy* (Boulder, CO: Westview Press 1994)
Francesca Klug, 'The Human Rights Act—A "Third Way" or "Third Wave" Bill of Rights' (2001) 4 *European Human Rights Law Review* 361–72
John O. Koehler, *Stasi: The Untold Story of the East German Secret Police* (Boulder, CO: Westview Press 1999)
T. Konstadinides, N. O'Meara, and R. Sallustio, 'The UK Supreme Court's Judgment in *Miller/Cherry*: Reflections on Its Context and Implications', UK Constitutional Law Blog (2 October 2019) <https://ukconstitutionallaw.org/>
D. Kosař, J. Baroš, and P. Dufek, 'The Twin Challenges to Separation of Powers in Central Europe: Technocratic Governance and Populism' (2019) 15(3) *European Constitutional Law Review* 427–61
David Kosarˇ and Samuel Spáč, 'Judicial Independence' in Richard Bellamy and Jeff King (eds), *Cambridge Handbook of Constitutional Theory* (Cambridge: Cambridge University Press 2024) 867–83
Matthew Kramer, 'Impartiality' in Richard Bellamy and Jeff King (eds), *Cambridge Handbook of Constitutional Theory* (Cambridge: Cambridge University Press 2024) 157–75
Matthew Kramer, *In Defence of Legal Positivism* (Oxford: Oxford University Press 1999)
Matthew Kramer, *Objectivity and the Rule of Law, Debates* (Cambridge: Cambridge University Press 2007)
Sandra Kröger and Richard Bellamy, 'Beyond a Constraining Dissensus: The Role of National Parliaments in Domesticating and Normalising the Politicization of European Integration' (2016) 14 *Comparative European Politics* 131–53

Mattias Kumm, 'The Legitimacy of International Law: A Constitutionalist Framework of Analysis' (2004) 15 *European Journal of International Law* 907–31
Will Kymlicka, *Multicultural Citizenship: A Liberal Theory of Minority Rights* (Oxford: Oxford University Press 1995)
Will Kymlicka, *Politics in the Vernacular: Nationalism, Multiculturalism and Citizenship* (Oxford: Oxford University Press 2001)
Dimitrios Kyritsis, 'Representation and Waldron's Objection to Judicial Review' (2006) 26 *Oxford Journal of Legal Studies* 733–51
Cristina Lafont, *Democracy without Shortcuts: A Participatory Conception of Deliberative Democracy* (Oxford: Oxford University Press 2020)
Hélène Landemore, *Democratic Reason: Politics, Collective Intelligence, and the Rule of the Many* (Princeton, NJ: Princeton University Press 2013)
Charles Larmore, 'What Is Political Philosophy?' (2013) 10 *Journal of Moral Philosophy* 276–306
Sir John Laws, 'Law and Democracy' (1995) 72 *Public Law* 85, 88
Lawrence LeDuc, *The Politics of Direct Democracy: Referendums in Global Perspective* (New York: Broadview Press 2003)
Andrew Legg, *The Margin of Appreciation in International Human Rights Law* (Oxford: Oxford University Press 2012)
Anthony Lester et al. (eds), *A British Bill of Rights* (London: IPPR 1990)
Jacob T. Levy, 'Federalism, Liberalism and the Separation of Loyalties' (2007) 101(3) *American Political Science Review* 459–77
Jonathan Lewis, 'The European Ceiling on Human Rights' (2007) *Public Law* 720–47
Peter Lindseth, *Power and Legitimacy: Reconciling Europe and the Nations State* (Oxford: Oxford University Press 2010)
John Locke, *Two Treatises of Government* (Peter Laslett ed., Cambridge: Cambridge University Press 1988)
Karl Loewenstein, 'Militant Democracy and Fundamental Rights I' (1937) 31(3) *American Political Science Review* 417–32
Karl Loewenstein, 'Militant Democracy and Fundamental Rights II' (1937) 31(4) *American Political Science Review* 638–58
Christopher Lord, 'Referendums and Democratic Theory' in Julie Smith (ed.), *The Palgrave Handbook of European Referendums* (Basingstoke: Palgrave Macmillan 2021) 29–48
Martin Loughlin, *The British Constitution: A Very Short Introduction* (Oxford: Oxford University Press 2013)
Martin Loughlin, 'What Would John Griffen Have Made of Jonathan Sumption's Reith Lectures?' (2019) 90(4) *The Political Quarterly* 785–93
Martin Loughlin, *Against Constitutionalism* (Cambridge, MA: Harvard University Press 2022)
Frank Lovett, 'Domination: A Preliminary Analysis' (2001) 84 *The Monist* 98–112
Frank Lovett, *A General Theory of Domination and Justice* (Oxford: Oxford University Press 2010)
A. L. Lowell, *The Government of England*, 2 vols (London: Macmillan 1908)
Noam Lupu and Zach Warner, 'Affluence and Congruence: Unequal Representation around the World' (2022) 84(1) *Journal of Politics* 276–90
Cormac Mac Amhlaigh, 'Putting Political Constitutionalism in Its Place' (2016) 14 *International Journal of Constitutional Law* 175–97
Niccolò Machiavelli, 'Discorsi' in Niccolò Machiavelli, *Il Principle e Discorsi* (S. Bertelli ed., Milan: Feltrinelli 1960) 107–506
Peter Mair, *Ruling the Void: The Hollowing out of Western Democracy* (London: Verso 2013)
Neil MacCormick, 'Argumentation and Interpretation in Law' (1993) 6 *Ratio Juris* 16–29
Neil MacCormick, 'Beyond the Sovereign State' (1993) 56 *Modern Law Review* 1–18
Neil MacCormick, 'The Maastricht-Urteil: Sovereignty Now' (1995) 1 *European Law Journal* 259–66
Neil MacCormick, *Questioning Sovereignty* (Oxford: Oxford University Press 1999)

Gerry Mackie, *Democracy Defended* (Cambridge: Cambridge University Press 2003)

Miguel Maduro, 'Europe and the Constitution: What if this is as Good as it Gets?' in J. H. H. Weiler and M. Wind (eds), *European Constitutionalism beyond the State* (Cambridge: Cambridge University Press 2003) 74–102

Noel Malcolm, *Human Rights and Political Wrongs* (London: Policy Exchange 2017)

Jane Mansbridge, 'Rethinking Representation' (2003) 97 *American Political Science Review* 515–28

Jane Mansbridge and Stephen Macedo, 'Populism and Democratic Theory' (2019) 15 *Annual Review of Law & Social Science* 59–77

Roger Masterman, 'Aspiration or Foundation? The Status of the Strasbourg Jurisprudence and the "Convention Rights" in Domestic Law' in Helen Fenwick, Gavin Phillipson, and Roger Masterman (eds), *Judicial Reasoning Under the U.K. Human Rights Act* (Cambridge: Cambridge University Press 2007) 57–86

Ruben Mathisen, 'Affluence and Influence in a Social Democracy' (2023) 117(2) *American Political Science Review* 751–8

Kenneth O. May, 'A Set of Independent, Necessary and Sufficient Conditions for Simple Majority Decision' (1952) 20(4) *Econometrica* 680–4

M. D. McDonald, S. M. Mendes, and I. Budge, 'What Are Elections For? Conferring the Median Mandate' (2004) 34 *British Journal of Political Science* 1–26

A. J. McGann, 'The Tyranny of the Supermajority: How Majority Rule Protects Minorities' (2004) 16 *Journal of Theoretical Politics* 53–77

Anthony McGann, *The Logic of Democracy: Reconciling Equality, Deliberation, and Minority Protection* (Ann Arbor, MI: University of Michigan Press 2006)

Robert McKeever, *Raw Judicial Power? The Supreme Court and American Society* (2nd edn, Manchester: Manchester University Press 1995)

Kathleen McNamara, *The Politics of Everyday Europe: Constructing Authority in the European Union* (Oxford: Oxford University Press 2015)

Frank I Michelman, 'How Can the People Ever Make the Laws? A Critique of Deliberative Democracy' (1997) 17(4) *The Modern Schoolman* 311–30

John Stuart Mill, *On Liberty* (J. M. Robson ed., Toronto: University of Toronto Press 1977)

John Stuart Mill, *Considerations on Representative Government*, in John Stuart Mill, *On Liberty and Other Essays* (Oxford: Oxford University Press 1998) 203–467

David Miller, 'Democracy's Domain' (2009) 37 *Philosophy and Public Affairs* 201–28

W. Mishler and R. S. Sheehan, 'The Supreme Court as a Counter-majoritarian Institution? The Impact of Public Opinion on Supreme Court Decisions' (1993) 87 *American Political Science Review* 87–101

Daniel Moeckli, 'Of Minarets and Foreign Criminals: Swiss Direct Democracy and Human Rights' (2011) 11 *Human Rights Law Review* 774–94

Rune Møller Stopp and Benjamin Ask Popp-Madsen, 'Defending Democracy: Militant and Popular Models of Democratic Self-Defense' (2022) 29 *Constellations* 310–28

C.-L. De S Montesquieu, *De l'esprit des lois*, 2 vols (Paris: Garnier-Flammarion 1979)

Andrew Moravcsik, 'The Origins of Human Rights Regimes: Democratic Delegation in Postwar Europe' (2000) 54 *International Organisation* 217–52

Andrew Moravcsik, 'The Myth of Europe's "Democratic Deficit"' (2008) *Intereconomics* 331–40

Sam Moyn, 'Resisting the Juristocracy', *Boston Review* (5 October 2018) <https://www.bostonreview.net/articles/samuel-moyn-resisting-juristocracy/>

Cass Mudde and Cristóbal Rovira Kaltwasser, *Populism: A Very Short Introduction* (New York: Oxford University Press 2017)

Russell Muirhead and Nancy Rosenblum, 'Political Liberalism vs. "the Great Game of Politics": The Politics of Political Liberalism' (2006) 4(1) *Perspectives on Politics* 99–108

Jan-Werner Müller, *Contesting Democracy: Political Ideas in Twentieth-Century Europe* (New Haven, CT: Yale University Press 2011)

Jan Werner Müller, 'Militant Democracy' in Michel Rosenfeld and András Sajó (eds), *The Oxford Handbook of Comparative Constitutional Law* (Oxford: Oxford University Press 2012) 1254–69

Jan-Werner Müller, *What is Populism?* (London: Penguin 2016)

Jan-Werner Müller, 'Populism and Constitutionalism' in Cristóbal Rovira Kaltwasser, Paul Taggart, Paulina Ochoa Espejo, and Pierre Ostiguy (eds), *The Oxford Handbook of Populism* (Oxford: Oxford University Press 2017) 590–606

Frederik Neuhouser, 'Rousseau's Critique of Economic Inequality' (2013) 41 *Philosophy and Public Affairs* 193–225

Danny Nicol, 'Statutory Interpretation and Human Rights After Anderson' (2004) *Public Law* 274–82

Danny Nicol, 'The Human Rights Act and the Politicians' (2004) 24 *Legal Studies* 451–79

Danny Nicol, 'Law and Politics After the Human Rights Act' (2006) *Public Law* 722–51

Danny Nicol, 'Business Rights as Human Rights' in Tom Campbell, Keith David Ewing, and Adam Tomkins (eds), *The Legal Protection of Human Rights* (Oxford: Oxford University Press 2011) 229–43

Danny Nicol, 'Legitimacy of the Commons Debate on Prisoner Voting' (2011) *Public Law* 681–90

Kalypso Nicolaïdis, 'European *Demoi*cracy and its Crisis' (2013) 51 *Journal of Common Market Studies* 351–69

Kalypso Nicolaïdis, 'For a Demoicratization of Eurozone Governance' in Stéphanie Hennette, Thomas Piketty, Guillaume Sacriste, and Antoine Vauchez (eds), *How to Democratize Europe* (Cambridge, MA: Harvard University Press 2019) 100–8

Wilfried Nippel, 'Ancient and Modern Republicanism: Mixed Constitution and "Ephors"' in Biancamaria Fontana (ed.), *The Invention of the Modern Republic* (Cambridge: Cambridge University Press 1994) 6–26

Pippa Norris and Ronald Inglehart, *Cultural Backlash: Trump, Brexit, and Authoritarian Populism* (Cambridge: Cambridge University Press 2019)

Colm O'Cinneide, *Human Rights and the UK Constitution* (London: The British Academy 2012)

Claus Offe, 'Referendum vs. Institutionalized Deliberation: What Democratic Theorists Can Learn from the 2016 Brexit Decision' (2017) 146(3) *Daedalus* 14–27

Dawn Oliver, *Constitutional Reform in the United Kingdom* (Oxford: Oxford University Press 2003)

Martin O'Neill and Stuart White, 'Trade Unions and Political Equality' in Hugh Collins, Gillian Lester, and Virginia Mantouvalou (eds), *Philosophical Foundations of Labour Law* (Oxford: Oxford University Press 2018) 252–68

Onora O'Neill, 'The Most Extensive Liberty' (1979/1980) 80 *Proceedings of the Aristotelian Society* 45–59

Peter C. Ordeshook, *Game Theory and Political Theory* (Cambridge: Cambridge University Press 1986)

Thomas Paine, *Political Writings* (B. Kuklick ed., Cambridge: Cambridge University Press 1989)

Zeynep Pamnuk, *Politics and Expertise: How to Use Science in a Democratic Society* (Princeton, NJ: Princeton University Press 2021)

Philip Pettit, *Republicanism: A Theory of Freedom and Government* (2nd edn, Oxford: Oxford University Press 1999)

Philip Pettit, 'Republican Freedom and Contestatory Democratization' in Ian Shapiro and Casiano Hacker-Cordón (eds), *Democracy's Value* (Cambridge: Cambridge University Press 1999) 163–90

Philip Pettit, 'Democracy: Electoral and Contestatory' in Ian Shapiro and Stephen Macedo (eds), *Designing Democratic Institutions* (New York: New York University Press 2000) 105–44

Philip Pettit, 'A Republican Law of Peoples' (2010) 9(1) *European Journal of Political Theory* 70–94

Philip Pettit, 'Legitimate International Institutions: A Neo-Republican Perspective' in Samantha Besson and John Tasioulas (eds), *The Philosophy of International Law* (Oxford: Oxford University Press 2010) 139–60

Philip Pettit, 'Representation, Responsive and Indicative' (2010) 17(3) *Constellations* 426–34

Philip Pettit, *On the People's Terms: A Republican Theory and Model of Democracy* (Cambridge: Cambridge University Press 2012)

Gavin Phillipson, 'Deference, Discretion and Democracy in the Human Rights Act Era' (2006) 60 *Current Legal Problems* 40–78

Michael Pinto-Duschinsky, *Bringing Rights Back Home: Making Human Rights Compatible with Parliamentary Democracy in the UK* (London: Policy Exchange 2011)
Hanna Fenichel Pitkin, *The Concept of Representation* (Berkeley, CA: University of California Press 1967)
J. G. A. Pocock, *The Machiavellian Moment: Florentine Political Thought and the Atlantic Republican Tradition* (Princeton, NJ: Princeton University Press 1975)
J. G. A. Pocock, *The Ancient Constitution and the Feudal Law* (2nd edn, Cambridge: Cambridge University Press 1987)
Polybius, *Rise of the Roman Empire* (F. W. Walbank ed., I. Scott-Kilvert tr., Harmondsworth: Penguin 1979)
Thomas Pogge, *World Poverty and Human Rights: Cosmopolitan Responsibilities and Reform* (Cambridge: Polity 2008)
Adam Przeworski, 'Minimalist Democracy: A Defense' in Ian Shapiro and Casiano Hacker-Cordon (eds), *Democracy's Value* (Cambridge: Cambridge University Press 1999) 23–55
Adam Przeworski, *Crises of Democracy* (Cambridge: Cambridge University Press 2019)
Robert Putnam, 'Diplomacy and Domestic Politics: The Logic of Two-Level Games' (1988) 42 *International Organization* 427–60
Jeremy A. Rabkin, *Law without Nations? Why Constitutional Government Requires Sovereign States* (Princeton, NJ: Princeton University Press 2005)
Joseph Raz, 'The Rule of Law and its Virtue' in Joseph Raz, *The Authority of Law: Essays on Law and Morality* (Oxford: Clarendon Press 1979) 210–29
Joseph Raz, *The Morality of Freedom* (Oxford: Clarendon Press 1986)
Joseph Raz, *Ethics in the Public Domain* (Oxford: Clarendon Press 1994)
Joseph Raz, 'The Politics of the Rule of Law' in Joseph Raz, *Ethics in the Public Domain: Essays in the Morality of Law and Politics* (Oxford: Clarendon Press 1994) 370–8
John Rawls, *A Theory of Justice* (Oxford: Oxford University Press 1971)
John Rawls, *Political Liberalism* (New York: Columbia University Press 1993)
John Rawls, 'The Idea of Public Reason Revisited' (1997) 64(3) *The University of Chicago Law Review* 765–807
John Rawls, *The Law of Peoples* (Cambridge, MA: Harvard University Press 1999)
John Rawls, *Just as Fairness: A Restatement* (Erin Kelly ed., Cambridge, MA: Belknap Press of Harvard University Press 2001)
Alan Renwick, *The Politics of Electoral Reform: Changing the Rules of Democracy* (Cambridge: Cambridge University Press 2011)
Henry Richardson, *Democratic Autonomy: Public Reasoning about the Ends of Policy* (Oxford: Oxford University Press 2002)
C. Richmond, 'Preserving the Identity Crisis: Autonomy, System and Sovereignty in European Law' (1997) 16(4) *Law and Philosophy* 377–420
W. H. Riker, *Liberalism Against Populism: A Confrontation Between the Theory of Democracy and the Theory of Social Choice* (San Francisco: Freeman and Co. 1982)
Arthur Ripstein, *Force and Freedom: Kant's Legal and Political Philosophy* (Cambridge, MA: Harvard University Press 2009)
Dani Rodrik, *The Globalization Paradox: Why Global Markets, States, and Democracy Can't Coexist* (Oxford: Oxford University Press 2011)
Frederick Rosen, *Jeremy Bentham and Representative Democracy: A Study of the Constitutional Code* (Oxford: Clarendon Press 1983)
Gerald Rosenberg, *The Hollow Hope: Can Courts Bring About Social Change?* (Chicago: Chicago University Press 1991)
Frances M. Rosenbluth and Ian Shapiro, *Responsible Parties: Saving Democracy from Itself* (New Haven, CT: Yale University Press 2018)
Evan Rosevear and Ran Hirschl, 'Constitutional Law Meets Comparative Politics: Socio-economic Rights and Political Realities' in Tom Campbell, Keith David Ewing, and Adam Tomkins (eds), *The Legal Protection of Human Rights* (Oxford: Oxford University Press 2011) 207–28
Jean Jacques Rousseau, *The Social Contract and Discourses* (G. D. H. Cole ed., London: Dent 1973)
J. G. Ruggie, 'International Regimes, Transactions and Change: Embedded Liberalism in the Postwar Economic Order (1982) 36 *International Organisation* 379–415

András Sajó and Renáta Uitz, *The Constitution of Freedom: An Introduction to Legal Constitutionalism* (Oxford: Oxford University Press 2017)
David Sanders, 'One Man's Damage: The Consequences of Boris Johnson's Assault on the British Political System' (2023) 94(2) *The Political Quarterly* 166–74
Andrea Sangiovanni, 'Solidarity in the European Union' (2013) 33(2) *Oxford Journal of Legal Studies* 213–41
Deborah Savage and Albert Weale, 'Political Representation and the Normative Logic of Two-Level Games' (2009) 1 *European Political Science Review* 63–81
Thomas Scanlon, *What We Owe To Each Other* (Cambridge, MA: Harvard University Press 1998)
Leslie Scarman, *English Law: The New Dimension* (London: Stevens and Sons 1974)
Fritz Scharpf, 'Legitimacy in the Multilevel European Polity' (2009) 1 *European Political Science Review* (2009) 173–204
Fritz Scharpf, The Asymmetry of European Integration or Why the EU Cannot Be a Social Market Economy (2010) 8 *Socio-Economic Review* 211–50
Fritz Scharpf, 'After the Crash: A Perspective on Multilevel European Democracy' (2015) 21 *European Law Journal* 384–405
Fritz Scharpf, 'De-constitutionalisation and Majority Rule: A Democratic Vision for Europe' (2017) 23 *European Law Journal* 315–34
Kim Lane Scheppele, 'Autocratic Legalism' (2018) 85 *University of Chicago Law Review* 545–83
B. Schlipphak and O. Treib, 'Playing the Blame Game on Brussels: The Domestic Political Effects of EU Interventions Against Democratic Backsliding' (2017) 24(3) *Journal of European Public Policy* 352–65
Philip Schofield, 'Jeremy Bentham' in Dennis J. Galligan (ed) *Constitutions and the Classics. Patterns of Constitutional Thought from Fortescue to Bentham* (Oxford: Oxford University Press 2014) 231–49.
Joseph A. Schumpeter, *Capitalism, Socialism and Democracy* (London: Routledge 1976)
Melissa Schwartzberg, *Counting the Many: The Origins and Limits of Supermajority Rule* (Cambridge: Cambridge University Press 2013)
Jeffrey Segal and Harold Spaeth, *The Supreme Court and the Attitudinal Model* (Cambridge: Cambridge University Press 1993)
Jeffrey A. Segal and Albert D. Cover, 'Ideological Values and the Votes of U.S. Supreme Court Justices' (1989) 83(2) *American Political Science Review* 557–65
Maija Setälä, 'On the Problems of Responsibility and Accountability in Referendums' (2006) 45 *European Journal of Political Research* 699–721
Amal Sethi, 'Politicising Constitutional Court Appointments in Europe' (2025) 21(2) *European Constitutional Law Review* 193–229
Martin Shapiro, 'The European Court of Justice' in Paul Craig and Gráinne de Búrca (eds), *The Evolution of EU Law* (Oxford: Oxford University Press 1999) 321–7
Judith Shklar, 'Political Theory and the Rule of Law' in A. C. Hutchinson and P. Monahan (eds), *The Rule of Law: Ideal or Ideology* (Toronto: University of Toronto Press 1987) 1–16
Judith Shklar, *Ordinary Vices* (Cambridge, MA: Harvard University Press 1984)
John Simmons, *Moral Principles and Political Obligations* (Princeton, NJ: Princeton University Press 1979)
Nigel Simmonds, *Central Issues in Jurisprudence* (London: Sweet and Maxwell 1986)
Beth Simmons, *Mobilizing for Human Rights: International Law in Domestic Politics* (Cambridge: Cambridge University Press 2009)
Quentin Skinner, 'The Context of Hobbes's Theory of Political Obligation' in M. Cranston and R. Peters (eds), *Hobbes and Rousseau: A Collection of Critical Essays* (New York: Doubleday 1972) 109–42
Quentin Skinner, *Reason and Rhetoric in the Philosophy of Hobbes* (Cambridge: Cambridge University Press 1996)
Quentin Skinner, *Liberty before Liberalism* (Cambridge: Cambridge University Press 1998)
Quentin Skinner, 'The Sovereign State: A Genealogy' in Hent Kalmo and Quentin Skinner (eds), *Sovereignty in Fragments: The Past, Present and Future of a Contested Concept* (Cambridge: Cambridge University Press 2010) 26–46

Matt Sleat, 'Bernard Williams and the Possibility of a Realist Political Theory' (2010) 11 *European Journal of Political Theory* 247–72

Alexander Somak, *The Cosmopolitan Constitution* (Oxford: Oxford University Press 2014)

Laurence Sterne, *The Life and Opinions of Tristram Shandy Gentleman* (London: T. Becketand P. A. Dehondt 1762)

Anna Stilz, *Liberal Loyalty: Freedom, Obligation, and the State* (Princeton, NJ: Princeton University Press 2009)

Anna Stilz, *Territorial Sovereignty: A Philosophical Exploration* (Oxford: Oxford University Press 2019)

Wolfgang Streeck, *Buying Time: The Delayed Crisis of Democratic Capitalism* (London: Verso 2014)

Alec Stone Sweet, *Governing with Judges: Constitutional Politics in Europe* (Oxford: Oxford University Press 2000)

Peter Stone, *The Luck of the Draw* (Oxford: Oxford University Press 2011)

Jonathan Sumption, 'The Limits of Law', the 27th Sultan Azlan Shah Lecture, Kuala Lumpur (20 November 2013) reprinted in N. W. Barber, Richard Ekins, and Paul Yowell (eds), *Lord Sumption and the Limits of Law* (Oxford: Hart Publishing 2016) 15–26

Jonathan Sumption, *Trials of the State: Law and the Decline of Politics* (London: Profile Books 2019)

Cass Sunstein, *Legal Reasoning and Political Conflict* (Oxford: Oxford University Press 1996)

Tom Theuns, 'Containing Populism at the Cost of Democracy? Political vs. Economic Responses to Democratic Backsliding in the EU' (2020) 12(2) *Global Justice: Theory Practice Rhetoric* 141–60. DOI: https://doi.org/10.21248/gjn.12.02.220

Dennis F. Thompson, 'Why Representative Democracy Requires Referendums' in J. A. Gardener (ed.), *Comparative Electoral Law* (Cheltenham: Elgar 2022) 193–211

Stephen Tierney, 'Constitutional Referendums: A Theoretical Enquiry' (2009) 72(3) *Modern Law Review* 360–83

Stephen Tierney, *Constitutional Referendums. The Theory and Practice of Republican Deliberation* (Oxford: Oxford University Press 2012)

Stephen Tierney, 'Whose Political Constitution? Citizens and Referendums' (2013) 14 *German Law Journal* 2185–96

Alex de Tocqueville, *Democracy in America* (Eduardo Nolla ed.,. James T. Schleifer Tr., vol. 1, Indianapolis: Liberty Fund 2012)

Adam Tomkins, *Our Republican Constitution* (Oxford: Hart Publishing 2005)

Adam Tomkins, 'The Role of Courts in the Political Constitution' (2010) 60 *University of Toronto Law Journal* 1–22

David Torrance, 'The United Kingdom Constitution: A Mapping Exercise', Research Briefing House of Commons Library (18 December 2024) <https://commonslibrary.parliament.uk/research-briefings/cbp-9384/>

Michel Troper, 'The Survival of Sovereignty' in Hent Kalmo and Quentin Skinner (eds), *Sovereignty in Fragments: The Past, Present and Future of a Contested Concept* (Cambridge: Cambridge University Press 2010) 132–50

Leah Trueblood, 'Are Referendums Directly Democractic?' (2020) 40(3) *Oxford Journal of Legal Studies* 425–48

Leah Trueblood, 'Brexit and Two Roles for Referendums in the United Kingdom' in Richard Albert and Richard Stacey (eds), *The Limits and Legitimacy of Referendums* (Oxford: Oxford University Press 2022) 183–201

Richard Tuck, *The Left Case for Brexit: Reflections on the Current Crisis* (Cambridge: Polity Press 2020)

James Tully, *Strange Multiplicity: Constitutionalism in an Age of Diversity* (Cambridge: Cambridge University Press 1995)

James Tully, 'Struggles over Recognition and Distribution' (2000) 7 *Constellations* 469–82

Mark Tushnet, *Taking the Constitution Away from the Courts* (Princeton, NJ: Princeton University Press 1999)

Mark Tushnet, 'Alternative Forms of Judicial Review' (2003) 101 *Michigan Law Review* 2781–2802

Mark Tushnet, 'New Forms of Judicial Review and the Persistence of Rights- and Democracy-Based Worries' (2003) 38 *Wake Forest Law Review* 813–38

Mark Tushnet, *Weak Courts, Strong Rights: Judicial Review and Social Welfare Rights in Comparative Constitutional Law* (Princeton, NJ: Princeton University Press 2008)

Mark Tushnet, *Taking Back the Constitution: Activist Judges and the Next Age of American Law* (New Haven, CY: Yale University Press 2020)

Mark Tushnet and Bojan Bugarič, *Power to the People: Constitutionalism in the Age of Populism* (Oxford: Oxford University Press 2021)

D. Tillyris, 'The Virtue of Vice: A Defense of Hypocrisy in Democratic Politics' (2016) 22(1) *Contemporary Politics* 1–19

R. Unger, *What Should Legal Analysis Become?* (London: Verso 1996)

M. Urbániková, and S. Šipulová, 'Failed Expectations: Does the Establishment of Judicial Councils Enhance Confidence in Courts?' (2018) 19(7) *German Law Journal* 2105–36

Nadia Urbinati, *Me the People: How Populism Transforms Democracy* (Cambridge, MA: Harvard University Press 2019)

R. Van Crombrugge, 'Are Referendums Necessarily Populist? Countering the Populist Interpretation of Referendums Through Institutional Design' (2021) 57(1) *Representation* 109–30

Lisa Vanhala, 'Civil Society Organisations and the Aarhus Conventions in Court' (2013) 49 *Representation* 309–20

Philippe Van Parijs, 'The Disenfranchisement of the Elderly, and Other Attempts to Secure Intergenerational Justice' (1998) 27 *Philosophy & Public Affairs* 292–333

Philippe Van Parijis, *Just Democracy: The Rawls-Machiavelli Programme* (Colchester: ECPR Press 2011)

Philippe Van Parijs and Yannick Vanderborght, *Basic Income: A Radical Proposal for a Free Society and A Sane Economy* (Cambridge, MA: Harvard University Press 2017) 235–41

S. Verdugo, 'On the Democratic (but Limited) Virtues of the Chilean Exit Referendum', IACL-AIDC Blog (4 October 2022) <https://blog-iacl-aidc.org/new-blog-3/2022/10/4/on-the-democratic-but-limited-virtues-of-the-chilean-exit-referendum>

S. Verdugo, 'The Paradox of Constitution-Making in Democratic Settings. A Tradeoff between Party Renewal and Political Representation?', International Journal of Constitutional Law Blog (24 September 2022) <http://www.iconnectblog.com/2022/09/the-paradox-of-constitution-making-in-democratic-settings-a-tradeoff-between-party-renewal-and-political-representation/>

Adrian Vermeule, *Common Good Constitutionalism* (Cambridge: Polity 2022)

Mila Versteeg and Emily Zackin, 'Constitutions Unentrenched: Toward an Alternative Theory of Constitutional Design' (2016) 110(4) *American Political Science Review* 657–74

Maurice Vile, *Constitutionalism and the Separation of Powers* (Oxford: Clarendon Press 1967)

Lars Vinx, 'Democratic Equality and Militant Democracy' (2020) 27 *Constellations* 685–701

Maurizio Viroli, *Machiavelli* (Oxford: Oxford University Press 1998)

Jeremy Waldron, 'A Right to Do Wrong' (1981) 92 *Ethics* 21–39

Jeremy Waldron, 'The Rule of Law in Contemporary Liberal Theory' (1989) 2 *Ratio Juris* 79–96

Jeremy Waldron, *Law and Disagreement* (Oxford: Clarendon Press 1999)

Jeremy Waldron, 'Legislating with Integrity' (2003) 72(2) *Fordham Law Review* 373–94

Jeremy Waldron, 'The Rule of Law as a Theatre of Debate' in Justine Burley (ed.), *Dworkin and his Critics* (Oxford: Blackwell 2004) 319–36

Jeremy Waldron, 'The Core of the Case Against Judicial Review' (2006) 115 *Yale Law Journal* 1346–1406

Jeremy Waldron, 'Legislation and the Rule of Law' (2007) 1(1) *Legisprudence* 91–123

Jeremy Waldron, 'The Concept and the Rule of Law' (2008) 43 *Georgia Law Review* 1–61

Jeremy Waldron, 'Can There Be a Democratic Jurisprudence?' (2008–09) 58 *Emory Law Journal* 675–712

Jeremy Waldron, 'Constitutionalism: A Skeptical View' in Thomas Christiano and John Christman (eds), *Contemporary Debates in Political Philosophy* (Malden: Wiley-Blackwell 2009) 265–82

Jeremy Waldron, 'Judges as Moral Reasoners' (2009) 7 *International Journal of Constitutional Law* 2–24

Jeremy Waldron, 'Citizenship and Dignity' (3 January 2013). NYU School of Law, Public Law Research Paper No. 12-74. Available at SSRN: <https://ssrn.com/abstract = 2196079> or <http://dx.doi.org/10.2139/ssrn.2196079

Jeremy Waldron, 'Five to Four: Why Do Bare Majorities Rule on Courts?' (2014) 123 *Yale Law Journal* 1692–1730

Jeremy Waldron, *Political Political Theory: Essays on Institutions* (Cambridge, MA: Harvard University Press 2016)

Neil Walker, 'Constitutional Pluralism Revisited' (2016) 22(3) *European Law Journal* 333–55

Wil Waluchow and Dimitrios Kyritsis, 'Constitutionalism' in *The Stanford Encyclopedia of Philosophy* (E. Zalta ed., 2022) <https://plato.stanford.edu/archives/sum2022/entries/constitutionalism/>

Silas Wasserstrom, 'The Empire's New Clothes' (1986) 75(1) *Georgetown Law Journal* 199–314

Albert Weale, *Democracy* (2nd edn, Basingstoke: Palgrave 2007)

Albert Weale, *Democratic Justice and the Social Contract* (Oxford: Oxford University Press 2013)

Albert Weale, 'The Democratic Duty to Oppose Brexit' (2017) 88 *Political Quarterly* 170–81

Albert Weale, *The Will of the People. A Modern Myth* (Cambridge: Polity 2018)

Albert Weale, 'Three Types of Majority Rule' (2019) 90 *Political Quarterly* 62–76

'The Profession and Vocation of Politics' in Max Weber, *Political Writings* (Peter Lassman and Ronald Speirs eds., Ronald Speirs tr., Cambridge: Cambridge University Press 1994) 309–69

Max Weber, 'Parliament and Government in Germany under a New Political Order' in Max Weber, *Political Writings* (Peter Lassman and Ronald Speirs eds., Ronald Speirs tr., Cambridge: Cambridge University Press 1994) 130–271

Grégoire Webber, Paul Yowell, Richard Ekins, Maris Köpcke, Bradley W. Miller, Francisco J. Urbina, *Legislated Rights: Securing Human Rights through Legislation* (Cambridge: Cambridge University Press 2018).

J. H. H. Weiler, *The Constitution of Europe: 'Do the New Clothes Have an Emperor?' and Other Essays on European Integration* (Cambridge: Cambridge University Press 1999)

J. H. H. Weiler, 'In Defence of the Status Quo: Europe's Constitutional Sonderweg' in J. H. H. Weiler and M. Wind (eds), *European Constitutionalism Beyond the State* (Cambridge: Cambridge University Press 2003) 7–25

J. H. H. Weiler, 'In the Face of Crisis: Input Legitimacy, Output Legitimacy and the Political Messianism of European Integration' (2012) 34 *Journal of European Integration* 825–41

Rivka Weill, 'Dicey Was Not Diceyan' (2003) 62 *Cambridge Law Journal* 474–94

Daniel Weinstock, 'Towards a Normative Theory of Federalism' (2001) 53 *International Social Science Journal* 75–83

Corinne C. Weston, 'England: Ancient Constitution and Common Law' in J. H. Burns (ed.), *The Cambridge History of Political Thought 1450–1700* (Cambridge: Cambridge University Press 1991)

J. White, *In the Long Run: The Future as a Political Idea* (London: Profile Books 2024)

Bernard Williams, 'Realism and Moralism in Political Theory' in Bernard Williams, *In the Beginning Was the Deed* (Princeton, NJ: Princeton University Press 2005) 1–17

Jeffrey A. Winters, and Benjamin I. Page, 'Oligarchy in the United States?' (2009) 7(4) *Perspectives on Politics* 731–51

Thomas Winzen, 'From Capacity to Sovereignty: Legislative Politics and Differentiated Integration in the European Union' (2016) 55(1) *European Journal of Political Research* 100–19

R. P. Wolff, *In Defence of Anarchism* (New York: Harper & Row 1970)

Ludwig Wittgenstein, *Philosophical Investigations* (Oxford: Blackwell 1953)

Alison Young, *Parliamentary Sovereignty and the Human Rights Act* (Oxford: Hart Publishing 2009)

I. M. Young, *Inclusion and Democracy* (Oxford: Oxford University Press 2000)

Michael Zürn, 'How Non-Majoritarian Institutions Make Silent Majorities Vocal: A Popular Explanation of Authoritarian Populism', *Perspectives on Politics First View* (2021) 1 <https://doi.org/10.1017/S1537592721001043>

Index

For the benefit of digital users, indexed terms that span two pages (e.g., 52–53) may, on occasion, appear on only one of those pages.

References to footnote is indicated by page number followed by the letter 'n' and then the note number.